Expert PHP 5 To

Proven enterprise development tools and best practices for designing, coding, testing, and deploying PHP applications

Dirk Merkel

BIRMINGHAM - MUMBAI

Expert PHP 5 Tools

First published: April 2010

Production Reference: 1240310

Published by Packt Publishing Ltd.
32 Lincoln Road
Olton
Birmingham, B27 6PA, UK.

ISBN 978-1-847198-38-9

www.packtpub.com

Cover Image by Karl Swedberg (karl@englishrules.com)

Credits

Author
Dirk Merkel

Reviewers
Andrew J. Peterson

Deepak Vohra

Acquisition Editor
Douglas Paterson

Development Editor
Ved Prakash Jha

Technical Editor
Neha Damle

Indexer
Monica Ajmera

Editorial Team Leader
Gagandeep Singh

Project Team Leader
Lata Basantani

Project Coordinator
Joel Goveya

Proofreader
Claire Cresswell-Lane

Graphics
Geetanjali Sawant

Production Coordinator
Shantanu Zagade

Melwyn D'sa

Cover Work
Melwyn D'sa

About the Author

Dirk Merkel has been developing software in a variety of programming languages for many years, including PHP, Java, Perl, and Ruby. His focus has been on web-related technologies and he has over 10 years experience coding in PHP. He has experience covering the whole software development cycle and has been managing several teams of developers working on large-scale projects.

He has been working as a professional consultant through his company Waferthin Web Works LLC (`http://www.waferthin.com`) and can be reached at `dirk@waferthin.com`. He is also the Chief Technology Officer at VivanTech Inc., a San Diego based provider of IT solutions.

He has written several articles on software development and security. *Expert PHP 5 Tools* is his first book.

He lives in San Diego with his lovely wife and two wonderful daughters.

I would like to thank my family (near and far)—especially my parents and sisters, my lovely wife, Rania, and my two awesome daughters, Nadia and Yasmin.

About the Reviewers

Andrew J. Peterson lives with his wife and three daughters in San Francisco, California. He has 20 years experience building and managing software systems for consumers, enterprises, start-ups, and non-profits. He brings expertise in the full life-cycle of software development, engineering, methodologies, architecture, and usability. He has diverse experience in the industry. In the consumer space, he led a team in the creation of the top-selling SoundEdit 16. He served numerous roles producing enterprise software, for the leading supplier of software solutions for container terminals, shipping ports and lines, and distribution centers. Over the past ten years, he transferred this experience to web-based software. He has built a variety of web applications, including non-profit, social networking, social search, pharmaceuticals and social ecommerce. He has build successful projects in a variety of languages, including Java, Ruby, C++, Ruby and Perl.

In the primal days of the Web, he wrote a manual helping users connect their Macintosh to the Web. More recently, he reviewed *PHP and Scriptaculous Web Application Interfaces* for Packt Publishing.

I'd like to thank my wife for the bliss she brings.

Deepak Vohra is a consultant and a principal member of the NuBean.com software company. Deepak is a Sun Certified Java Programmer and Web Component Developer, and has worked in the fields of XML and Java programming and J2EE for over five years. Deepak is the co-author of the Apress book *Pro XML Development with Java Technology* and was the technical reviewer for the O'Reilly book *WebLogic: The Definitive Guide*. Deepak was also the technical reviewer for the Course Technology PTR book *Ruby Programming for the Absolute Beginner*, and the technical editor for the Manning Publications book *Prototype and Scriptaculous in Action*. Deepak is also the author of the Packt Publishing books *JDBC 4.0 and Oracle JDeveloper for J2EE Development* and *Processing XML Documents with Oracle JDeveloper 11g*.

Table of Contents

Preface

This book will enable you to take your PHP development skills to an enterprise level by teaching the skills and tools necessary to write maintainable and efficient code. You will learn how to perform activities such as unit testing, enforcing coding standards, automating deployment, and interactive debugging using tools created for PHP developers—all the information in one place. Your code will be more maintainable, efficient, and self-documenting.

What this book covers

Chapter 1, Coding Style and Standards, explains how to define a coding standard that suits your development process and how to enforce it using PHP_CodeSniffer.

Chapter 2, Documentation with phpDocumentor, explains how to properly document your code with phpDocumentor and generate well formatted developer documentation.

Chapter 3, The Eclipse Integrated Development Environment, explains how to install, customize, and use the free PDT plug-in for Eclipse to create a powerful IDE for PHP development

Chapter 4, Source Code and Version Control, explores the ins and outs of subversion for distributed version control for development teams. It also teaches you to extend subversion functionality with PHP scripts.

Chapter 5, Debugging, teaches you to write your own flexible debugging library and master remote interactive debugging with Xdebug.

Chapter 6, PHP Frameworks, explains how to evaluate, compare, and choose frameworks that suit your projects and development style. Master the most commonly used modules of Zend Framework.

Chapter 7, Testing, explains testing methods and types, unit testing, creating comprehensive test suites with PHPUnit, and test-driven development.

Chapter 8, Application Deployment, states guidelines for automated and reversible application deployment, automating upgrades and deployments with Phing

Chapter 9, PHP Application Design with UML, introduces the reader to UML, class diagrams, sequence diagrams, and use cases.

Chapter 10, Continuous Integration, explains how to use CI, keep costs down and save time by discovering bugs and conflicts in your projects, at an early stage.

What you need for this book

To follow along with the examples, you will need a working version of PHP 5 installed on your system. Some of the chapters rely on command line tools such as `pear` and `pecl`, which are included in the standard distribution of PHP. Version 5.2.x of PHP or higher is recommended for maximum compatibility with the sample code. If you do not already have PHP installed on your system, you can download it from php.net here:

```
http://www.php.net/downloads.php
```

Although this book was written and coded on OS X, any flavor of MS Windows or Linux will do the job as well. Basic familiarity with your system's command line and a handy text editor for tweaking the examples will also be helpful.

Who this book is for

This book has been written for professional developers new to PHP and experienced PHP developers, who want to take their skills to the next level by learning enterprise level tools and techniques.

Conventions

In this book, you will find a number of styles of text that distinguish between different kinds of information. Here are some examples of these styles, and an explanation of their meaning.

Code words in text are shown as follows: "We can include other contexts through the use of the `include` directive."

A block of code will be set as follows:

```
<fileset dir="${project.home}/build" >
<include name="*.properties" />
<exclude name="deprecated.properties" />
</fileset>
```

When we wish to draw your attention to a particular part of a code block, the relevant lines or items will be shown in bold:

```
<fileset dir="${project.home}/build" >
<include name="*.properties" />
<exclude name="deprecated.properties" />
</fileset>
```

Any command-line input or output is written as follows:

```
$ phing upgrade-db
```

New terms and **important words** are shown in bold. Words that you see on the screen, in menus or dialog boxes for example, appear in our text like this: "clicking the **Next** button moves you to the next screen".

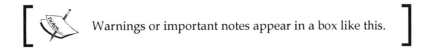

Warnings or important notes appear in a box like this.

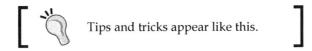

Tips and tricks appear like this.

Reader feedback

Feedback from our readers is always welcome. Let us know what you think about this book—what you liked or may have disliked. Reader feedback is important for us to develop titles that you really get the most out of.

To send us general feedback, simply drop an email to feedback@packtpub.com, and mention the book title in the subject of your message.

If there is a book that you need and would like to see us publish, please send us a note in the **SUGGEST A TITLE** form on www.packtpub.com or email suggest@packtpub.com.

If there is a topic that you have expertise in and you are interested in either writing or contributing to a book, see our author guide on www.packtpub.com/authors.

Customer support

Now that you are the proud owner of a Packt book, we have a number of things to help you to get the most from your purchase.

Downloading the example code for the book

Visit `http://www.packtpub.com/files/code/8389_Code.zip` to directly download the example code.

The downloadable files contain instructions on how to use them.

Errata

Although we have taken every care to ensure the accuracy of our contents, mistakes do happen. If you find a mistake in one of our books—maybe a mistake in text or code—we would be grateful if you would report this to us. By doing so, you can save other readers from frustration, and help us to improve subsequent versions of this book. If you find any errata, please report them by visiting `http://www.packtpub.com/support`, selecting your book, clicking on the **let us know** link, and entering the details of your errata. Once your errata are verified, your submission will be accepted and the errata added to any list of existing errata. Any existing errata can be viewed by selecting your title from `http://www.packtpub.com/support`.

Piracy

Piracy of copyright material on the Internet is an ongoing problem across all media. At Packt, we take the protection of our copyright and licenses very seriously. If you come across any illegal copies of our works in any form on the Internet, please provide us with the location address or website name immediately so that we can pursue a remedy.

Please contact us at `copyright@packtpub.com` with a link to the suspected pirated material.

We appreciate your help in protecting our authors, and our ability to bring you valuable content.

Questions

You can contact us at `questions@packtpub.com` if you are having a problem with any aspect of the book, and we will do our best to address it.

1
Coding Style and Standards

A developer's coding style takes time to develop and often reflects his or her personality. Consequently, you are likely to encounter more than just a little resistance when trying to get your team members to adopt a different style. However, that is exactly what I will be arguing in this chapter. We will learn about the benefits of standardizing on a certain coding style. Along the way, we will develop our own style and learn how to automatically enforce that or any standard of your choice using the handy PHP_CodeSniffer utility. I am hoping that at the end of this chapter, you will be able to take a look at your own and your co-workers' coding styles and make the necessary changes to reap the benefits that include code readability and maintainability.

Coding standard considerations

Since you are reading this book, there is a good chance that you have a couple of years of programming experience under your belt. Even if it is in a programming language other than PHP, you have probably had plenty of time to develop your own style of writing code. In all likelihood, you have chosen or developed a style that appears to make the most sense to you and that you can adhere to and read easily.

However, if you are reading this book, it also means that you are looking to improve your knowledge of PHP. Consequently, I assume that you are willing to change your coding style or at least fine-tune it. First, let me try to convince you that this is worth the effort.

Even if you are writing code only for yourself and have no reasonable expectation that any other programmer will ever look at or work on it, you will probably want to follow your own coding standards. Whether you are aware of it or not, chances are you are doing this already. For example, at some point every programmer decides whether to put the opening brackets on the same line or the one following the if-statement. I would also guess that you are doing it the same way every time.

Personally, I have had many occasions to revisit code that I had written years ago. I can always tell how well defined my coding style was at the time. The more consistent the style, the easier it is to get back into the code and understand the intricacies of what it is doing.

I think we have all had trouble understanding our own code after not looking at it for a while. If you haven't been in that position already, imagine inheriting a project of substantial size and having to get used to someone else's coding habits and oddities. This is where agreeing on a common coding standard pays off. If all developers working on the same project agree on the same standard, collaboration becomes so much easier as it takes less time to find and figure things out. I'm not just talking about where to place the opening brackets, but rather things such as locations of classes and libraries, names of methods and attributes, and inline documentation.

Let's consider some of the pros and cons of having formally defined coding standards—starting with the pros.

Pros

It will be easier to understand code. Whether you are looking at your own code or that of another development team member, reading and understanding the code will be more fluent. This benefit extends not only to current contributors, but also to programmers who are new to the team or PHP in general. Not having to grapple with different styles and conventions will allow them to come up to speed more quickly and allow them to absorb the common style from the beginning.

Nowadays, software is often designed, developed, tested, and used in a distributed fashion. Team members could be located anywhere in the world. With todays tools for communication, the rules for where and how to assemble software teams are being rewritten. Just take a look at some of the very successful Open Source projects, many of which have no physical presence at all. Consider the Apache Software Foundation or in the PHP space, the Zend Framework project, both of which are very successful examples of highly successful projects with many distributors from all over the globe. Projects such as these are some prime candidates for reaping the benefits of a common coding standard.

I would go so far as to say that the right coding standard should go beyond style. It can improve the quality and robustness of the code. For example, having developers consistently validate method parameters will undoubtedly result in a more robust code base.

Cons

Developers tend to ignore coding standards. Adhering to a common standard requires everyone to change their ways – some more so, some less. Unless someone takes on the responsibility of enforcing the standard, change is not going to come about by itself. When developers are too set in their ways or push back when being asked to change, you run the risk of alienating them. The best thing is to get everyone involved in developing the standard. With their own time and expertise invested in the project, they are more likely to abide by the rules the group agreed on.

There are also some common myths when it comes to coding standards in general. First, people tend to think that it stifles creativity. What people who are not familiar or experienced with software development often don't realize is that software is as much a creative process as writing a poem or composing a melody is. There are basic rules to follow in all those endeavors. Depending on what kind of poem you are writing, you might have to make sure it rhymes, follows a certain rhythm, or only has a certain number of syllables. Writing software is no different. At a basic level, you have some rules to define the playing field. Having a coding standard is just a small part of the rules. There are still endless possibilities for the developer to express his creativity and ingenuity.

The second myth you commonly encounter is that it is unnecessary. You will often hear programmers say something like: "My code has been working flawlessly all along. Why do I need a coding standard?" or "If you can't understand the code I write, then you're not good enough to work on this project."

The former statement misses the point. A coding standard's primary purpose is not to make the code work (although it may help). There are many other tools available to help developers with that part of their work. What a coding standard does is make it easier and faster for the developer to understand their own and others' code.

The latter statement betrays the developer's attitude towards working in a group environment. In my opinion, exactly the opposite is true. The bigger the development team and the more complex the project, the more it can benefit from some common ground rules.

A PHP coding standard

There are many ways to define a coding standard. Some like to set some basic guidelines and leave the rest to the developers. Others like to be as explicit as possible. What I am getting at is that there is no correct answer. Any given standard may or may not be appropriate for a given situation or project.

With that in mind, let's be true to the approach of this book and come up with a general-purpose coding standard that you can use as a starting point for your own projects. Our assumption will be that we are developing PHP5+ application, which is why our coding standard will specifically address and forbid some constructs and conventions commonly used in PHP4's object-oriented implementations.

Formatting

Formatting paints the overall picture of the code. It's the first thing you see when you glance at it. It is also the one chance the developer has to make the code easily readable that does not require understanding of what the code actually does.

PHP tags

All PHP code is to be enclosed by full PHP tags: `<?php` and `?>`. Short tags (`<?` and `?>`) or ASP-style tags (`<%` and `%>`) are not allowed.

Indenting

Tabs are to be replaced by four space characters. Most IDEs and text editors can be set to do this automatically.

Line length

The suggested maximum number of characters per line is 80 characters, although just about all GUI-based editing tools can easily accommodate more characters. This convention takes into consideration that command line interfaces are often limited to 80 characters. The absolute maximum number of characters per line is 120. Lines of code with more characters are not acceptable.

Line endings

Lines must end only with a standard Unix linefeed (LF). Linefeeds are represented as ordinal 10, or hexadecimal 0x0A.

Carriage returns (CR) (0x0D), commonly used on Macintosh computers, and carriage return/linefeed combinations (CRLF) (0x0D, 0x0A), commonly used on Windows computers, are not allowed.

Spacing

For readability, spaces are required at the following code sections:

- After a comma separating method/function parameter lists or array members
- Following control structure keywords, such as `if`, `else`, `unless`, `switch`, and so on
- Before curly braces unless they are at the beginning of a line
- Before and after logical operators, such as `&&`, `||`, `&`, `|`, `==`, `!=`, `===`, and `!==`
- Before and after arithmetic operators, such as `+`, `-`, `*`, and `%`
- Before and after assignment operators, such as `=`, `+=`, `-=`, and `*=`

```php
<?php
    public function doSomething($arg1, $arg2, $arg3)
    {
        if ($arg1 == $arg2 == $arg3) {
            // notice blank line above
            $this->identical = true;
            echo "All three arguments are identical.\n";
        } else {
            echo "At least one argument is different.\n";
        }
    }
?>
```

Statements

Put only one statement per line. Multiple statements on a single line are expressly forbidden because they are easily overlooked when reading the code. Spreading a single statement over multiple lines is discouraged unless it clearly improves readability of the code.

```php
<?php
// unnecessary and confusing
echo ($errorCondition === true)
    ?
        "too bad\n"
    :
        "nice\n";

// keep ';' on the same line as the statement
// don't do this:
echo "goodbye!\n"
;
```

```
// must not put multiple statements on a line
echo 'An error has occurred'; exit;
?>
```

Strings

Use only double quotes to define strings if you are taking advantage of variable interpolation or the string contains formatting characters or single quotes, such as ', \n or \t. In all other instances, single quotes should be used as they result in less work for the parser and faster execution of your script.

Strings exceeding the maximum line length should be broken into smaller segments and concatenated using the dot notation.

Long strings should use the heredoc notation if possible.

```php
<?php
// defining a simple string
$myOutput = 'This is an awesome book!';

$adjectives = array('nicer',
                    'better',
                    'cleaner');

// string with variable interpolation and formatting characters
echo "Reading this book makes a good PHP programer $adjectives[1].\n";

// double quotes containing single quote
echo "This book's content will make you a better developer!";

// defining long strings by breaking them up
$chapterDesc = 'In this chapter, we are tyring to explore how'
               'a thorough and clear common coding standard'
               'benefits the project as well as each individual'
               'developer.';

// I'm not much of a poet, but this is how you use the heredoc syntax
$poem = <<<ENDOFSTRING
Roses are red,
violets are blue,
this is my poem
for the code in you.
ENDOFSTRING;
?>
```

Arrays

Numerically indexed arrays should have base index 0 whenever possible. For numerically indexed array, multiple values per line are allowed, but spaces must be inserted to align the first item of each line.

Associative arrays should be declared such that key-value pairs should be listed one to each line. White space must be inserted so as to align the names, assignment operators, and values of all items. Single quotes are always to be used if the key value is a string.

```php
<?php
// simple numerically indexed array
$myFruits = array('apples', 'bananas', 'cherries');

// use bracket syntax within string to access array
echo "My favorite fruits are {$myFruits[2]}.\n\n";

// longer numerically indexed array
$myLongList = array('The', 'quick', 'brown' ,'fox',
                    'jumped', 'over', 'the', 'lazy',
                    'fox', '.');

// use bracket syntax with variable as index to access array
$listSize = count($myLongList);
for ($i = 0; $i < $listSize; $i++) {
    echo $myLongList[$i];
    echo ($i < $listSize - 2) ? ' ' : '';
}
echo "\n\n";

// associative array; everything lines up
$spanAdj = array('green'  => 'verde',
                 'little' => 'poquito',
                 'big'    => 'grande');

// using a foreach construct to access both keys and values
foreach ($spanAdj as $english => $spanish) {
  echo "'" . $spanish . "' means '" . $english . "' in Spanish.\n";
}
?>
```

The above code fragment outputs the following text when executed:

```
Terminal — bash — bash — Dirk — ttys004 — 80×15 — ⌘2
DirkMacBook:Code dirk$ cd chapter2
DirkMacBook:chapter2 dirk$ php ch2\|15.php
My favorite fruits are cherries.

The quick brown fox jumped over the lazy fox.

'verde' means 'green' in Spanish.
'poquito' means 'little' in Spanish.
'grande' means 'big' in Spanish.
DirkMacBook:chapter2 dirk$
```

Control structures

Conditional tests should be written on one line if possible. For long and complex conditional tests, line breaks should be inserted before each combining operator with the line indented for combining operators to line up. The starting curly brace should appear on the same line as the last conditional test. Control statements should have one space between the control keyword and the opening parenthesis, so as to distinguish them from function calls.

```php
<?php
// all conditionals on the same line
if ($myValue <= -1 || $myValue > 100) {
    doSomethingImportant();
}

// too many conditional for one line
// break up conditionals like this ...
if ($myValue > 5
    || $myValue < 5
    || $myValue == 0
    || $myValue == -3) {

    doSomethingElseImportant();
}
?>
```

If-elseif-else statements

The elseif and else keywords are to appear on the same line as the previous block's closing parenthesis:

```php
<?php
if (is_array($myHash)) {
    throw new Exception("myHash must be an array!");
} elseif (array_key_exists('index', $myHash)) {
    echo "The key 'index' exists.\n";
} else {
    echo "The key 'index' does NOT exists.\n";
}
?>
```

Switch statements

The body of the switch statement and the body of each case statement must be indented. The opening curly bracket should appear on the same line as the test expression. A space character should precede the parentheses of the test expression. Finally, the last case statement must be followed by a default statement:

```php
<?php
switch ($temperature) {

    case 50:
        echo "Let's stay home and write some code.\n";
        break;

    case 80:
        echo "Let's go to the beach\n";
        break;

    default:
        echo "Go to jail. Do not pass go.\n";
        break;
}
?>
```

Class and method definitions

Both class and method definitions follow the "one true brace" convention. That is to say, the opening and closing curly brackets are to appear on a line by themselves:

```php
<?php
// showing "one true brace" convention
class Otb
{
    // for metods as well
    public method doSomething()
    {
      // your clever and immensely important code goes here
        ...
    }
}
?>
```

Naming conventions

Choosing appropriate and descriptive names for your classes, methods, properties, and constants may seem like a trivial task, but it may well be the most important part of your job as a programmer — short of developing functional code. The names you choose will have a significant impact on the readability of your code and the ease with which other developers in your team will be able to follow your design and logic. It is also far from easy because it requires a deep and thorough understanding of the overall structure of your application.

Stringing words together to construct the name of a method, function, variable, property, or class is commonly referred to as a **camelCase** if each new word starts with a capital letter, but all other letters are lowercase. No other word delimiters are used. Examples of camelCase formatting are: getStackLength(), updateInterval, and DbLogWriter.

Class names

Classes should be named after the objects they represent. Try to stay away from descriptive phrases (too long), incorporating parent class or interface names, or using verbs.

Examples of bad class names are:

- `ExcessInventoryProductOrderReceivedAndFilled` (too long and contains verb)

- `IterableWidgetList` (incorporates interface name)

Examples of good names are as follows:

- `WidgetStack`

- `DbFileCache`

Class names should reflect the path relative to the root class directory. Directories are to be delimited by the underscore character ("_"). The first letter of each word/directory name is to be capitalized. No other characters are to be capitalized. In particular, abbreviations should adhere to this convention as well. Furthermore, only alphanumeric characters and the underscore character are allowed. Use of numbers is discouraged.

The following PHP segment takes a class file path and converts it to the corresponding class name:

```php
<?php
class ClassNameConverter
{
    public static $classRootDir = array('var', 'www', 'sites',
                            'my_app', 'includes', 'classes');

    public static function makeClassName($absolutePath)
    {
        $platformClassRootDir = DIRECTORY_SEPARATOR .
implode(DIRECTORY_SEPARATOR, self::$classRootDir) .
DIRECTORY_SEPARATOR;

        // remove path leading to class root directory
        $absolutePath = str_replace($platformClassRootDir, '',
                                                $absolutePath);

        // replace directory separators with underscores
        // and capitalize each word/directory
        $parts = explode(DIRECTORY_SEPARATOR, $absolutePath);

        foreach ($parts as $index => $value) {
            $parts[$index] = ucfirst(strtolower($value));
        }
```

```
            // join with underscores
            $absolutePath = implode('_', $parts);

            // remove trailing file extension
            $absolutePath = str_replace('.php', '', $absolutePath);

        return $absolutePath;
        }
    }

    $classNameExamples =
    array('/var/www/sites/my_app/includes/classes/logging/db/Mysql.php',
     '/var/www/sites/my_app/includes/classes/logging/db/MysqlPatched.php',
     '/var/www/sites/my_app/includes/classes/caching_lib/Memcached.php'
                                );

    foreach ($classNameExamples as $path) {
        echo $path . ' converts to ' .
    ClassNameConverter::makeClassName($path) . "\n";
    }
    ?>
```

Here is the corresponding output:

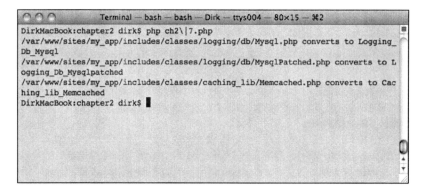

Property and variable names

Properties and variables should start with a lower case letter, contain only alphanumeric characters, and generally follow the "camelCase" convention. Every effort should be made to make property names as descriptive as possible without their length getting excessive. Underscore characters are not allowed in property and variable names.

Short variable names, such as $i or $cnt are only allowed in very short looping constructs.

Constant names

Names of constants should only contain alphanumeric characters. Words are to be separated by the underscore character. Names should be as descriptive as possible, but more than three words are discouraged.

Method and function names

Similar to property names, method and function names should contain only alphanumeric characters and follow the "camel case" convention. They should start with a lower case letter and contain no underscore characters. Class methods must always be preceded by one of the three visibility specifiers: public, protected, or private.

Method names should be descriptive as to their purpose. However, excessive length is discouraged.

Accessor methods for object properties should always be named set<PropertyName> and get<PropertyName>.

The following listing illustrates proper names for properties, methods, classes, and constants:

```php
<?php
class MessageQueue
{
    // upper case constant with underscores
    const MAX_MESSAGES = 100;

    // descriptive properties using camelCase
    private $messageQueue          = array("one\ntwo");
    private $currentMessageIndex  = -1;

    // setter method for $currentMessageIndex
    public setCurrentMessageIndex($currentMessageIndex)
    {
        $this->currentMessageIndex = (int)$currentMessageIndex;
    }

    // getter method for $currentMessageIndex
    public getCurrentMessageIndex()
    {
```

```php
        return $this->currentMessageIndex;
    }

    // is<Attribute> method returns boolean
    public function isQueueFull()
    {
        return count($this->messageQueue) == self::MAX_MESSAGES;
    }

    // has<Attribute> method returns boolean
    public function hasMessages()
    {
        return (is_array($this->messageQueue) && count($this->messageQueue) > 0);
    }

    // descriptive take action method
    public function resetQueue()
    {
        $this->messageQueue = null;
    }

    // descriptive take action method
    public function convertMessagesToHtml()
    {
        // local copy of message queue
        $myMessages = $this->messageQueue;

        // $i is acceptable in a short for-loop
        for ($i = 0; $i < sizeof($myMessages); $i++) {
            $myMessages[$i] = nl2br($myMessages[$i]);
        }

        return $myMessages;
    }

    // additional methods to manage message queue ...
}
?>
```

Methodology

In this section, we will look at some conventions that take advantage of object-oriented features found in PHP5 and later. Some of the recommendations listed as follows are generally considered best practices.

Type hinting

Whenever possible, functions should type-hint by specifying the class of the parameter. Furthermore, as of PHP 5.1, arrays can be type-hinted. Therefore, arrays should always be type hinted—especially when passing a hashed array instead of individual parameters.

```php
<?php
class SomeClass
{
    // method requires an object of type MyClass
    public function doSomething(MyClass $myClass)
    {
        echo 'If we made it this far, we know that the name ' .
        'of the class in the parameter: ' . get_class($myClass);
    }

    // method requires an array
    public function passMeAnArray(array $myArray)
    {
        // we don't need to test is_array($myArr)
        echo "The parameter array contains the following items:\n";
        print_r($myArr);
    }
}
?>
```

Separating object creation from initialization

If something goes wrong during object creation, the calling code may be left in a state of uncertainty. For example, throwing an exception in the constructor will prevent the object from being instantiated. Therefore, it is advisable to separate construction and initialization of the object. A short constructor will be responsible for instantiating the object, after which, an `init` function is responsible for handling object initialization.

```php
<?php
class MyClass
{
```

```
        private myAttrib;

        // short constructor - no parameters this time
        public function __construct()
        {
            // intentionally left blank
        }

        // initialization method to be called
        // immediately after object instantiation
        public function init($var)
        {
            $this->myAttrib = trim$(var);
        }
    }

    // first we instantiate the object
    $myObject = new MyClass();

    // then we initialize the object
    $myObject->init('a string literal');
    ?>
```

Class files

Each class definition should be in a separate source file. And, there should be no additional code (outside the class) in that file. The name of the file should reflect the name of the class. For example, class `Message` should be defined in the file `Message.php`.

Class names and directory structures

The directory hierarchy in which the class files are organized should be reflected in the name of the class. For example, assume that we decided to put our classes directory inside an `includes` directory:

```
includes/
    classes/
        Parser/
            FileParser/
                CommonLog.php
```

The file `CommonLog.php` should contain a class called `Parser_FileParser_` `CommonLog`. This convention will make it easier to comprehend a class's position in the class hierarchy. It also makes it easier for the `autoload()` function to locate classes.

Visibility and access

All properties and methods of a class must have one of three visibility specifiers: `public`, `protected`, or `private`. Direct access to properties is discouraged in favor of corresponding getter and setter methods: `get/set<Attribute>()` —even when accessing properties from within a class. Magic methods may be used to provide access to the properties.

```php
<?php
class AlwaysUseGetters
{
    // private property not accessible outside this class
    private $myValue;

    // setter method
    public function setMyValue($myValue)
    {
        $this->myValue = $myValue;
    }

    // getter method
    public function getMyValue()
    {
        return $this->myValue;
    }

    public function doSomething($text)
    {
        // use getter to retrieve property
        return $text . $this->getMyValue() . '!';
    }
}

// instantiate object
$myAwc = new AlwaysUseGetters();

// use setter to set property
$myAwc->setMyValue('book');
```

```
// call method to illustrate use of getter
echo $myAwc->doSomething('This is an awesome ');
?>
```

Including source files

Use `require_once` to unconditionally include a PHP file. Analogously, use `include_once` to conditionally include a PHP file, for example in a factory method. Since `require_once` and `include_once` share the same internal file list, a file will never be included more than once even if you're mixing the two constructs.

Never use `require` or `include` as they provide the same functionality as `require_once` and `include_once`, but leave open the possibility of unintentionally including the same PHP file multiple times.

```php
<?php
// use of require_once
require_once('logging/Database/DbLogger.php');

class DbConnector
{
    // these are the RDBMs we support
    public static $supportedDbVendords = array('mysql',
                                               'oracle',
                                               'mssql');

    // factory method using include_once
    public static function makeDbConnection($dbVendor = 'mysql')
    {
        if (in_array($dbVendor, self::$supportedDbVendords)) {

            // construct the class name from the DB vendor name
            $className = ucfirst($dbVendor);
            include_once 'database/drivers/' .
                        $className . '.php';

            return new $className();

        } else {

            // unsupported RDBMs -> throw exception
            throw new Exception('Unsupported RDBSs: ' . $dbVendor);
        }
    }
}
```

```php
// use factory method to get DB connection
$dbHandle = MakeAnObject::makeDbConnection();
?>
```

Comments

Developers are encouraged to provide inline comments to clarify logic. Double forward slashes (//) are used to indicate comments. C or Perl-style hash marks (#) to signal comments are not allowed. For readability, all inline comments are to be preceded by a blank line. Here is the previous listing with inline comments. Notice how blank lines were added to make it more readable.

```php
<?php
// inline comment preceding if statement
if (is_array($myHash)) {

    // inline comment indented with code
    throw new Exception("myHash must be an array!");

// inline comment preceding elseif (preceded by blank line)
} elseif (array_key_exists('index', $myHash)) {
    echo "The key 'index' exists.\n";

// inline comment preceding else (preceded by blank line)
} else {
    echo "The key 'index' does NOT exists.\n";
}
?>
```

Inline documentation

The phpDocumentor type documentation blocks are required in four places:

- At the beginning of each PHP source code file
- Preceding each class definition
- Preceding each method definition
- Preceding each class-level property definition

Following is a table of required and recommended phpDocumentor tags. Please refer to the chapter on documentation for more details.

Tag name	File	Class	Method	Property	Usage
abstract	x	x	x		
access			x	x	public, private, or protected
author	x	x	[x]	[x]	author name <author@email.com>
copyright	x				name date
deprec			[x]	[x]	
deprecated			[x]	[x]	
example	[x]	[x]	[x]		path or url to example
extends		[x]			class name
global				[x]	type $variableName
link	[x]	[x]	[x]	[x]	url
package	x	x			package name
param			x		type [$name] description [default]
return			x		type description
see	[x]	[x]	[x]		file, class, or function name
since			x		date added to class
static			[x]	[x]	
subpackage	[x]	[x]			sub-package name
throws			[x]		exceptionName
todo	[x]	[x]	[x]		task description
var				x	type $name description [default]
version		x	[x]		auto-generated by source control

where
x = required
[x] = recommended where applicable
blank = do not use

Coding standard adherence and verification

Now that we have gone through the effort of defining a detailed coding standard, how do we make sure that everybody on the team adheres to it? Even if you are the only one writing code, it would help to have a way of checking that you are following your own standard. Looking through every single file and inspecting it for coding standard adherence would do the job, but it would also be mind-numbingly boring and repetitive. Luckily, repeating things is something at which computers excel.

PHP_CodeSniffer for automated checking

PHP_CodeSniffer is a free package that parses PHP source files and checks them for compliance with pre-defined coding standards. The software comes pre-defined with some common coding standards, namely the PEAR, Zend, Squiz, MySource, and PHPCS standards. But luckily, the author made the package easily extensible. Defining your own coding standard against which PHP_CodeSniffer can check is simply a matter of extending some classes and implementing some methods. Naturally, PHP_CodeSniffer is written in object-oriented PHP.

In their own words: "**PEAR** is a framework and distribution system for reusable PHP components."

What this means is that PHP comes with a simple installer that can be used to automatically install any of the various libraries that are categorized, organized, documented, and made available for download from the PEAR site:

```
http://pear.php.net
```

Installing PHP_CodeSniffer

Let's start by installing PHP_CodeSniffer directly from the PEAR site using their handy command line installer. When I built and installed PHP on my system, I had it put everything in a sub-folder of my local Apache installation. In my case, the PHP root folder is therefore in /usr/local/apache2/php/. This is where you can find the PEAR executable among other handy PHP utilities. The most recent version at the time of this writing is 1.2.1.

Installing the package is simply a matter of telling the pear executable to download and install it. You should see something similar to the following lines cascading down your screen.

```
Terminal — bash — bash — Dirk — ttys004 — 80×15 — ⌘2
DirkMacBook:bin dirk$ cd /usr/local/apache2/php/bin/
DirkMacBook:bin dirk$ sudo pear install PHP_CodeSniffer
downloading PHP_CodeSniffer-1.2.1.tgz ...
Starting to download PHP_CodeSniffer-1.2.1.tgz (297,076 bytes)
.............................................................done: 297,076 bytes
install ok: channel://pear.php.net/PHP_CodeSniffer-1.2.1
DirkMacBook:bin dirk$ █
```

Afterwards, listing the contents of your PHP installations `bin` directory should show the `phpcs` executable in addition to everything else you had in that directory.

```
Terminal — bash — bash — Dirk — ttys004 — 80×25 — ⌘2
DirkMacBook:bin dirk$ ls -al
total 112440
drwxr-xr-x  21 root  wheel       714 Dec  1 08:33 .
drwxr-xr-x   7 root  wheel       238 Nov 10  2006 ..
-rwxr-xr-x   1 root  wheel      2539 Nov  5 21:03 dbunit
-rwxr-xr-x   1 root  wheel       859 Sep 16 22:34 pear
-rwxr-xr-x   1 root  wheel       880 Sep 16 22:34 peardev
-rwxr-xr-x   1 root  wheel       796 Sep 16 22:34 pecl
lrwxr-xr-x   1 root  wheel        36 Sep 14 23:45 phar -> /usr/local/apache2/php
/bin/phar.phar
-rwxr-xr-x   1 root  wheel     14813 Sep 14 23:45 phar.phar
-rwxr-xr-x   1 root  wheel       901 Sep 16 22:37 phing
-rwxr-xr-x   1 root  1004   10757424 Sep 15 09:27 php
-rwxr-xr-x   1 root  wheel      2874 Sep 15 09:30 php-config
-rwxr-xr-x   1 root  wheel   9069408 Jul  6 15:38 php.9-14-09
-r-xr-xr-x   1 root  wheel  18340260 Sep 25  2007 php.bck
-rwxr-xr-x   1 root  wheel   10757424 Sep 15 09:30 php.dSYM
-rwxr-xr-x   1 root  wheel       966 Dec  1 08:33 phpcs
-rwxr-xr-x   1 root  wheel      1476 Sep 17 20:15 phpdoc
-rwxr-xr-x   1 root  wheel      4530 Sep 15 09:30 phpize
-rwxr-xr-x   1 root  wheel      2302 Nov  2 19:26 phpuc
-rwxr-xr-x   1 root  wheel      2132 Nov  5 21:03 phpunit
-rw-r--r--   1 root  wheel   8561676 Aug 23 05:35 pyrus.phar
drwxr-xr-x   3 root  wheel       102 Dec  1 08:33 scripts
DirkMacBook:bin dirk$ █
```

Just like PHP itself, the PEAR installer supports many operating systems. I installed PHP_CodeSniffer on Mac OS X, but the same procedure will work on any of the operating systems on which PHP itself runs. Also, if you are running into problems during the installation, I urge you to visit the PEAR site's support section and FAQ page.

Basic usage

Using PHP_CodeSniffer to validate one or more files against a coding standard is pretty straightforward. You simply invoke the `phpcs` executable and pass the file or directory to check as an argument.

Here is some sample output from checking one of the listings for this chapter:

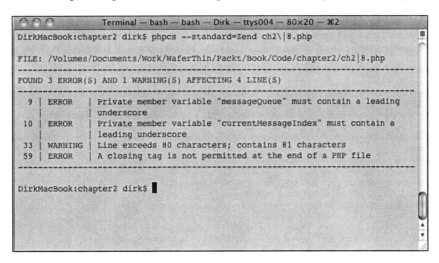

As you can see from the output, checking against the default coding standard (Zend), `phpcs` has found three errors and one warning. For each of the problems it finds, `phpcs` reports the line number of the source file, the severity of the issue (error, warning, and so on) and a description. The three errors it found aren't really part of the coding standard that we defined earlier in this chapter. However, the warning indicates that the maximum line number, which we defined in our own standard to be 80 characters, was exceeded. We could have suppressed the warnings by adding the `-n` switch to the command line. At this point, we should fix the issue and re-run `phpcs` to confirm that there are no additional issues detected.

Slightly advanced usage

Rather than duplicating the PHP_CodeSniffer documentation here, I want to use this section to briefly list the available runtime options and highlight some of the more useful ones.

There are various command line options that let you customize what to check, how to check, and how to format the ouput. Type `phpcs --help` to see all of the arguments understood by the script.

PHP_CodeSniffer comes with several predefined coding standards. Typing `phpcs -i` will tell which coding standards are installed. The version of the tool I installed came with the following standards: MySource, PEAR, PHPCS, Squiz, and Zend. To tell `phpcs` to check against a specific standard, simply add the following option to the command line: `--standard=Zend`.

The last useful command line switch I would like to point out is the `--report=summary` argument. When recursively checking a directory of source files, the output can get rather long. This switch prints a summary report with one line per file rather than outputting each individual issue it identified. Here is the summary report for all code listings in this chapter up to this point.

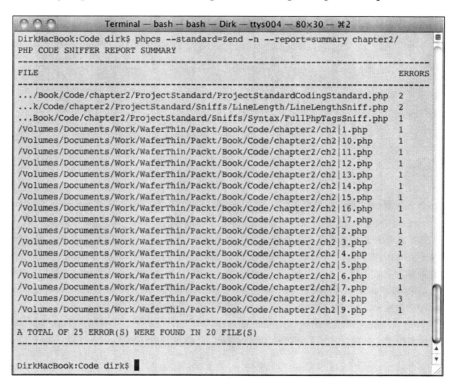

Here is a list of additional features you can customize from the command line. Please refer to the PHP_CodeSniffer online documentation for details.

- Including/excluding files based on their extension
- Excluding files or directories based on their name
- Limiting the checking to select sub-sections of the coding standard (sniffs)
- Verbosity of the output

- Permanently setting / deleting configuration options for future invocations of `phpcs` including defaults for:
  - Coding standard
  - Report format
  - Show/hide warnings in output
  - Tab width (numbers of space characters)
  - Coding standard specific configuration options

Validating against your own coding standard

Being able to check code against an existing and established coding standard, such as Zend, is useful, but the real power of PHP_CodeSniffer lies in its extensibility. By defining our own coding standard in a format PHP_CodeSniffer understands, we can use it to check conformance to our own standard.

Defining your own coding standard involves a three-step process. The steps are as follows:

1. Create the directory structure to contain your PHP_CodeSniffer coding standard definition.
2. Create a class file to allow PHP_CodeSniffer to interact with and learn about our coding standard.
3. Create the individual rule files, called **Sniffs** in PHP_CodeSniffer lingo.

 Terminology: In PHP_CodeSniffer parlance, **Sniffs** are individual class files that contain the logic to validate a single coding standard rule. For example, you might have a file called `LineLengthSniff.php` that contains the definition for class `LineLengthSniff`. The logic in this class will be invoked each time PHP_CodeSniffer wants to check whether the length of a line of code conforms to the defined standard.

Creating the directories

The directory structure for each coding standard definition is simple. From the command line, the following set of commands can be used to create the initial set of directories and files of a hypothetical coding PHP_CodeSniffer standard definition.

```
          Terminal — bash — bash — Dirk — ttys004 — 80×25 — ⌘2
DirkMacBook:chapter2 dirk$ mkdir ProjectStandard
DirkMacBook:chapter2 dirk$ cd ProjectStandard
DirkMacBook:ProjectStandard dirk$ touch ProjectStandardCodingStandard.php
DirkMacBook:ProjectStandard dirk$ mkdir Sniffs
DirkMacBook:ProjectStandard dirk$ cd Sniffs
DirkMacBook:Sniffs dirk$ mkdir LineLength
DirkMacBook:Sniffs dirk$ touch LineLength/LimitLineLengthSniff.php
DirkMacBook:Sniffs dirk$ mkdir NamingConventions
DirkMacBook:Sniffs dirk$ touch NamingConventions/ClassNamesSniff.php
DirkMacBook:Sniffs dirk$ touch NamingConventions/VariableNamesSniff.php
DirkMacBook:Sniffs dirk$ touch NamingConventions/PropertyNamesSniff.php
DirkMacBook:Sniffs dirk$ tree ../../ProjectStandard/
../../ProjectStandard/
|-- ProjectStandardCodingStandard.php
`-- Sniffs
    |-- LineLength
    |   `-- LimitLineLengthSniff.php
    `-- NamingConventions
        |-- ClassNamesSniff.php
        |-- PropertyNamesSniff.php
        `-- VariableNamesSniff.php

3 directories, 5 files
DirkMacBook:Sniffs dirk$ █
```

We start by creating a directory to hold all the files associated with our coding standard definition, `ProjectStandard`. In that directory, we create a class file called `ProjectStandardCodingStandard.php` that identifies our directory as one containing a PHP_CodeSniffer coding standard definition. This class is also responsible for communicating with the main `phpcs` executable regarding some of the details of our coding standard (more about that later).

Next we create a directory called `Sniff`, which will contain descriptions of individual coding standard rules, or collections (directories thereof). In our case, we plan on creating rules regarding naming conventions and line length, which is why we are creating directories `NamingConventions` and `LineLength` inside the `Sniffs` directory. Each of these sub-directories then contains one or more individual sniff files: `LimitLineLengthSniff.php`, `ClassNamesSniff.php`, `VariableNamesSniff.php`, and `PropertyNamesSniff.php`.

The main coding standard class file

In the previous step, we have already created a placeholder for the main class file in our ProjectStandard directory. Now let's put some code in there and identify ourselves as a PHP_CodeSniffer coding standard.

```php
<?php
// make sure the parent class is in our include path
if (class_exists('PHP_CodeSniffer_Standards_CodingStandard', true)
    === false) {
    throw new PHP_CodeSniffer_Exception('Class
            PHP_CodeSniffer_Standards_CodingStandard not found');
}


// our main coding standard class definition
class PHP_CodeSniffer_Standards_ProjectStandard_
ProjectStandardCodingStandard extends PHP_CodeSniffer_Standards_
CodingStandard
{
    // include sniffs from other directories or even whole coding
       standards
    // great way to create your standard and build on it
       public function getIncludedSniffs()
    {
        // return an array of sniffs, directories of sniffs,
        // or coding standards to include
        return array(
                'Generic'
                );
    }


    // exclude sniffs from previously included ones
    public function getExcludedSniffs()
    {
        // return a list of sniffs or directories of sniffs to
      exclude
      return array(
                'Generic/Sniffs/LineLengthSniff.php'
                );
    }
}
?>
```

Our main class extends `PHP_CodeSniffer_Standards_CodingStandard`. This
is required of all classes identifying a coding standard to be used with `phpcs`.
However, the two methods we are implementing, `getIncludedSniffs()` and
`getExcludedSniffs()` are pretty important because they let us assemble our own
coding standard from parts of existing standards, thus saving us a lot of time since
we don't have to write all the sniffs ourselves. Both classes return simple arrays. The
items in the array are either names of existing coding standards, paths to directories
of sniffs of existing coding standards, or paths to individual sniff files. For example,
it turns out that our own coding standard is pretty close to the "Generic" coding
standard included with PHP_CodeSniffer. Therefore, to make things easier for us,
we include the whole "Generic" coding standard in the `getIncludedSniffs()`
method, but choose to exclude that standard's `LineLengthSniff.php` in the
`getExcludedSniffs()` method.

Creating Sniffs

Each of the rules we formulated to express our coding standard earlier in the chapter,
can be described using a sniff class file that PHP_CodeSniffer can use. However,
before we jump in and really get our hands dirty, it is a good idea to review how
tokenization works. After all, PHP_CodeSniffer builds on and expands PHP's inbuilt
tokenizer extension.

 Tokenization is the process of breaking input text into meaningful parts.
When combined with a classification and/or description, each such part
is considered a **token**.

Tokenization

PHP uses the Zend Engine's tokenizer at its core to parse and interpret PHP source
files. Lucky for us, the tokenizer is also directly accessible via two functions in the
language's top-level namespace: `token_get_all()` and `token_get_name()`.

Tokenization consists of taking input text and breaking it up into meaningful
segments. Each segment can optionally carry a label, explanation, or additional
detail. Let's look at an example of PHP code being tokenized by the Zend Engine.

```php
<?php
// get the contents of this file into a variable
$thisFile = file_get_contents(__FILE__);

// get the token stack
$tokenStack = token_get_all($thisFile);

$currentLine = 0;
```

```
// output each token & look up the corresponding name
   foreach ($tokenStack as $token) {

    // most tokens are arrays
       if (is_array($token)) {

        if ($currentLine < $token[2]) {
            $currentLine++;
            echo "Line $currentLine:\n";
        }
        echo "\t" . token_name($token[0]) . ': ' . rtrim($token[1]) .
"\n";

    // some tokens are just strings
    } else {
        echo "\tString: " . rtrim($token) . "\n";
    }
  }
?>
```

The above code snippet runs itself through the tokenizer, which results in the following output:

We formatted our output a littler nicer, but the first token essentially looks like this:

```
Array(
        [0] => 367
        [1] => <?php
        [2] => 1
      )
```

In this case, 367 is the value of the parser token, which corresponds to T_OPEN_TAG when we look it up with the token_name() function. <?php is the actual text of the token and 1 is the line number on which the token occurs. You can look up the complete list of tokenizer token constants in the online PHP manual, or the following code snippet will list the ones that are defined for your version of PHP.

```
<?php
// get all constants organized by category
$allTokens = get_defined_constants(true);

// we're only interested in tokenizer constants
print_r($allTokens["tokenizer"]);
?>
```

As you can see for yourself, tokens contain a lot of information that is useful to programmatically understand what an analyzed portion of code is doing. PHP_CodeSniffer builds upon the existing tokenization extension and built-in tokens by providing additional tokens to provide even finer granularity when examining PHP code.

Writing our first sniff

Now that you know what tokens are, it will be much easier to understand what the individual sniffs are doing. First of all, a sniff registers with the main executable the tokens in which it is interested using the register() method. That way, the main code can hand over execution to the sniff's process() method whenever it encounters such a token. For example, a sniff trying to validate that a code file has the proper PHP opening and/or closing tag might register interest in the T_OPEN_TAG with the parent code. That is exactly what we're doing in the following listing:

```
<?php
// sniff class definition must implement the
// PHP_CodeSniffer_Sniff interface
class ProjectStandard_Sniffs_Syntax_FullPhpTagsSniff implements
PHP_CodeSniffer_Sniff
{
    // register for the tokens we're interested in
    public function register()
```

```
    {
        return array(T_OPEN_TAG);
    }

    // process each occurrence of the token in this method
    public function process(PHP_CodeSniffer_File $phpcsFile,
                                                        $stackPtr)
    {
        $tokens = $phpcsFile->getTokens();

        // warn if the opening PHP tag is not the first token in the
                                                                file
        if ($stackPtr != 0) {
            $phpcsFile->addWarning('Nothing should precede the PHP
                                        open tag.', $stackPtr);
        }

        // error if full PHP open tag is not used
        if ($tokens[$stackPtr]['content'] != '<?php') {
            $phpcsFile->addError('Only full PHP opening tags are
                                        allowed.', $stackPtr);
        }

        // all files must have closing tag
        if ($token[sizeof($tokens) - 1]['type'] != T_CLOSE_TAG) {
            $phpcsFile->addError('All files must end with a closing
                                        PHP tag.', $stackPtr);
        }
    }
}
?>
```

Let's take a closer look at the process() method, which takes two parameters.
The first one is a reference to a PHP_CodeSniffer_File object, which we can use
to access the token stack. The second argument is an array index to the current
token in the stack.

Armed with that information, we can start validating the code via the token stack.
First, we use the PHP_CodeSniffer_File's addWarning() method to display a
warning message whenever the very first token is not the PHP open tag. Next, we
use the addError() method to display an error message to the user whenever the
opening tag doesn't match the string "<?php" since that is the only opening tag that
our coding standard allows. Lastly, we display an error message if the last token in
the stack is anything other than the closing PHP tag.

That's it. The main `phpcs` executable does the rest. It tokenizes the input file(s), calls all registered sniffs for each occurrence of their respective token, and displays nicely formatted output to the user.

You may have noticed in the above listing that we used the values of the token's 'content' and 'type' attributes. If you recall, the tokens returned by the standard PHP tokenizer did not have those attributes. Instead, `PHP_CodeSniffer` adds those and other attributes. Following is a list of token attributes that are always available. Depending on the type of token, additional attributes might be available. You should consult the `PHP_CodeSniffer` API documentation for details.

Attribute name	Example	Description
code	301	The token type code (see `token_get_all()`)
content	if	The token content
type	T_IF	The token name
line	56	The line number when the token is located
column	12	The column in the line where this token starts (starts from 1)
level	2	The depth a token is within the scopes open
Conditions	Array(2 => 50, 9 => 353)	A list of scope condition token positions => codes that opened the scopes that this token exists in (see conditional tokens)

Extending existing sniffs

We have already seen that we can include sniffs from other coding standards in our own. However, we can take it a step further and make an existing sniff do all the work while still implementing our own standard. For example, the "Generic" coding standard includes a sniff to check for maximum line length. As it happens, the suggested maximum line length is 80 characters— the same as in our own standard. However, the absolute maximum line length is 100; whereas, our standard allows for up to 120 characters per line. Therefore, all we have to do is extend the existing sniff and overwrite the protected property `$absoluteLineLimit` as in the following listing.

```php
<?php
if (class_exists('Generic_Sniffs_Files_LineLengthSniff', true) ===
false) {
    throw new PHP_CodeSniffer_Exception('Class Generic_Sniffs_Files_
LineLengthSniff not found');
}
```

```
// class to check line length in number of characters
// note: we're overwriting an existing sniff from the generic coding
standard
class Zend_Sniffs_Files_LineLengthSniff extends Generic_Sniffs_Files_
LineLengthSniff
{
    // we generate an error when exceeding the absolute
    // maximum line length
    protected $absoluteLineLimit = 120;

}
?>
```

Automated code checks

Even though PHP_CodeSniffer is available, there is no guarantee that individual developers will actually take advantage of it. However, in a team environment, the lead developer can take several steps to make sure the team members adhere to the chosen common standard. First, the code base should be scheduled for an automated check once a day during active development. A simple (insert you favorite scheduler utility here) job can process all the source files and send an email to everybody in the team.

However, it is possible to take things a step further. Assuming that you are using a source code control system, most of these systems provide hooks at various stages of checking out or committing source code. The most commonly used hook is the pre-commit hook. In other words, the source code control system executes any number of user-configurable steps before committing the code. The outcome of these steps impact whether the use is allowed to commit the code or not. In the case of our coding standard, we can configure the pre-commit hook to run any PHP source files being committed through PHP_CodeSniffer and only proceed if no errors and/or warnings are being generated. In essence, this is a way that your team only accepts contributions from individual developers if they adhere to the team's coding standard.

For a detailed example of how to configure the Subversion source code control system with a PHP_CodeSniffer pre-commit hook, please consult the chapter on source code and version control.

Summary

I think we have come full circle within the course of this chapter. We started with a philosophical discussion; as well as an examination of the pros and cons of a common coding standard. We then proceeded to formulate a coding standard that can serve as a foundation for any PHP development project— whether it consists of a single developer or dozens spread throughout the globe.

Realizing that having a standard alone is not enough, we looked at PHP_CodeSniffer as a tool for validating code against a pre-defined standard. We even learned how to translate our coding guidelines to PHP code that PHP_CodeSniffer can use when checking the source files. Lastly, we briefly discussed that automating or integrating source validation is an effective way of actually enforcing the standard without having to waste too much time reviewing code manually.

The standard we defined in this chapter is not the answer to all your coding standard needs. I'm sure you were objecting to some of the rules I defined as you were reading through them. That's ok. The important thing is to have a coding standard at all. You can never make everybody happy, but you can make sure that the team benefits from the coding standard, even if the members don't agree with each and every detail.

Rather than blindly adopting the coding standard in this or any other standard for that matter, you might want to take the time to examine it and customize it for your purposes. Also, a coding standard evolves over time along with the language itself. With PHP6 due to be released in the near future, we will have to revisit our standard and see how to best improve it to reflect all the exciting new features.

2
Documentation with phpDocumentor

In this chapter, we will take a look at documentation. Since this is a book for the professional PHP developer, we will primarily be dealing with code-level documentation targeted at other developers.

We will learn to create code-level documentation using phpDocumentor, PHP's entry into the xDoc family of documentation tools and the de facto standard for documenting PHP code. Specifically, we will install phpDocumentor. Next, we will learn the general syntax for DocBlocks and how to run phpDocumentor to generate the documentation. Finally, we will cover all phpDocumentor tags in some detail and look at some examples.

Before we proceed further, I have to start off with a confession. The code samples and listing in the rest of this book don't fully reflect the extent of code-level documentation I would expect a reader of this book to produce. Although I have tried to make sure that there are plenty of inline comments to guide the reader, I haven't really been using proper phpDoc tags and sections. The reasons are simple and two-fold. First, space in print editions is limited and adding all the proper documentation sections to our source code would have increased the size of the listings significantly. Second, the inline comments in the listings are intended for the developer directly. In contrast, phpDoc comments get parsed and processed with the rest of the code and the resulting output formatted for easier reading and browsing.

In other words, when you tackle your own projects, I would expect you to do as I do in this chapter and not as I do in the rest of the book (at least as far as phpDoc is concerned).

Code-level documentation

The documentation we will be creating describes the interface of the code more than minute details of the actual implementation. For example, you might document an API that you have developed for the outside world to interact with some insanely important project on which you are working.

Having an API is great, but for other developers to quickly get an overview of the capabilities of the API and being able to crank out working code within a short amount of time is even better. If you are following the proper conventions while writing the code, all you would have to do is run a utility to extract and format the documentation from the code.

Even if you're not inviting the whole world to interact with your software, developers within your own team will benefit from documentation describing some core classes that are being used throughout the project. Just imagine reading your co-worker's code and coming across some undecipherable object instance or method call. Wouldn't it be great to simply pull up the API documentation for that object and read about its uses, properties, and methods? Furthermore, it would be really convenient if the documentation for the whole project were assembled and logically organized in one location. That way, a developer cannot only learn about a specific class, but also about its relationships with other classes. In a way, it would enable the programmer to form a high-level picture of how the different pieces fit together.

Another reason to consider code-level documentation is that source code is easily accessible due to PHP being a scripting language. Unless they choose to open source their code, compiled languages have a much easier time hiding their code. If you ever plan on making your project available for others to download and run on their own server, you are unwittingly inviting a potential critic or collaborator. Since it is rather hard (but not impossible) to hide the source code from a user that can download your project, there is the potential for people to start looking at and changing your code.

Generally speaking, that is a good thing because they might be improving the quality and usefulness of the project and hopefully they will be contributing their improvements back to the user community. In such a case, you will be glad that you stuck to a coding standard and added comments throughout the code. It will make understanding your code much easier and anybody reading the code will come away with the impression that you are indeed a professional.

Great, you say, how do I make sure I always generate such useful documentation when I program? The answer is simple. You need to invest a little time learning the right tool(s). That's the easy part for someone in the technology field where skill sets are being expanded every couple of years anyway. The hard part is to consistently apply that knowledge. Like much else in this book, it is a matter of training yourself to have good habits. Writing API level documentation at the same time as implementing a class or method should become second nature as much as following a coding standard or properly testing your code.

Luckily, there are some tools that can take most of the tedium out of documenting your code. Foremost, modern IDEs (Integrated Development Environments) are very good at extracting some of the needed information automatically. Templates can help you generate documentation tags rather rapidly. Take a look at the chapter on IDEs to see how you can configure our IDE of choice to quickly generate much of the syntax surrounding the documentation, while leaving it to the programmer to fill in the crucial details.

Levels of detail

As you create your documentation, you have to decide how detailed you want to get. I have seen projects where easily half the source code consisted of comments and documentation that produced fantastic developer and end-user documentation. However, that may not be necessary or appropriate for your project. My suggestion is to figure out what level of effort you can reasonably expect of yourself in relation to what would be appropriate for your target audience. After all, it is unlikely that you will start documenting every other line of code if you are not used to adding any documentation at all. On one hand, if your audience is relatively small and sophisticated, you might get away with less documentation. On the other hand, if you are documenting the web services API for a major online service as you are coding it, you probably want to be as precise and explicit as possible. Adding plenty of examples and tutorials might enable even novice developers to start using your API quickly. In that case, your employer's success in the market place is directly tied to the quality and accessibility of the documentation. In this case, the documentation is very much part of the product rather than an afterthought or merely an add-on.

On one end of the spectrum, you can have documentation that pertains to the project as a whole, such as a "README" file. At the next level down, you might have a *doc* section at the beginning of each file. That way, you can cover the functionality of the file or class without going into too much detail.

Introducing phpDocumentor

phpDocumentor is an Open Source project that has established itself as the dominanot tool for documenting PHP code. Although there are other solutions, phpDocumentor is by far the one you are most likely to encounter in your work – and for good reason. Taking a clue from similar documentation tools that came before it, such as JavaDoc, phpDocumentor offers many features in terms of user interface, formatting, and so on.

PhpDocumentor provides you with a large library of tags and other markup, which you can use to embed comments, documentation, and tutorials in your source code. The phpDoc markup is viewed as comments by PHP when it executes your source file and therefore doesn't interfere with the code's functionality. However, running the phpDocumentor command line executable or using the web-based interface, you can process all your source files, extract the phpDoc related content, and compile it into functional documentation. There is no need to look through the source files because phpDocumentor assembles the documentation into nicely looking HTML pages, text files, PDFs, or CHMs.

Although phpDocumentor supports procedural programming and PHP4, the focus in this chapter will be on using it to document applications developed with object-oriented design in mind. Specifically, we will be looking at how to properly document interfaces, classes, properties, and methods. For details on how to document some of the PHP4 elements that don't typically occur in PHP5's object-oriented implementation, please consult the phpDocumentor online manual:

```
http://manual.phpdoc.org/
```

Installing phpDocumentor

There are two ways of installing phpDocumentor. The preferred way is to use the PEAR repository. Typing `pear install PhpDocumentor` from the command line will take care of downloading, extracting, and installing phpDocumentor for you. The pear utility is typically included in any recent standard distribution of PHP. However, if for some reason you need to install it first, you can download it from the PEAR site:

```
http://pear.php.net/
```

Before we proceed with the installation, there is one important setting to consider. Traditionally, phpDocumentor has been run from the command line, however, more recent versions come with a rather functional web-based interface. If you want pear to install the web UI into a sub-directory of your web server's document root directory, you will first have to set pear's `data_dir` variable to the absolute path to that directory. In my case, I created a local site from which I can access various applications installed by pear. That directory is `/Users/dirk/Sites/phpdoc`. From the terminal, you would see the following if you tell pear where to install the web portion and proceed to install phpDocumentor.

```
DirkMacBook:bin dirk$ cd /usr/local/apache2/php/bin/
DirkMacBook:bin dirk$ sudo pear config-set data_dir /Users/dirk/Sites/phpdoc
config-set succeeded
DirkMacBook:bin dirk$ sudo pear install PhpDocumentor
downloading PhpDocumentor-1.4.3.tgz ...
Starting to download PhpDocumentor-1.4.3.tgz (2,423,486 bytes)
.....................................................................done: 2,423,486 byt
es
install ok: channel://pear.php.net/PhpDocumentor-1.4.3
DirkMacBook:bin dirk$ ls
dbunit          phar            php-config      phpcs           phpunit
pear            phar.phar       php.9-14-09     phpdoc          pyrus.phar
peardev         phing           php.bck         phpize          scripts
pecl            php             php.dSYM        phpuc
DirkMacBook:bin dirk$
```

As part of the installation, the pear utility created a directory for phpDocumentor's web interface. Here is the listing of the contents of that directory:

```
DirkMacBook:PhpDocumentor dirk$ cd /Users/dirk/Sites/phpdoc/PhpDocumentor/
DirkMacBook:PhpDocumentor dirk$ ls -F
HTML_TreeMenu-1.1.2/     new_phpdoc.php          poweredbyphpdoc.gif
docbuilder/             phpDocumentor/          user/
index.html             phpDocumentor.ini
media/                  phpdoc.php
DirkMacBook:PhpDocumentor dirk$
```

The other option for installing phpDocumentor is to download an archive from the project's `SourceForge.net` space. After that, it is just a matter of extracting the archive and making sure that the main `phpdoc` executable is in your path so that you can launch it from anywhere without having to type the absolute path. You will also have to manually move the corresponding directory to your server's document root directory to take advantage of the web-based interface.

DocBlocks

Let's start by taking a look at the syntax and usage of phpDocumentor. The basic unit of phpDoc documentation is a DocBlock. All DocBocks take the following format:

```
/**
 * Short description
 *
 * Long description that can span as many lines as you wish.
 * You can add as much detail information and examples in this
 * section as you deem appropriate. You can even <i>markup</i>
 * this content or use inline tags like this:
 * {@tutorial Project/AboutInlineTags.proc}
 *
 * @tag1
 * @tag2 value2 more text
 * ... more tags ...
 */
```

 A **DocBlock** is the basic container of phpDocumentor markup within PHP source code. It can contain three different element groups: short description, long description, and tags – all of which are optional.

The first line of a DocBlock has only three characters, namely "/**". Similarly, the last line will only have these three characters: " */". All lines in between will start with " * ".

Short and long descriptions

An empty line or a period at the end of the line terminates short descriptions. In contrast, long descriptions can go on for as many lines as necessary. Both types of descriptions allow certain markup to be used: <b>, <br>, <code>, <i>, <kbd>, <li>, <ol>, <p>, <pre>, <samp>, <ul>, <var>. The effect of these markup tags is borrowed directly from HTML. Depending on the output converter being used, each tag can be rendered in different ways.

Tags

Tags are keywords known to phpDocumentor. Each tag can be followed by a number of optional arguments, such as data type, description, or URL. For phpDocumentor to recognize a tag, it has to be preceded by the @ character. Some examples of common tags are:

```
/**
 * @package ForeignLanguageParser
 * @author Dirk Merkel dirk@waferthin.com
 * @link http://www.waferthin.com Check out my site
 */
class Translate
{
}
```

In addition to the above "standard" tags, phpDocumentor recognizes "inline" tags, which adhere to the same syntax, with the only notable difference that they are enclosed by curly brackets. Inline tags occur inline with short and long descriptions like this:

```
/**
 * There is not enough space here to explain the value and usefulness
 * of this class, but luckily there is an extensive tutorial available
 * for you: {@tutorial ForeignLanguageParser/Translate.cls}
 */
```

DocBlock templates

It often happens that the same tags apply to multiple successive elements. For example, you might group all private property declarations at the beginning of a class. In that case, it would be quite repetitive to list the same, or nearly the same DocBlocks, over and over again. Luckily, we can take advantage of DocBlock templates, which allow us to define DocBlock sections that will be added to the DocBlock of any element between a designated start and end point.

DocBlock templates look just like regular DocBlocks with the difference that the first line consists of /**#@+ instead of /**. The tags in the template will be added to all subsequent DocBlocks until phpDocumenter encounters the ending letter sequence /**#@-*/.

The following two code fragments will produce the same documentation. First, here is the version containing only standard DocBlocks:

```
<?php
class WisdomDispenser
{
    /**
     * @access protected
     * @var string
     */
    private $firstSaying = 'Obey the golden rule.';
```

```php
/**
 * @access protected
 * @var string
 */
private $secondSaying = 'Get in or get out.';

/**
 * @access protected
 * @var string
 * @author Albert Einstein <masterof@relativity.org>
 */
private $thirdSaying = 'Everything is relative';
}
?>
```

And here is the fragment that will produce the same documentation using a more concise notation by taking advantage of DocBlock templates:

```php
<?php
class WisdomDispenser
{
    /**#@+
     * @access protected
     * @var string
     */
    private $firstSaying = 'Obey the golden rule.';
    private $secondSaying = 'Get in or get out.';

    /**
     * @author Albert Einstein <masterof@relativity.org>
     */
    private $thirdSaying = 'Everything is relative';
    /**#@-*/
}
?>
```

Tutorials

DocBlocks are targeted at developers. phpDocumetor generates beautiful documentation, but even if you are looking at the code itself, DocBlocks are very valuable to a programmer. In contrast, tutorials are often targeted at end-users or present extended examples and instructions to developers, which often require a little more handholding than even a DocBlock's long description can accommodate.

Naming conventions and how to reference tutorials

Tutorials are typically organized in their own directory that mimics the package structure you designed using the `@package` and `@subpackage` tags. Each tutorial is a self-contained file that will be referenced from DocBlocks using the `@tutorial`, `{@tutorial}`, or `{@link}` tags.

For example, perhaps you have used the `@package` tag to group various files and classes together under a package named "WebServices." Furthermore, let's assume you have created multiple sub-packages using the `@subpackage` tag, one if which might be called "Authentication." If you wanted to write a tutorial on how to consume the authentication web service and use it to log into your system, you would employ the following directory structure and file naming convention:

```
WebServices/

`-- Authentication

    `-- Login.cls
```

The corresponding DocBlock preceding the Login class might then look something like this:

```
/**
 * Login class for web services authentication
 *
 * This class provides various methods that are exposed
 * by the web services layer of the package. This class
 * and its methods can be used to obtain a token from
 * the authentication system that will be required during
 * subsequent API calls. For more detail on how to call
 * the authentication system from you PHP code, take a
 * look at our tutorial:
 * {@tutorial WebServices/Authentication/Login.cls}.
 *
 * @package WebServices
 * @subpackage Authentication
 * @tutorial WebServices/Authentication/Login.cls
 */
class Login
{
    // lots of useful methods here!
}
```

Essentially, the directory structure reflects your package and sub-package names. The names of tutorial files match the name of the element being documented in the case of package and class-level documentation. The file extension indicates the PHP element being documented: tutorials for a package have file extension .pkg, class tutorial end in .cls, and procedure-level tutorials end in .proc.

```
PackageName/

`-- SubpackageName

    |-- ClassTutorialName.cls

    |-- PackageTutorialName.pkg

    `-- ProcedureTutorialName.proc
```

DocBook syntax

Rather than coming up with their own format, the developers of phpDocumentor relied on an established format for technical documentation: DocBook. DocBook is an XML-based markup language originally developed to document software and hardware. However, it has since been applied to all kinds of documentation, including tutorials.

Rather than to go into the details of DocBook syntax, which is beyond the scope of this chapter, I want to present a basic outline of a DocBook tutorial that continues our theme of writing a tutorial for a web services authentication call. This rudimentary DocBook document has been adapted from the phpDocumentor manual and can be used as a starting point for your own tutorials.

```
<refentry id="{@id}">
    <refnamediv>
        <refname>Web Services Authentication Tutorial</refname>
        <refpurpose>How to use the authentication web service to
                    obtain a security token that will be required for
                    subsequent  web services requests.
        </refpurpose>
    </refnamediv>
    <refsynopsisdiv>
        <author>
            Dirk Merkel
            <authorblurb>{@link mailto:dirk@waferthin.com Dirk
                                        Merkel}</authorblurb>
        </author>
    </refsynopsisdiv>
    {@toc}
    <refsect1 id="{@id intro}">
```

```
        <title>Web Services Authentication Tutorial</title>
        <para>Pay attention because this is how you will have to
                implement authentication to access our web service
        </para>
    </refsect1>
</refentry>
```

One important thing to take away from this example is that DocBook tutorials can contain certain inline phpDocumentor tags. This is very important because it allows tutorials to tie into the rest of the project's documentation. The following inline tags can be used in DocBook tutorials:

{@link}

{@tutorial}

{@id}

{@toc}

Please consult the phpDoc tag reference section in this chapter to see the proper usage for each tag.

Documenting a project

To really illustrate the usefulness of good documentation, nothing takes the place of actually seeing a complete example. Now that we have covered the basic syntax and you have some idea of the available tags, let's see what phpDocumentor can do.

For the purpose of this example, I have created a small project. I have tried to cram as many different object-oriented features in as possible. This way, there will be plenty for us to document and explore the different phpDoc tags at our disposal.

The purpose of this example project is to provide user authentication. Given a username and password, this code tries to verify that a corresponding valid account exists. In an effort to keep things at a manageable size, I have taken the liberty to simplify much of the functionality.

Here is a hierarchical outline of the files in the sample project:

```
project/
|-- classes
|    |-- Accountable.php
|    |-- Authentication
|    |    `-- HardcodedAccounts.php
```

```
|    |-- Authentication.php

|    `-- Users.php

`-- index.php
```

The `classes` directory contains all our interfaces and class definitions. The `index.php` file handles all necessary includes, creates some objects, and serves as a form handler. It essentially ties everything together. Next, let's take a look at each of the files.

```
File project/classes/Accountable.php:
```

```php
<?php
interface Accountable
{
    const AUTHENTICATION_ERR_MSG = 'There is no user account
associated with the current session. Try logging in fist.';

    public function isLoggedIn();
    public function getAccount($user = '');
}
?>
```

The `Accountable` interface defines a constant and two methods that will have to be implemented by any that implement the interface.

```
File project/classes/Authentication.php:
```

```php
<?php
abstract class Authentication implements Accountable
{
    private $account = null;

    public function getAccount($user = '')
    {
        if ($this->account !== null) {
            return $this->account;
        } else {
            return AUTHENTICATION_ERR_MSG;
        }
    }

    public function isLoggedIn()
    {
        return ($this->account !== null);
    }
```

```
    abstract public function login($user, $password);
}
?>
```

Authentication is a class that implements the Accountable interface. It provides concrete implementations of the two methods dictated by the interfaces. However, since it also declares an abstract method, the class itself is abstract. Authentication serves as a blueprint for any class providing authentication services. Any child class will have to implement the login() method.

File project/classes/Authentication/HardcodedAccounts.php:

```
<?php
class Authentication_HardcodedAccounts extends Authentication
{
    private $users;

    public function __construct()
    {
        $this->users = new Users();
    }

    public function login($user, $password)
    {
        if (empty($user) || empty($password)) {
            return false;
        } else {

            // both validation methods should work ...

            // user static method to validate account
            $firstValidation = Users::validate($user, $password);

            // use magic method validate<username>($password)
            $userLoginFunction = 'validate' . $user;
            $secondValidation = $this->users-
                                    >$userLoginFunction($password);

            return ($firstValidation && $secondValidation);
        }
    }
}
?>
```

Class `Authentication_HardcodedAccounts` extends abstract class `Authentication` and provides the required implementation of method `login()`. To actually validate whether a given username and password correspond to an account, it delegates the work to a `User` class, which we will see in the next listing.

One thing to note is that `login()` calls two different methods of the `User` object to validate the username and password. There is absolutely no reason for doing so other than showing two different ways of passing the required parameters. The first is a call to a static method, which passes both username and password as method arguments. The second is a call to magic method `login<user>($password)`, which passes the username as part of the method name and the corresponding password as an argument.

File `project/classes/Users.php`:

```php
<?php
class Users
{
    private static $accounts = array('dirk'      => 'myPass',
                                      'albert'    => 'einstein');

    public static function validate($user, $password)
    {
        return self::$accounts[$user] == $password;
    }

    public function __call($name, $arguments)
    {
        if (preg_match("/^validate(.*)$/", $name, $matches) &&
count($arguments) > 0) {
            return self::validate($matches[1], $arguments[0]);
        }
    }
}
?>
```

Class `Users` has a hard-coded list of users and their passwords stored in a private array property. I sure hope you're not thinking of implementing this in production, but it does keep things nice and simple for our example.

`Users` also provides the two account validation methods we saw being called from the `Authentication_HardcodedAccounts` class. `validate<user>()` is implemented with the help of the `__call()` magic method.

File `project/index.php`:

```php
<?php
require_once('classes/Accountable.php');
require_once('classes/Authentication.php');
require_once('classes/Users.php');
require_once('classes/Authentication/HardcodedAccounts.php');

$authenticator = new Authentication_HardcodedAccounts();

// uncomment for testing
$_POST['user'] = 'dirk';
$_POST['password'] = 'myPass';

if (isset($_POST['user']) && isset($_POST['password'])) {

    $loginSucceeded = $authenticator->login($_POST['user'],
                                            $_POST['password']);

    if ($loginSucceeded === true) {
        echo "Congrats - you're in!\n";
    } else {
        echo "Uh-uh - try again!\n";
    }
}
?>
```

Lastly, we have `index.php`, which ties everything together. After including the necessary class files, it creates an instance of `Authentication_HardcodedAccounts`, and uses it to validate the username and password that were presumably posted from a web form.

Documentation without DocBlocks

You have probably already noticed that short of some inline comments, the sample project has no DocBlocks, tags, or anything else added by the programmer for the purpose of documenting the code. Nevertheless, there is quite a bit that phpDocumentor can do with uncommented PHP code. If we are in the directory containing the project directory, we can run phpDocumentor and ask to generate documentation for the project like this:

```
DirkMacBook:chapter3 dirk$ phpdoc --target ./project-no-phpDoc/docs --directory
./project-no-phpDoc/ --title 'Generated Documentation - No DocBlocks' --sourceco
de on --defaultpackagename 'UserAuthentication'
PHP Version 5.3.2-dev
phpDocumentor version 1.4.3

Parsing configuration file phpDocumentor.ini...
    (found in /Users/dirk/Sites/phpdoc/PhpDocumentor/)...

done
Maximum memory usage set at 2048M after considering php.ini...
using tokenizer Parser
Hidden /Volumes/Documents/Work/WaferThin/Packt/Book/Code/chapter3/project-no-php
Doc/.DS_Store Ignored


Grabbing README/INSTALL/CHANGELOG

done
```

The above command will recursively process all files in the project directory (`--directory ./project/`), create documentation with a custom title (`--title 'Generated Documentation - No DocBlocks'`), include a source code listing of each file processed (`--sourcecode on`), save all documentation to the docs directory (`--target ./project/docs`), and group everything under a specified package name (`--defaultpackagename 'UserAuthentication'`). Later on in this chapter, we will take a look at the complete list of command line options of the `phpdoc` executable.

Listing all documentation pages that phpDocumentor generated is impractical, but let's take a look at the outline and at least one of the classes. All we have to do to view the documentation is to open the `index.html` file in the `docs` directory where we told phpDocumentor to direct the output with a web browser.

UserAuthentication

UserAuthentication

Description
  Class trees
  Index of elements
Interfaces
  Accountable
Classes
  Authentication
  Authentication_HardcodedAccounts
  Users
Files
  Accountable.php
  Authentication.php
  HardcodedAccounts.php
  index.php
  Users.php

phpDocumentor v 1.4.3

Root interface Accountable

- Accountable

Root class Authentication

- Authentication (**implements** Accountable)
    - Authentication_HardcodedAccounts

Root class Users

- Users

Documentation generated on Thu, 03 Dec 2009 13:01:40 -0800 by phpDocumentor 1.4.3

Looking at the above screenshot, we see that phpDocumentor correctly found all the class files. Moreover, it identified `Accountable` as an interface and found `index.php`, even though it contains no class definitions. All classes and interfaces are grouped together under the AuthenticationUser package name that was specified from the command line. At the same time, we see some of the shortcomings. There is no further classification or grouping and all components are simply listed under the root level.

Before we move on, let's also take a look at what information phpDocumentor was able to extract from the Users.php file:

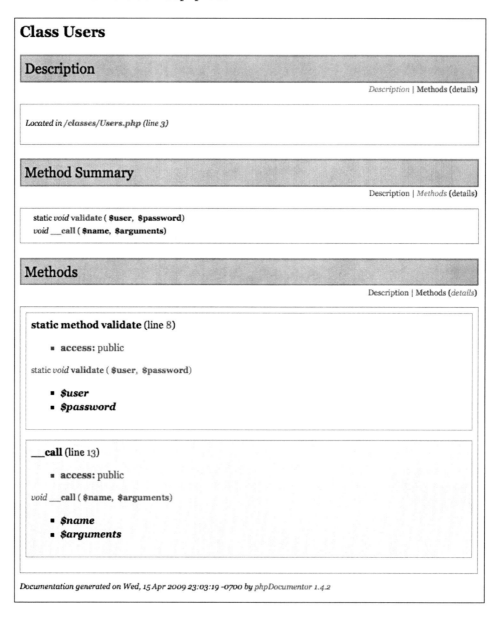

It correctly identified the methods of the class, their visibility, and which parameters are required. I think that is a pretty useful start, albeit the description is a bit sparse and we have no idea what methods were actually implemented using the magic __call() method.

Another point to note here is that the class property `$accounts` does not appear in the documentation at all. That is intended behavior because the property has been declared private. If you want elements with private visibility to appear in your documentation, you will have to add the -pp / --parse private command line option or put this option in a `config` file.

Documentation with DocBlocks

Of course, this example wouldn't be complete if we didn't proceed to add proper DocBlocks to our code. The following is the exact same code as before, but this time it has been properly marked up with DocBlocks.

File `project/classes/Accountable.php`:

```php
<?php
/**
 * @author Dirk Merkel <dirk@waferthin.com>
 * @package WebServices
 * @subpackage Authentication
 * @copyright Waferthin Web Works LLC
 * @license http://www.gnu.org/copyleft/gpl.html Freely available
under GPL
 */
/**
 * <i>Accountable</i> interface for authentication
 *
 * Any class that handles user authentication <b>must</b>
 * implement this interface. It makes it almost
 * trivial to check whether a user is currently
 * logged in or not.
 *
 * @package WebServices
 * @subpackage Authentication
 * @author Dirk Merkel <dirk@waferthin.com>
 * @version 0.2
 * @since r12
 */
interface Accountable
{
    const AUTHENTICATION_ERR_MSG = 'There is no user account
associated with the current session. Try logging in fist.';

    /**
     * Did the current user log in?
     *
```

```
        * This method simply answers the question
        * "Did the current user log in?"
        *
        * @access public
        * @return bool
        */
       public function isLoggedIn();

       /**
        * Returns user account info

        *
        * This method is used to retrieve the account corresponding
        * to a given login. <b>Note:</b> it is not required that
        * the user be currently logged in.
        *
        * @access public
        * @param string $user user name of the account
        * @return Account
        */
       public function getAccount($user = '');
   }
   ?>
```

File project/classes/Authentication.php:

```
   <?php
   /**
    * @author Dirk Merkel <dirk@waferthin.com>
    * @package WebServices
    * @subpackage Authentication
    * @copyright Waferthin Web Works LLC
    * @license http://www.gnu.org/copyleft/gpl.html Freely available
   under GPL
    */
   /**
    * <i>Authentication</i> handles user account info and login actions

    *
    * This is an abstract class that serves as a blueprint
    * for classes implementing authentication using
    * different account validation schemes.
    *
    * @see Authentication_HardcodedAccounts
    * @author Dirk Merkel <dirk@waferthin.com>
```

```
 * @package WebServices
 * @subpackage Authentication
 * @version 0.5
 * @since r5
 */
abstract class Authentication implements Accountable
{
    /**
     * Reference to Account object of currently
     * logged in user.
     *
     * @access private
     * @var Account
     */
    private $account = null;

    /**
     * Returns account object if valid.
     *
     * @see Accountable::getAccount()
     * @access public
     * @param string $user user account login
     * @return Account user account
     */
    public function getAccount($user = '')
    {
        if ($this->account !== null) {
            return $this->account;
        } else {
            return AUTHENTICATION_ERR_MSG;
        }
    }

    /**
     * isLoggedIn method
     *
     * Says whether the current user has provided
     * valid login credentials.
     *
     * @see Accountable::isLoggedIn()
     * @access public
     * @return boolean
     */
    public function isLoggedIn()
```

```
        {
            return ($this->account !== null);
        }

        /**
         * login method
         *
         * Abstract method that must be implemented when
         * sub-classing this class.
         *
         * @access public
         * @return boolean
         */
        abstract public function login($user, $password);
    }
    ?>
```

File project/classes/Authentication/HardcodedAccounts.php:

```
    <?php
    /**
     * @author Dirk Merkel <dirk@waferthin.com>
     * @package WebServices
     * @subpackage Authentication
     * @copyright Waferthin Web Works LLC
     * @license http://www.gnu.org/copyleft/gpl.html Freely available
    under GPL
     */
    /**
     * <i>Authentication_HardcodedAccounts</i> class
     *
     * This class implements the login method needed to handle
     * actual user authentication. It extends <i>Authentication</i>
     * and implements the <i>Accountable</i> interface.
     *
     * @package WebServices
     * @subpackage Authentication
     * @see Authentication
     * @author Dirk Merkel <dirk@waferthin.com>
     * @version 0.6
     * @since r14
     */
    class Authentication_HardcodedAccounts extends Authentication
    {
        /**
```

```
 * Referece to <i>Users</i> object
 * @access private
 * @var Users
 */
private $users;

/**
 * Authentication_HardcodedAccounts constructor
 *
 * Instantiates a new {@link Users} object and stores a reference
 * in the {@link users} property.
 *
 * @see Users
 * @access public
 * @return void
 */
public function __construct()
{
    $this->users = new Users();
}

/**
 * login method
 *
 * Uses the reference {@link Users} class to handle
 * user validation.
 *
 * @see Users
 * @todo Decide which validate method to user instead of both
 * @access public
 * @param string $user account user name
 * @param string $password account password
 * @return boolean
 */
public function login($user, $password)
{
    if (empty($user) || empty($password)) {
        return false;
    } else {

        // both validation methods should work ...

        // user static method to validate account
        $firstValidation = Users::validate($user, $password);
```

```
            // use magic method validate<username>($password)
            $userLoginFunction = 'validate' . $user;
            $secondValidation = $this->users-
                                  >$userLoginFunction($password);

            return ($firstValidation && $secondValidation);
        }
    }
}
?>
```

File project/classes/Users.php:

```
<?php
/**
 * @author Dirk Merkel <dirk@waferthin.com>
 * @package WebServices
 * @subpackage Accounts
 * @copyright Waferthin Web Works LLC
 * @license http://www.gnu.org/copyleft/gpl.html Freely available
under GPL
 */
/**
 * <i>Users</i> class
 *
 * This class contains a hard-coded list of user accounts
 * and the corresponding passwords. This is merely a development
 * stub and should be implemented with some sort of permanent
 * storage and security.
 *
 * @package WebServices
 * @subpackage Accounts
 * @see Authentication
 * @see Authentication_HardcodedAccounts
 * @author Dirk Merkel <dirk@waferthin.com>
 * @version 0.6
 * @since r15
 */
class Users
{
    /**
     * hard-coded user accounts
     *
     * @access private
     * @static
```

```
 * @var array $accounts user name => password mapping
 */
private static $accounts = array('dirk'        => 'myPass',
                                  'albert'      => 'einstein');


/**
 * static validate method
 *
 * Given a user name and password, this method decides
 * whether the user has a valid account and whether
 * he/she supplied the correct password.
 *
 * @see Authentication_HardcodedAccounts::login()
 * @access public
 * @static
 * @param string $user account user name
 * @param string $password account password
 * @return boolean
 */
public static function validate($user, $password)
{
    return self::$accounts[$user] == $password;
}


/**
 * magic __call method
 *
 * This method only implements a magic validate method
 * where the second part of the method name is the user's
 * account name.
 *
 * @see Authentication_HardcodedAccounts::login()
 * @see validate()
 * @access public
 * @method boolean validate<user>() validate<user>(string
 *                                  $password) validate a user
 * @staticvar array $accounts used to validate users & passwords
 */
public function __call($name, $arguments)
{
    if (preg_match("/^validate(.*)$/", $name, $matches) &&
count($arguments) > 0) {
        return self::validate($matches[1], $arguments[0]);
    }
```

```
        }
    }
    ?>
```

File project/index.php:

```php
<?php
/**
 * Bootstrap file
 *
 * This is the form handler for the login application.
 * It expects a user name and password via _POST. If
 *
 * @author Dirk Merkel <dirk@waferthin.com>
 * @package WebServices
 * @copyright Waferthin Web Works LLC
 * @license http://www.gnu.org/copyleft/gpl.html Freely available
under GPL
 * @version 0.7
 * @since r2
 */
/**
 * required class files and interfaces
 */
require_once('classes/Accountable.php');
require_once('classes/Authentication.php');
require_once('classes/Users.php');
require_once('classes/Authentication/HardcodedAccounts.php');

$authenticator = new Authentication_HardcodedAccounts();

// uncomment for testing
$_POST['user'] = 'dirk';
$_POST['password'] = 'myPass';

if (isset($_POST['user']) && isset($_POST['password'])) {

    $loginSucceeded = $authenticator->login($_POST['user'],
                                    $_POST['password']);

    if ($loginSucceeded === true) {
        echo "Congrats - you're in!\n";
    } else {
        echo "Uh-uh - try again!\n";
    }
}
?>
```

Since none of the functionality of the code has changed, we can skip that discussion here. What has changed, however, is that we have added DocBlocks for each file, class, interface, method, and property. Whereas the version of the project without documentation had a total of 113 lines of code, the new version including DocBlocks has 327 lines. The number of lines almost tripled! But don't be intimidated. Creating DocBlocks doesn't take nearly as much time as coding. Once you are used to the syntax, it becomes second nature. My estimate is that documenting takes about 10 to 20 percent of the time it takes to code. Moreover, there are tools to really speed things up and help you with the syntax, such as a properly configured code editor or IDE (see the chapter on Development Environment for more details).

Now let's see how phpDocumentor fared with the revised version of the project. Here is the index page:

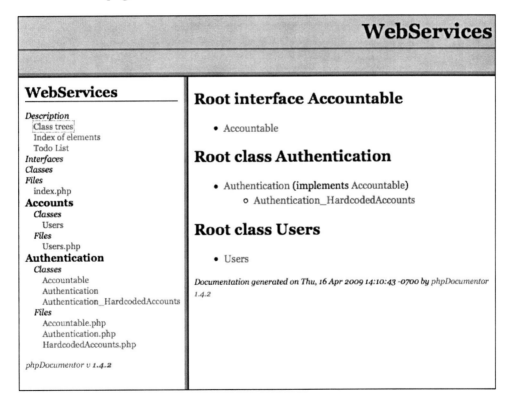

This time, the heading shows that we are looking at the **Web Services** package. Furthermore, the classes and interfaces have been grouped by sub-packages in the left-hand index column. Next, here is the documentation page for the Users class:

Class Users

Description

Description | Methods (details)

Users class

This class contains a hard-coded list of user accounts and the corresponding passwords. This is merely a development stub and should be implemented with some sort of permanent storage and security.

- **author:** Dirk Merkel <dirk@waferthin.com>
- **version:** 0.6
- **see:** Authentication
- **see:** Authentication_HardcodedAccounts
- **since:** r15

Located in /classes/Users.php (line 25)

Method Summary

Description | Methods (details)

static boolean validate (string $user, string $password)
void __call ($name, $arguments)

Methods

Description | Methods (details)

static method validate (line 51)

static validate method

Given a user name and password, this method decides whether the user has a valid account and whether he/she supplied the correct password.

- **see:** Authentication_HardcodedAccounts::login()
- **access:** public

static boolean validate (string $user, string $password)

- *string $user: account user name*
- **access:** public

static boolean validate (string $user, string $password)

- *string $user: account user name*
- *string $password: account password*

__call (line 69)

magic __call method

This method only implements a magic validate method where the second part of the method name is the user's account name.

- **staticvar:** array $accounts: used to validate users & passwords
- **method:** boolean validate(): validate<user>(string $password) validate a user
- **see:** Authentication_HardcodedAccounts::login()
- **see:** Users::validate()
- **access:** public

void __call ($name, $arguments)

- *$name*
- *$arguments*

Documentation generated on Thu, 16 Apr 2009 14:10:44 -0700 by phpDocumentor 1.4.2

As you can see, this documentation page is quite a bit more informative than the earlier version. For starters, it has a description of what the class does. Similarly, both methods have a description. All the tags and their content are listed and there are helpful links to other parts of the documentation. And, from the method tag we can actually tell that the magic method `__call()` was used to implement a method of the form `validate<user>($password)`. That is quite an improvement, I would say!

To really appreciate how much more informative and practical the documentation has become by adding DocBlocks, you really need to run through this example yourself and browse through the resulting documentation.

phpDocumentor options

There are a good number of options when running phpDocumentor that affect everything from where it looks for the code to parse, how to parse, what kind of output to generate, and how to format it. All the options are available from both the command line and the web-based interface.

Command line reference

Here is a listing of all command line options supported by phpDocumentor 1.4.2, which is the version that was used while writing this chapter. The descriptions are taken directly from the output produced by running `phpdoc --help` from the command line and it is only reproduced here for the readers' convenience.

Short option	Long option	Description
-f	--filename	Name of file(s) to parse ',' file1,file2. Can contain complete path and * ? wildcards
-d	--directory	Name of a directory(s) to parse directory1,directory2
-ed	--examplesdir	Full path of the directory to look for example files from @example tags
-tb	--templatebase	Base location of all templates for this parse.
-t	--target	Path where to save the generated files
-i	--ignore	File(s) that will be ignored, multiple separated by ','. Wildcards * and ? are ok
-is	--ignoresymlinks	Ignore symlinks to other files or directories, default is off
-it	--ignore-tags	Tags to ignore for this parse. @package, @subpackage, @access and @ignore may not be ignored

Short option	Long option	Description
-dh	--hidden	Set equal to on (-dh on) to descend into hidden directories (directories starting with '.'), default is off
-q	--quiet	Do not display parsing/conversion messages
		Useful for cron jobs on/off, default off
-ue	--undocumentedelements	Control whether or not warnings will be shown for undocumented elements. Useful for identifying classes and methods that haven't yet been documented on/off default off
-ti	--title	Title of generated documentation, default is 'Generated Documentation'
-h	--help	Show this help message
-c	--useconfig	Use a Config file in the users/ subdirectory for all command-line options
-pp	--parseprivate	Parse @internal and elements marked private with @access. Use on/off, default off
-po	--packageoutput	Output documentation only for selected packages. Use a comma-delimited list
-dn	--defaultpackagename	Name to use for the default package. If not specified, uses 'default'
-dc	--defaultcategoryname	Name to use for the default category. If not specified, uses 'default'
-o	--output	Output information to use separated by ','. Format: output:converter:templatedir like "HTML:frames:phpedit"
-cp	--converterparams	Dynamic parameters for a converter, separate values with commas
-ct	--customtags	Custom tags, will be recognized and put in tags[] instead of unknowntags[]
-s	--sourcecode	Generate highlighted sourcecode for every parsed file (PHP 4.3.0+ only) on/off, default off
-j	--javadocdesc	JavaDoc-compliant description parsing. Use on/off, default off (more flexibility)
-p	--pear	Parse a PEAR-style repository (package is directory, _members are @access private) on/off, default off
-ric	--readmeinstallchangelog	Specify custom filenames to parse like README, INSTALL, or CHANGELOG files

Config files

Rather than having to specify all options you want on the command line each time you run generate documentation, phpDocumentor supports `config` files. You can put all your command line switches in one `config` file and then conveniently tell the `phpdoc` executable to use the `config` file. Here is a `config` file that has all the same options that we used in the above example:

```
;; phpDocumentor parse configuration file
;;
;; interface will automatically generate a list of .ini files that can
be used.
;;
;; project_phpdoc_config.ini is used to generate the documentation
;; for the sample project in the chapter on phpDocumentor
;;
;; Copyright 2009, Dirk Merkel <dirk@waferthin.com>


[Parse Data]
;; title of all the documentation
;; legal values: any string
title = Generated Documentation - No DocBlocks

;; comma-separated list of directories to parse
;; legal values: directory paths separated by commas
directory = /Users/dirk/php/project

;; where should the documentation be written?
;; legal values: a legal path
target = /Users/dirk/php/project/docs

;; turn this option on if you want highlighted source code for every
file
;; legal values: on/off
sourcecode = on
```

To use the `config` file from the command line, simply type:

```
phpdoc -c /Users/dirk/php/project/project_phpdoc_config.ini
```

For additional examples of user-defined `config` files, consult the `user/` directory of your phpDocumentor installation.

There is also a system-wide default `config` file called `phpDocumentor.ini` that can be found in the top level of the phpDocumentor installation directory. It contains some additional options that are not accessible from the command line, such as toggling debug mode, which file extensions to parse, and so on.

Browser-based interface

You may remember from the installation, phpDocumentor includes a browser-based interface that gives you the same options as the command line. However, you get the added convenience of a tabbed interface that lets you easily explore the available options without having to consult the help section. Of course, you can also select your custom config file from this interface just as you did from the command line.

Here is an example of the browser-based interface while processing the documentation for our sample project:

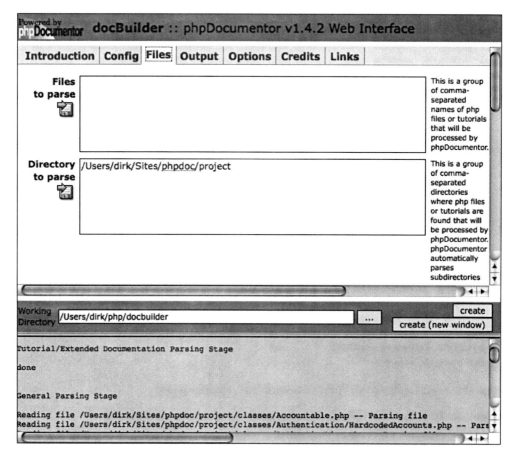

One of the 'gotchas' of working with the browser-based interface is that you must have all permissions properly set up. For example, if your project is residing in a directory outside your web server's DocumentRoot, phpDocumentor might not be able to read the files. Also, if the template you are using to format the output comes with one or more stylesheets that need to be copied to the output directory, your web server and/or PHP will need the necessary permissions.

Tag reference

This section contains an alphabetical listing of all tags supported by phpDocumentor by default. For each tag, we list the name and indicate whether it can or should be used in any of the four different contexts: file, class, method, and property. Each tag listing also comes with an example and a comments section that point out any botches. Lastly, tags are separated into standard and inline tags.

Standard tags

Standard tags are used to describe and document specific characteristics code immediately following the DocBlock. For example, you can specify where in the package hierarchy a class falls (using @package and @subpackage tags), link to a different section of the documentation (using the @link tag), or track a version number for a given method (using the @version tag).

For phpDocumentor to recognize a tag, it has to be the first thing on the line after the asterisk ("*") and of course it has to be one of the tags phpDocumentor recognizes.

@access

Name:	File:	Class:	Method:	Property:
@access (public | protected | private)	[x]	[x]	x	x

Example(s):

```
/**
 * @access private
 */
$myProp = null;

...
/**
 * @access protected
 */
protected function sortEntries() {}
```

Comments:

Possible values for the access tag are public, private, and private. By default, elements with access level private will not be documented. To turn off this behavior, use the command line switch ?parseprivate. A PDERROR_PARSEPRIVATE warning will be generated if the @access tag is set to private in a file-level DockBlock because it will result in the while file being omitted from documentation.

@author

Name:	File:	Class:	Method:	Property:
@author author_name [<email>]	x	x	[x]	[x]

Example(s):

```
/**
 * @author Dirk Merkel <dirk@waferthin.com>
 */
class WorldDomination { }
```

Comments:

phpDocumentor will try to parse any content between < and > to see whether it is a valid e-mail address. If so, it will be displayed as a mailto link in documentation output that supports it.

@category

Name:	File:	Class:	Method:	Property:
@category category_name	[x]			

Example(s):

```
/**
 * @package REST API
 * @category Web Services
 */
```

Comments:

Packages are grouped into categories. As of phpDocumentor version 1.4.2, this tag will be ignored by all default converters other than the XMLDocBook one.

@copyright

Name:	File:	Class:	Method:	Property:
@copyright [copyright holder info]	x	[x]	[x]	

Example(s):

```
/**
 * @copyright Copyright © Waferthin
 */
```

Comments:

Most of the time, this tag will be used in file-level DocBlocks. In rare occasions, you might want document copyright to a particular class or even method. For example, if you are using a copyrighted algorithm or are reusing another entity's code.

@deprecated

Name:	File:	Class:	Method:	Property:
@deprecated [info string]		x	x	x

Example(s):

```
/**
 * @deprecated superseded by class UltimateWorldDomination

 */
class WorldDomination { }
```

Comments:

Although the functionality is still supported by the code, you can use the deprecated phpDoc tag to let developers know that they should no longer use the respective element.

@example

Name:	File:	Class:	Method:	Property:
@example file_path "link text"	[x]	[x]	[x]	

Example(s):

```
/**
 * @example http://www.waferthin.com/examples/proper_markup.php
Example of proper markup usage
 * @example xmpls/config.php configuration file illustrated
 */
public function parseConfig() { }
```

Comments:

The example tag retrieves, parses, and creates a link to an external example file. The file URL scheme is compatible with fopen(), which means you can retrieve remote files as well as local ones. phpDocumentor will add line numbers and syntax highlighting to the retrieved file. For relative paths, phpDocumentor will look in directories specified via the --ed or --examplesdir command line switches, but it will look for an examples directory in the top-level parsing directory by default.

@filesource

Name:	File:	Class:	Method:	Property:
@filesource	[x]			

Example(s):

```
/**
 * @filesource
 */
class { }
```

Comments:

When the documentation gets created for the file containing the @filesource tag, it will include a link to the syntax-highlighted source code of the file containing the tag. @filesource can only be used in file-level DocBlocks.

@global

Name:	File:	Class:	Method:	Property:
Usage 1: @global data_type $variable_name	[x]			
Usage 2: @global variable_name [description]			[x]	

Example(s):

```
/**
 * Usage 1: Documenting declaration of a global variable
 * @global array $HTML_COLORS
 */
$HTML_COLORS = array('#ffffff' => 'white',
                     '#ff0000' => 'red'
                     '#000000' => 'black');
/**
 * Usage 2: Documenting use of a global variable in a method
 * @global HTML_COLORS lookup for HTML color representations
 */
public function outputHtml()
{
    global $HTML_COLORS;
}
```

Comments:

Usage 1: This tag is used to document the declaration of global variables (see @name tag to change the name of the global variable for display purposes).

Usage 2: Use @global to document the use of a global variable in a function or method.

@ignore

Name:	File:	Class:	Method:	Property:
@ignore	[x]	[x]	[x]	[x]

Example(s):

```
/**
 * @ignore
 */
const('TIME_ZONE', 'local');
```

Comments:

Prevents the element immediately following the @ignore tag from being documented. For example, you might have a class that handles encryption. The encryption algorithm might need to be seeded and for good measure you are including a salt (a pseudo-random string). Naturally, you might not want that salt publicized in your documentation because it would compromise the strength of your encryption implementation. Simply put the @ignore tag before the line where you declare the variable holding the salt and it will not appear in your projects documentation.

@internal

Name:	File:	Class:	Method:	Property:
@internal	[x]	[x]	[x]	[x]

Example(s):

```
/**
 * @internal
 */
public function applySecretFormula() { }
```

Comments:

The @internal tag prevents the corresponding element from being included in the documentation unless the --pp / --parseprivate command line switch is being used. This has the same effect as setting the @access tag to private and serves the purpose of creating documentation for different audiences.

@license

Name:	File:	Class:	Method:	Property:
@license license_text_url [link text]	[x]	[x]	[x]	

Example(s):

```
/**
 * @license http://waferthin.com/gpl.txt available under GPL
 */
class AesEncryption { }
```

Comments:

This tag creates a hyperlink to an external file that contains the text of the license under which the corresponding element is available.

@link

Name:	File:	Class:	Method:	Property:
@link external_url [link text]	[x]	[x]	[x]	[x]

Example(s):

```
/**
 * @link http://www.w3.org/TR/xhtml1/ W3C XHTML Standard
 */
public function textToXhtml($text = '') { }
```

Comments:

Although this tag supports internal inks, it is primarily intended for linking to external resources. For internal links refer to @see and {@link}.

@method

Name:	File:	Class:	Method:	Property:
@method return_type method_name(type $arg1[= val1], type $arg2[= val2], …) [description]		[x]		

Example(s):

```
/**
 * @method array mix(Array array1 = array(), Array array2 = array())
joins and randomizes two arrays
 */
```

Comments:

This is an extremely useful tag for any developer who takes advantage of PHP's magic methods. Since even reflection cannot know about methods the developer creates using the __call() magic method, one can use the @method tag to document any magic methods provided by the class. Any method documented this way will be listed on the class-level documentation.

@name

Name:	File:	Class:	Method:	Property:
@name $var_name	[x]			

Example(s):

```
/**
 * @name $colors
 * @global array
 */
$HTML_COLORS = array('#ffffff' => 'white',
                     '#ff0000' => 'red'
                     '#000000' => 'black');
```

Comments:

Creates an alias for a global variable for documentation purposes (also see @global tag).

@package

Name:	File:	Class:	Method:	Property:
@package package_name	x	x		

Example(s):

```
/**
 * File-level package tag
 * @package Authentication_API
 */
/**
 * Class-level package tag (needed because it is not inherited!!!)
 * @package Authentication_API
 */
class ResultSet { }
```

Comments:

This tag defines a logical grouping of elements within the documentation. A file-level `@package` tag will apply to all elements within that file; however, package membership of classes will be **default** unless explicitly set for the class itself. This is true even if the file-level package tag has been set! The only exception is that sub-classes inherit their parent class's package membership.

@property

Name:	File:	Class:	Method:	Property:
@property data_type $var_name [description]		[x]		
@property-read datatype $varname [description]		[x]		
@property-write datatype $varname [description]		[x]		

Example(s):

```
/**
 * @property string $greeting greeting to user upon login
 */
class Login
{
    private $greeting = 'Hello, Stranger!';
    public function __get($property)
    {
        if ($property == 'greeting') {
            return $this->greeting;
        }
    }
}
```

Comments:

The @property tag documents "magic" properties made available by a class's __get() and __set() methods. In contrast the @property-read and @property-write tags are used to document magic properties that are readable or writable only, respectively.

@return

Name:	File:	Class:	Method:	Property:
@return data_type			x	

Example(s):

```
/**
 * @return int
 */
```

Comments:

This tag indicates the data type of the return value of the method. Valid data types are native PHP data types (int, string, and so on), array, class names, null, and nothing (void). It is possible to list multiple possible data types separated by the pipe character ("|"): array|string.

@see

Name:	File:	Class:	Method:	Property:
Usage 1: @see [ClassName::]methodName()	[x]	[x]	[x]	[x]
Usage 2: @see [ClassName::]$property_name	[x]	[x]	[x]	[x]
Usage 3: @see php_function_name	[x]	[x]	[x]	[x]

Example(s):

```
/**
 * Usage 1: link to documentation of method in another class
 * @see DbConnection::connect()
 * Usage 2: link to a property in this class
 * @see $greeting
 * Usage 3: link to a PHP built-in function
 * @see mysql_connect()
 */
```

Comments:

This tag allows you to link to other sections of your documentation. This tag is very important because it allows readers of your documentation to follow a logical flow. In a sense it is as empowering to documentation as hyperlinks are to the Web in general. You can specify names of classes and the properties and methods inside those classes. The string '::' is used to separated class name from property/methods name. Use @link, @inline, or {@link} for creating hyperlinks to external resources.

@since

Name:	File:	Class:	Method:	Property:
@since [version_info]	x	x	[x]	[x]

Example(s):

```
/**
 * @since r0.9.2
 */
```

Comments:

This tag is used to indicate at which revision or version of the software this element was added. The version info string can identify the revision/version within your source code control system or it can be the official release of the software in which the element was first available to the users.

@static

Name:	File:	Class:	Method:	Property:
@static			[x]	[x]

Example(s):

```
/**
 * @static
 */
public static function proprietaryEncode() { }
```

Comments:

This tag is used to document static properties and methods.

@staticvar

Name:	File:	Class:	Method:	Property:
@staticvar data_type [description]			[x]	

Example(s):

```
/**
 * @staticvar bool determines whether this object needs updating
 */
public function checkState()
{
    if (self::current === false) {
        echo "Update me!";
    }
}
```

Comments:
This tag is used to indicate when a method uses a static property.

@subpackage

Name:	File:	Class:	Method:	Property:
@subpackage	[x]	[x]		

Example(s):

```
/**
 * @package World_Domination
 * @subpackage Conquer_Europe
 */
class Attack { }
```

Comments:

This tag is used to further organize the files and classes in your documentation by assigning them to sub-packages. The @subpackage tag cannot be used without the @package tag in the same DocBlock.

@todo

Name:	File:	Class:	Method:	Property:
@todo description	[x]	[x]	[x]	[x]

Example(s):

```
/**
 * @todo refactor to improve performance
 */
public function sortComplexData() { }
```

Comments:

This tag is used to leave a note for the developer(s) to implement future changes or enhancements.

@tutorial

Name:	File:	Class:	Method:	Property:
@tutorial tutorial_name	[x]	[x]		

Example(s):

```
/**
 * @package Killer_App
 * @tutorial Killer_App.pkg
 */
class AwesomeFeature { }
```

Comments:

This tag links to tutorials defined within your documentation. Tutorials follow certain naming conventions and are written in DocBook syntax. See the section on phpDocumentor tutorials for more information. To create a hyperlink to external resources, use the @see, @link, or inline {@link} tags instead.

@uses

Name:	File:	Class:	Method:	Property:
@uses [ClassName::]methodName() description	[x]	[x]	[x]	[x]

Example(s):

```
/**
 * @uses Utility::secretAlgorithm() seeds algorithm with special salt
 */
class Shuffle { }
```

Comments:

This tag behaves exactly like the @see tag with two differences. First, a reciprocal @usedby tag in the DocBlock of the element that is being pointed to. Second, unlike @see, @uses takes a description.

@var

Name:	File:	Class:	Method:	Property:
@var data_type [description]				[x]

Example(s):

```
/**
 * @var string full user name for logging purposes
 */
$uname = 'Dirk Merkel';
```

Comments:

This tag is used to document the data type of variables and properties. It also takes an optional description that can be used to elaborate on the content and/or use of the property.

@version

Name:	File:	Class:	Method:	Property:
@version version_string	[x]	[x]	[x]	

Example(s):

```
/**
 * @version v2.3b - prerelease candidate
 */
```

Comments:

You can use this tag to record your own versioning. A common use if this tag is to put a placeholder that will automatically be replaced by the version control system's revision or version number upon committing the change (see the chapter on source code control for more detail).

Inline tags

Inline tags differ from standard text in that they can occur anywhere within the text of the short or long description of a DocBlock. To properly differentiate inline tags from the description, their syntax differs a bit from standard tags in that they are enclosed by curly brackets. When parsed by phpDocumentor and rendered by the desired converter, these tags are replaced by content that is being placed inline with the rest of the text.

In addition to DocBlock descriptions, inline tags can be used in tutorials. There are a total of six inline tags, four of which can be used in DocBlocks and a different set of four can be used in tutorials.

{@Example}

Name:	File:	Class:	Method:	Property:
{@example start_line end_line}	[x]	[x]	[x]	

Context:	DocBlock:	Tutorial:
	[x]	

Example(s):

```
/**
 * Authentication login method
 *
 * Before being able to access the web services API,
 * a client has to authenticate via this login method.
 * Simplified client code might look like this:
 * {@example examples/login.php 0 15}
 */
public function login($login, $password) { }
```

Comments:

The inline {@example} tag behaves very much like the standard @example tag in that it retrieves, parses, and displays all or part of a source code file with highlighted syntax. See the description of the @example tag for details on which files are compatible and how to reference them.

The differences from the standard @example tag is that the referenced source code will be displayed inline and that it is possible to limit the listing by start and end line number within the file.

{@id}

Name:			File:	Class:	Method:	Property:
{@id section_name}						
Context:			DocBlock:		Tutorial:	
					[x]	

Example(s):

```
// in DocBook tutorial
...
<refentry id="{@id my_main_section}">
    ...
    <refsect1 id="{@id main_argument}">
    ...
    </refsect1>
<refentry>
...


// tutorial tag
/**
 * @tutorial WebServices.Authentication.Login.cls.main_section.
main_argument
 */
```

Comments:

When using a @tutorial tag to link to a particular tutorial, it is possible to directly link to specific sections within the referenced document. The {@id} tag allows one to assign the desired section an identifier that can be used in the link. The general structure of building a link to a sub-section of a tutorial looks like this:

```
package.package_name[.sub-package_name].file[.section_name].
[sub-section_name]
```

{@internal}}

Name:		File:	Class:	Method:	Property:
{@internal}}		[x]	[x]	[x]	[x]
Context:		**DocBlock:**		**Tutorial:**	
		[x]			

Example(s):

```
/**
 * Web Services Authentication
 *
 * Use this class and its methods to obtain an authentication
 * token that will be used during the session. {@internal This
 * must be discussed with the architectural committee. See
 * our {@link http://massivecorp.com/gl.html Massive Corp
 * Development Guidelines}.}}
 */
class Authentication { }
```

Comments:

Analogous to the standard @internal tag, the inline {@internal}} tag prevents the corresponding content from being included in the documentation unless the --pp / --parseprivate command line switch is being used. This has the same effect as setting the @access tag to private and serves the purpose of creating documentation for different audiences.

Note: This tag ends in two closing curly brackets, which is necessary because itself can contain inline tags.

{@inheritdoc}

Name:		File:	Class:	Method:	Property:
{@inheritdoc}			[x]		

Context:		DocBlock:	Tutorial:	
		[x]		

Example(s):

```
/**
 * Login User
 *
 * This class handles authentication to obtain a
 * session token.
 */
class Authentication { }
...
/**
 * Login User w/ SecureID
 *
 * {@inheritdoc} Specifically, the user will have to supply
 * a SecureID token during login.
 */
class SecureIdAuthentication extends Authentication { }
```

Comments:

By default, child classes will inherit certain tags and comments from the parent class they are extending. Specifically, the following will be inherited: @author tag, @version tag, @copyright tag, and long description. This is only true if the child class isn't explicitly setting the tags and description. Using the {@inheritdoc} provides the developer the flexibility of deciding where to put the inherited comments.

{@link}

Name:	File:	Class:	Method:	Property:
{@link external_url [link text]}	[x]	[x]	[x]	[x]

Context:	DocBlock:	Tutorial:
	[x]	[x]

Example(s):

```
/**
 * This class handles authentication using Secured tokens.
 * For more details on SecureID, you can consult
 * the {@link http://en.wikipedia.org/wiki/SecurID the SecureID
 * article on Wikipedia}.
 */
class SecureIdAuthentication { }
```

Comments:

Analogous to the standard @link tag, the inline {@link} tag creates a hyperlink to an external documentation source or reference document (see @link for details).

{@source}

Name:	File:	Class:	Method:	Property:
{@source [start_line] [end_line]}	[x]	[x]	[x]	

Context:	DocBlock:	Tutorial:
	[x]	

Example(s):

```
/**
 * Authentication Method
 *
 * This method is to be called from the client before
 * it can make any other API call. All the heavy lifting
 * is being done by this try-catch block: {@source 10 17}
 * This is where we're calling the internal authentication
 * server.
 */
public function authenticate($login, $password)
{
    $success = false;
```

```
    if (empty($login) || empty($password)) {
        throw new Exception("login and password cannot be blank!");
    } else {

        // the next 8 lines will be included in the DocBlock
        try {
            if ($this->authentServer->isLoginValid($login, $password))
{

                $success = true;
            }
        } catch (Exception $e) {
            $this->logger->log("Error: " . $e->message);
        }
    }
    return $success;
}
```

Comments:

The inline {@source} will insert the source code of the element being documented in its place. The optional parameters of start and end line number will limit the listing to the corresponding lines. The first line of the documented element is considered line 1. Omitting the ending line number will list the element's source code from the starting line to the end of the listing.

{@toc}

Name:		File:	Class:	Method:	Property:
{@toc}					

Context:		DocBlock:	Tutorial:
			[x]

Example(s):

```
// in DocBook tutorial
...
<refentry id="{@id my_main_section}">
    {@toc}
    ...
    <refsect1 id="{@id main_argument}">
    ...
    </refsect1>
<refentry>
...

// tutorial tag
/**
 * @tutorial WebServices.Authentication.Login.cls.main_section.main_
argument
 */
```

Comments:

In a tutorial, inline {@id} tags can be used as anchors for links (see {@id} tag). The inline {@toc} tag creates a table of contents from all {@id} tags. The {@toc} tag typically occurs within the opening and closing refentry DocBook tag.

{@tutorial}

Name:	File:	Class:	Method:	Property:
{@tutorial }	[x]	[x]		

Context:	DocBlock:	Tutorial:
	[x]	[x]

Example(s):

```
/**
 * Use this class to authenticate.
 * For more details take a look at this
 * tutorial: {@tutorial MyApp/Authenticate/Authenticate.cls}
 */
class Authenticate { }
```

Comments:

The inline {@tutorial} displays a link to a tutorial. See the section on tutorials on how to properly reference and name a tutorial.

PHP4 elements

There are two standard tags that can only be used in PHP4 because they are named after reserved keywords in PHP5 and greater: @abstract and @final. I find these two tags nearly useless, as they merely document how the element should behave, not how it actually behaves. In other words, you can say that a method should be final, but you cannot actually declare it final because the keyword and the corresponding concept do not exist in PHP4.

Although you should be aware that these two tags exist, I recommend against using them.

Custom tags

Custom tags are surprisingly easy to implement. There is no need to extend or overwrite any classes. As a matter of fact, unless you have somewhat unusual requirements, all it takes is a command-line option. Say you find a need to add a tag to indicate the date on which the last peer review of the source occurred and the name of person that performed it. You could start using a `@sourcereviewdate` tag:

```
/**
 * This class is absolutely critical to the survival
 * and success or our application.
 *
 * @author Dirk Merkel <dirk@waferthin.com>
 * @package WebServices
 * @sourcereview 03-15-2009 by Kimba Merkel
 */
class SuperSecretAlgorithm
{
}
```

Now all you have to do for phpDocumentor to recognize the new tag is to include this option on the command line: `--customtags sourcereview`. Alternatively, you can define your custom tag(s) in your own config file.

Summary

If the example in this chapter did not sell you on the benefits of documenting your code using the phpDoc syntax, you only need to take a look at the API documentation of some of the biggest PHP projects out there, such as Zend Framework and Pear. There is a reason that this method of documenting source code has been around for over ten years. Programmers quickly get the big picture of how the various components come together. Moreover, it also allows them to drill down to the granular level of parameters, return values, and so on.

If you are not in the habit of commenting your code, I suggest you start slowly. Rather than documenting every single element, start with file and class-level DocBlocks. I suspect that you will quickly get used to creating documentation at the same time as code – especially when you see the results in the form of detailed and useful documentation. Hopefully, you will feel encouraged enough to start documenting more elements and produce documentation that any programmer that might come across your code can benefit from.

3

The Eclipse Integrated Development Environment

My first PHP script was typed in an HTML editor that was eventually discontinued eight years ago. There was no syntax coloring or auto-completion feature. But, don't worry; this isn't going to turn into one of those when-I-was-your-age kind of stories. I'm merely trying to make the point that PHP development environments have come a long way. There is a lot that properly configured modern development tools can do for you. There are tools for writing code faster, such as auto-completion, built-in reference, and templates. There are tools to make fixing code faster, such as advanced debuggers and automated refactoring tools.

An editing tool is one of those basic tools in your tool chest that you just can't do without. It follows you from task to task. Whether you're writing code, editing a plain text configuration file, or designing an XML format for exchanging data with one of your customers, chances are that you do all that in your favorite editor. If you have become proficient at using one particular editor, you will most likely be sticking with it for a long time. In my case, vi editing commands have become second nature to me a long time ago. (If you don't know, vi is a console-based text editor you will find on most Unix/Linux operating systems). When in a bind, I'm always likely to access a server directly to quickly correct a critical bug in vi. However, I would be a fool not to expand my horizons and leverage some of the amazing tools that are available now.

Don't get me wrong—I know that you can get syntax coloring and PHP debugging support in vi. Nevertheless, you can harness a lot more power by learning one of the **Integrated Development Environments (IDEs)** that have matured over the last few years.

In this chapter, I want to take a close look at one of those IDEs, namely Eclipse with the PDT plugin. We haven't even gotten beyond the first page of this chapter and I can already hear the objections: "… but what about <insert_favorite_ide_here>? I know many developers that swear by it!"

I realize that Eclipse isn't the only game in town, but there are some compelling reasons to take a close look at what it has to offer, not the least of which is the fact that we cannot look at all the offerings. After all, PHP has become a pretty popular language and there are quite a few options when assembling your tool chest. Also, you should keep in mind that many of the concepts covered in this chapter translate across development environments. For example, any IDE that supports debugging is likely to give you a way of manipulating breakpoints, inspecting variables, and viewing stack traces. Even if you decide not to use Eclipse, you can probably benefit from knowing about its benefits. At the very least, it might help to convince you to invest the time to learn an IDE if you haven't done so already. Here is a list of the topics we will be covering in this chapter:

- Introducing and installing Eclipse with PDT
- Basic Eclipse concepts, such as workspaces, views, and perspectives
- Creating a sample project
- Understanding and using features of the editor, including syntax highlighting, code assist, code folding, marking occurrences, overriding indicators, and navigating types, methods, and resources
- Inspecting projects, files, and libraries
- Interactive visual debugging
- Setting of preferences to customize the Eclipse
- Eclipse's plugin architecture and useful plugins environment
- Additional features offered by Zend's commercial Zend Studio for Eclipse

Why Eclipse?

Eclipse grew out of technology and concepts at IBM. Prior to being announced as an open source project in 2001, it already had several years of development and evolution under its belt. Since then, thousands of developers have contributed and continue to contribute to the project. This means that many of the core concepts and implementations of Eclipse are quite mature. Moreover, the project was put into the hands of a newly formed not-for-profit foundation in 2004. In other words, Eclipse is here to stay and is unlikely to disappear overnight like some software projects.

Another advantage of using Eclipse is that it has found wide acceptance. No matter whether you are doing development in PHP, Java, Perl, or C++, there is a community of users and developers ready to lend a hand if you need support. As we will see shortly, efforts to make Eclipse a strong tool for PHP development are backed and driven by Zend—probably the biggest commercial name in PHP.

Eclipse is not so much a development environment itself as it is the foundation for building such tools. It provides all the basic tools that are common across the various offerings to leverage this strong underpinning. For example, Eclipse provides a framework for accessing and manipulating data called the "Data Tools Platform" but it makes few assumptions on the underlying storage and provides no specific support for particular vendors. Other developers can use that framework to build more specific tools. The real benefit here is extensibility and reusability. Since Eclipse depends on additional software to really shine, it comes as no surprise that it has a strong and easy to use plugin architecture. It is very straightforward to locate and install plugins that add completely new functionality to your installation of Eclipse. In addition, the mechanism for keeping all those plugins up-to-date is also built right into Eclipse itself.

Last, but not least, on our list of reasons to consider Eclipse as an IDE for PHP development is that it is open source. This point is certainly debatable. There is nothing wrong with commercial software. After all, I would expect that the audience for this book, including myself, is looking to get paid for PHP development on some level. Nevertheless, I put a lot of faith in the open source movement. Most of the tools I use are open source even though most of the development I get paid for is sold under some kind of commercial license. However, I still make an effort to contribute to open source projects and often release code from my personal projects under free licenses.

In order to present a balanced view, I think it would be only fair to also consider some of the criticisms that have been leveraged against the Eclipse project. Some of these apply to Eclipse in general; others only apply when viewing Eclipse as a tool for PHP development.

It is no secret that Eclipse's resource requirements are quite high. It is a huge application and gets only bigger as you continue to add plugins. Also, you might get frustrated with its slow response times if you don't give Eclipse plenty of RAM to do its thing. This is no lightweight text editor that you can launch in the blink of an eye. Eclipse is a serious application and there is a lot going on behind the scenes at any given time. In other words, if you've been eyeing that cute little net book with the seven-inch screen that is oh-so-portable, you might want to consider that it is not the right vehicle for PHP development using Eclipse. It is akin to a high-performance engine requiring premium fuel. You can drive it with standard gas, but it won't be the same.

Another issue to consider is the learning curve you will have to conquer to really become productive in Eclipse. Yes, it has a graphical user interface, but that doesn't mean that you will automatically know how to do what you want or even everything that is possible. There is no way around investing some time in learning Eclipse. Luckily, you don't have to do it all at once. I believe that reading this chapter will give you a solid head start on knowing how to develop PHP applications in Eclipse. The rest you will pick up automatically as you continue to explore Eclipse and the world of PHP in general.

Introducing PDT

PDT is an acronym for PHP Development Tool. In accordance with Eclipse's approach to extensibility, PDT is installed and updated as a plugin. PDT provides basic functionality for developing PHP applications in an integrated environment. Primarily, PDT provides the developer with tools to perform the three tasks of editing, inspecting, and debugging source code. We will explore each of these high-level features throughout this chapter.

Installing Eclipse

When it comes to installing Eclipse, you basically have two options. First, you can download one of the standard Eclipse packages and install PDT along with several other plugins. Second, you can download a PHP all-in-one and then use that as a starting point for installing the remaining plugins. Either way, you will be installing several plugins to extend the functionality of Eclipse.

The right approach for you depends on whether you will be using Eclipse for development in other languages. If so, my recommendation is to start with a standard Eclipse package and to install PDT and other plugins via Eclipse's built-in software installation and update feature. It will be a good exercise in configuring Eclipse and keeping it up-to-date. Otherwise, assuming that you will be using Eclipse for PHP only, you are best served by download the all-in-one package for PHP devlopers.

Requirements

All of the packages are available for Windows, Mac OS X, and both 32bit and 64bit versions of Linux. Nevertheless, there are some additional requirements. First and foremost, you will need a **Java Runtime Environment** (**JRE**). The Eclipse site recommends Java 5 JRE. Yes, Eclipse is a Java program and requires Java to run. This has nothing to do with the fact that we will be developing PHP code. However, it does bring us to our next requirement. Actually, it is more of a recommendation than a requirement. Eclipse is known to be many things, but speedy is not one of them. Even if you ignore the debatable issue of performance of UI-based Java applications, Eclipse is a behemoth of an application. It requires significant RAM, CPU, and disk space. The latter is not much of an issue anymore these days. But, your development machine should have plenty of RAM and extra processing cycles so as not to leave you frustrated when using Eclipse.

Another recommendation I would like to make is to use at least a 20-inch display. The PHP development and debugging perspectives divide the main window into up to six or seven panes that all hold different information. Take as an example the screenshot, which shows Eclipse while editing the code for this chapter. The code editor in the center of the window is surrounded by panes, such as a hierarchical directory and file listing or your project(s) ("PHP Explorer"), a hierarchical outline of the resources defined by your project, such as constants, functions, and classes ("PHP Project Outline"), a structural outline of the currently viewed file ("Outline"), a pane for looking up PHP built-in functions ("PHP Functions"), and a pane displaying the syntactical errors Eclipse has detected ("Problems"), and so on. You get the picture.

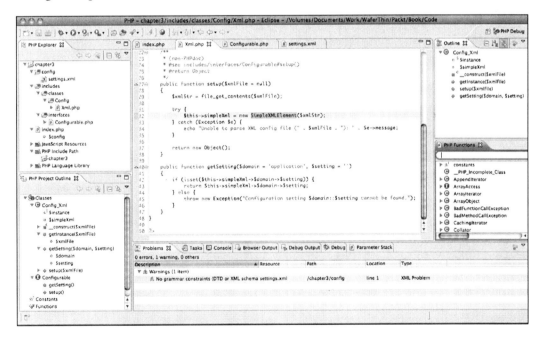

Again, since Eclipse is so customizable, you can change the layout and get rid of some panes and tabs to accommodate a smaller screen. But, in my opinion, you would be compromising away some of the features that make Eclipse so powerful. You will be hard-pressed to run Eclipse effectively on a 7-inch netbook, but that doesn't mean you might have to sometimes. The answer is to design your own perspective that only contains the absolute essentials you can fit on a small screen. When you are back to using a bigger display, you can switch back to the more full-featured perspective.

Choosing a package

Eclipse is incredibly extensible. Aside from adding numerous plugins to enable functionality in Eclipse, you can start out with a pre-configured Eclipse package. There are several packages available from the Eclipse download page. For the version that is current as of this writing, which is 3.5.1, these are the available options:

- Eclipse IDE for Java EE Developers (188 MB)
- Eclipse IDE for Java Developers (91 MB)
- Eclipse for PHP Developers (137 MB)
- Eclipse IDE for C/C++ Developers (78 MB)
- Eclipse for RCP/Plugin Developers (182 MB)
- Eclipse Modeling Tools (includes Incubating components) (366 MB)
- Eclipse IDE for Java and Report Developers (218 MB)
- Pulsar for Mobile Java Developers (112 MB)
- Eclipse SOA Platform for Java and SOA Developers (136 MB)
- Eclipse Classic 3.5.1 (161 MB)

If you are going to be doing Java development in Eclipse as well, you should download one of the two Java-centric packages at the beginning of the list. However, if you are going to be focusing on the much more enjoyable world of PHP, you should start with the "Eclipse for PHP Developers" package. Since none of the packages available from the `eclipse.org` site come with all the PHP goodies, you will have to add those no matter which package you download.

Eclipse IDE download page: `http://www.eclipse.org/downloads/`

After downloading the chosen package, simply uncompress the archive and move the resulting folder to its final destination. Eclipse is pretty self-contained and does not require an installer or a lot of external preferences files.

Adding the PDT plugin

If you have chosen to start with the "Eclipse for PHP Developers" package, you can skip this section because you already have everything you need to get started exploring Eclipse and PDT. However, keep reading if you started with one of the non PHP-centric packages or you already have Eclipse installed from working with another programming language.

Similar to Eclipse itself, you have two installation options for adding the **PHP Development Tools** (PDT) plugin to your Eclipse installation. First, you can download an archive of the plugin, extract it and put it into the "plugins" directory inside your Eclipse folder.

However, I recommend the second way of installing PDT, which is via Eclipse's built-in installer. After starting up Eclipse, select the **Help | Software Updates** menu option. If not already selected, switch to the **Available Software** tab. You should see a list of all sites from which Eclipse knows to get new software or updates to installed components. Assuming that they are the sites that we need to install PDT, you should go ahead and click the **Add Site ...** button to add each of these sites in turn:

- `http://download.eclipse.org/technology/dltk/updates-dev/1.0/`
- `http://download.eclipse.org/tools/pdt/updates/2.0/`
- `http://download.eclipse.org/releases/galileo/`

The first link will get you access to the Dynamic Languages Tool, which is a prerequisite for PDT. The second link is for PDT itself. And, the third link is an Eclipse update site. The last site may already be in your list.

Once you expand the PDT site by clicking on the little error next to its name, you can select either the PDT SDK Feature. Once you click the **Install** button, Eclipse will do some checking and prompt you to install the required dependencies as well. After accepting the respective licenses, Eclipse is off downloading and installing the plugins. Although not strictly required, it is a good idea to restart Eclipse after the installation.

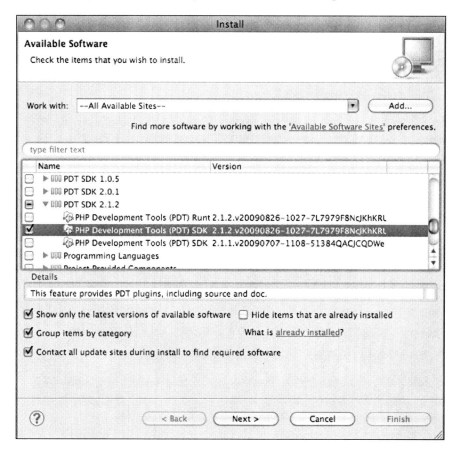

Now that you know how to install Eclipse plugins, take a look at the listing at the end of this chapter for additional plugins you might want to install.

Basic Eclipse concepts

Eclipse uses certain concepts in constructing a user interface. Getting the definition of those basic concepts out of the way, will make the following discussion much easier.

Workspace

On a physical level, your workspace is based on a folder or directory in which you keep your projects. It also includes all external files and resources that Eclipse knows about. However, a workspace is much more than a collection of files. It also represents the relationships between the files, objects, and actions you can take on them. You can think of the workspace as everything there is, but not necessarily all you can see at any given moment.

You can have any number of workspaces. For example, you might have a workspace for PHP projects and another for Java projects. Although, there is no requirement that you cannot keep projects with a variety of underlying technologies in the same workspace. Another reason to keep distinct workspaces might be to separate work projects from personal ones. I for one, have four different workspaces right now; one for work, a second one for work because a legacy project required a specific home directory for compiling it, a third one for private projects, and a separate fourth workspace for projects related to this book.

Switching between workspaces is easy; simply select the **File | Switch Workspace | Other ...** menu option if you are opening or starting a new workspace. Otherwise, if you are switching to a workspace you have used before, Eclipse probably remembered it and put the option in the **Switch Workspace** submenu for you to select directly. Here is a screenshot of a typical PHP workspace in the process of switching to another workspace:

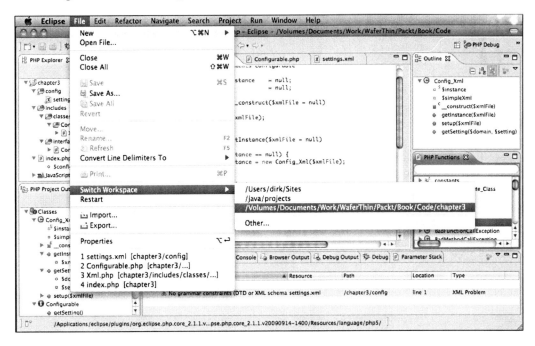

Eclipse keeps workspace related information in a folder named .metadata in your workspace directory. There is quite a bit of information stored in that directory and there have been reports of the amount or nature of that data impacting the stability of Eclipse. For example, all actions related to installing, uninstalling, upgrading, and downgrading of plugins will be tracked meticulously in the .metadata directory. Luckily, there is an option to launch Eclipse with the -clean command-line argument to perform some household maintenance on that directory. After that, Eclipse often becomes more stable again. This is how the Eclipse documentation describes the -clean command-line option:

> *Cleans cached data used by the OSGi framework and Eclipse runtime. Try to run Eclipse once with this option if you observe startup errors after install, update, or using a shared configuration.*

Following is a screenshot of me launching Eclipse with the -clean option from the command line. Note that on my operating system, the eclipse binary is hidden inside some directories inside the Eclipse.app directory. If you are on Windows or Linux, you can run the -clean option on the binary directly.

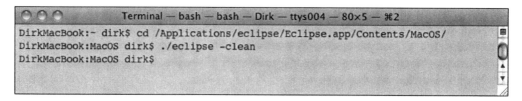

The above command line will start Eclipse while cleaning various plugin related data that has been cached on disk.

Views

Views are typically windows, screens, or tabs that allow you to interact with one particular aspect of your workspace. For example, there are views to show object hierarchies, display console output, interact with databases, and so on. Eclipse comes with a couple of built-in views that are likely to be useful no matter what kind of development you might be doing, such as an internal web browser and navigator to display the hierarchical structure of your project files on the hard disk.

In addition to the standard views, each plugin is free to add any number of views to your copy of Eclipse. PDT for example, adds these six views:

- **Browser output**: Since many PHP projects rely on a browser-based user interface, it makes a lot of sense to be able to see what exactly the browser gets to see when it interacts with your code.

- **Debug output**: PHP debuggers can generate output specifically for debugging. This might happen automatically depending on the configuration of the debugger or it might be caused by debug function calls you place in the code to gain greater insight into a particular passage of code. Having a view dedicated to this output eliminates some of the other chatter going on (browser output, PHP warnings and errors, or console output).

- **Parameter stack**: This view is used during debugging and it displays the values of function parameters during execution.

- **PHP explorer**: A tree structure outline of the files that make up your system. This view starts with, but is not limited to the project's home directory. It can include references to external files that have been added to the project.

- **PHP functions**: Rather than launching a web browser or opening a book (unless it's this one!) to learn about a particular PHP function, PDT provides a view that lists all PHP functions grouped by module for easy reference. See the *Other Features* section towards the end of this chapter for more details.

- **PHP project outline**: This view displays all classes, constants, and functions in your project in a tree structure and allows you to drill down the hierarchy for more detail, such as method visibility, parameters, variables, and so on.

Also, views are not limited to a specific project. Some views might display information pertaining to a single file; whereas, others might display information gathered from your whole workspace. Search results and workspace-wide to-do items are examples of views that cut across projects.

Selecting and opening a view is pretty easy and will add it to your current perspective. Simply select the **Window | Show View** menu option. You can either select one of the recently used views or select **Other ...** to see a complete list of available views.

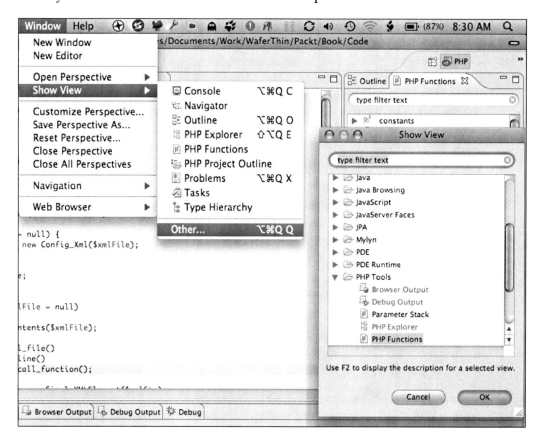

Perspectives

Perspectives are nothing more than strategically combined views. In other words, one can arrange any number of views within a window and then assign the name of a perspective to it. If at any later point in time you want to switch back to that particular layout, all you have to do is select the name of the perspective from the **Window | Show Perspective** menu.

PDT defines two perspectives, each of which includes the following views:

- PHP perspective
  - ○ PHP Explorer view
  - ○ Outline view
  - ○ Type hierarchy view
  - ○ Problems view
  - ○ Tasks view
  - ○ Console view
- PHP Debug perspective
  - ○ Debug view
  - ○ Variables view
  - ○ Breakpoints view
  - ○ Parameter stack view
  - ○ Debug output view
  - ○ Browser output view
  - ○ Expressions view
  - ○ Editor
  - ○ Console view
  - ○ Tasks

While you cannot easily create your own views in Eclipse, it is trivial to create your own perspective. Once you have included, resized, and rearranged all the views you wish to include in your new perspective, simply select the **Window | Save Perspective As...** menu option.

You can also customize already defined perspectives by enabling or disabling commands and shortcut icons available under that perspective. Simply go to the **Window | Customize Perspective ...** menu option.

A PDT sample project

For the purpose of showing off PDT's features, I have created a small sample project, consisting of four files:

1. `config/settings.xml`: Application configuration settings in XML format.

2. `classes/Configurable.php`: An interface stipulating methods `setup()` and `getSetting()`. By defining this interface, we leave the details such as the source of the configuration data or the internal data structure to the implementing class.

3. `classes/Config/Xml.php`: A class implementing interface Configurable and providing implementations of methods `setup()` to parse the above XML file and `getSetting()` to allow the application to retrieve a stored configuration setting. This class was implemented as a singleton with the assumptions that configuration settings don't and shouldn't be read more than once during the execution of the application.

4. `index.php`: The main executable that requires the other source files, instantiates a `Config_Xml` object, and outputs one of the settings just to show it is working correctly.

This little project does no more than parsing an XML config file and providing a method for various parts of the application to retrieve these settings as needed. Nevertheless, this is enough to illustrate the feature PDT provides to the object-oriented PHP developer. Here are the listings for the four source files:

`config/settings.xml`:

```
<?xml version='1.0' standalone='yes'?>
<settings>
    <application>
        <name>Converter</name>
        <homedir>/var/www/converter</homedir>
    </application>
    <logging>
        <dir>logs</dir>
        <file>debug.out</file>
        <level>3</level>
        <type>text</type>
    </logging>
</settings>
```

settings.xml is the XML file that the rest of our code will be parsing. There are two groups of settings: application and logging. Each group consists of a listing of name-value pairs where the tag name is the name and the content of the tag is the value. For example, the first option in the logging group sets the value of the dir option to logs.

classes/Configurable.php:

```php
<?php
interface Configurable
{
    public function setup();
    public function getSetting();
}
?>
```

The interface defined by Configurable.php requires any class that implements the interface to provide implementations of the methods setup() and getSetting(). The idea is that the setup() would handle parsing the XML file and storing the settings as properties in a class. getSetting() would then be used as a method to access the value of a specific setting.

classes/config/Xml.php:

```php
<?php
class Config_Xml implements Configurable
{
    private static $instance   = null;
    private $simpleXml                = null;

    private function __construct($xmlFile = null)
    {
        $this->setup($xmlFile);
    }

    public function getInstance($xmlFile = null)
    {
        if (self::$instance == null) {
            self::$instance = new Config_Xml($xmlFile);
        }

        return self::$instance;
    }
```

```php
        public function setup($xmlFile = null)
        {
            $xmlStr = file_get_contents($xmlFile);

            try {
                $this->simpleXml = new SimpleXMLElement($xmlStr);
            } catch (Exception $e) {
                echo "Unable to parse XML config file (" . $xmlFile . "):
                                            " . $e->message;
            }
        }


        public function getSetting($domain = 'application',
                                                    $setting ='')
        {
            if (isset($this->simpleXml->$domain->$setting)) {
                return $this->simpleXml->$domain->$setting;
            } else {
                throw new Exception("Configuration setting
                                $domain::$setting cannot be found.");
            }
        }
    }
?>
```

The Config_XML class defined in the above listing is a singleton, which means that one has to call the getInstance() method to obtain a reference to the only allowed instance of the class. Config_XML implements the Configurable interface. Specifically, the setup() method takes the name of an XML file and tries to use PHP's SimpleXML module to parse the settings from the XML document into a simple object-based representation. The accessor method getSetting() is then used to return the value of a particular setting.

index.php:

```php
<?php
require_once('includes/interfaces/Configurable.php');
require_once('includes/classes/Config/Xml.php');

$config = Config_Xml::getInstance('/path/to/appdir/config/settings.
xml');

echo 'Application name: ' . $config->getSetting('application', 'name')
. "\n";
?>
```

To exercise the above classes, I have created `index.php`, which starts by including the source files of the respective classes. It then obtains a reference to the `Config_Xml` singleton and asks it to parse our sample XML settings file. The last line of code simply retrieves and outputs the value of the `name` setting in the `application` group.

PDT features

Following is a more detailed listing of what each high-level PDT feature includes:

- Editor
- Inspection
- Debugging
- PDT preferences

Editor

The PHP editor provided by PDT goes way beyond simple text editing. Since it is aware of PHP syntax and top-level functions, it can offer functionality that other text editors cannot. As a result, it helps developers to output code faster and with fewer simple errors.

Syntax highlighting

PDT can parse and understand PHP. It will highlight keywords, properties and variables; thus making code easier to read.

Code assist

Type a few letters of a PHP function or class name and PDT will present you with matching properties or method names, complete with arguments and documentation if available.

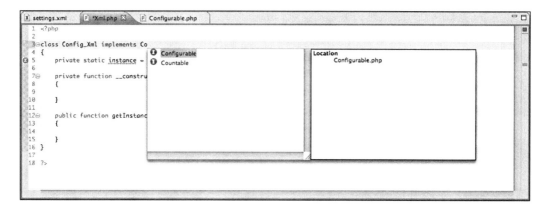

Code folding

Configure PDT to hide DocBlocks, include sections, methods, and so on. Rather than showing each line of those sections, it can display only the first line and expand to show the full listing when you click the small plus sign next to the intro line. Code folding makes it easier to get an overview of a piece of code by temporarily hiding irrelevant sections.

```
X settings.xml    P Xml.php ⊠    P Configurable.php
 1  <?php
 2
 3⊖ class Config_Xml implements Configurable
 4  {
 5        private static $instance    = null;
 6        private $simpleXml          = null;
 7
 8⊕      private function __construct($xmlFile = null)□
14⊕      public function getInstance($xmlFile = null)□
△23⊕     public function getSetting($domain = 'application', $setting = '')□
32
33  ?>
```

Mark occurrences

Clicking on a particular element, such as a property or method, will cause the editor to highlight every occurrence of the element in the file currently being displayed. This is extremely useful when trying to track how a property changes throughout the flow of the code, for example. Read and write occurrences are being highlighted in different colors. Also, the availability of this feature can be toggled in the preferences.

The following screenshot illustrates how the editor highlighted all occurrences of the property $simpleXml after I clicked on it on line 11.

```php
class Config_Xml implements Configurable
{
    private static $instance     = null;
    private $simpleXml           = null;

    private function __construct($xmlFile = null)
    {
        $xmlStr = file($xmlFile);
        $this->simpleXml = new SimpleXMLElement($xmlStr);
    }

    public function getInstance($xmlFile = null)
    {
        if (self::$instance == null) {
            self::$instance = new Config_Xml($xmlFile = null);
        }

        return self::$instance;
    }

    public function getSetting($domain = 'application', $setting = '')
    {
        if (isset($this->simpleXml->$domain->$setting)) {
            return $this->simpleXml->$domain->$setting;
        } else {
            throw new Exception("Configuration setting $domain::$setting cannot be fou
        }
```

Override indicators

PDT displays various little icons in the margin of the current document to indicate certain meta-info about the corresponding line in the editor. These icons include error messages, debugging breakpoints, code folding markers, and to-do items. Another icon that can be displayed is a small up arrow to indicate when a child class is overwriting a parent class method. Similarly, providing a concrete implementation of a method defined in an interface will also bring about the little arrow. This behavior can be seen in the screenshot above on line 23 because `getSetting()` implements the method of the same name from the `Configurable` interface.

Type, method, and resource navigation

One of the standard Eclipse features that you will quickly come to rely on is the ability to easily locate files, methods, and types through simple pattern matching. Rather than scrolling up and down the hierarchical file layout while hunting for the right file, it will become second nature to simply hit the shortcut key combination and locate the method you need by typing part of its name. All three quick lookup options in the following screenshots are available from Eclipse's "Navigate" menu.

Typing a partial method name will quickly generate a list of matching methods as well as the filenames and locations. Double-clicking any of the entries will result in the corresponding file being opened in the editor.

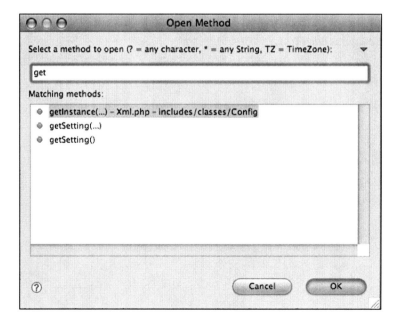

The **Open Resource** dialog allows you to locate files by name. The use of wildcards is not only allowed, but encouraged.

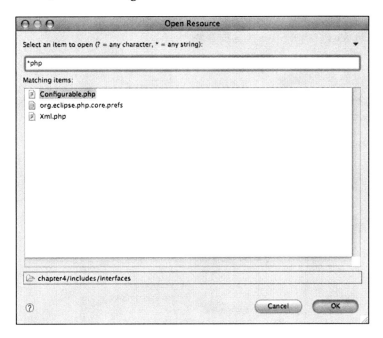

The last member of this trio of navigation shortcuts is the **Open Type** dialog, which allows you to do a wildcard search on types, such as class or inteface names. Obviously, Eclipse will have to know about PHP syntax to be able to extract and index that sort of information from source files.

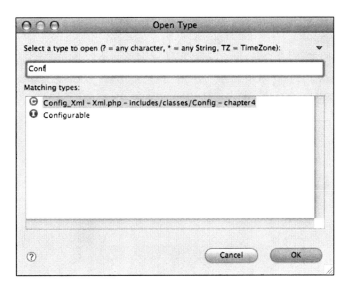

Inspection

PDT and Eclipse offer several views that allow you to view your project's resources hierarchically. These views allow you to gain an overview of your projects, files, types, methods, and properties at a glance.

Projects and files

PDT lets you work with multiple projects that are in your workspace. It makes it easy to navigate the hierarchy of files that comprise your project.

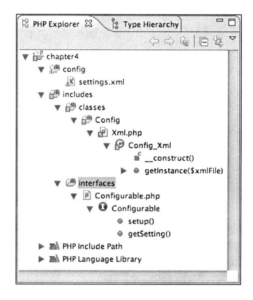

PHP explorer

You have access to a hierarchical outline of any PHP file you are currently editing. You can easily jump to any property or function within a class. It also makes it easier to grasp the overall functionality of the piece of code on which you are working.

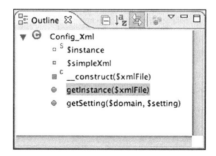

Type hierarchy

This feature really shines in the context of object-oriented development. Given an object or class, you can ask PDT to display the type hierarchy, which shows all parent and child classes of the object. This includes interfaces as you can see in the following screenshot. We can see that class `Config_Xml` implements the `Configurable` interface by providing concrete implementations of the two methods `getSetting()` and `setup()`.

This feature is very handy when trying to determine where within the object hierarchy a particular class falls. Skipping two generations up the hierarchy to see which methods are being provided by the parent's parent class is as easy as double-clicking the corresponding item in the tree display of the hierarchy.

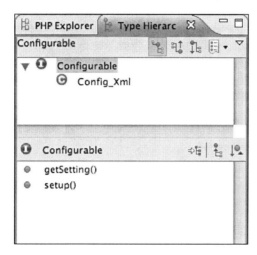

Debugging

Although PDT does not provide its own debugger, it provides support for at least two PHP debuggers that give you powerful control over and insight into how your scripts execute. You can set breakpoints and examine the variable stack just like in any other full-fledged debugger.

The example later on in this section assumes that the Xdebug debugger has been compiled as a module for the version of your PHP executable. For more detailed instructions on how to do this, please consult the chapter on debugging techniques and tools.

In addition to debugging your code directly, PDT also allows you to execute and preview web pages right within the IDE. There is also functionality for debugging from within web pages in addition to PHP source code.

PDT supports multiple configurations for running or debugging your application. For the same application, you might have a configuration for simply running it in the browser, executing and debugging it locally, and a third one to debug a version that has been deployed to your staging or production server.

After you have told PDT about the debugger(s) you have installed and the web servers you will be using in the Preferences (**Eclipse | Preferences**), you are ready to start defining your configurations. Let's start by selecting the **Run | Debug Configuration ...** menu option. Since Eclipse supports many different kinds of development, it is no wonder that you might be overwhelmed by numerous options in the resulting dialog box; however, for now you can safely ignore anything that doesn't start with "PHP".

Since our application doesn't really have a web UI, we will be debugging by executing it directly. To do that, highlight the **PHP Script** option in the left hand column of the configurations dialog and click the little icon with a plus sign to create a new configuration. The configuration itself consists of four tabs; however, in our case all the important information is in the first tab. Here is a capture of what your screen should look like at this point:

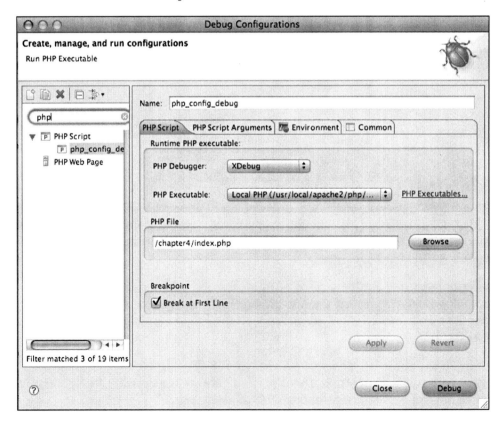

We have told PDT which of our debuggers we will be using ("XDebug"), which PHP executable ("Local PHP"), and which script to execute with that executable (`/chapter3/index.php`). The path of the script to execute is relative to the project folder. Lastly, checking the "Break at First Line" options ensures that the PHP executable doesn't just run away with our application. Instead, we would like it to stop at the beginning and wait for our instructions.

The other thing we might want to do is place a breakpoint at a line of the code in which we are particularly interested. Placing a breakpoint couldn't be easier. All you have to do is double-click the margin of the source code editor at the line where you want to place the breakpoint. I have done so at line 27 of file `Xml.php`.

At this point, we are ready to debug by clicking the **Debug** button at the bottom of the configuration screen. PDT will prompt you to switch to the debug perspective, which is a perspective that is optimized for debugging. Go ahead and do so. In addition, I would recommend selecting the little checkbox to do this automatically from now on. The resulting screen has multiple views that will help you debug your application. In particular, you will see following views:

- **Debug view**: As you can have multiple debug session going on simultaneously, the view shows you a hierarchical list of all of them and the state of the debugger for each.

- **Breakpoints/Variables**: "Breakpoints" will show you a list of files and lines where you have placed breakpoints. You are able to toggle each of the breakpoints. "Variables" will show you a list of all variables that are defined in the current scope in which the application is executing. This always includes super global arrays $_COOKIE, $_ENV, $_FILES, $_GET, $_POST, $_REQUEST, and $_SERVER.

- **Editor**: The Editor view will automatically switch to display the currently executing PHP file and highlight the active source code line. This is very handy to see what the code is doing while you are examining the debug output.

- **Console**: The debugger or your application may generate output that goes directly to the console, which is positioned at the bottom of the window.

- **Debug Output/Browser Output**: Any output that is usually sent to the browser will appear on the **Browser Output** tab. In our case however, the application only generates console output. Output generated by the debugger automatically or through function calls supported by the debugger will appear in the **Debug Output** tab.

Of course, it is up to you to customize the debug view to your liking. However, the default layout is able to cram a lot of information onto the screen and should be sufficient for most users.

To better illustrate the power of the debugger, I have added a couple of lines to the Xml.php file. The function calls xdebug_call_file(), xdebug_call_line(), xdebug_call_function() are only supported because I have compiled support for Xdebug into my PHP executable. The following screenshot illustrates the debug perspective. Notice how execution has stopped at our breakpoint (now on line 30). The **Debug Output** tab shows the output generated by the Xdebug specific function calls. The **Variables** tab shows a list of both global and local variables and their respective values.

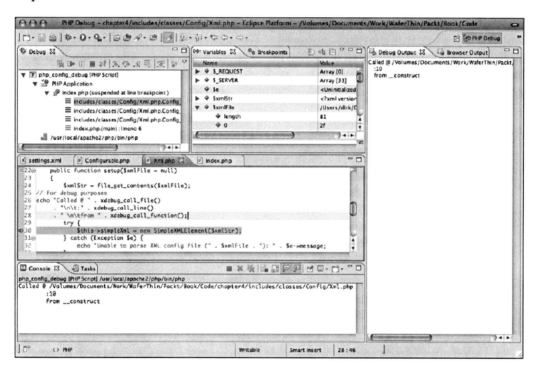

The key to Eclipse in general and PDT in particular is extensibility. It should therefore come as no surprise that PDT functions as a framework as much as it functions as a development environment.

PDT preferences

You can further customize PDT's features by setting some preferences. The various Eclipse plugins typically expose a slew of settings that can be changed via the **Preferences** dialog. Some of these settings affect how you work in minor ways; whereas, others can impact or even complement your development style in a significant way. I want to highlight the settings that I consider the most beneficial to the developer. To access any of these settings you should select the **Preferences** option under the **Eclipse** menu. The dialog that pops up allows you to select the plugin for which preferences can be set in a hierarchical list on the left. For most modules, you can drill down further by expanding the listing. PHP, for example, has the following sub-sections:

- Appearance
- Code style
- Debug
- Editor
- New project layout
- PHP executables
- PHP interpreter
- PHP manual
- PHP servers
- Templates

Appearance

The only setting provided is whether to display method return types. To be honest, I have been having trouble getting this option to work. In theory, the PHP Project Outline view should be listing the type of the value returned by the respective method. However, I was unable to see any difference when toggling this option. Moreover, I am unclear how PDT would know about the return type because a method might return more then one type.

Code style

The following two settings affect the visual appearance and spacing of the code you type and that is generated by Eclipse. Beyond purely cosmetic reasons, these settings are important to comply with coding standards of your project and for better compatibility with other editors and IDEs.

Formatter

This is where you tell Eclipse how to indent the source code whenever you hit the tab key. This is actually an important setting because it will affect how easily your code will be viewable and editable in other editors. According to our coding standards developed in Chapter 1 (and commonly accepted otherwise), you should change the default setting from indenting with tabs to indenting with four spaces.

Code templates

One immensely useful function PDT provides is to generate DocBlocks automatically for any element in your code including classes, methods, and properties. Simply click your cursor on the element you are looking to comment and then select "Generate Element Comment" from the "Source" menu. PDT will generate the appropriate DocBlock and fill in as much detail as reflection will provide about the element. For example, when using this feature to generate the DocBlock for method `Config_Xml::getInstance()`, PDT is able to put the correct variable name on the `@param` line.

```
13
14    /**
15     * @param $xmlFile
16     * @return unknown_type
17     */
18    public function getInstance($xmlFile = null)
19    {
20        if (self::$instance == null) {
21            self::$instance = new Config_Xml($xmlFile = null);
22        }
23
24        return self::$instance;
25    }
```

The templates for the actual DocBlocks and comments that are generated using this feature can be edited on the "Code Templates" screen.

There is also an option to edit templates for code generation, but that feature has not yet been implemented in PDT 2.0. However, I expect that in future versions you will be able to have PDT quickly generate class skeleton or automatically add getter and setter methods for any newly added property. This corresponds to functionality that has been available in Eclipse for Java for a number of years.

Debug

Being able to interactively debug in a visual environment is one of the great features of Eclipse. However, before you can debug, you have to tell Eclipse which debugger you are using and how to interact with it. Furthermore, this section of the preferences lets you define some default behavior as you are stepping through the code in debug mode.

Installed debuggers

On this screen, you can let PDT know which debuggers are installed and on which port they are listening. The correct settings on this screen are prerequisites for successfully being able to actively step through our PHP code and debug it. PDT comes preconfigured with settings for "Zend Debugger" and "XDebug" and their respective default ports of 10000 and 9000.

Step filtering

Using this screen, you can specify a list of resources, such as files or directories that will be skipped during debugging. What this means is that when you are stepping through source files, any files found on the step filtering list will be ignored. This comes in handy when you have a piece of code that is constantly being executed, even though you know that it works perfectly well. Examples of code sections you might want to exclude from stepping through include bootstrap files or class loaders.

It is possible to define path names with wildcard characters.

As of this writing, this feature is not supported in XDebug and unlikely to be supported in version 2.x of PDT at all. However, it does work with Zend Debugger.

Workbench options

Here you can specify some preferences that dictate when to switch to or from the debug perspectives. Whether multiple debug sessions are possible can also be set from this screen. The default settings are typically fine here.

Editor

In a previous section, we looked at the useful features the PHP editor that comes with PDT provides when editing source code. In this section, we will look at the preferences that determine how those features behave. These settings are likely the ones that have the highest impact on how you interact with your code.

Code assist

On this screen, you can fine-tune how auto-completion gets activated, what suggestions it will present, and how to add your selection to your code.

Code folding

Here you can toggle the code folding feature overall and decide whether classes, functions, and DocBlocks should be folded by default. I recommend not having any element fold be default. You can always fold them later to temporarily get rid of distracting or confusing sections.

Hovers

This screen lets you decide what the editor should display when you bring your cursor to hover over a particular element of the source code. The **Combined Hover** option, which is the default, will try to make a context-sensitive best guess. Hover pop-ups can display debug variable values, problem descriptions, documentation, annotations, or the source code of an element.

Mark occurrences

Here you can toggle which elements will be marked throughout the source code when you click on them. Available options are types, class methods and declarations, functions, constants, global variables, local variables, method exits, methods implementing an interface, and targets of break and continue statements.

My recommendation is to keep all options enabled, unless you find yourself getting distracted by too many items being highlighted. In that case, you can start selectively disabling some of the options.

Save actions

Although sparse otherwise, this screen has one of my favorite options. It allows you to enable an editor feature to automatically remove trailing white space from each line before actually saving the file.

When juggling code snippets around by copying, cutting, and pasting them, it always happens that you create extra whitespace. Other than making your files slightly larger it has no other side effect other than being annoying.

Syntax coloring

On this screen you can toggle syntax coloring for source code elements; as well as select the color and style you would like the editor to use. You are limited to the elements supported by this feature: comments, heredoc, keywords, normal source, numbers, PHP tags, PHPDoc sections, strings, task tags, and variables.

Task tags

It is common practice among developers to leave notes in inline comments or 'DocBlocks' to indicate that some kind of task has to be completed. For example, you might not have enough time to implement proper input validation while cranking out the prototype for your client. If you leave yourself a note in the source code using one of the strings PDT knows about, it is possible for PDT to present you with a list of tasks for your whole project.

On this screen, you can define the keywords that you intend to use so that PDT can be aware that you are creating a task tag. The default entries are `@to-do`, `FIXME`, `TODO`, and `XXX`.

There are other Eclipse plugins that let you leverage tasks and tags by taking them to a whole other level. You might want to take a look at the Mylyn plugin:

```
http://www.eclipse.org/mylyn/
```

For more details, see the *Eclipse Plugins* section later in this chapter.

Typing

Here you can toggle whether PDT automatically adds the closing equivalent for every quote, parenthesis, brace, square bracket, PHP tag, and phpDoc tag you type. If you are not used to it, this feature can feel like it is interrupting your coding flow. However, I definitely recommend you take the time to get used to it because it will end up reducing the time required to track down syntax errors because you forgot to close the code block.

New project layout

When you create a new project from the **File | New | PHP Project** menu option, you can tell PDT where you intend to keep your source files. By "source files" we mean your classes, interfaces, libraries, and so on. You can choose to have PDT consider the root directory of your project a source folder. Alternatively, you can have Eclipse automatically create an "application" folder for your source files and a "public" folder for publicly accessible resources. The "application" and "public" folders are the defaults, but you can change those directories on this screen.

There are two situations where I recommend switching away from the default setting of the root directory being a source folder and instead opting to separate your source files from your publicly available files.

First, if your application will be accessible via the Web, it is common security practice to only expose resources that you really intend to be accessible that way. All other resources that are not meant to be executed directly should be included explicitly.

Second, if you are following the MVC architecture, you would be expected to separate your business logic from your presentation layer. For more details on MVC, take a look at the chapter on the Zend Framework.

PHP executables

Here you can let PDT know about the different PHP executables you intend you use in your different projects. There is a plenty of reason to have more than one executable. For starters, you might want to have PHP4, PHP5.x, and a beta version of the next major version of PHP to test compatibility of your application with different possible deployment configurations. Another possibility is that you have multiple PHP executables that are the same version of PHP, but that were compiled with different options. You might have a lightweight version and an everything-but-the-kitchen-sink version. One might include many optional modules; whereas, the other might not.

PHP interpreter

Here you can select with which version of PHP you are working. In my version of Eclipse 3.5 with PDT 2.1.3, the choices are PHP 4 and PHP 5.1 / PHP 5.2 and PHP 5.2. Even though support for PHP 4 has been discontinued, this option continues to be available here because many developers have to deal with that version of PHP for existing and legacy projects. I expect that if it becomes necessary to differentiate between higher versions of PHP to support certain features, we will see option for PHP 6 appear here.

You can also enable ASP style tags here.

My recommendation is similar for both settings. Only enable PHP 4 if that is really the environment in which you will have to deploy your application. If you have a choice, you should certainly opt for PHP 5. Similarly, you should only enable ASP style tags if that is the convention being used by an existing project. If you recall our discussion of coding standards in an earlier chapter, we decided that ASP style tags should generally not be allowed.

Luckily, the defaults on this screen are to use PHP 5 and disallow ASP style tags.

PHP manual

The layout of the online PHP manual follows certain conventions, which is why PDT is able to link directly to manual pages from within hovers in the editor or the PHP function lookup view. On this screen, you can list several URLs that host the PHP manual. By default, only the manual on the main php.net site is listed.

```
http://www.php.net/manual/en/
```

One of the options you have is to point PDT at a different language version of the manual if you happen to do development in a language other than English, such as:

```
http://www.php.net/manual/de/
```

One thing I recommend is to download the manual for your version of PHP in HTML format and extract it into a local directory. PDT allows you to reference local directories in addition to remote URLs. That way, you always have access to the complete PHP manual – even if you have no Internet connectivity.

The complete PHP manual is available for download in various formats and languages at:

```
http://www.php.net/download-docs.php
```

PHP servers

For the purpose of launching, testing, and debugging specific pages within your project, you can edit the list of PHP servers on this screen. You need to create an entry for your web server if you are going to create a launch or debug configuration. For more details, see the section on debugging in this chapter.

Templates

Templates are such a time-saver that it is a shame that developers are often overlooking them. After all, we're all guilty of copy-pasting sections of code from tutorials or other sections where we spent time implementing a certain feature correctly. With templates, you can have those code snippets at your fingertips. All you have to do is define a template once and associate a short name with it. Afterwards, any time you type the name, followed by hitting *Ctrl-space*, Eclipse will insert the whole template into your source file. What's better, by tabbing through the code, the editor will allow you to customize the template in the appropriate places. Lucky for us, PDT comes pre-defined with dozens of different templates, including the following examples:

The shortcut `cls` will generate this code snippet that serves as the skeleton of a class definition:

```
class ${class_name} {
    function ${function_name}() {
        ${cursor};
    }
}
```

The shortcut `itdir` generates the following code to iterate over a directory:

```
${dollar}${dirh} = opendir(${dirname});
if (${dollar}${dirh}) {
    while (${dollar}${dir_element} = readdir(${dollar}${dirh})) {
        ${cursor};
    }
    unset(${dollar}${dir_element});
    closedir(${dollar}${dirh});
}
```

Take a look at the predefined templates and use them as a starting point for creating your own.

Other features

In this section, we take a look at two additional features that don't neatly fit into the categories we have examined up until now. First, we look at the PHP functional reference feature, which will save many trips to the php.net site once you get used to it. Second, we look at extending Eclipse through plugins and we take a closer look at some of the more useful plugins for PHP development.

PHP function reference

This view provides you with a hierarchical, searchable listing of all built-in PHP functions. If you are like me, you have benefited from the well-organized online reference at the php.net site. However, being able to search for a function name from within your development environment is still a great time saver. Once you have located the function you need, you can double-click it and have it inserted into the source file you are currently editing. Or, you can right-click and decide to view the corresponding php.net manual page. As Eclipse has a built-in browser, you don't need to switch to a different application to read the details of how to use the function; as well as the often-useful comments at the bottom of the manual pages.

To add this view to your environment, select the **Window | Show View | Other** menu option to bring up the **Show View** dialog. Then select **PHP Tools | PHP Functions**.

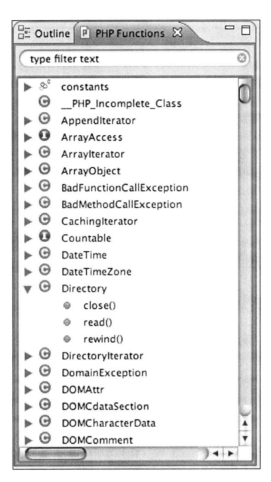

Eclipse plugins

As mentioned before, extensibility through plugins is one of the key advantages of Eclipse. There are many sites where you can find out about additional plugins that might enhance your productivity. However, I'd like to recommend one site that does a good job of collecting, listing, organizing, and describing plugins. Whether you have a particular plugin for which you are trying to get more information or you have a particular need to fill, 'Eclipse Marketplace' is a good place to start:

```
http://marketplace.eclipse.org
```

Following is a list of plugins that might be helpful to PHP developers. Depending on which base Eclipse package you chose, you may or may not have the plugin installed.

Subversive

Description:

This subversion plugin is modeled after the CVS plugin. It provides easy ways of executing all the usual svn commands, such as:

- Browsing local and remote repositories, supporting various protocols, such as `https` and `snv+ssh`
- Adding projects to repositories and checking out branches, tags, and trunk to your local workspace
- Synchronizing your local working copy with the repository
- File operations to commit, update, and revert changes
- Merge and resolve changes via a highly functional graphical UI

Subclipse is another subversion plugin for Eclipse, but in the past, I have consistently had better success with Subversive.

Home page:

`http://community.polarion.com`

Update site(s):

`http://download.eclipse.org/technology/subversive/0.7/update-site/`
`http://www.polarion.org/projects/subversive/download/eclipse/2.0/`
`update-site/`

Mylyn

Description:

Mylyn can connect to various issue, task, and bug trackers (insert your favorite term here) to integrate that workflow directly into Eclipse. After all, who wants to open a browser window for Bugzilla and another for Jira just to have to switch back to Eclipse to actually do the work? Mylyn integrates those tasks by giving you a view to add to any perspective. It natively supports a couple of "task repositories," such as Jira and Bugzilla, but many different repositories are supported with additional plugins (see the Mantis Mylyn Connector below). In addition to shared repositories, you can also work with local repositories that don't require external systems.

Home page:

`http://www.eclipse.org/mylyn/`

Update site(s):

`http://download.eclipse.org/tools/mylyn/update/e3.4`

Mylyn Mantis Connector

Description:

This plugin allows Mylyn to integrate with Mantis. After all, this is a book about PHP and I would be neglectful if I weren't to mention at least one PHP based issue tracker. Besides, Mantis is one of my favorites due to the simplicity of its workflow.

Home page:

```
http://mylyn-mantis.wiki.sourceforge.net/
```

Update site:

```
http://mylyn-mantis.sourceforge.net/eclipse/update/site.xml
```

Quantum DB

Description:

This plugin lets you connect to a number of different databases to review schema information and run queries. It relies on JDBC drivers (Java database drivers), which there are many of, including Oracle, MySQL, PostgreSQL, and so on. However, it is not meant as a replacement for a full-fledged DB design tool.

Home page:

```
http://quantum.sourceforge.net/
```

Update site:

```
http://quantum.sourceforge.net/update-site
```

Zend Studio for Eclipse

Zend has a commercial IDE offering that builds on PDT. I don't necessarily want to drum up sales for Zend, but their IDE offers a lot of added features for the professional PHP developer. As I have mentioned at the beginning of this chapter, Eclipse isn't the only game in town. Other development environments offer feature sets that compete with both Eclipse/PDT and Zend Studio. However, having looked at Eclipse and PDT in detail, it is a natural progression to at least mention Zend Studio because it directly leverages and expands the PDT features we have discussed thus far.

You can download and purchase Zend Studio for Eclipse from zend.com. The download comes with a 30 day free trial after which you have to purchase a license to continue using the product. However, 30 days should be enough to evaluate the product and make a buying decision. At the time of this writing, a license for Zend Studio for Eclipse ranges from $399 to $717, depending on how many years of upgrades and support you want to include. There are also volume discounts available if you plan on setting up a whole team with the same IDE. You can find the download here:

```
http://www.zend.com/en/products/studio/downloads
```

Now let's take a look at the default interface Zend Studio gives you. As it is based on Eclipse and PDT, this should appear pretty familiar by now.

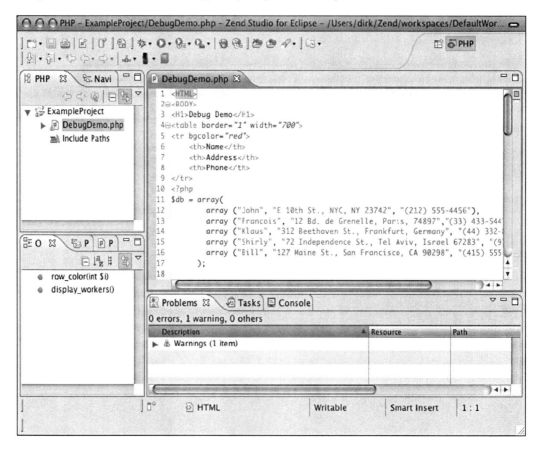

If you take a look at Zend's site, you can see their own take on the differences between PDT and Zend Studio. Following are the issues that I consider the most significant.

Support

With Zend being a commercial entity, you might be able to benefit from a different level of support. Personally, I am the type of guy to try and figure things out myself by researching and looking behind the scenes. But, if you want to save time and effort, with Zend Studio, you have the added option of reaching out to commercial support by opening a trouble ticket or picking up the phone.

Refactoring

Zend Studio allows you reorganize your project by renaming and moving files, methods, and properties. Often when you do this in PDT, it breaks your application because there is some reference or occurrence that you neglected to update, no matter how careful you are. Zend Studio handles the grunt work for you. No need to try and do a global search-replace. Zend Studio gives you control over what and how to update your code.

Code generation

Writing code is a creative endeavor; especially if you do it at will—but not always. Some tasks are repetitive and mundane. It's when you have to spend a lot of time on those tasks that you wish you could simply delegate them to someone else. Code generation lets you do that—sort of. Zend Studio provides three kinds of code generation:

- **Getter/setter methods**: After defining properties of a class, you can selectively generate the getter and setter methods while specifying the visibility for each of them.

- **Overriding/implementing of inherited methods**: Using reflection, Zend Studio knows which methods are defined in parent classes and interfaces. Using a simple wizard, it lets you select any of those methods and generate a skeleton implementation for each.

- **A wizard interface for generating new elements**: Adding new classes or interfaces is easy as the wizard prompts you for visibility, constructor/destructors, phpDocumentor DocBlocks, parent classes/interfaces, and which methods to inherit.

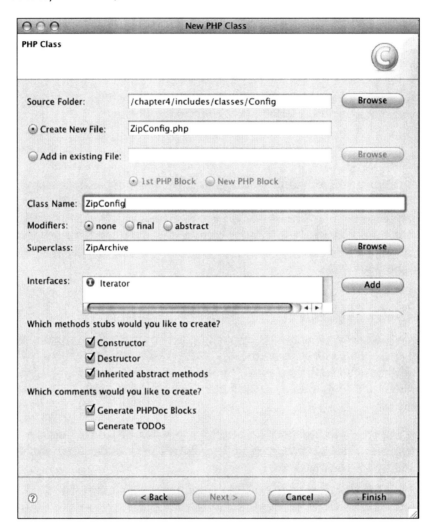

PHPUnit testing

In addition to aiding you in the creation of PHPUnit tests at the same time you create your code (see code generation above), Zend Studio also gives you a visual interface for running your test suite or individual tests and to inspect the result.

PhpDocumentor support

Having read the previous chapter, you are aware of the importance and benefits of creating phpDocumentor DocBlocks in your code (you did read the whole chapter, didn't you?). Zend Studio not only generates DocBlock skeletons when generating code, such as new classes or methods, it also prompts the developer to add detail to the DocBlock each time he adds a new element by hand.

Zend Framework integration

In one of the later chapters, we will be looking at using frameworks in our development with particular focus on the excellent Zend Framework. Zend Studio lets you create new Zend Framework projects based on the ZF's implementation of MVC. ZF libraries and modules are automatically added to the include path and there are wizards for generating new ZF elements:

- Zend Action Helper
- Zend Controller
- Zend Controller Test Case
- Zend Module
- Zend Table
- Zend View
- Zend View Helper

In my opinion, support for the Zend Framework is one of the strongest arguments for considering the jump from Eclipse/PDT to Zend Studio. If you rely on ZF in just about every PHP project you undertake, Zend Studio might be the way to go.

Zend server integration

If your organization uses Zend Platform for deploying PHP applications in production and you are using ZP's ability to monitor and test the environment, you might benefit from the integration Zend Studio offers in this area. It lets you view test results generated in Zend Platform and inspect the corresponding code in the editor and debugger. All this is pretty powerful stuff and you are unlikely to find this kind of integration elsewhere, but unless you are heavily invested in Zend Platform, which is another commercial offering, you cannot benefit from the features Zend Studio offers in this area.

Summary

For those who until now have not been using an integrated development environment to write PHP, I hope that this chapter was a good introduction to the benefits you can reap by investing the time to learn such a tool. All the little conveniences, such as code completion, syntax checking, debugging, add up to real time savings and quality improvements. As a result, you will be able to develop better code faster.

For those who have been using an IDE already, perhaps you came across a couple of tips and tricks that you didn't know were possible. It really pays to invest the time to properly learn the tools with which you write the code that pays your bills.

We also got to take a closer look at the great effort that both the Eclipse Foundation and the PHP Development Tools (PDT) team have produced. Even if you decide that Eclipse with PDT is not the right tool for your every day needs, Eclipse is a great tool to be familiar with because it continues to evolve, improve, and find its way into an increasing number of IT shops. Eclipse's greatest strength is its flexibility to add functionality via plugins. Due to that, there is no telling what kind of development it will be used for in the future.

Lastly, I don't expect you to blindly accept that Eclipse is the right tool for you. Your needs and requirements for a PHP development environment are possibly quite different from my own. However, with what you have learned in this chapter, you will have a good understanding of what to look for in a solid IDE. At this point, I encourage you to take a survey of what other developers are using. Find out why they chose what they did. After collecting the information you will be in a good position to make a decision on what IDE is best suited for the way you work. Hopefully, this chapter showed you how to ask the right questions.

4
Source Code and Version Control

My challenge in writing this chapter was to make it relevant to PHP development. There are great books that discuss source code and version control in general and I didn't want to rehash in one chapter what those books cover in much more detail. For example, if you want to learn more about Subversion in detail, you can read the excellent "Version Control with Subversion." In addition to being available in print, you can access a free online version of the book here:

```
http://svnbook.red-bean.com/
```

Instead, in this chapter, I want to go over the most important concepts and techniques with specific focus on making it part of your everyday workflow as a PHP developer. The questions I want to answer include:

- How should I structure my PHP application when using Subversion?
- How can I integrate other PHP tools to automate various processes with Subversion?
- What PHP tools are available for working with Subversion?
- What problems do these tools solve?

Common use cases

Here are a couple of use cases that typify how you can leverage Subversion in your day-to-day development activity.

Scenario 1: After a phone call with a panicked client, you are forced to access the production server to fix an issue that is affecting thousands of users. Unfortunately, after a couple of edits, the page returns a 500 HTTP error, which probably means that you made it worse than before. Unfortunately, in your rush to fix the problem, you didn't make a proper backup of the file(s) you were editing and have no way of reverting to the previous version. For the time being, let's ignore the fact that you probably shouldn't be working on your production environment. After all, we have all done it—even if it is wrong.

Scenario 2: That open source project you started while commuting an hour on the train every day has been kicked into overdrive. SourceForge.net named it project of the month and suddenly you have several qualified volunteers that want to contribute code, do translations of the user interface, and work on documentation. Overnight, you are not only faced with having to coordinate with several other people wanting to make changes to your source code, you also have to deal with the fact that they are located in different geographical locations and are possibly working on the same files simultaneously. Sure, you can have them send you patch files for everything they do, but then you might as well quit your day job because your project just graduated from hobby to time and money pit.

Scenario 3: In an effort to track down how an especially elusive bug was introduced, it is necessary to determine which developer contributed which part of the code. Being able to step through the source code in reverse chronological order would be a valuable tool in this situation.

A brief history of source code control

The **Revision Control System (RCS)** tool is a lightweight utility for versioning individual files. All revisions, access logs, permissions, and so forth are being kept in a single text file, which is really easy to create on the fly. I have used RCS to version server config files. That way, you can easily back out of any changes quickly in case you break the configuration and the service goes down completely. It also makes it easy to review and revert to previous configurations even if it is long after you have already forgotten the actual changes you made to the file.

You can visit the official RCS homepage as a starting point for learning more about this tool. There, you can also find download links to the current source code, binaries for various platforms, and the original paper that inspired the creation of RCS:

```
http://www.cs.purdue.edu/homes/trinkle/RCS/
```

RCS comes with a cast of supporting utilities that turn its basic functionality into a functioning version control system, including:

- `ci`: Check a file into RCS
- `co`: Retrieve a file from RCS
- `rcsfile`: Describes the file format employed by RCS
- `rcsdiff`: Analyze the differences between two revisions of the same file
- `rlog`: Outputs detailed information about a file, such as paths, names, revisions, logs, access list, and branches; as well as entries for each revision
- `rcsmerge`: Merging different versions of a file
- `rcsclean`: Deleting abandoned working files

There is not enough space to cover all the RCS tools in full detail, especially considering that we will shortly be moving on to bigger and better things. However, I think the following example will give you a feeling of how to use RCS and the fact that it is still relevant even after more than 25 years since it was first conceived. The following example assumes that you have the above list of executables installed on your system and that you wish to start versioning your default PHP script, index.php.

```
Terminal — bash — bash — Dirk — ttys000 — 80×16 — ⌘2
DirkMacBook:project dirk$ ls -l
total 8
-rw-r--r--@ 1 dirk  dirk   196 Jan 14 08:15 index.php
DirkMacBook:project dirk$ mkdir RCS
DirkMacBook:project dirk$ ci index.php
RCS/index.php,v  <--  index.php
enter description, terminated with single '.' or end of file:
NOTE: This is NOT the log message!
>> Landing first version of bootstrap file.
>> .
initial revision: 1.1
done
DirkMacBook:project dirk$ ls -l
total 0
drwxr-xr-x  3 dirk  dirk   102 Jan 14 08:19 RCS
DirkMacBook:project dirk$
```

Following along with the commands and their resulting actions in the above example, we start out by listing the contents or our working directory with `ls -al`, which contains only the `index.php` file. We then create a directory named "RCS" with `mkdir RCS`, which will be used by the `rcs` utility to store all RCS files. A single file will be created for each file that we are versioning with RCS. Next we check our `index.php` file into RCS with the `ci index.php`. Listing the directory contents again reveals that the file is now gone.

```
DirkMacBook dirk$ co -l index.php
RCS/index.php,v  -->  index.php
revision 1.1 (locked)
done
DirkMacBook dirk$ vi index.php
DirkMacBook dirk$ rcsdiff index.php
===================================================================
RCS file: RCS/index.php,v
retrieving revision 1.1
diff -r1.1 index.php
6,7c6,7
< // kick things off
< $registry->controller->dispatch();
---
> // initializing controller for MVC architecture
> $controller->dispatch();
DirkMacBook dirk$ DirkMacBook dirk$ rcsdiff index.php
===================================================================
RCS file: RCS/index.php,v
retrieving revision 1.1
diff -r1.1 index.php
6,7c6,7
< // kick things off
< $registry->controller->dispatch();
---
> // initializing controller for MVC architecture
> $controller->dispatch();
DirkMacBook dirk$ ci -l index.php
RCS/index.php,v  <--  index.php
new revision: 1.2; previous revision: 1.1
enter log message, terminated with single . or end of file:
>> Fixed controller initialization.
>> .
done
DirkMacBook:~ dirk$
```

At this point, `index.php` only resides in RCS's repository and we need to use the checkout command `co -l index.php` to get it back into our working directory. The optional `-l` argument locks the file and ensures that no other user can check in a revision while we have an active lock on it.

After using an editor to make some modifications to the file (`vi index.php`), we can use the `rcsdiff index.php` command to see the differences between our modified version and the most recent one in the RCS repository.

Satisfied with our changes, we check the file back into the RCS repository with `ci -l index.php` while keeping a working copy in our directory due to the use of the `-l` switch.

```
                Terminal — bash — bash — Dirk — ttys005 — 80×30 — ⌘2
DirkMacBook dirk$ rlog index.php

RCS file: RCS/index.php,v
Working file: index.php
head: 1.2
branch:
locks: strict
        dirk: 1.2
access list:
symbolic names:
keyword substitution: kv
total revisions: 2;     selected revisions: 2
description:
Landing first version of bootstrap file.
----------------------------
revision 1.2    locked by: dirk;
date: 2009/05/14 23:17:50;  author: dirk;  state: Exp;  lines: +2 -2
Fixed controller initialization.
----------------------------
revision 1.1
date: 2009/05/14 23:14:29;  author: dirk;  state: Exp;
Initial revision
============================================================================
DirkMacBook dirk$ ls -al
total 8
drwxr-xr-x   4 dirk   dirk   136 Dec 25 16:18 .
drwxr-xr-x  10 dirk   dirk   340 Dec 25 09:38 ..
drwxr-xr-x   3 dirk   dirk   102 Dec 25 16:18 RCS
-rw-r--r--   1 dirk   dirk   196 Dec 25 16:16 index.php
DirkMacBook:~ dirk$
```

Lastly, we use the `rlog index.php` command to get a summary of the actions we have taken thus far.

Obviously we have skipped over a lot of options and features of RCS, but I'm hoping that the above example serves not only as an overview of RCS, but also as an introduction to the concepts involved in versioning and source code management. In an upcoming section, we will explore these and other concepts in more detail.

CVS

The main reason we covered RCS in the previous section was to set the stage for our next trip down memory lane. As useful as RCS was and continues to be, it has some shortcomings that prevent it from scaling up and being used for projects involving multiple developers. But, as things go in the open source community, someone needing a more advanced tool had the skill and time to create this tool. In this case, that someone was Dick Grune and the tool he created was CVS.

Initially, the **Concurrent Versioning System (CVS)** was not much more than a wrapper around RCS; a collection of scripts that added some features and provided a more powerful interface, but one that essentially continued to call on RCS to do the work behind the scenes. However, that architecture was replaced after a couple of years by one where all the underlying file manipulation is being done by code that is part of the CVS executable.

Among many small improvements, some of the major features CVS offered over RCS include the following:

- **Support for projects**: RCS's approach was file-centric. In contrast, CVS focused on the whole project. With the introduction of CVS, developers were able to take actions that affected every file in the project. Suddenly, it became easy to check hundreds of files from the repository, make some changes, review changes to multiple files, and commit those changes back to the shared repository. It was also possible to update one's local version of the project with the changes submitted by other developers.

- **Client-server architecture**: CVS made it possible for the repository to reside in one location and for the developers working on the project to be in any number of locations. As long as there was network connectivity whenever it became necessary to interact with the server, the developers could work anywhere and anytime.

- **Branching**: Once you start dealing with different versions of a software product, it quickly becomes inevitable to deal with different branches of the underlying code base. The model of branching introduced by CVS is being followed by most source code control and versioning systems that have come after it. For a more detailed description of branching, please see the list of concepts and terminology later on in this chapter.

These improvements were huge. All of a sudden, big, geographically dispersed development teams had a standardized tool for managing their source code. Not surprisingly, CVS quickly become the de facto standard in source code control. Versions of it exist for every major platform.

I intentionally deferred a description of a developer's typical workflow with CVS for when we get into the discussion of Subversion because it is essentially unchanged between the two tools.

As mentioned above, CVS builds on RCS to provide functionality for whole projects instead of just individual files. Unfortunately, this file-centric approach of the underlying tool; as well as the fact that CVS is getting up there in age, has translated into some shortcomings. Specifically, following are some common complaints users leverage against CVS:

- **Insufficient support for directories**: In CVS, directories are just containers. They can't be versioned, especially not in regards to the various versions of the files they contain.

- **No atomic commits**: When checking in multiple files at once, say all files that needed to be modified to add a certain feature, atomic commits would ensure that either all files get committed properly or none at all. In CVS, it is possible to end up with an inconsistent code tree if the commit is unable to complete for any reason, such as loss of connectivity or a power outage.

- **No local copies of base revisions**: This means that every time a developer wants to use the `status`, `revert`, or `diff` commands, they require connectivity to the repository, which translates into a significant inconvenience and forces you to modify your natural workflow.

- **Conflicts break code**: Conflicting code from different versions of a file often requires manual resolution. In contrast, Subversion (as of release 1.5) includes conflict resolution (merging) and it won't let you commit files with unresolved conflicts. Along those same lines, CVS does not include support for atomic commits.

- **Binary files are not handled gracefully**: Each version of a binary file, such as an image, compiled executable, or audio clip, is being stored in full. Although CVS is able to store only the differences between versions for text files, it is not able to do the same for binary files despite the fact that those algorithms exist.

  Furthermore, binary files have to be explicitly marked as such to avoid mangling by keyword expansion and translation of line-endings.

Despite the welcome feature set of CVS, there were enough annoyances for users and developers to try to improve on the existing tool.

Introducing Subversion

Subversion was conceived as a replacement for CVS. Rather than try to fix CVS, which was being held back in its evolution by its legacy underpinning, the developers set out to create a new tool from the ground up. The idea was to make it significantly similar to CVS so that developers would feel right at home and the learning curve, while switching from one tool to the other, would be minimal. Subversion is not a drop-in replacement for CVS, but rather an evolution of the ideas and concepts first successfully realized by CVS. At that, it has been very successful. Subversion is generally known as CVS without the annoyances.

There are many resources available on the web to learn more about Subversion, but your starting point should be the project's home page:

```
http://subversion.tigris.org
```

Client installation

As with most open source packages, there are essentially two ways of getting it installed on your system. First, you can download and compile the source code. If you're not completely comfortable with the build process, run into trouble, or you simply want to simplify the installation, I encourage you to go for a binary package instead. Unlike the source code, the binary packages are not being maintained by the Subversion project, but rather by contributors. Binary packages are available for just about every major platform and typically lag behind official source code releases by a couple of days.

Whichever path you choose for installing Subversion, you should probably start at the project's download page:

```
http://subversion.tigris.org/getting.html
```

Another thing to consider is that Subversion is based on client-server architecture. This means that the Subversion server will need to run on the machine that will host your repository. If you are working for or with a company, you might want to check whether a Subversion server is already available. If so, you will only need a client, of which there is a great variety. However, if you are setting up your own server for the first time, you will need the source code or one of the binary packages mentioned previously.

Server configuration

Many readers will have an existing Subversion repository with which to start work. For those that have to install and configure the server portion of Subversion from scratch, I urge you to refer to the free and excellent "Version Control with Subversion" mentioned earlier in the chapter. I will not be able to cover that topic in detail in this chapter, however, I do want to summarize the available architecture options.

Although Subversion was build to be network layer agnostic, there are currently only two widely used options: `svnserver` and Apache with `mod_dav_svn`. Both options essentially expose a Subversion API that can be wrapped by client applications into IDE plug-ins, shell extensions, or dedicated Subversion clients.

Apache with mod_dav_svn

The venerable Apache HTTP server combined with the `mod_dav_svn` extension provides a solid implementation for accessing Subversion over the WebDAV protocol. Because it leverages Apache's extensibility, you get features such as SSL encryption, logging, and web-based repository browsing for free. This option is slightly more complex to configure and not as fast in terms of network operations as the `svnserve` option described below.

svnserve

The second option, `svnserve`, is a fast and lightweight server process that speaks a custom protocol. It is easy to set up and configure and generally runs faster than the Apache with `mod_dav_svn` option described above. While it does support encryption, it doesn't provide quite as many additional benefits as the first option.

You also have the option of using SSH as a front-end to `svnserve` to handle authentication. In that case, svnserve's own user account database is replaced by system accounts against which the SSH server process will authenticate.

Subversion concepts

Following is a short glossary of terms used by source code control and versioning systems in general and Subversion in particular. Subversion's primary interface is the command line. Although various other dedicated Subversion clients and plug-ins for other applications exist, I think it is important to first learn what is going on behind the scenes. Later on in this chapter we will take a look at how to interact with Subversion using a graphical user interface. In particular, we will take a closer look at one of the two Subversion plug-ins offered for Eclipse, the development environment we discussed in the previous chapter.

Repository

A repository is a central location where the master copy and all previous versions of all files are stored. It also holds information about users, comments, logs, actions taken, and so on. A repository gives you a way to store all that info, but it neither dictates how you organize your projects within the repository nor does it expect you to organize the project's files in a particular way. Nevertheless, there are certain conventions that most developers follow that make it easy to perform various tasks related to source code management. It also makes it easier for any newcomers to find their way around the repository.

Tags

A tag is a name for a particular collection of versions of the files in your project. This was an important concept in CVS where each file has its own version counter. In Subversion, however, all files in a revision have the same version number. Thus, when you tag a revision in Subversion you merely create an alias for that revision. Typically tags might be `release-1.2` or `beta1-rc2`.

Tagging in Subversion becomes more interesting when you assemble files from different revisions. This is not as uncommon as you might think it is. For example, to assemble the new version of your software product, you want to use the most recent code checked in by the developers. Unfortunately, the new hotshot programmer you hired did not read this book and was consequently not able to complete the update to the reporting module. You decide to roll out the product without the new reporting features and pull the most recent stable revision of the reporting module code from the repository. You now have a combination of new and old code and it makes sense to assign this collection of project files a name by tagging it.

Trunk

The main branch of your project is called the trunk. Typically, the top-level of your project would contain a directory called "trunk." This is not a requirement, but rather done by convention.

Branches

A branch is nothing more than a copy of all or part of your project's code. If you think of your code as path through time, a branch would be a second path that diverges from the original. A branch can in itself be branched again to create a hierarchical tree structure.

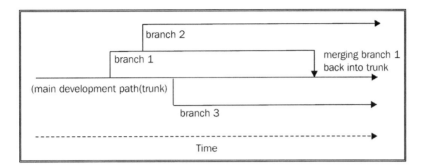

Branches are typically created to be able to work on a copy of the main code either temporarily or permanently without interfering with development happening on the trunk.

When a branch was created to temporarily support some custom development, it is common practice to merge (see definition as follows) the diverging branch back into the trunk. In other cases, branches are created because the code permanently diverges from the main branch, the trunk. An example of a permanently diverging branch might be a release.

By convention, Subversion repositories are typically structured such that branches are stored in a separate directory that is parallel to the trunk.

Working (Local) copy

Checking out the project code from the repository creates a local copy of the whole project. The developer will be making any changes to this local working copy. The working copy should be updated periodically with changes submitted to the repository by other developers to ensure that the two copies are not diverging too much. The idea is that changes to the local copy will eventually be committed back to the repository and made available to other developers. Before committing changes, the developer will have to resolve any conflicts between the repository and his local copy.

Merging

Merging is the activity of resolving conflicts between a developer's local working copy and the corresponding code in the repository. Whenever a developer updates his working copy by retrieving new changes to the project in the repository since the last update, Subversion will make an effort to automatically merge any changes if possible. However, at times it is impossible for Subversion to know how to resolve conflicts. In those cases, the developer will have to examine the code and manually resolve the differences and thus merge the two versions of a file.

Revisions and versions

The terms revision and version are often used interchangeably; however, the correct terminology used by Subversion is *revision*. A revision constitutes an incremental change to the code. Correspondingly, the revision number for the whole repository increases by one each time a revision is committed.

In contrast, software releases are typically given a release number, which associates the release with a set of features.

Updating

Updating refers to the act of retrieving changes to the project's files in the repository by downloading them to the developer's local working copy. During the update, changes will be merged into the local working copy either automatically if possible or manually by the developer.

Developers should update their local working copy regularly to avoid the two versions of the code from diverging too much and minimizing the risk of incompatibilities.

Comparing

Comparing refers to the activity of systematically stepping through the differences between two different revisions of the same file or two different files. This is typically done during merging to resolve a conflict. However, Subversion's support for visually comparing two versions of a file also comes in handy when trying to retrace the incremental changes to a file. Comparing is also referred to as "diffing" two files or folders and uses an algorithm to detect and highlight the differences. It can even be used to create a patch to transform one version of the file into the other.

History/Log

You can (and should) accompany each commit with a comment. Viewing the history of a file involves looking at these comments, actions taken, date, and other files affected. It's a way of viewing the transformations a file has undergone over time. You can also view this information for the whole project rather than only a single file.

Annotating code

Annotated source code output will display any revision of a file with the name of the developer responsible for each line of code and the revision number when it was last changed or added.

Following is some sample output as produced by the Subversion's aptly named blame command that is used to generate annotated source code listings. The first column contains the revision number in which the corresponding line of code was last changed. The second column holds the name of the developer, followed by the line of code itself:

```
$ svn blam userAction.php
...
77  DirkMerkel    /**
77  DirkMerkel     * listAction
77  DirkMerkel     * Used to get the content in list form for the object
77  DirkMerkel     * and assign the data to a Zend_View object in JSON format.
77  DirkMerkel     *
77  DirkMerkel     * @author Dirk Merkel <dirk@waferthin.com>
77  DirkMerkel     * @since 5-16-09
77  DirkMerkel     * @return void
77  DirkMerkel     * @access public
77  DirkMerkel     */
74  DirkMerkel    public function listAction()
74  DirkMerkel    {
74  DirkMerkel        $this->_context
74  DirkMerkel            ->addActionContext(list, json)
74  DirkMerkel            ->initContext();
92  JoeSchmoe
92  JoeSchmoe         // instantiate content object
92  JoeSchmoe         $model = new Content();
74  DirkMerkel
74  DirkMerkel         // get id from request
74  DirkMerkel         $id = $this->_request->getParam(id);
105 BenIntern
105 BenIntern         // use object to get list by ID
105 BenIntern         $list = $model->getList($id);
105 BenIntern
74  DirkMerkel         // loop over list items
74  DirkMerkel         $tmp = "";
74  DirkMerkel         foreach ($list as $item) {
80  DirkMerkel
99  DaBigBoss             if ($dm->SegmentName != $tmp) {
99  DaBigBoss                 $tmp = $dm->SegmentName;
99  DaBigBoss             } else {
99  DaBigBoss                 $dm->SegmentName = "";
99  DaBigBoss             }
74  DirkMerkel         }
74  DirkMerkel         $this->view->list = $list;
74  DirkMerkel    }
...
```

Reverting

Subversion retains a "pristine" local copy of each file that was checked out into the local workspace from the repository. As the developer starts making changes to the file, this hidden copy of the file remains unchanged. Consequently, the two files further diverge with more changes that the developer makes. Reverting means discarding all local changes and starting over with the file the way it was when originally checked out of the repository.

Committing

Once changes have been made to the developer's local working copy, the change will have to be communicated back to the central repository before they can become available to other developers on the team. During or before the process of committing the changes, it is often necessary for the developer to update his working copy and resolve any differences before being allowed to perform the commit operation.

Subversion command reference

"Version Control with Subversion" does a fine job of documenting all Subversion commands, including all optional parameters, in great detail. The same can be said for the many man pages that come with Subversion. Rather than simply repeating that information, based on those sources, I would like to present a more concise reference to the most frequently used commands to get you started quickly. Once you require additional commands or more detail on a particular command, you can consult one of the two free resources mentioned.

svn

svn is the command-line client used by developers to interact with the repository and their local working copy. Below is the complete list of svn subcommands because these are the tools developers use on a daily basis. Consequently, you should probably spend some time familiarizing yourself with all of them.

Command:	**svn add** [--auto-props] [--depth ARG] [--force] [--no-auto-props] [--no-ignore] [--parents] --quiet (-q)] [--targets] **FILENAME** LWC_PATH		
Accesses:	Repo, LWC	**Changes:**	LWC
Description:	Add a file, folder (recursively), or symbolic link to the repository during the next commit.		
Example:	`% svn add ./myfile.php` `A         myfile.php`		

blame

Command:	**svn blame**/praise/annotate/ann [--extensions (-x) ARG] [--force] [--incremental] [--revision (-r) ARG] [--use-merge-history (-g)] [--verbose (-v)] [--xml] **TARGET**
Accesses:	Repo Changes: LWC
	List the specific TARGET file with each line being preceded by the author's name and the revision when it was changed.
Example:	% svn blame https://secure.waferthin.com/myproject/ trunk/index.php

```
156      dirk <?php
156      dirk
157      dirk // including bootstrap file
```

cat

Command:	**svn cat** [--revision (-r) REV] **TARGET**
Accesses:	Repo Changes:
Description:	Output file contents.
Example:	% svn cat -r 164 \

```
        https://svn/svn/svn-hooks/branches/nt-feat/pre-commit
```

changelist

Command:	**svn changelist** [--changelist ARG [--depth ARG] [--quiet (-q)] [--recursive (-R)] [--remove] [--targets ARG] **CLNAME TARGET**
Accesses:	LWC Changes:
Description:	Create and assign a name to a logical grouping of files in the local working copy.
Example:	svn changelist ticket312 file1.php file2.php

```
svn changelist ticket312 file1.php file2.php
...
svn commit –changelist ticket312
```

checkout

Command:	svn checkout/co --depth ARG [--force] [--ignore-externals]
	[--quiet (-q)] [--revision (-r) REV] **URL[@REV]... [PATH]**
Accesses:	Repo, LWC **Changes:** LWC
Description:	Check project out for repository and creates local working copy. Can take multiple directories to check out.
Example:	`% svn checkout -r 164 \` `https://svn/svn/svn-hooks/branches/php-nt-feature`

cleanup

Command:	svn cleanup [--diff3-cmd CMD] [**PATH**...]
Accesses:	LWC **Changes:** LWC
Description:	Recursively remove locks and resume incomplete operations. Run this if you encounter a working copy locked error.
Example:	`% svn cleanup ./lwc_project_dir`

commit

Command:	svn commit/ci --changelist ARG [--depth ARG] [--editor-cmd ARG] [--encoding ENC] [--file (-F) FILE] [--force-log] [--keep-changelists] [--message (-m) TEXT] [--no-unlock] [--quiet (-q)] [--targets FILENAME] [--with-revprop ARG] [**PATH**...]
Accesses:	Repo **Changes:** Repo, LWC
Description:	Send changes from your local working copy to the repository.
Example:	`% svn commit -m "Fixes for bug 312." ./parser.php`

copy

Command:	svn copy/cp [--editor-cmd EDITOR] [--encoding ENC] [--file (-F) FILE] [--force-log] [--message (-m) TEXT] [--parents] [--quiet (-q)] [--revision (-r) REV] [--with-revprop ARG] **SRC[@REV]... DST**]
Accesses:	Repo, LWC **Changes:** Repo, LWC
Description:	Copy files or directories (recursively). Both, source and destination, can be a local working copy path or a repository URL. Used to create branches (which are just copies).
Example:	`% svn copy https://svn/svn/svn-hooks/trunk \` `https://svn/svn/svn-hooks/branches/php-nt-feature`

delete

Command:	**svn delete**/del/remove/rm [--editor-cmd EDITOR] [--encoding ENC] [--file (-F) FILE] [--force] [--force-log] [--keep-local] [--message (-m) TEXT] [--quiet (-q)] [--targets FILENAME] [--with-revprop ARG] **PATH**/URL...		
Accesses:	Repo	**Changes:**	Repo, LWC
Description:	Delete items in local working copy on next commit or items from the repository immediately.		
Example:	`% svn delete ./parser_old.php` `% svn commit ./parser_old.php`		

diff

Command:	**svn diff**/di --change (-c) ARG [--changelist ARG] [--depth ARG] [--diff-cmd CMD] [--extensions (-x) "ARGS"] [--force] [--new ARG] [--no-diff-deleted] [--notice-ancestry] [--old ARG] [--revision (-r) ARG] [--summarize] [--xml] [-c M | -r N[:M]] [**TARGET**[@REV]...]		
Accesses:	Repo, LWC	**Changes:**	
Description:	Display differences between two files or different revisions of the same file.		
Example:	`% svn diff -r 126:129 parser.php`		

export

Command:	**svn export** [--depth ARG] [--force] [--ignore-externals] [--native-eol EOL] [--quiet (-q)] [--revision (-r) REV] [-r REV] **URL**/PATH1[@PEGREV] [PATH2]		
Accesses:	Repo	**Changes:**	Destination Path
Description:	Exports a clean copy of the directory referenced by the URL or PATH1 argument. This command can export from repositories or local working copies. Use this command to deploy or install an application.		
Example:	`% svn export -r 250 https://svn/svn/svn-hooks/trunk\` `  /usr/local/SVN/hooks`		

help

Command:	**svn help**/h/? [SUBCOMMAND...]	
Accesses:		**Changes:**
Description:	View built-in help.	
Example:	`% svn help diff`	

import

Command:	**svn import** [--auto-props] [--depth ARG] [--editor-cmd EDITOR] [--encoding ENC] [--file (-F) FILE] [--force] [--force-log] [--message (**-m**) TEXT] [--no-auto-props] [--no-ignore] [--quiet (-q)] [--with-revprop ARG] [**PATH**] **URL**		
Accesses:	Repo, LWC	**Changes:**	Repo
Description:	Recursively imports a local directory into the repository.		
Example:	`% svn import -m "landing initial version of project" ./` `cool_project https://ourcompany.com/svn/trunk`		

info

Command:	**svn info** [--changelist ARG] [--depth ARG] [--incremental] [--recursive (-R)] [--revision (-r) REV] [--targets FILENAME] [--xml] [**TARGET**[@ REV]...]	
Accesses:	Repo, LWC	**Changes:**
Description:	Display array of info about file(s) in the local working copy or the repository.	
Example:	`% svn info ./parser.php`	

list

Command:	**svn list**/ls [--depth ARG] [--incremental] [--recursive (-R)] [--revision (-r) REV] [--verbose (-v)] [--xml] [**TARGET**[@REV]...]	
Accesses:	Repo, LWC	**Changes:**
Description:	List files in a directory in the repository.	
Example:	`% svn list https://ourcompany.com/svn/proj/trunk/docs`	

lock

Command:	**svn lock** [--encoding ENC] [--file (-F) FILE] [--force] [--force-log] [--message (-m) TEXT] [--targets FILENAME] **TARGET**		
Accesses:	Repo	**Changes:**	Repo, LWC
Description:	Supply a reference to local working copy file(s) to lock corresponding file(s) in the repository. Locked files prevent other users from committing changes. See "unlock" command.		
Example:	`% svn lock parser.php`		

log

Command:	**svn log** [--change (-c) ARG] [--incremental] [--limit (-l) NUM] [--quiet (-q)] [--revision (-r) REV] [--stop-on-copy] [--targets FILENAME] [--use-merge-history (-g)] [--verbose (-v)] [--with-all-revprops] [--with-revpropARG— xml] [**PATH**]
Accesses:	Repo Changes:
Description:	Display log messages for file(s).
Example:	`% svn log parser.php`

merge

Command:	**svn merge** [--accept ARG] [--change (-c) REV] [--depth ARG] [--diff3-cmd CMD] [--dry-run] [--extensions (-x) ARG] [--force] [--ignore-ancestry] [--quiet (-q)] [--record-only] [--reintegrate] [--revision (-r) REV] **sourceURL1[@N] sourceURL2[@M] [WCPATH]**
Accesses:	Repo, LWC Changes: LWC
Description:	Compare two sources (a branch and trunk, for example) and apply the differences to a working copy. Use this command to merge a branch back into trunk.
Example:	`% svn merge -r 224:226 parser.php`

mergeinfo

Command:	**svn mergeinfo** [--revision (-r) REV] **SOURCE_URL[@REV] [TARGET[@ REV]...]**
Accesses:	Repo, LWC Changes:
Description:	Display merge info (past or potential) for files or directories.

Example:	`% svn mergeinfo \`
	`   https://ourcompany.com/svn/svn-hooks/trunk \`
	`   https://ourcompany.com/svn/svn-hooks/branches/newfeat`

mkdir

Command:	**svn mkdir** [--editor-cmd EDITOR] [--encoding ENC] [--file (-F) FILE] [--force-log] [--message (-m) TEXT] [--parents] [--quiet (-q)] [--with-revprop ARG] **PATH**/URL		
Accesses:	Repo	**Changes:**	LWC, Repo
Description:	Create a directory in the repository or the local working copy.		
Example:	```% svn mkdirk ./library``` ``` % svn commit ./library```		

move

Command:	**svn move**/mv/rename/ren [--editor-cmd EDITOR] [--encoding ENC] [--file (-F) FILE] [--force] [--force-log] [--message (-m) TEXT] [--parents] [--quiet (-q)] [--revision (-r) REV] [--with-revprop ARG] **SRC DST**		
Accesses:	Repo, LWC	**Changes:**	Repo, LWC
Description:	Move files or directories in the local working copy or the repository.		
Example:	```% svn move ./parser.php includes/libraries/```		

propdel

Command:	**svn propdel**/pdel/pd [--changelist ARG] [--depth ARG] [--quiet (-q)] [--recursive (-R)] [--revision (-r) REV] [--revprop] **PROPNAME** [PATH]		
Accesses:	Repo, LWC	**Changes:**	Repo, LWC
Description:	Remove a property from files or directories.		
Example:	```% svn propdel contributed-by-ben-inc ./libraries```		

propedit

Command:	**svn propedit**/pedit/pe [--editor-cmd EDITOR] [--encoding ENC] [--file (-F) ARG] [--force] [--force-log] [--message (-m) ARG] [--revision (-r) REV] [--revprop] [--with-revprop ARG] **PROPNAME TARGET**		
Accesses:	Repo, LWC	**Changes:**	Repo, LWC
Description:	Edit a property assigned to one or more files.		
Example:	```% svn propedit contributed-by-ben-inc ./parser.php```		

propget

Command:	**svn propget**/pget/pg [--changelist ARG] [--depth ARG] [--recursive (-R)] [--revision (-r) REV] [--revprop] [--strict] [--xml] **PROPNAME [TARGET[@ REV]...]**		
Accesses:	Repo, LWC	**Changes:**	Repo, LWC
Description:	Output property value.		
Example:	`% svn propget contributed-by-ben-inc ./libraries/`		

proplist

Command:	**svn proplist**/plist/pl --changelist ARG] [--depth ARG] [--quiet (-q)] [--recursive (-R)] [--revision (-r) REV] [--revprop] [--verbose (-v)] [--xml] **[TARGET[@REV]...]**		
Accesses:	Repo, LWC	**Changes:**	Repo, LWC
Description:	List properties assigned to one or more files in the working copy.		
Example:	`% svn proplist ./parser.php`		

propset

Command:	**svn propset**/pset/ps [--changelist ARG] [--depth ARG] [--encoding ENC] [--file (-F) FILE] [--force] [--quiet (-q)] [--recursive (-R)] [--revision (-r) REV] [--revprop] [--targets FILENAME] **PROPNAME [PROPVAL	-F VALFILE] PATH...**		
Accesses:	Repo, LWC	**Changes:**	Repo, LWC
Description:	Assign a property and corresponding value to one or more files or directories in the local working copy or the repository.		
Example:	`% svn propset contributor \` `    contributed-by-ben-inc parser.php`		

resolve

Command:	**svn resolve** [--accept ARG] [--depth ARG] [--quiet (-q)] [--recursive (-R)] [--targets FILENAME] **PATH...**		
Accesses:		**Changes:**	LWC
Description:	Replace conflict file and remove conflict artifacts.		
Example:	`% svn resolve --accept mine-full parser.php`		

resolved

Command:	**svn resolved** [--depth ARG] [--quiet (-q)] [--recursive (-R)] [--targets FILENAME] **PATH**...		
Accesses:		**Changes:**	LWC
Description:	Removes conflict artifacts. Does actually change files to resolve conflict.		
Example:	`% svn resolved parser.php`		

revert

Command:	svn revert --changelist ARG] [--depth ARG] [--quiet (-q)] [--recursive (-R)] [--targets FILENAME] PATH...		
Accesses:		**Changes:**	LWC
Description:	Reset file(s) in local working copy to base revision.		
Example:	`% svn revert parser.php`		

status

Command:	**svn status**/stat/st [--changelist ARG] [--depth ARG] [--ignore-externals] [--incremental] [--no-ignore] [--quiet (-q)] [--show-updates (-u)] [--verbose (-v)] [--xml] **[PATH...]**		
Accesses:	Repo, LWC	**Changes:**	
Description:	Output status and info on changes to local working copy files.		
Example:	`% svn status ./libraries`		

switch

Command:	**svn switch**/sw [--accept ARG] [--depth ARG] [--diff3-cmd CMD] [--force] [--ignore-externals] [--quiet (-q)] [--relocate] [--revision (-r) REV] [--set-depth ARG] **URL**[@PEGREV] [PATH]		
Accesses:	Repo, LWC	**Changes:**	LWC
Description:	Associate your local working copy with a different repository location.		
Example:	`% svn switch https://ourcompany.com/svn/branch/newone .`		

unlock

Command:	**svn unlock** [--force] [--targets FILENAME] **TARGET**…
Accesses:	Repo, LWC **Changes:** Repo, LWC
Description:	Unlock target file(s). See "lock" command.
Example:	`% svn lock parser.php`

update

Command:	**svn update**/up [--accept ARG] [--changelist] [--depth ARG] [--diff3-cmd CMD] [--editor-cmd ARG] [--force] [--ignore-externals] [--quiet (-q)] [--revision (-r) REV] [--set-depth ARG] [PATH…]
Accesses:	Repo, LWC **Changes:** LWC
Description:	Updated local working copy with changes committed to the repository since the last successful update.
Example:	`% svn update`

svnadmin

The `svnadmin` is the administrators' toolkit. In addition to subcommand allowing you to make backups, inspect, and repair repositories is the ability to create one.

create

Command:	**svnadmin create** [--bdb-log-keep] [--bdb-txn-nosync] [--config-dir DIR] [--fs-type TYPE] [--pre-1.4-compatible] [--pre-1.5-compatible] **REPOS_PATH**
Description:	Create a new repository at the specified path.
Example:	`% svn create /usr/local/SVN`

dump

Command:	**svnadmin dump** [–deltas] [--incremental] [--quiet (-q)] [--revision (-r) REV] dump **REPOS_PATH**
Description:	Dumps the whole repository to STDOUT in a portable file format suitable for migrating repositories and backing them up.
Example:	`% svnadmin dump /usr/local/SVN > svn_backup.6-30-09.dump`

Additional `svnadmin` subcommands not covered here in detail include: `crashtest`, `deltify`, `help`, `hotcopy`, `list-dblogs`, `list-unused-dblogs`, `load`, `lslocks`, `lstxns`, `recover`, `rmlocks`, `rmtxns`, `setlog`, `setrevprop`, `setuuid`, `upgrade`, and `verify`.

svnlook

`svnlook` is a utility for querying info about a repository. It only 'looks' and doesn't make any changes to the repository. The subcommands available to target specific information include: `author`, `cat`, `changed`, `date`, `diff`, `dirs-changed`, `help`, `history`, `info`, `lock`, `log`, `propget`, `proplist`, `tree uuid`, `youngest`.

Here is an example of how the author subcommand behaves. The other subcommands behave in very much the same fashion.

Command:	svnlook author [--revision (-r) REV] [--transaction (-t) TXN] REPOS_PATH
Description:	Print the author of the (most recent) revision to the repository.
Example:	`% svnlook author -r 125 /usr/local/SVN`

svnserve

`svnserver` is server executable that speaks Subversion's custom network protocol. It is one of the options you have for enabling remote access to your repository. `svnserver` has no subcommands.

svndumpfilter

This command line utility operates on existing Subversion dump files. Using subcommands and optional arguments, it can selectively remove paths/files from a dump file. Subcommands are: `exclude`, `include`, and `help`. Here is an example of how to exclude the paths containing `test_scripts` from a dump file while creating a new dump file:

```
% svndumpfilter exclude test_script \
  < svn_7-1-09.dump \
  > svn_notests_7-1-09.dump
```

svnversion

This command line utility outputs summary revision information of what is currently contained in your local working copy.

Creating a Subversion project

Nothing illustrates the use and usefulness of Subversion as much as an example. Let's create a small project and see it through the whole Subversion workflow.

Subversion allows you to execute external scripts to affect some of its actions. These scripts are called **hooks**. I have put together a small project where we create two of these hooks; namely a pre-commit hook and a post-commit one. I imagine you can already guess when these hooks will be executed. Hooks are discussed in more detail later in this chapter. Following is a short description accompanying each of the four files in the project.

The `pre-commit` script will be executed just before a changeset is being committed to the repository. On one hand, if the script terminates with exit code 1, the commit will be aborted and the output from `STDERR` will be displayed to the user. On the other hand, if the script returns exit code 0, the commit will complete as requested. In our case, we are running two checks to decide whether to allow the commit command. First, we disallow empty comments. Second, we use the `PHP_CodeSniffer` pre-commit hook to enforce the Zend Framework coding standard in our source code files.

Also worth a note is the use of `svnlook`, which is a Subversion utility to retrieve all kinds of info about the repository and individual files. In our pre-commit script, we are using it to retrieve the comment being submitted with the commit command.

```
/pre-commit:
    #!/usr/local/apache2/php/bin/php
    <?php
    // class for command line parsing
    require_once('includes/classes/Cli/Options.php');

    // path to local svnlook executable
    define('SVNLOOK', '/usr/local/bin/svnlook');

    // path to local PHP_CodeSniffer pre-commit hook script
    define('PHPCSPC', '/usr/local/apache2/php/bin/scripts/
                                        phpcs-svn-pre-commit');

    // get object reference and parse current command line
    $options = Cli_Options::getInstance();

    // make sure we were given the two arguments we need to continue
    if (count($options->getArguments()) < 2) {
        fwrite(STDERR, "Error: " . $options->getScriptName() . " requires
                                            two parameters.");
        exit(1);
```

```php
}

// get repository and transaction passed in from
// Subversionas as command line arguemtns
list($repos, $txn) = $options->getArguments();

// get latest log message
exec(SVNLOOK . " log -t '$txn' '$repos'", $svnlookOutput);

if (is_array($svnlookOutput)) {
    $svnlookOutput = trim(implode("\n", $svnlookOutput));
}

// make sure log message is not empty
if (empty($svnlookOutput)) {
    fwrite(STDERR, "Error: log message is required.");
    exit(1);
}

// see if PHP_CodeSniffer ok's our code
exec(PHPCSPC . " --standard=Zend --tab-width=4 '$repos' -t '$txn'",
                              $phpcsOutput, $phpcsReturnValue);

if (is_array($phpcsOutput)) {
    $phpcsOutput = trim(implode("\n", $phpcsOutput));
}

// did PHP_CodeSniffer return an error?
if ($phpcsReturnValue == 1) {
    fwrite(STDERR, "phpcsOutput: $phpcsOutput");
    exit(1);
}

// everthing went fine
exit(0);
?>
```

In contrast to pre-commit, the post-commit script gets executed just after the commit command has been processed. Although it is too late to allow or disallow the commit, we can use it to send out an informative e-mail to individual developers, managers, or a mailing list distribution account. Composing a nicely formatted e-mail and sending it out is actually being handled by svnnotify, an open source Perl script that has been maintained over several years for just that purpose.

post-commit:

```php
#!/usr/local/apache2/php/bin/php
<?php
// class for command line parsing
require_once('includes/classes/Cli/Options.php');

// path to local svnnotify executable
define('SVN_NOTIFY', '/opt/local/bin/svnnotify');

// get object reference and parse current command line
$options = Cli_Options::getInstance();

// make sure we were given the two arguments we need to continue
if (count($options->getArguments()) < 2) {
    fwrite(STDERR, "Error: " . $options->getScriptName() . " requires
                                                two parameters.");
    exit(1);
}

// get repository and revision passed in from
// Subversionas as command line arguemtns
list($repos, $rev) = $options->getArguments();

// send post-commit email(s)
exec(SVN_NOTIFY . " --from dirk@waferthin.com --to dirk@waferthin.com
     --handler HTML::ColorDiff -d  --repos-path '$repos' --revision
                                                '$rev'");
?>
```

If you have been reading the code for the pre-commit and post-commit scripts above, you will have noticed the use of the `Cli_Options` class. This is a utility class, implemented as a singleton, for parsing command-line arguments and options. Although we only use it to retrieve arguments needed by `svnlook` and `svnnotify`, it also supports parsing of options and flags.

includes/classes/Options/Cli.php:

```php
<?php
class Cli_Options
{
    private static $instance    = null;
    private $scriptName         = null;
    private $supportedOptions   = array();
    private $optionValues       = array();
    private $arguments          = array();
```

```php
    private function __construct($supportedOptions)
    {
        // required for getopt() support
        if (!function_exists('getopt')) {
            throw new Exception("getopt() is not available.");
        }

        $this->setSupportedOptions($supportedOptions);
        $this->processCommandLine();
    }

    public static function getInstance($supportedOptions = array())
    {
        if (self::$instance == null) {
            self::$instance = new Cli_Options($supportedOptions);
        }
        return self::$instance;
    }

    public function setSupportedOptions($supportedOptions)
    {
        if (!is_array($supportedOptions)) {
            throw new Exception("Supported command line options must
                                        be passed in as an array.");
        } else {
            $this->supportedOptions = $supportedOptions;
        }
    }

    public function getSupportedOptions()
    {
        return $this->supportedOptions;
    }

    public function getScriptName()
    {
        return $this->scriptName;
    }

    public function getArguments()
    {
        return $this->arguments;
    }

    public function getArgument($i = 0)
    {
```

```
            return $this->arguments[$i];
    }

    public function processCommandLine($args = null)
    {
        // if no command line was given, pull in global one
        if ($args === NULL) {
            $args = $GLOBALS['argv'];
        }

        // parse options
        $opts = getopt(implode('', $this->supportedOptions));

        // store the script name
        $this->scriptName = array_shift($args);

        // remove options from $args array
        foreach ($opts as $opt => $arg) {

            $allowed = str_replace(array(':', $opt), '',
implode($this->supportedOptions));

            $max = strlen($allowed);

            $key = key(preg_grep("'^-$opt([$allowed]{0,$max}|$arg)$'",
$args));

            // process option & store it
            $this->processOption($args[$key]);

            unset($args[$key]);
        }

        // reorder array keys
        $args = array_values($args);

        // store arguments
        $this->arguments = $args;
    }

    protected function processOption($option = '')
    {
        // remove dash
        if ($option{0} == '-') {
            $option{0} = '';
        }
```

```php
            // does the option have an argument?
            if (strstr($option, ':')) {
                list($key, $value) = explode(':', $option, 2);
                $this->optionValues[$key] = $value;

            } else {
                $this->optionValues[$option] = true;
            }
        }

        public function getOptionValue($option)
        {
            // is the option supported?
            if (in_array($option, $this->supportedOptions) ||
                in_array($option . ':', $this->supportedOptions)) {
                return $this->optionValues[$option];
            } else {
                throw new Exception("Unsupported option requested.");
            }
        }
    }
?>
```

Cli_Options.php is a generic class for parsing command line arguments to scripts wrapping PHP's built-in getOpt() function.

Since the constructor method is private, the static getInstance() method is the only way to instantiate the object. If an instance of the class doesn't already exist, getInstance() will create it by calling the constructor and return the resulting object. The constructor itself checks whether the getOpt() function is defined in this version of PHP because without it the class will not work. The constructor also accepts an array of strings as a parameter that determines which command line options will be supported when parsing the command line. The last thing the constructor does is to call the processCommandLine() method, which is where it gets interesting.

After obtaining a reference to the command line arguments array to be processed, processCommandLine() uses getOpt() to parse the supported options and stores them in an associative array $allowed. It also stores the name of the executing script in a variable. It then iterates over the arguments, processing one at a time by removing it from the array and parsing any argument to the option using the utility method processOption().

In the end, we are left with an associative array `$optionValues` that holds the argument for a given option. The remaining methods are merely setters and getters for the name of the executing script, the arguments, and most importantly the values of the options given on the command line.

`test.php` is a command-line script used to test `Cli_Options`. Simply execute it with a couple of command line arguments and switches to see how they are being handled by the `Cli_Options` utility class.

test/test.php

```
#!/usr/local/apache2/php/bin/php
<?php
require_once('../includes/classes/Cli/Options.php');

$options = Cli_Options::getInstance(array('i', 'v', 'h', 'p:'));
$options->processCommandLine();

// testing script name parsing
echo 'script name: ' . $options->getScriptName() . "\n";

// testing option value parsing
echo "p:" . $options->getOptionValue('p') . "\n";

// testing argument parsing
echo "first argument: " . $options->getArgument(0) . "\n";
?>
```

`test.php` starts out requiring the `Cli_Options` class listed previously. It then obtains an instance of the class and tells it that 'i', 'v', 'h', and 'p' are acceptable command line options and that 'p' requires an argument, which is indicated by the colon following the 'p'. After processing the command line, the script outputs the name of the script (`test.php`), the argument given with the 'p' command line option, and the first argument.

Now that we have spent some time putting together the initial version of our project let's add it to an existing repository. We start by creating the commonly used directories `branches`, `tags`, and `trunk`. We then put all our files into the trunk with the two hook scripts (`pre-commit` and `post-commit`) in the root directory, the `test.php` script into a test directory, and lastly the `Options.php` into `includes/classes/Cli/`.

```
Terminal — bash — bash — Dirk — ttys001 — 79×30 — ⌘2
DirkMacBook:book dirk$ mkdir svn-hooks
DirkMacBook:book dirk$ cd svn-hooks/
DirkMacBook:svn-hooks dirk$ mkdir branches
DirkMacBook:svn-hooks dirk$ mkdir tags
DirkMacBook:svn-hooks dirk$ mkdir trunk
DirkMacBook:svn-hooks dirk$ cd trunk
DirkMacBook:trunk dirk$ mkdir test
DirkMacBook:trunk dirk$ mv /tmp/test.php ./test/
DirkMacBook:trunk dirk$ mkdir includes
DirkMacBook:trunk dirk$ mkdir includes/classes
DirkMacBook:trunk dirk$ mkdir includes/classes/Cli
DirkMacBook:trunk dirk$ mv /tmp/Options.php includes/classes/Cli/
DirkMacBook:trunk dirk$ mv /tmp/*commit ./
DirkMacBook:trunk dirk$ cd ../../
DirkMacBook:book dirk$ tree svn-hooks
svn-hooks
|-- branches
|-- tags
`-- trunk
    |-- includes
    |   `-- classes
    |       `-- Cli
    |           `-- Options.php
    |-- post-commit
    |-- pre-commit
    `-- test
        `-- test.php

7 directories, 4 files
DirkMacBook:book dirk$ █
```

Now that we have the initial layout of our project, let's add it to our local repository using svn's import command:

```
                Terminal — bash — bash — Dirk — ttys004 — 80×13 — ⌘3
DirkMacBook:~ dirk$ mkdir svn-hooks
DirkMacBook:~ dirk$ svn checkout https://svn/svn/svn-hooks/trunk ./svn-hooks
A       svn-hooks/test
A       svn-hooks/test/test.php
A       svn-hooks/includes
A       svn-hooks/includes/classes
A       svn-hooks/includes/classes/Cli
A       svn-hooks/includes/classes/Cli/Options.php
A       svn-hooks/post-commit
A       svn-hooks/pre-commit
Checked out revision 161.

DirkMacBook:~ dirk$ █
```

We're using the -m switch to supply a comment. Also, I added the desired directory name at the end of the repository URL because the import command processes the contents of the local directory, also named svn-hooks, but not the directory itself. Depending on your Subversion setup, you should get prompted for your credentials before being allowed to import a project or do anything else with the repository.

Now that we have our project safely stored in Subversion, we no longer need the original. Assuming that we intend to commit future enhancements back to Subversion, we will shortly be checking the project out of the repository again. For now, we will delete the original project folder to prevent us from accidentally working with that version and then having to take extra steps to commit our changes.

```
$ rm -rf ./svn-hooks
```

Basic version control workflow

All files that constitute a project are assembled at a central location. Development group members are able to authenticate before accessing any part of the project files. They download all or some of the files of the project:

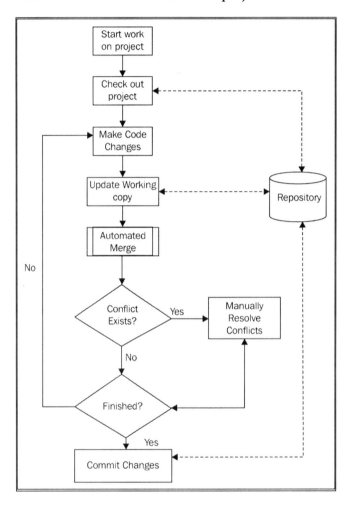

Hopefully a picture (really a diagram in this case) says a thousand words. However, it might make sense to step through the typical Subversion workflow.

As a developer joins or starts a project, he checks the code of the project out of the repository. This means copying all files to his local workspace. This way, he can work without constantly being tied to the repository. As part of his main work activity of programming, he makes changes to the code and tests them.

Periodically, it becomes necessary for the developer to update his local working copy by connecting to the central repository and downloading new changes committed by other developers since the last time he performed such an update (or checkout). This is done to ensure that the code he develops will be compatible with the contributions of the other developers. It is even possible for the developer to have to update his working copy with his own changes if he uses more than one working copy, say one on his work machine and another at home.

In many cases, Subversion is able to merge changes automatically without requiring input from the developer. However, the developer should still examine the changes to make sure there are no unanticipated conflicts with his as yet uncommitted code. If there are conflicts, Subversion cannot resolve on its own, the developer will be prompted to manually resolve those conflicts before continuing.

After going through multiple iterations of making changes and synchronizing with the repository, the developer will reach a point where his development has been completed and he should then commit his changes back to the repository.

Let's pick up work on our svn-hook project to see the above workflow in action. First, we check out the project for us to have a repository-aware local copy of the code:

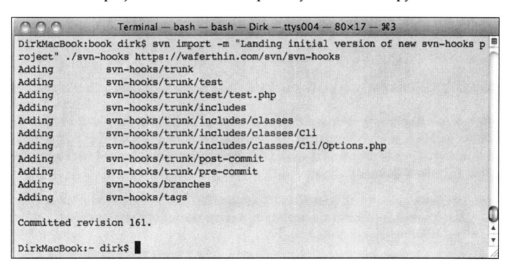

```
DirkMacBook:book dirk$ svn import -m "Landing initial version of new svn-hooks p
roject" ./svn-hooks https://waferthin.com/svn/svn-hooks
Adding          svn-hooks/trunk
Adding          svn-hooks/trunk/test
Adding          svn-hooks/trunk/test/test.php
Adding          svn-hooks/trunk/includes
Adding          svn-hooks/trunk/includes/classes
Adding          svn-hooks/trunk/includes/classes/Cli
Adding          svn-hooks/trunk/includes/classes/Cli/Options.php
Adding          svn-hooks/trunk/post-commit
Adding          svn-hooks/trunk/pre-commit
Adding          svn-hooks/branches
Adding          svn-hooks/tags

Committed revision 161.

DirkMacBook:~ dirk$
```

If you paid close attention to the above example, you will have noticed that we check out the trunk of the project, but we put it into a local directory named after the project itself. This is simply a naming convention I follow for projects I work on. If I were to check out a branch, I probably would have named the local folder accordingly, something like "svn-hooks-windows-branch."

Next, let's make some changes to our project, by adding a destructor method and adding some inline comments to the constructor. After making those changes, we want to update our local working copy.

```
● ● ●                  Terminal — bash — bash — Dirk — ttys001 — 80×5 — ⌘2
DirkMacBook:~ dirk$ svn update ./
C    includes/classes/Cli/Options.php
Updated to revision 163.

DirkMacBook:~ dirk$ ▮
```

The "C" preceding the file name signals a conflict. Apparently, someone else has modified the Options.php file in such a way that Subversion is unable to merge his/her changes into our local working copy without our involvement. We need to investigate further. First, let's take a look at the contents of the directory where the problem file resides.

```
● ● ●                  Terminal — bash — bash — Dirk — ttys000 — 80×9 — ⌘2
$ ls -l  includes/classes/Cli/
total 32
drwxr-xr-x  9 dirk  dirk   306 May 26 08:36 .svn
-rw-r--r--  1 dirk  dirk  2933 May 26 08:36 Options.php
-rw-r--r--  1 dirk  dirk  2838 May 26 08:36 Options.php.mine
-rw-r--r--  1 dirk  dirk  2628 May 26 08:36 Options.php.r161
-rw-r--r--  1 dirk  dirk  2687 May 26 08:36 Options.php.r163

DirkMacBook:~ dirk$ ▮
```

There are actually four versions of the same file and looking at the file sizes, they are all different. Here is what happened. Subversion encountered a conflict and so as not to lose any changes while providing us with the information we need to resolve the conflict, it created these four files:

- Options.php.r161 is revision 161 of the file. This is our base revision. In other words, this is the revision we checked out of the repository, but before we made our changes.

- Options.php.r163 is revision 163 of the file. This is the most recent revision as it is in the repository right now and the one that is causing a conflict with our local version.

- Options.php.mine is the file from our local working copy to which we made the changes. Subversion renamed it from Options.php to Options.php.mine when it detected the conflict.

- `Options.php` is our file pre-commit file, but with the conflict section marked up using the diff utility. Here are the relevant lines in the code:

```
<?php
class Cli_Options
{
        private static $instance        = null;
        private $scriptName             = null;
        private $supportedOptions       = array();
        private $optionValues           = array();
        private $arguments              = array();


<<<<<<< .mine
        // private constructor for singleton
=======
        // TODO: no comment for this constructor?
>>>>>>> .r163
        private function __construct($supportedOptions)
        {
```

Now we can tell what happened. It all has to do with comments. Someone who committed his changes to the repository under revision 163, added a TODO item asking the developer to add a comment describing the constructor method. My own comment (.mine) conflicted with that line. Not knowing the actual meaning of the conflicting lines, Subversion did not know how to resolve the conflict and instead alerted us.

Let's use the `blame` command to find out who added that comment.

```
DirkMacBook:~ dirk$ svn blame ./Options.php
   161    dirk <?php
   161    dirk
   161    dirk class Cli_Options
   161    dirk {
   161    dirk     private static $instance        = null;
   161    dirk     private $scriptName             = null;
   161    dirk     private $supportedOptions       = array();
   161    dirk     private $optionValues           = array();
   161    dirk     private $arguments              = array();
   161    dirk
   163    paul     // TODO: no comment for this constructor?
   161    dirk     private function __construct($supportedOptions)
   ...

DirkMacBook:~ dirk$
```

Apparently user "Paul" did a code review and noticed that I had neglected to properly comment the constructor.

How do we resolve the conflict? We could manually edit the `Options.php` file to how we want the code to look. However, since our change is essentially a response to Paul's comment, even though we didn't know about it until we tried to commit, we would like to be able to tell Subversion to go ahead with our version. That is exactly what the resolve command does. After resolving the conflict, we are free to commit our changes to the repository.

```
Terminal — bash — bash — Dirk — ttys001 — 80×9 — ⌘2
> '
DirkMacBook:~ dirk$ svn resolve --accept mine-full Options.php
Resolved conflicted state of foo.c
$ svn commit -m "Added destructor method and commented constuctor" Options.php
Sending        Options.php
Transmitting file data .
Committed revision 164.

DirkMacBook:~ dirk$ █
```

This command also removes the conflict artifacts. For additional options this command offers, please see the manual.

A closer look at the repository

As mentioned before, the repository is the central place where Subversion keeps all information, including the files (current and past versions), tags, branches, meta-info, and so on. You can basically think of a repository of a file system with memory. Just like in a file system, projects, folders, and files are organized in a hierarchical tree structure.

From a Subversion client, you can perform all kinds of actions on those files, including adding, deleting, changing, and resolving conflicts. Subversion will keep track of all your actions and revert to any previous state. In a sense, you get infinite undo!

Data store

Internally to the repository, there are two backend engines that can be used to store the files: **Berkeley DB (BDB)** and the normal flat file storage supported by the underlying operating system (FSF). If you are familiar with MySQL, you can think of these options as the storage engine underlying a table definition.

While BDB was used during the initial development of Subversion, support for FSF was added in version 1.1 and quickly became the default. FSF provides more flexibility when it comes to accessibility and reliability. It also makes moving repositories across platforms a snap. In contrast, you cannot copy the BDB-based repository to another operating system and expect it to work. For most purposes, you should stick with FSF as the default. However, that is not to say that BDB has some nice features to offer as well. For a more detailed look at BDB in Subversion, please consult the online manual.

Thankfully, clients of the repository are blissfully unaware of the choice of data store. Only when something goes wrong, such as a system crash where actions on the files in the repository are interrupted mid-process, does it fall to the repository administrator to step in.

You choose the data store with a simple command line switch when you create the repository. See the options for the `svnadmin create` command for more details.

Layout

The repository provides you with the ability to store your files and projects; as well as all their history. But, it does not tell you how to organize them. If you so choose, you can dump every single project or file into the top-level of the repository, but that would quickly lead to chaos as projects and files get mixed up. The repository is not unlike the file system of the machine you use to program. Some people have their desktop or home directory littered with hundred of files. Others have everything organized and neatly categorized. Naturally, there is a lot of room in between.

Your best bet is to devote some time to choosing the layout before creating the repository. Following are two diagrams to illustrate the most commonly adopted repository layouts: multiple projects within a single repository and a single project per repository.

```
        Single Repository
         For All Projects
 (Independent or Loosely Coupled)

 |--Repository
 |    |
 |    |--Project1
 |    |  |--trunk
 |    |  |   `--[files]
 |    |  |--tags
 |    |  |   `--[files]
 |    |  `--branches
 |    |      `--[files]
 |    |
 |    |--Project2
 |    |  |--trunk
 |    |  |   `--[files]
 |    |  |--tags
 |    |  |   `--[files]
 |    |  `--branches
 |    |      `--[files]
 |    |
 |    |--[more projects]
```

This first option reduces the time required for administration because you are dealing with only one repository. With this option, your hook scripts will have to be aware of individual project requirements. For example, you might want to send a notification email when a developer commits a piece of code to Project1, but not Project2. You can only achieve that by integrating that logic into the hook script. In contrast, the next option does not suffer from this drawback.

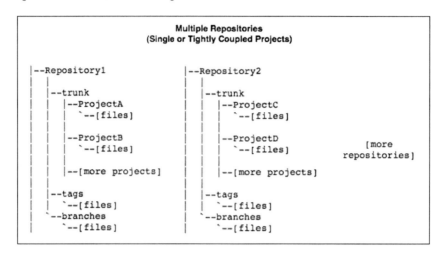

With this second option, you would have a single project per repository. You still have the option of organizing sub-projects in corresponding directories of the trunk directory and this makes sense when sub-projects are tightly coupled or related. This is the layout you encounter most often.

If you think back to how we added our sample project to our repository, you might realize that we went with the first option. We added a project folder containing "trunk", "branches", and "tags" directories to an existing repository.

Branching and merging

In this section, we will be looking at the concepts and practical implications of branching your code. Some might consider this an advanced feature, however, since mastering these concepts gives you such a powerful tool, it is well worth spending your time on. If you are working in a team environment or you have the need to support multiple versions of the same project, you will want to pay attention now.

What is a branch?

You create a branch of the code when you tell Subversion that you want to fork off the main development path, the trunk, and make a separate parallel branch of code. You can think of Subversion making a copy of all the files in the project and letting you work on that copy instead of the original. Any changes you commit back to the repository will modify the copy of the files in the branch you are working on, not the trunk. Of course, this implies that other developers will not be affected or benefit from any changes you commit unless they are working in the same branch as you are.

Why branch?

Let's look at some of the reasons for creating a branch of your trunk. After all, it will result in more work having to maintain two separate lines of development.

One reason to branch is because you have two different sets of requirements that will have to be implemented with the existing code base. For example, it has not been that long that MySQL AB, the company developing the popular open source database MySQL was acquired by Sun Microsystems, which in turn was acquired by Oracle. Considering the commercial nature of Oracle, you might have some doubts regarding their commitment to open source in general and the further advancement of MySQL in particular. Luckily, since MySQL has been made available under an open source license, it is trivial to start with the most recent official release and create your own branch. Assuming you have the skill and time to significantly advance the development of a relational database system, you can now start your work on "OurSQL" – or whatever you want to call your new project. In this scenario, you are probably permanently branching away from the trunk of the project and will not have to merge changes later on.

Another reason to branch might be that a developer on your team has been asked to implement an elaborate feature that touches upon many parts of the project and is therefore likely to interfere with the work of other developers working on unrelated tasks. In this case, you can create a branch for the developer to do his or her work. The intention of this approach is to merge the changes to the branch back into the trunk after coding has been completed and thoroughly tested.

Another scenario to consider is that after a successful launch of version 2 of your project, you are making great progress towards version 3 when a number of unfortunate bugs are discovered that really require you to release a fix. One way to do this is to branch the code at the version 2 tag. You can then make the fixes to the version 2 code base, release a revision to that version, say v2.0.1, and later merge those same fixes into trunk if necessary.

How to branch?

Creating a branch is pretty straightforward. Before you make any changes to your branch it is nothing more than a copy of the version with which you start. It should therefore come as no surprise that we need to use svn's `copy` command to create a branch. Although the command's syntax supports making local copies/branches, the preferred way of doing it is remotely by using remote repository URLs for both the source and the target of the copy operation.

Continuing our `svn-hook` example, let's branch the trunk of the project so that we can work on implementing a feature to syntax check PHP scripts before they are being committed. This is equivalent to running the CLI version of PHP with the -l command line switch. Here is the Subversion command for creating the branch:

```
Terminal — bash — bash — Dirk — ttys001 — 80×7 — ⌘2
DirkMacBook:- dirkDirkMachine$ svn copy https://svn/svn/svn-hooks/trunk \
https://svn/svn/svn-hooks/branches/php-lint-feature \
-m "branching trunk to implement a feature to lint-check PHP scripts"

Committed revision 166.

DirkMacBook:- dirk$ █
```

As far as the developer is concerned, there are now two separate copies of the project: the original in the `trunk` directory and a newly created copy in the `branches/php-ling-feature` directory. However, Subversion is smart about copying files. To save space, it only creates a pointer to the original file. This is the equivalent of a shortcut, alias, or symbolic link—depending on which terminology you are used to. As long as both copies are the same, there is really only one file that can be accessed from two different directory paths. However, as soon as one of the files changes, Subversion creates a second file to track those changes. This approach is generally referred to as **cheap copies**.

Maintaining and merging a branch

Now that we have created a branch, let's check it out of the repository and start working on the lint-checking feature.

```
Terminal — bash — bash — Dirk — ttys001 — 80×14 — ⌘2
DirkMacBook:~ dirkDirkMacBook:Sites dirk$ mkdir svn-hooks-php-lint
DirkMacBook:Sites dirk$ svn co https://svn/svn/svn-hooks/branches/php-lint-featu
re ./svn-hooks-php-lint
A    svn-hooks-php-lint/test
A    svn-hooks-php-lint/test/test.php
A    svn-hooks-php-lint/includes
A    svn-hooks-php-lint/includes/classes
A    svn-hooks-php-lint/includes/classes/Cli
A    svn-hooks-php-lint/includes/classes/Cli/Options.php
A    svn-hooks-php-lint/post-commit
A    svn-hooks-php-lint/pre-commit
Checked out revision 166.

DirkMacBook:~ dirk$
```

We now make some changes to the pre-commit script. First we add a function that can retrieve a list of files that are being committed. From that list, we omit files that are being deleted. Furthermore, we have the ability to limit the list to certain file extensions (".php" comes to mind) and exclude any file names matching a certain pattern. This function was adapted from code present in the phpcs-svn-pre-commit script.

```php
// ... other code …
// function uses svnlook to get list of files
// adapted from phpcs-svn-pre-commit
function getPhpFileList($repo,
                        $txn,
                        $allowedExtensions = array(),
                        $disallowedPatterns = array())
{
    // Get list of files in this transaction.
    $command = SVNLOOK . " changed $repo -t '$txn'";

    $handle  = popen($command, 'r');
    if ($handle === false) {
        echo 'ERROR: Could not execute svnlook' . $PHP_EOL;
        exit(2);
    }

    $contents = stream_get_contents($handle);

    fclose($handle);
```

```
// Do not check deleted paths.
$contents = preg_replace('/^D.*/m', null, $contents);

// Drop the four characters representing the action which precede
  the path on
// each line.
$contents = preg_replace('/^.{4}/m', null, $contents);

$files = array();

$allowedPattern = implode('|', $allowedExtensions);
$disallowedPattern = implode('|', $disallowedPatterns);

foreach (preg_split('/\v/', $contents, -1, PREG_SPLIT_NO_EMPTY) as
$path) {

    // No need to process folders as each changed file is
                                                    checked.
    if (substr($path, -1) === '/') {
        continue;

    // only keep allowed file extensions
    } elseif (empty($allowedPattern) &&
     !preg_match("/($allowedPattern)$/", $path)) {
        continue;

    // do NOT allow certain file name patterns
    } elseif (!empty($disallowedPattern) &&
     preg_match("/($disallowedPattern)/", $path)) {
        continue;

    // this one's a keeper
    } else {
        $files[] = $path;
    }
}
return $files;
}
```

We commit that function to Subversion and continue with our modifications. Now we add the code to process the list of files output by the above function and run a syntax check on each file using PHP CLI binary defined at the top of the file. Here are the lines of code we are adding:

```
// … other code …
// path to local PHP CLI executable
define('PHPCLI', '/usr/local/apache2/php/bin/php');
// … other code …
// get list of PHP files
$phpFiles = getPhpFileList($repos, $txn, array('commit'));

// run syntax for check each PHP file
list($totalSyntaxOutput, $totalSyntaxReturnValue) = array('', 0);
foreach ($phpFiles as $phpFile) {

    // svnlook command to get file contents
    $fileContentsCommand = SVNLOOK . " cat -t '$txn' '$repos'
'$phpFile'";

    // run syntax check
  list($phpSyntaxOutput, $phpSyntaxReturnValue) = array('', 0);
    exec($fileContentsCommand . ' | ' . PHPCLI . ' -l',
                            $phpSyntaxOutput, $phpSyntaxReturnValue);

  // add return values
  $totalSyntaxReturnValue += $phpSyntaxReturnValue;

  // append output
  if (is_array($phpSyntaxOutput) && count($phpSyntaxOutput) > 0) {
      $totalSyntaxOutput .= "Syntax error in file '$phpFile':" .
                                                    PHP_EOL;
      $totalSyntaxOutput .= trim(implode(PHP_EOL, $phpSyntaxOutput));
  }
}
// did PHP syntax check return an error?
if ($totalSyntaxReturnValue > 0) {
    fwrite(STDERR, "PHP CLI syntax check output:" . PHP_EOL .
"$totalSyntaxOutput");
    exit(1);
}
// … other code …
```

That completes our enhancements to the pre-commit script. Once again, we commit our changes, but we also want to merge the branch back into the trunk. Before merging, the revision graph for the `pre-commit` file looks like this:

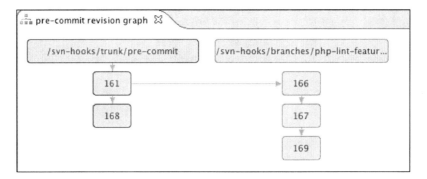

To merge our branch back into the trunk, we start with an up-to-date copy of the trunk and then use the merge command:

```
% svn merge --reintegrate ^/branches/svn-hooks-php-lint
```

From here on, all developers will see our changes in the trunk.

Branching workflow

The following diagram describes the process we just went through when we branched, developed in our branch, and merge our branch back into the trunk.

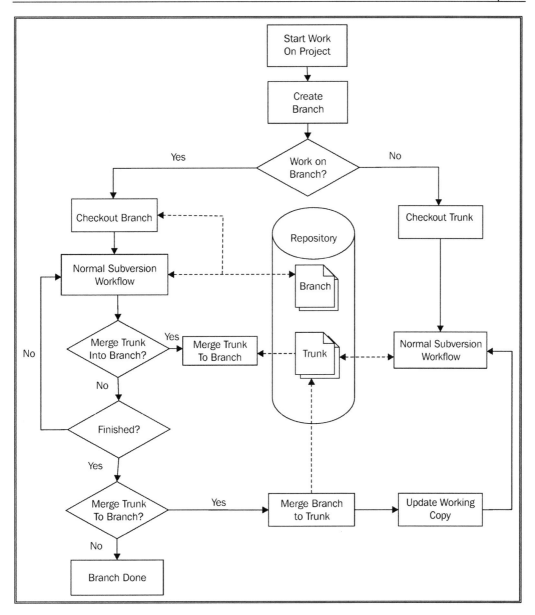

As work on the project starts, we create a branch of the trunk on which to do our development. For a developer to work on the branch, he will have to check it out of the repository. We are now following the activity depicted on the left side of the above diagram. Any changes to the files will also be committed back to the branch. The regular Subversion workflow of coding, updating the local working copy, merging and committing changes continues until work on the trunk has been completed. At that point, the developer has the option of merging the branch back into the trunk, thus integrating the changes.

In comparison, the right side of the diagram depicts a Subversion workflow of checking out the trunk and working on it.

UI clients

There are all kinds of Subversion clients available that will let you interact with a remote repository. In this section, I want to give a brief introduction to a select few that are especially interesting or relevant.

Eclipse plug-ins

Since we devoted a whole chapter to exploring Eclipse with the PDT plug-in as an IDE for PHP development, I think it is only fitting that we follow this up with a look at the state of Subversion support in Eclipse. Essentially there are two competing plug-ins: Subclipse and Subversive. I'm happy to say that users have been benefiting from a little competition between the two. Both are quite mature, stable, and feature-rich. Although I have used both of them, I had a little more luck with Subclipse in my most recent Eclipse installation. Consequently, the following screenshots are from that plug-in. However, Subversive will look almost identical because they both build upon Eclipse Team Provider Architecture.

You can do everything with these plug-ins that you can do from the command line. This includes, importing / exporting projects, browsing remote repositories, synchronizing projects to reflect recent changes, update/commit/revert code changes, examine log and history data, and merge changes/resolve conflicts. In some cases, having a graphical UI is of tremendous benefit. For example, the activity of resolving conflicts is greatly simplified by these utilities. Not only do they show you two different versions side-by-side, they also highlight the differences and let you copy code from one revision to the other (or vice versa) at the click of a button.

Here is a screenshot of Subclipse's repository exploring perspective:

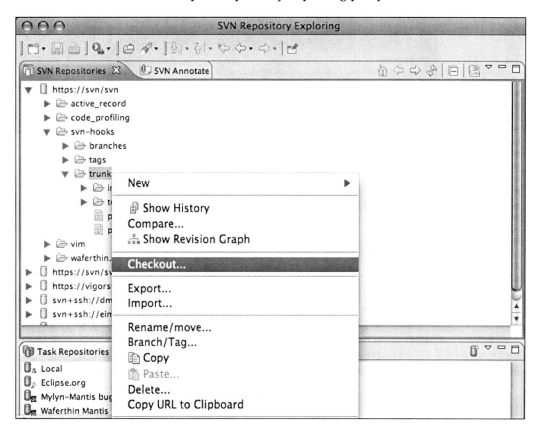

Checking out a project from the repository is easy with a wizard interface for creating the local project in Eclipse:

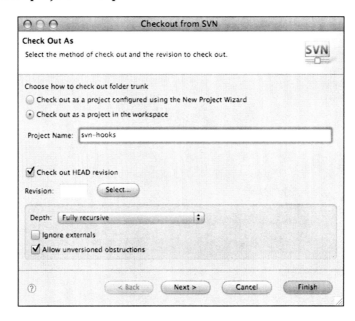

Lastly, one of the real strengths of these plug-ins within a visual IDE is merging changes or resolving conflicts:

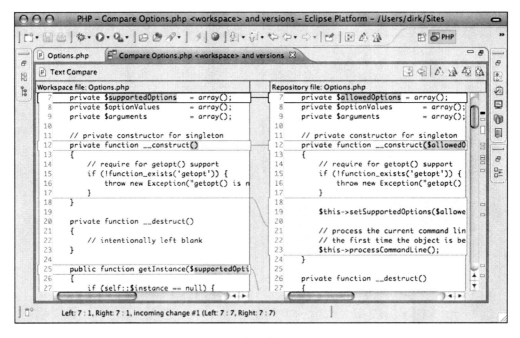

To install either of these plug-ins, take a look at the description of Eclipse's "Software Updates ..." feature in the chapter on IDEs.

You can download and learn more about these Eclipse plug-ins from their respective home pages:

Subversive: `http://www.eclipse.org/subversive/`

Subclipse: `http://subclipse.tigris.org`

TortoiseSVN

TortoiseSVN is Subversion client implemented as a Windows shell extension. The main reason I want to mention it here is because it is completely independent of an IDE or other tool. That and the fact that the implementation is quite elegant explains that TortoiseSVN has found wide use among Windows users working with Subversion.

WebSVN

WebSVN is one of the sub-projects of the main SVN project. The developers have done a great job of creating a web-based interface for viewing one or more repositories. Of course, it is freely available under the GPL. Better yet—it was written in PHP. Therefore, if you have to make any code changes or want to contribute to the project, you will feel right at home. You can visit the WebSVN home page here:

`http://www.websvn.info/`

Among others, WebSVN offers the following features as mentioned on their site:

- Intuitive interface closely matching the SVN approach
- Templating system allowing you to customize the look of any page
- File listings with colorized syntax
- Blame view
- Log and history views and search capability

Here is a screenshot of the page displaying the projects in my repository. As you can see, I navigated into the trunk of our sample project:

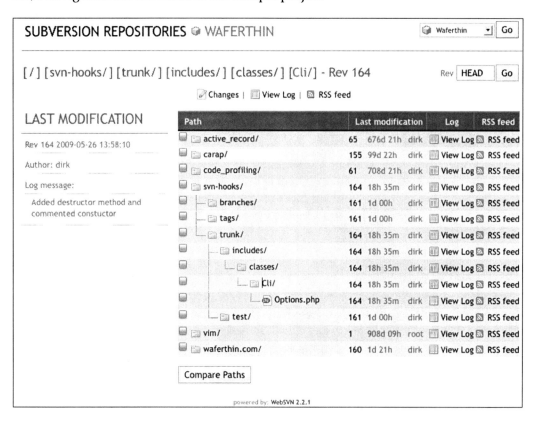

The next screenshot illustrates colorized syntax when viewing an individual source file. In this case, we are looking at file `Options.php`, which contains the definition for class `Cli_Options`:

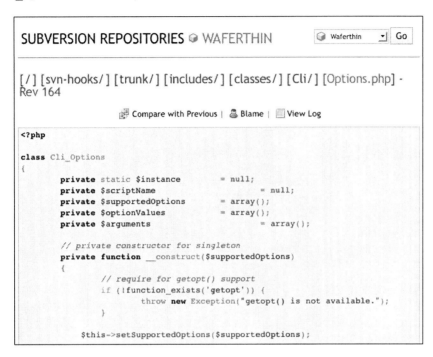

Next we have a screenshot of WebSVN showing the side-by-side differences between two revisions of the same file:

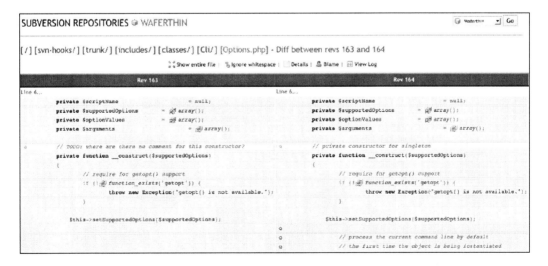

To see who is responsible for each line of code and in what revision, WebSVN has a nice page for showing output from the SVN blame command:

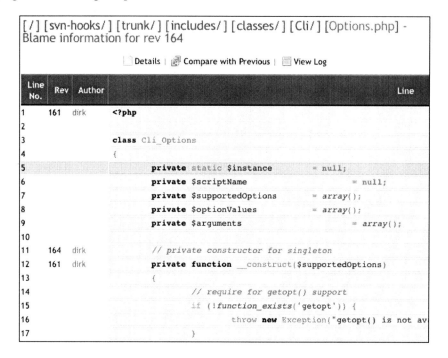

And finally, here is the page displaying log messages for successive revisions of a particular file:

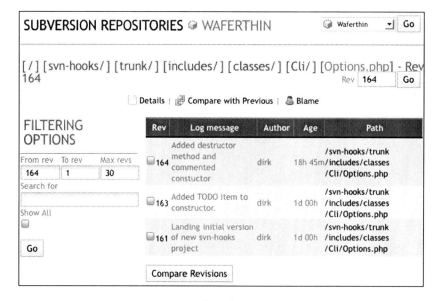

A demo of the latest official release of WebSVN is available online at:

```
http://demo.websvn.info/
```

Remember how we used the `svnnotify` script in our post-commit hook script to send a notification e-mail when a file had been submitted to the repository? Using the -U --revision-url switch, we can get `svnnotify` to include link to the repository. Although this can be a direct Subversion link, it can also be a link to WebSVN. That way, anyone on the recipient list will be able to click the link and view the file in his browser with all the amenities WebSVN provides.

Subversion conventions and best practices

This section is a combination of things we have learned in this chapter and best practices typically associated with software development in a team environment and with the help of Subversion.

- Use the convention of organizing your code into three folders: "trunk", "branches", and "tags." Loosely coupled projects should get their own structure; whereas tightly coupled projects can share the same folder threesome.

- Commit and update often. Many small conflict resolution cycles are usually much easier than having to resolve major conflicts at the end of your tasks development cycle. Frequently committing your code also serves as a backup. As a rule of thumb, commit your code before you call it a day and preferably also before you take lunch. However, don't commit code that will break existing functionality.

- Write descriptive and informative commit comments. Reading commit comments is much faster than having to read multiple files of code when trying to figure out what was done.

- Use branches to keep the trunk stable while implementing extended features. Also use branches for diverging, but parallel lines of development.

- Use pre-commit and post-commit hooks for automated auditing. As seen in our example, you can enforce coding standards and initiate small code reviews using hooks and other add-on scripts.

Customizing Subversion

There are many ways of customizing Subversion and there is no point in covering them all here because the online manual does an excellent job of documenting them. However, I do want to take a look at some feature that I use personally on a daily basis, simply because they add so much to my workflow. Also, as you will see, some of these features connect back to other tools we are examining in this book.

Hooks

During many of the action Subversion takes, you can ask that execution be handed off to an external executable either before or after the action occurs. These points where you can interject yourself into the actions of Subversion are called **hooks**. Pre-commit hooks execute before the respective event in the repository and post-commit hooks execute after.

When you create a repository, Subversion automatically creates a `hooks` directory that contains a template for each of the different kinds of hooks that are possible. Take a look at the `hooks` directory of my own repository:

```
Terminal — bash — bash — Dirk — ttys002 — 80×16 — ⌘3
DirkMacBook:hooks dirk$ cd /usr/local/SVN/hooks
DirkMacBook:hooks dirk$ ls -Fl
total 88
drwxr-xr-x  3 root  wheel   102 May 30  2009 includes/
-rwxr-xr-x  1 root  wheel   834 Jun  8  2009 post-commit*
-rw-r--r--  1 _www  wheel  2015 Jan 11  2007 post-commit.tmpl
-rw-r--r--  1 _www  wheel  1638 Jan 11  2007 post-lock.tmpl
-rw-r--r--  1 _www  wheel  2255 Jan 11  2007 post-revprop-change.tmpl
-rw-r--r--  1 _www  wheel  1567 Jan 11  2007 post-unlock.tmpl
-rwxr-xr-x  1 root  wheel  1510 May 29  2009 pre-commit.bck*
-rw-r--r--  1 _www  wheel  2940 Jan 11  2007 pre-commit.tmpl
-rw-r--r--  1 _www  wheel  2044 Jan 11  2007 pre-lock.tmpl
-rw-r--r--  1 _www  wheel  2764 Jan 11  2007 pre-revprop-change.tmpl
-rw-r--r--  1 _www  wheel  1985 Jan 11  2007 pre-unlock.tmpl
-rw-r--r--  1 _www  wheel  2137 Jan 11  2007 start-commit.tmpl
DirkMacBook:hooks dirk$
```

There are a total of nine template files ending in `.tmpl` and two actual hooks, which lack the ".tmpl" file extension in the above listing. None of the templates will actually be executed because there are two things you need to do when turning a template into a working hook. First, you must remove the file extension from the filename so that it exactly matches the name of the hook. Second, you have to assign the correct ownership and permissions to the hook file. The file has to be executable by the owner of the Subversions process. In my case, I am accessing the repository locally as user "dirk." Most of the time, Subversion commands will be executed under the login of the user performing the action.

Lets turn our attention to the two hooks that have been implemented in this repository, namely the pre-commit and the post-commit hook.

Enforcing coding standards with a pre-commit hook

If you look back on the chapter on coding standards, you might recall that we learned to use the PHP_CodeSniffer tool to check our source files for compliance with our chosen standard. With the help of a pre-commit hook, we can now go a step further and enforce this process. We will create a hook that will check the code being committed against a specified coding standard (defined in the PHP_CodeSniffer format). If the code passes the test, it will get committed to the repository. However, if PHP_CodeSniffer finds something wrong with the code, it will return a corresponding error message to the user and prevent the commit process from completing. Thus, we can ensure that only source files adhering to your standard make it into our repository.

The following code listing is a shell script that is based on the pre-commit.tmpl in the hooks directory. I omitted some of the comments for brevity, but you can always look at the original template for more detail. This script will run in a Linux/Unix environment, but a .bat script for Windows would follow the same logic.

```
#!/bin/sh
# PRE-COMMIT HOOK
#
# The pre-commit hook is invoked before a Subversion txn is
# committed.  Subversion runs this hook by invoking a program
# (script, executable, binary, etc.) named 'pre-commit' (for which
# this file is a template), with the following ordered arguments:
#
#   [1] REPOS-PATH   (the path to this repository)
#   [2] TXN-NAME     (the name of the txn about to be committed)
REPOS="$1"
TXN="$2"

# Make sure that the log message contains some text.
SVNLOOK=/usr/local/bin/svnlook
$SVNLOOK log -t "$TXN" "$REPOS" | \
   grep "[a-zA-Z0-9]" > /dev/null || exit 1

# Check that the file being committed conforms
# to the coding standard employed by our project.
/usr/local/apache2/php/bin/scripts/phpcs-svn-pre-commit
--standard=Zend --tab-width=4 "$REPOS" -t "$TXN" >&2 || exit 1

# All checks passed, so allow the commit.
exit 0
```

Our pre-commit script requires two command line arguments to do its work; the Subversion process invoking it will supply both. First, it needs to know which repository to work with. Second, it needs to know the file that is supposed to get committed.

After running through all the checks, the script exits with one of two exit codes: 1 indicates a problem and 0 indicates that all the checks passed. Moreover, any messages written to standard error will be shown to the user.

The first check our script runs is to see whether a log message was entered with the commit. I encourage everybody to do that. It saves other developers from having to "diff" the code to figure out what was changed. We are actually using another tool in the Subversion arsenal here, namely the svnlook command. svnlook lets you query your repository or individual files therein for specific information. In this case, we are using it to retrieve the comment submitted by the user along with his commit command. A simple pattern match using the grep command then tells us whether the comment is empty or not.

The second check executes the PHP_CodeSniffer pre-commit script. The command line arguments to that script should look familiar if you were paying attention to the chapter on coding standards. We're basically telling the script to validate against the Zend coding standard and to require indentations to use four spaces instead of tabs.

Here is what happens when I try to commit a file without a comment. After supplying a comment, my script then does not pass the Zend Framework coding standard test:

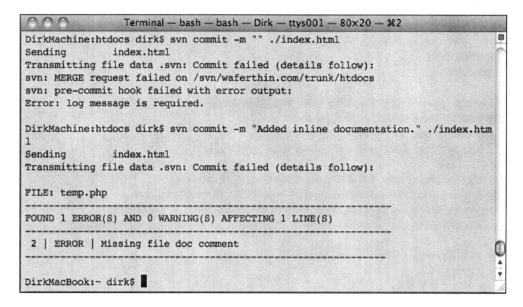

But, why are we bothering with shell script? Isn't this a book about PHP? Right you
are — which is why the sample project that we have been developing throughout this
chapter contains a replacement for the previous script. At this point, all we have to
do is export the svn-hooks project into the "hooks" directory of our repository and
change the permissions to make the two scripts executable:

```
      ○ ○ ○                  Terminal — bash — bash — Dirk — ttys001 — 80×30 — ⌘2
DirkMacBook:~ dirk$ svn export https://svn/svn/svn-hooks/trunk/includesPassword:
A    includes
A    includes/classes
A    includes/classes/Cli
A    includes/classes/Cli/Options.php
Exported revision 168.
$ svn export https://svn/svn/svn-hooks/trunk/pre-commit
A    pre-commit
Export complete.
$ svn export https://svn/svn/svn-hooks/trunk/post-commit
A    post-commit
Export complete.
$ chmod 0755 pre-commit
$ chmod 0755 post-commit
$ ls -Al
total 88
drwxr-xr-x    3 root   wheel     102 May 30 05:56 includes
-rw-r--r--    1 root   wheel     838 May 26 07:54 post-commit
-rw-r--r--    1 _www   wheel    2015 Jan 11  2007 post-commit.tmpl
-rw-r--r--    1 _www   wheel    1638 Jan 11  2007 post-lock.tmpl
-rw-r--r--    1 _www   wheel    2255 Jan 11  2007 post-revprop-change.tmpl
-rw-r--r--    1 _www   wheel    1567 Jan 11  2007 post-unlock.tmpl
-rwxr-xr-x    1 root   wheel    1510 May 29 16:59 pre-commit
-rw-r--r--    1 _www   wheel    2940 Jan 11  2007 pre-commit.tmpl
-rw-r--r--    1 _www   wheel    2044 Jan 11  2007 pre-lock.tmpl
-rw-r--r--    1 _www   wheel    2764 Jan 11  2007 pre-revprop-change.tmpl
-rw-r--r--    1 _www   wheel    1985 Jan 11  2007 pre-unlock.tmpl
-rw-r--r--    1 _www   wheel    2137 Jan 11  2007 start-commit.tmpl

DirkMacBook:~ dirk$
```

The new `pre-commit` script is a PHP-based drop-in replacement for the existing shell
script. However, it has the added benefit that it also does a syntax check on files
with the `.php` extension before allowing them to be committed.

Notifying developers of commits with a post-commit hook

By exporting our svn-hooks project into the repository's "hooks" directory, we also installed the `post-commit` script. Its job is to generate an informative e-mail detailing each commit transaction. You will have to modify it slightly to specify the e-mail address(es) to send these notifications. See the listing of the script earlier in the chapter for more details. Once it is working correctly, you will be receiving e-mails similar to the following one:

```
From:    Dirk Merkel
Subject: [165] Renamed property $supportedOptions to $allowedOptions.
Date:    May 28, 2009 10:02:10 AM PDT
To:      Dirk Merkel
```

```
Revision:  165
Author:    dirk
Date:      2009-05-28 08:12:39 -0700 (Thu, 28 May 2009)
```

Log Message

```
Renamed property $supportedOptions to $allowedOptions.
```

Modified Paths

* svn-hooks/trunk/includes/classes/Cli/Options.php

Diff

Modified: svn-hooks/trunk/includes/classes/Cli/Options.php (164 => 165)

```
---- svn-hooks/trunk/includes/classes/Cli/Options.php    2009-05-26 20:58:10 UTC (rev 164)
+++ svn-hooks/trunk/includes/classes/Cli/Options.php    2009-05-28 15:12:39 UTC (rev 165)
@@ -4,19 +4,19 @@
 {
        private static $instance       = null;
        private $scriptName                   = null;
-       private $supportedOptions      = array();
+       private $allowedOptions = array();
        private $optionValues          = array();
        private $arguments                    = array();

        // private constructor for singleton
-       private function __construct($supportedOptions)
+       private function __construct($allowedOptions)
        {
                // require for getopt() support
```

Summary

Remember the three scenarios I posed in the introduction to this chapter. With all that you have learned about Subversion, the solution to those problems should appear much less daunting. Assuming that you have been using Subversion or a similar version control system to develop your project, let's revisit those scenarios now.

Scenario 1: After accidentally messing up a file on a production server, you can simply pull the revision of the file you need from the remote repository — effectively reverting the local changes.

Scenario 2: Switching your open source project from a single developer to a distributed team becomes a snap after you put the project into Subversion and give the volunteering developers access using `svnserve` to get up and running quickly.

Scenario 3: Being forced to review development efforts, you can easily use Subversion's blame command and ability to access past revisions to see how and when the bug was introduced. Armed with that knowledge, you can work to improve the development process to prevent a similar problem from occurring in the future.

If you haven't been using it already, I hope that the examples and explanations in this chapter have inspired you to start working with Subversion to manage your source code and versions.

5
Debugging

I started debugging the first time I was asked to code the obligatory "Hello World" program. It's just something that comes with the territory. If you write code, you create bugs. Hopefully you will be able to find most of them by the time your code reaches your application's users.

There are many kinds of bugs that range in complexity from glaringly obvious to nearly impossible to figure out. Knowing that they are out there hiding in your code, we will look at tools for finding and eradicating them in this chapter. Specifically, we will look at configuration options, constants, and functions that are useful when debugging. Armed with that knowledge, we will construct a general-purpose class we can include in our projects for easy debugging. Finally, we will learn how to use Xdebug and Eclipse to interactively debug code running locally or on the server.

First line of defense: syntax check

One of the first things PHP does when you ask it to execute a piece of code is a syntax check. Basically, it goes through the code and makes sure that it conforms to the basic grammar of the language. Some of the questions the parser asks include:

- Does a semicolon terminate every statement?
- Do all the function calls reference functions that actually exist in PHP's namespace?
- Are all language constructs in the code known to the parser?

If any problems are detected, the interpreter will generate an error message that is often detailed enough to pinpoint the problem and fix it. If you are reading the chapters of this book in order, you will already have seen the output of the syntax check in the chapter on Subversion. If you recall, we created a pre-commit hook script that checks the syntax of PHP scripts before they are being allowed to be committed to the repository.

The syntax check happens automatically when the interpreter starts up, but we can also invoke it separately without having it go on to actually execute the code. When using the PHP command line interface (CLI), the -l switch does the job. Consider the following, intentionally buggy "Hello World" script:

```
<?php
echo "Hello World!'
?>
```

We can easily run a syntax check from the command line as follows:

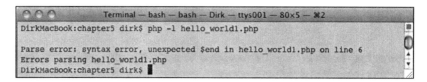

The error message basically says the script was terminated before the parser thought it should be. This is actually a good example of how the line number doesn't always correspond to the cause of the problem. The error message points the finger at line 5, but that is simply the closing PHP tag and the last line of the script. Perhaps the problem occurs two lines before that when we didn't terminate our echo statement with a semicolon. Let's fix that and run the syntax check again. Unfortunately, this time we're getting the exact same error output again.

Obviously there are additional problems. Furthermore, the error message isn't terribly helpful in finding the root of the problem. Luckily, our script isn't terribly complex to say the least. The problem has to lie with our single line of code. A close inspection reveals that we have mismatching quotes. We start the string literal with a double quote, but end it with a single quote. This rather confused the PHP parser and explains the odd error message. To us it is obvious what our intent was, but PHP has no idea whether we simply forgot to add a closing single quote, start the quote, change the single quote to a double one, or even have one type of quote inside the other so as to avoid having to escape them. All PHP sees is the beginning of a string literal, but no end. Since strings can span multiple lines, the parser encounters the end of the script without finding the closing quote, which is why the line in the error message points at the end of the script. Why it complains of line 6 instead of line 5, which is the last line of the script, I honestly don't know.

Now that we have found our second bug, let's run the syntax check one more time.

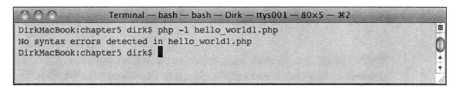

We're in good shape now—at least as far as the syntax is concerned. PHP certifies that the script will do something. Whether it is what we intended it to do is another question. The PHP parser doesn't know anything about our intent. If we meant for the script to solve differential equations, we failed miserably. I'm exaggerating, of course, but the point is still valid. Just because our code passes a syntax check, doesn't mean that there aren't much more subtle faults in our logic that we will have to correct. We'll be looking at tools to help us do that later in this chapter.

Logging

One of the most useful and equally underused tools for trouble-shooting PHP are log files. PHP can be configured to write all kinds of information and detail to a system-wide log file that will be a valuable resource when the time comes to track down some illusive bugs.

There are several reasons you should be using and reviewing log files regularly, including the following:

- Log files give you access to historical debug info. If you receive an error report, but are unable to duplicate the problem yourself, you can consult the log file(s) to see if there is anything that was recorded at the time of the incident.

- Log files contain cumulative information. Error messages in the browser describe the state of the code at a particular point in time—often at the time when it crashed. In contrast, log files span a period of time that can range from a few seconds to months or even years. Having access to so much historical data lets you learn about the frequency and severity of issues with your code. For example, when considering whether to spend the resources to fix a bug that you estimate will take two days to correct, you might consult the log files to see how frequently users encounter the bug. If it turns out that the bug is non-critical and only one user has encountered it over last twelve months, you might opt to forego fixing it or at least assign a low priority to it. Using some regular expressions and log analyzer software, you can compile some highly informative data about your application that you would not be able to access otherwise.

- Log files let you keep error messages and debug information away from users' browsers. A visitor to your site being shown an error message simply makes your site look amateurish.

 PHP's log file is different from the ones your web server generates. Apache, for example, typically generates two log files. The first one is to record which resources are accessed when, by whom, and how. The second Apache log file contains errors generated by Apache and its modules. This might include output generated by PHP, but is not nearly as detailed for the purpose of debugging PHP as the log file generated by PHP.

Configuration options

Let's take a look at the PHP config options that you can set in the `php.ini` file and how they affect where, when, and how information is written to the PHP log file. All of these options have been available since PHP 4.3.2. Furthermore, all of the options with one exception can be set in the system-wide `php.ini` file, Apache's `httpd.conf/.htacces`, or PHP scripts. The only exception is the `xmlrpc_errors` option, which can only be set in the main `php.ini` config file.

In this section of the chapter, we will only be focusing on the configuration options relevant to error logging and debugging. For a complete list of options, please consult the online PHP manual. You can also quickly retrieve a list of all options; as well as their global and local settings, using the array `ini_get_all()` function.

You can refer to the section on *Error Handling and Logging* of the online PHP manual at `php.net` for a detailed description of all the error-related configuration options. In the following table, I would like to simply present the settings for each of the options that I recommend for both development and production environment.

Option	Description	Dev.	Prod.
`error_reporting`	The level of detail to display in the log messages.	`E_ALL | E_STRICT`	`E_ERROR`
`display_errors`	Toggle the sending of log messages to `STDOUT` where it is typically visible in the user's browser.	`On`	`Off`
`display_startup_ errors`	Toggle the display of errors during PHP's startup phase *regardless* of the `display_errors` setting.	`On`	`Off`

Option	Description	Dev.	Prod.
log_errors	Toggle logging of errors to server's error log.	On	On
log_errors_max_len	Maximum number of bytes in error message (0 = unlimited).	0	0
ignore_repeated_errors	Toggle display of the exact same error message more than once in a row.	Off	Off
ignore_repeated_source	Toggle display of same error message if it occurs on different source code lines / files.	Off	Off
report_memleaks	Toggle display or memory leaks (requires debug compile).	Off	Off
track_errors	Toggle whether to store the last error message in variable $php_errormsg – limited to scope where error occurred.	On	On
html_errors	Toggle plain text vs. HTML formatted messages with links to PHP functions in the manual (uses docref_root and docref_ext).	On	Off
xmlrpc_errors	Toggle formatting of error messages in XML-RPC format.	Off	Off
xmlrpc_error_number	Toggle use value of the XML-RPC faultCode element for error number.	Off	Off
docref_root	Base URL for the PHP manual (remote or local) (used by html_errors).	http://www.php.net/manual/en/	
docref_ext	File extension of manual pages (used by html_errors).	.php	
error_prepend_string	String to output before the error message.		
error_append_string	String to output after the error message.		
error_log	Error log directory path and filename.	/var/log/php_errors.txt	/var/log/php_errors.tx

Since settings in the `php.ini` file affect all sites, you might want to set default settings in that file and then rely on site-specific settings to override them. A simple way of doing that is to have an include file that uses the `ini_set()` function to configure error handling and logging depending on the site's environment. Here is such a file that supports a `Development` environment and a default environment (presumably for production purposes):

`init_environment.php` (excerpt below):

```php
<?php
// logging & error settings for development
if (ENVIRONMENT == 'Development') {

    // level of log detail
    ini_set('error_reporting', 'E_ALL | E_STRICT');

    // display errors in browser
    ini_set('display_errors', 'On');

    // ... more dev settings (see code download for more) ...

// default logging & error settings
} else {
    // level of log detail
    ini_set('error_reporting', 'E_ERROR');

    // ... more default settings (see code download for more) ...
}
?>
```

Customizing and controlling config options: PhpIni

The above listing is a quick and easy solution, but with a little more effort, we can construct a solution that is both more flexible and powerful. Here are the additional requirements. First, the above solution might work well in a quick procedural script, but a more object-oriented solution will be more flexible and extensible. So, let's wrap everything into a class. Second, the actual settings should not be hard-coded in the class itself because you shouldn't have to change your code each time you need to tweak your debug settings. Doing so would make it increasingly difficult to reuse that class in different parts of your application at the same time. Instead, settings should be pulled in from one or more external configuration files. This way, you are separating configuration from code and can use the same class multiple times at once. Third, we want to be able to easily support multiple configuration files and environments. Fourth, it would be nice if we can override any of the configuration settings — on the fly. Lastly, we want this class to be able to tell us about any of the settings, such as the default or current setting.

With these requirements in mind, let's take a look at class `PhpIni` listed as follows:

```php
<?php
class PhpIni
{
    // initialize current development to null
    public $environment = null;

    // initialize location of config file(s) to empty array
    public $configDirs = array();

    // initialize active settings to empty array
    public $activeSettings = array();

    // define default settings for each environment defined
    // by this class (can be overriden later)
    public $defaultSettings = array();
    // constructor sets the location of the config files
    public function __construct(array $configDirs = array())
    {
        if (count($configDirs) > 0) {
            $this->configDirs = $configDirs;
        }
    }
    // applies the settings for the current environment
    // optionally overrides defaults with custom settings
    public function applySettings(array $customSettings = array())
    {
        // reset current settings
        $this->activeSettings = array();

        // get list of ini files
        $iniFiles = $this->getIniFiles();

        // initialize default settings
        $this->defaultSettings = array();

        // read all ini files
        foreach ($iniFiles as $iniFile) {
            // merge all default settings
```

```
            $this->defaultSettings = array_merge($this-
                >defaultSettings, parse_ini_file($iniFile, TRUE));
        }

        // merge ini files with custom settings
        $this->activeSettings = array_merge($this-
            >defaultSettings[$this->environment], $customSettings);
        // apply settings
        foreach ($this->activeSettings as $directive => $value) {
            ini_set($directive, $value);
        }
    }
    // returns array of all config directories
    public function getConfigDirs()
    {
        $this->configDirs = $configDirs;
    }


    // set array of config directories at once
    public function setConfigDirs(array $configDirs = array())
    {
        return $this->configDirs;
    }


    // push a directory onto the end of configDirs array
    public function addConfigDir($newConfigDir)
    {
        array_push($this->configDirs, $newConfigDir);
    }


    // returns the currently set environment
    public function getEnvironment()
    {
        return $this->environment;
    }


    // set the current environment
    public function setEnvironment($environment)
    {
        $this->environment = $environment;
    }
    // return the default setting in a given environment
                                            (or current one)
    // throws an exception if either environment or setting are
                                                    undefined
```

```
    public function getDefaultSetting($setting, $environment = null)
    {
        // use current environment if none given
        if ($environment === null) {
            $environment = $this->getEnvironment();
        }

        // check whether the environment exists
        if (!array_key_exists($environment, $this->defaultSettings)) {
            throw new Exception("Environment '$environment' not
                                                    defined.");

        // check whether the setting exists
        } elseif (!array_key_exists($setting, $this->defaultSettings[$
environment])) {
            throw new Exception("Default setting '$setting' in
                        environment '$environment' is not defined.");
        // return the requested default setting
        } else {
            return $this->defaultSettings[$environment][$setting];
        }
    }
    // return the value of the setting how it was actually set
    // WARNING: only works if setting was set with this class
    public function getActiveSetting($setting)
    {
        // check whether the setting exists
        if (!array_key_exists($setting, $this->activeSettings)) {
            throw new Exception("Setting '$setting' is not currently
                                        defined throug __CLASS__.");

        // return the requested setting
        } else {
            return $this->activeSettings[$setting];
        }
    }
    // given all directories in configDirs, this method finds
    // and returns all files ending in .ini in those directories
    public function getIniFiles()
    {
        // initialize array of ini files
        $iniFiles = array();

        // loop over directories
        foreach ($this->configDirs as $dir) {
```

```
            if (is_dir($dir)) {
                // open directory ...
                if ($dirHandle = opendir($dir)) {

                    // ... and iterate of the file therein
                    while (($file = readdir($dirHandle)) !== FALSE) {

                        // check file extension
                        $pathParts = pathinfo($dir .
                                    DIRECTORY_SEPARATOR . $file);
                        if ($pathParts['extension'] == 'ini') {

                            // we found a .ini file
                            $iniFiles[] = $dir . DIRECTORY_SEPARATOR
                                                        . $file;

                        }
                    }
                    closedir($dirHandle);
                }
            }
        }
        return $iniFiles;
    }
}
?>
```

The basic idea is that we have an array of directories that can hold configuration files. This array is stored in $configDirs and there are getter/setter methods getConfigDirs() and setConfigDirs(). Additionally, there is a convenience method addConfigDir() to push another configuration directory onto the end of the $configDirs array. Furthermore, the constructor takes an optional array of configuration directories to initialize $configDirs.

Provided that we have properly populated the list of configuration directories, the getIniFiles() method iterates over those directories and looks for files having the file extension .ini and returns a list of such files with complete paths in an array. If we wanted, we could make the class more flexible by letting the user define acceptable file extension rather than hard-coding that only .ini files are acceptable.

You may have already noticed the getter/setter methods for the $environment variable. Specifying the environment you want to use is required because we will be supporting an unlimited number of environments. This is probably a good time to look at the actual config file(s).

```
config/error.ini (excerpt):

    [DEVELOPMENT]
    ; description of development environment
    description = Development environment for pre-production use and
    debugging
    ; level of log detail
    error_reporting = E_ALL | E_STRICT
    ; ... more development settings (see code download for more) ...


    [PRODUCTION]
    ; description of production environment
    description = Production environment optimized for security
    ; level of log detail
    error_reporting = E_ERROR
    ; ... more default settings (see code download for more) ...
```

For a complete listing of the above file, please consult the file config/error.ini in the code download package accompanying this chapter.

The options and values should seem familiar by now. However, what should also be familiar to you is the format of the file. That is because it is the same format used by PHP's own config file, php.ini. The reason we chose this format is because parsing it is built into PHP in the form of the parse_ini_file() function. As we will see shortly, this convenient function does a lot of work for us and saves us from the unnecessary headache of dealing with parsing and validating a custom or obscure file format.

If the optional second parameter is set to TRUE, parse_ini_files() parses the section heading as well and returns an associative array with the section names being the key for the settings array. This is exactly what we want for our purposes.

Getting back to our PhpIni class—all our preparation of defining directories with configuration files and setting the environment comes together in the applySettings() method, which does a number of useful things. To start, it gets all eligible .ini files from getIniFiles(). It then uses method parse_ini_files() to read all possible settings and environments into the $defaultSettings property. Knowing which environment the user requested, it then stores all settings that are actually going to be applied in property $activeSettings. Next, if the user has passed custom settings into the applySettings() method, they will be added to the $activeSettings array and will override any default settings. The last thing this method does is to actually apply all settings saved in the $activeSettings property.

Once the config files have been parsed and the settings have been applied, it makes sense to call the methods getDefaultSetting() and getActiveSetting() at any time in your program to check any of the settings.

PhpIni example

Here is a little script that illustrates how to instantiate and use the PhpIni class:

```php
<?php
// include PhpIni class
require_once('classes/PhpIni.php');

// instantiate PhpIni object
$phpIni = new PhpIni(array('/my/projects/config/dir'));

// set the environment
$phpIni->setEnvironment('DEVELOPMENT');

// apply all settings from the .ini files,
// but override config setting 'error_log' with a custom value
$phpIni->applySettings(array('error_log' => '/custom/dir/for/project/
php_errors.txt'));

// output information about the environment
echo "Current environment (" . $phpIni->getEnvironment() . "): "
    . $phpIni->getActiveSetting('description') . "\n";

// current setting for 'error_log'
echo "Current setting for 'error_log' in this environment: "
    . $phpIni->getActiveSetting('error_log') . "\n";

// default setting for 'error_log' in current environment
(DEVELOPMENT)
echo "Default setting for 'error_log' in this environment: "
    . $phpIni->getDefaultSetting('error_log') . "\n";

// default setting for 'error_log' in inactive  environment PRODUCTION
echo "Default setting for 'error_log' in Production environment: "
    . $phpIni->getDefaultSetting('error_log', 'PRODUCTION') . "\n";
?>
```

After instantiating a `PhpIni` and telling it to look for config files in `/my/projects/config/dir`, we tell it that we want to work with the `DEVELOPMENT` environment. After that, it's just a matter of calling `applySettings()` with a custom `error_log` file location. Finally, we output various settings to confirm that everything is working as desired. Here is the output of our `PhpIni` test script:

```
Terminal — bash — bash — Dirk — ttys004 — 79×10 — ⌘2
DirkMacBook:chapter5 dirk$ php php_ini_test.php
Current environment (DEVELOPMENT): Development environment for pre-production u
se and debugging
Current setting for 'error_log' in this environment: /custom/dir/for/project/ph
p_errors.txt
Default setting for 'error_log' in this environment: /var/debug/log/php_errors.
txt
Default setting for 'error_log' in Production environment: /var/production/log/
php_errors.txt
DirkMacBook:chapter5 dirk$ ▮
```

 As useful as the PHP error log file is, it can become a problem when left to grow without being monitored. Like all log files, PHP error logs should be monitored not only for content, but also for size. Log files should be archived periodically so they don't grow too big and become a problem for the server (production or development). Besides, if you don't intend to monitor your log files, why bother enabling them and having them generate all this useful information?

Outputting debug information

So far, we have been focusing on the error messages PHP generates. Initially we looked at the output of the parser as it validates the source code syntax before trying to execute it. After that, we learned about logging in PHP—how it works, how to customize, and how to leverage to our benefit. Next, let's try to add to the information to give us more clues if something goes wrong. In particular, there are several built-in functions and constants that can be used for this purpose. Let's start by discussing these functions and constants and then try to integrate them into a class that will give us additional information and conveniences when debugging code.

Functions

There are several core PHP functions that are helpful in outputting and formatting debug information. I would expect that you are familiar with at least some of the functions listed below, but familiarizing yourself with some of the others will help you to choose the ones that most closely match your needs.

echo(string $arg1 [, string $...]) / print(string $arg)

For simply outputting values of variables or state information to the screen or browser, nothing beats the simplicity of `echo` or `print()`. Which one you use is entirely up to you. `echo` is slightly faster, but `print()` has a return value. Both of these differences are irrelevant to our purpose. However, I will say that you will see more `echo` than `print` statements in PHP code in general. For whatever reason, it appears to have become the de facto standard.

var_dump(mixed $expression [, mixed $expression [, $...]]) and print_r(mixed $expression [, bool $return= false])

These two functions will output information about their argument. If the argument is an array or object, they will traverse the hierarchy and display information about the components as well. However, there are some important differences.

Generally speaking, `print_r()` is a bit easier to read. It also takes an optional second argument that returns the information rather than outputting it to the browser. You can get the same result from `var_dump()` if you combine it with PHP's output control functions for output buffering (see functions `ob_start()` and `ob_end_flush()`).

The other important difference is that `var_dump()` will give you a bit more information. Specifically, it will tell you the data type of a variable or property and its size. Let's look at a quick example:

```php
<?php
class VDump
{
    // private, protected, and public properties
    private $path = '/this/way';
    protected $extensions = array('csv', 'txt');
    public $file  = null;

    // constructor
    public function __construct($file)
    {
        $this->$file;
    }

    // private method
    private function getPath()
    {
        return $this->path;
    }
```

```
    // protected method
    protected function getFile()
    {
        return $this->file;
    }

    // public method
    public function getPathAndFile()
    {
        return $this->getPath() . '/' . $this->getFile();
    }
}

// instantiate sample object
$vdump = new VDump('data.csv');

// var_dump example ...
var_dump($vdump);

// print_r example ...
// ... same as:
// echo print_r($vdump, TRUE);
print_r($vdump);
?>
```

Here is the output you get from executing the above example code:

```
DirkMacBook:chapter5 dirk$ php var_dump.php
object(VDump)#1 (3) {
  ["path":"VDump":private]=>
  string(9) "/this/way"
  ["extensions":protected]=>
  array(2) {
    [0]=>
    string(3) "csv"
    [1]=>
    string(3) "txt"
  }
  ["file"]=>
  NULL
}
VDump Object
(
    [path:VDump:private] => /this/way
    [extensions:protected] => Array
        (
            [0] => csv
            [1] => txt
        )

    [file] =>
)
DirkMacBook:chapter5 dirk$
```

As you can see, although `print_r()`'s output is cleaner, `var_dump()`'s is more informative. What is also interesting to note is that both functions have access to and display information about private properties. Unfortunately, neither function displays any information about the methods of the class.

highlight_string(string str [, bool return]) and highlight_file(string filename [, bool return])

The `highlight_string()` function outputs a syntax-highlighted string of the first argument passed to it. `highlight_file()` does the same thing for source code in a file. The following relationship is true: `highlight_string (file_get_contents(filename)) == highlight_file(filename)`. Either function will return rather than output the string if the optional second parameter is TRUE. These functions are extremely useful when displaying the lines of code surrounding an error. However, they can clearly be a security risk and should under no circumstance be used outside a development environment. After all, you do not want to display any production code in the browser and provide an attack vector to any would-be hacker of your site.

get_class([object object])

Given an object as argument, this function returns the name of the class or FALSE if the argument is not an object.

get_object_vars(object object)

This function returns an associative array of the properties of an object that are visible from the scope from which the function was called. The property name and the corresponding value constitute the key-value pairs of associative array being returned.

get_class_methods(mixed class_name)

This function returns an array of method names of the class that was passed in as a parameter. Note that `get_class_methods()` will only return the names of methods that are visible from the current scope.

get_class_vars(string class_name)

Similar to the preceding method, `get_class_var()` returns an associative array of properties and their default value as specified in the definition of the class. Note that only the properties that are accessible from the current scope will be returned. In other words, `private` and `protected` properties will not be returned when `get_class_vars()` is being called from outside the class.

debug_backtrace()

Any time this function is called, it generates an associative array containing a combination of the output of some of the functions mentioned in this section; as well as some of the magic constants listed below. Specifically, the array includes the following keys: `function`, `line`, `file`, `class`, `object`, `type`, and `args`.

debug_print_backtrace()

Although the names of the functions are quite similar, `debug_print_backtrace()` provides much more detail than its cousin `debug_backtrace()`. This function is much more akin to what you might be used to in other programming languages in terms of a backtrace. Output consists of `eval()` expressions, `included/required` files, and functions calls to bring code execution to the line of execution from which the `debug_print_backtrace()` function was called.

exit([string status]) or exit (int status)

When debugging, you often want to terminate the flow of execution after it gets to the trouble spot and you have to output your debug information. Most of the time you will want to call `exit()` to stop execution. However, did you know that you can also use `exit()` to output your debug info? For example, `exit("Result was: $result\n")` will output a debug statement with the value of `$result` and then exit the program.

The other version of `exit()` takes as argument an integer which will be returned by the program when it terminates. Exit status 0 means that the program terminated normally; whereas, any integer greater than zero indicates an error condition.

Magic constants

Magic constants are constants that are automatically defined for an executing script. Their respective values depend on which file, class, method, and line of the script is currently being executed.

__FILE__: This stands for the absolute path and name of the file that contains the line on which the constant occurs.

__LINE__: This constant contains the line within the file in which it occurs.

__CLASS__: It contains the name of the class in which the constant occurs. It is empty if it occurs outside of a class.

__**DIR**__: This constant represents the absolute path to the directory containing the file in which the constant occurs. This is equivalent to `dirname(__FILE__)`. (New in PHP 5.3.0).

__**FUNCTION**__: This constant is non-empty in top-level functions and methods of classes. It contains the name of the function or method.

__**CLASS**__: If used inside a class, this constant holds the name of the class. Outside of any class, it is empty.

__**METHOD**__: The `__METHOD__` magic constant is identical to `__FUNCTION__` with the only difference that I'm aware of is that it also returns the name of the class if used within a method of that class.

__**NAMESPACE**__: This constant holds the name of the current name space. (New in PHP 5.3.0).

Writing our own debugging class

Now that we have a nice arsenal of functions and constants that can give us more information about trouble spots in our code, let's see how we can best use them. Of course, there is nothing wrong with putting `echo()` and `exit()` statements in your code to output a variable or array. It's a quick way to confirm any suspicions you might have about the behavior of your code already. However, if you want to see more information without having to write much debug code on the spot, it is convenient to have a reusable class that will take care of that for you.

Functional requirements

Let's start with some requirements that we would like to see to make this class both simple to use and powerful for debugging at the same time. First, the code that needs to be included or executed should be as small and compact as possible. Having everything in a single file or class would be ideal.

Second, this utility should be invoked easily. Instead of having to write a lot of additional code to output the debug info we need, our little helper should be at our command with a single line of code to invoke it.

Third, it should be able to handle different output formats. Primarily, I would like it to output HTML because most PHP applications are web-based and viewing our debug output in a browser would allow us to organize the information a little better. However, it should also be able to output debug information in plain text so we can use it from the command line when debugging scripts on the server directly or when writing command line scripts.

Fourth, in addition to using this utility for spot-checking our code, it should be able to handle exceptions as well. Hopefully, the code you have been writing is taking advantage of exceptions. After all, exceptions are the preferred way of handling condition out of our control in PHP 5.x and higher. Besides, exceptions represent an easy way to collect and display a lot of information about the state of the executing program at the point in the logical flow where the exception occurred.

Fifth, since various core PHP functions and various modules generate errors instead of exceptions, it would be a nice feature if we could include such errors in our debug output. Just like exceptions being thrown by native PHP methods or our code, errors can represent unforeseen circumstances in the execution of our program.

Sixth, in addition to displaying information about currently executing line of code, we would want to look at the sequence of functions and methods executed to arrive at the current line of code. This is called a backtrace and often consists of several methods or functions calling each other.

Lastly, in addition to the debug information associated with exceptions and errors, we want to be able to have our utility output any additional variables, objects, or data structures we deem useful in diagnosing the problem.

DebugException

With that somewhat demanding list of requirements, please take a look at the code in the following listing:

```php
<?php
class DebugException extends Exception
{
    const PLAIN = 0;
    const HTML  = 1;

    public static $sourceCodeSpan  = 10;
    public static $outputFormat    = self::HTML;
    public static $errorScope      = E_ERROR;

    protected $addedDebug     = array();

    public function __construct($message, $code = 0)
    {
        // make sure everything is assigned properly
        parent::__construct($message, $code);

        // additional debug info?
        if (func_num_args() > 2) {
```

```
                $this->addedDebug = array_slice(func_get_args(), 2);
        }
    }


    public function __destruct()
    {
        // intentionally left blank
    }


    // to be called statically once to handle all exceptions & errors
    public static function init()
    {
        // handle all exceptions with this class
        set_exception_handler(array('DebugException',
                                            'exceptionHandler'));

        // handle all errors with this class
        set_error_handler(array('DebugException', 'errorHandler'),
                                            self::$errorScope);

        // auto-detect / guess the output format
        if (php_sapi_name() == 'cli') {

            // plain text for CLI use
            self::$outputFormat = self::PLAIN;

        } else {

            // HTML output otherwise
            self::$outputFormat = self::HTML;
        }
    }


    // unregister error and exception handlers
    public static function unInit()
    {
        // pop exception handler stack
        restore_exception_handler();

        // pop error handler stack
        restore_error_handler();
    }


    // turn errors into DebugExceptions
```

```php
public static function errorHandler($number,
                                    $message,
                                    $file,
                                    $line,
                                    $context)
{
    // convert error to excepton and throw it
    $debugException = new DebugException($number, 0, $context);

    // transfer info to DebugException
    $debugException->file = $file;
    $debugException->line = $line;

    // throw the new DebugException
    throw $debugException;
 }


// catching regular exceptions
public static function exceptionHandler($exception)
{
    // explicitly call this class's __toString()
    self::output($exception);
}


// collects & outputs the debug info
public static function output(Exception $exception)
{
    $output = array();

    // output file name and line number
    $output[] = array('Summary:', 'An exception occurred in file
                           ' . basename($exception->getFile())
             . ' on line ' . $exception->getLine() . '.');

    // output message
    $output[] = array('Error message: ', $exception-
                                          >getMessage());

    // get source code of file that threw exception
    $sourceExcerpt = self::getSourceExcerpt($exception-
                        >getFile(), $exception->getLine());

    $output[] = 'Source code excerpt of lines ' .
                                       $sourceExcerpt['start']
```

```php
                                . ' through ' . $sourceExcerpt['end'] . ' of file
                                       ' . $exception->getFile() . ':';

        // highlight syntax for HTML output
        if (self::$outputFormat == self::HTML) {
            $output[] = array('', highlight_string(implode('',
                                    $sourceExcerpt['source']), TRUE));
        } elseif (self::$outputFormat == self::PLAIN) {
            $output[] = implode('', $sourceExcerpt['source']);
        }


        // get backtrace nicely formatted
        $formattedTraces = self::getFormattedTrace($exception);


        // get additionally debug info nicely formatted
        $output = array_merge($output,
                        self::getFormattedDebugInfo($exception));


        // format output depending on how $outputFormat is set
        // output HTML first
        if (self::$outputFormat == self::HTML) {

            // have a show/hide link for each trace
            for ($i = 0; $i < sizeof($formattedTraces); $i++) {
                $output[] = '<a href="" onclick="var bt = document.
getElementById(\'backtrace' . ($i + 1) . '\');if (bt.style.display ==
\'\') bt.style.display = \'none\';else bt.style.display = \'\';return
false;">Backtrace step ' . ($i + 1) . ' (click to toggle):</a>';
                $output[] = self::arrayToTable($formattedTraces[$i],
                                    'backtrace' . ($i + 1));
            }

            echo self::arrayToTable($output, null, 'Debug Output',
                                                FALSE);


        // output plain text
        } elseif (self::$outputFormat == self::PLAIN) {

            // merge traces into output array
            $output = array_merge($output, $formattedTraces);

            // flatten the multi-dimensional array(s) for simple
                                                    outputting
            $flattenedOutput = self::flattenArray($output);
```

```
        echo implode(PHP_EOL, $flattenedOutput);
    }
}

// extracts +/- $sourceCodeSpan lines from line $line of file
                                                    $file
public static function getSourceExcerpt($file, $line)
{
    // get source code of file that threw exception
    $source = file($file);

    // limit source code listing to +/- $sourceCodeSpan lines
    $startLine = max(0, $line - self::$sourceCodeSpan - 1);
    $offset = min(2 * self::$sourceCodeSpan + 1, count($source) -
                            $line + self::$sourceCodeSpan + 1);

    $sourceExcerpt = array_slice($source, $startLine, $offset);

    if ($startLine > 0) {
        array_unshift($sourceExcerpt, "<?php\n", "// ...\n");
    }

    // return source excerpt and start/end lines
    return array('source' => $sourceExcerpt,
                 'start'  => $startLine,
                 'end'    => $startLine + $offset);
}

// creates array containing formatted backtrace
// uses syntax highlighting for source code if
// $outputFormat is HTML
public static function getFormattedTrace(Exception $exception)
{
    // init output array of formatted traces
    $formattedTraces = array();

    // get traces from exception
    $traces = $exception->getTrace();

    // init counter
    $count = 1;

    // iterate over traces
    foreach ($traces as $aTrace) {
```

```
                // skip the method where we turned an error into an
                                                            Exception
        if ($aTrace['function'] != 'errorHandler') {

            // init output for this trace
            $output = array();

            $output[] = "Backtrace step $count:";

            // output class if given
            if (array_key_exists('class', $aTrace)) {
                $output[] = array('Class: ', $aTrace['class']);
            }

            // output type if given
            if (array_key_exists('type', $aTrace)) {
                $output[] = array('Type: ', $aTrace['type']);
            }

            // output function if given
            if (array_key_exists('function', $aTrace)) {

                $output[] = array('Function: ',
                                        $aTrace['function']);

                // output argument to function
                if (array_key_exists('args', $aTrace)) {
                    $output[] = array('', 'with argument(s): ' .
                              implode(', ', $aTrace['args']));
                }
            }

            // get source code of file that threw exception
            $sourceExcerpt =
        self::getSourceExcerpt($aTrace['file'], $aTrace['line']);

            $output[] = 'Source code excerpt of lines ' .
                                        $sourceExcerpt['start']
                    . ' through ' . $sourceExcerpt['end'] . '
                          of file ' . $aTrace['file'] . ':';

            // highlight syntax for HTML output
            if (self::$outputFormat == self::HTML) {
                $output[] = array('', highlight_string(implode('',
```

```
$sourceExcerpt['source']), TRUE));
            } elseif (self::$outputFormat == self::PLAIN) {
                $output[] = implode('', $sourceExcerpt['source']);
            }

            $formattedTraces[] = $output;

            // increase step counter
            $count++;
        }
    }
    return $formattedTraces;
}


// formats the variables & objects passed to the constructor
// and stored in $addedDebug. Uses syntax highlighting for
// source code if $outputFormat is HTML
public static function getFormattedDebugInfo(Exception
                                                    $exception)
{
    // init output array
    $output = array();

    // only the DebugException class has the addedDebug property
    if (get_class($exception) == __CLASS__) {

        if (count($exception->addedDebug) > 0) {
            $output[] = 'Additional debug info:';
        }

        // iterate over each variable
        foreach ($exception->addedDebug as $addBug) {
            foreach ($addBug as $debugLabel => $debugVar) {

                // format with print_r
                if (self::$outputFormat == self::HTML) {
                    $output[] = array($debugLabel, '<pre>' .
                            print_r($debugVar, TRUE) . '</pre>');
                } elseif (self::$outputFormat == self::PLAIN) {
                    $output[] = array($debugLabel,
                                        print_r($debugVar, TRUE));
                }
            }
        }
```

```
        }
        return $output;
    }


    // converts an array of items to output to an HTML table
    // expects format:
    //          array('some text here',          <- single cell on row 1
    //                array('label', $value),    <- two cells on row 2
    //                                           (label and value)
    //                .);
    public static function arrayToTable(array $contents = array(),
                                        $id = null,
                                        $caption = null,
                                        $hideByDefault = TRUE)
    {
        $html = '';


        // open table tag
        if (count($contents) > 0) {
            $html .= '<table style="width: 100%;border: 2px solid
                                                                $html
.= ($hideByDefault) ? 'none' : '';
            $html .= ';"';
            $html .= ($id != null) ? " id=\"$id\"" : '';
            $html .= ">\n";
        }


        // add caption
        if (!empty($caption) > 0) {
            $html .= '<caption><h2>' . htmlentities($caption) .
                                             "</h2></caption>\n";
        }


        $rowCount = 1;
        $rowColors = array('#fff', '#ccc');


        // iterate over input array
        foreach ($contents as $row) {
            $html .= "<tr style=\"background: " .
                             $rowColors[($rowCount % 2)] . ";\">\n";


            // split arrays into label and field
            if (is_array($row) && count($row) >= 2) {
                    $html .= '<td><strong>' . htmlentities($row[0]) .
    "</strong></td>\n"
```

```
                                   . '<td>' . $row[1] . "</td>\n";

           // output single strings on a row by themselves
           } else {
               $html .= '<th colspan="2" style="text-align: left;">'
. $row . "</th>\n";
           }

           $html .= "</tr>\n";

           $rowCount++;
       }

       // close table tag
       if (count($contents) > 0) {
           $html .= "</table>\n";
       }
       return $html;
   }

   // takes a multi-dimensional array and flattens it for plain text
                                                              output
   public static function flattenArray(array $inputArray = array())
   {
       $outputArray = array();

       // iterate over input array items
       foreach ($inputArray as $item) {

           if (is_array($item)) {
               // use recursion to traverse the hierarchy
               $outputArray = array_merge($outputArray,
                                    self::flattenArray($item));
           } else {
               array_push($outputArray, $item);
           }
       }
       return $outputArray;
   }
}

DebugException::init();
?>.
```

There is a lot to absorb so let's take it one step at a time. The first thing you will notice is that the DebugException class we are defining extends PHP's built-in Exception class. That way, we can more or less treat it like any other exception in our code.

We start the class by defining two class constants that serve as labels to the two types of output formatting we will be supporting, namely HTML and plain text. The property $outputFormat should be set to the value of either of those two constants and we initialize it to be HTML. The assumption is that most of the time we will be using this utility class in a web-based debug session.

There are two additional static properties. First, $sourceCodeSpan is an integer that indicates the number of lines preceding and following an error line number that will be extracted from the source file and displayed to the user. Second, $errorScope determines which errors will be intercepted by our class and converted to an exception. Possible values for $errorScope correspond to the valid setting for error_reporting in the php.ini configuration file.

Since we are extending the Exception class, our constructor requires the exact same arguments as the parent class and calling the parent constructor is the first thing we are doing. However, using the func_num_args() and func_get_args() functions we are able to support additional parameters to the constructor. To be precise, we allow any number of additional arguments that will simply be stored in the $addedDebug property. The idea is that we can pass any variables or objects that we wish to display in our debug output to the constructor when we instantiate and throw our DebugException class.

The init() method is crucial to the way the DebugException class operates. It sets two static methods to be the exception and error handler. What this means is that the method DebugException::errorHandler will be called for any error that occurs in our application. Analogously, execution will be handed off to the DebugException ::exceptionHandler() method whenever the interpreter encounters an uncaught exception, including a DebugException. What this means in practice is that we only have to throw an exception at the line in our code where we want to generate debug output for the DebugException class to take over. In other words, all errors and exceptions will be handled by our class and to intentionally generate debug output all we have to do is generate one such error or exception. We will see how that is actually done in an example following the walk-through of the code.

The other thing that the init() method does is that it tries to make an educated guess as to whether the output is best rendered in HTML or PLAIN format. The php_sapi_name() function provides information about the **SAPI (Server Application Programming Interface)** with which the currently running PHP executable was built. Chances are that php_sapi_name() will return cli if we're running a script from the command line. For simplicity, we assume that all other SAPIs signal that HTML output should be generated.

As the `DebugException` class registers itself as the handler of all exceptions and errors, we provide a convenient method for undoing that in case you want to continue execution of your code unchanged after generating debug info. The `uninit()` method complements the `init()` method and uses the `restore_exception_handler()` and `restore_error_handler()` methods to unregister itself and reinstate the previous exception and error handlers.

Now we come to the static methods that are actually invoked in case an uncaught error or exception is encountered. The `DebugException::errorHandler()` method is straightforward. It takes the parameters generated by an error and uses them to throw a new `DebugException`. We can do this because exceptions and errors are quite similar in terms of the information they generate. Both have a message, a filename, a line number, and a backtrace of other functions called for execution to arrive at the line where the error or exception occurred.

The `DebugException::exceptionHandler()` method is even simpler. It takes any exception passed in, which should be any uncaught exception in our code, and passes it to the static method `DebugException::output()`.

The `output()` method is where most of the heavy lifting is done. It basically takes an exception and starts assembling an array of information to be displayed at the end of the method. It does all this by functioning as a dispatcher for five additional methods: `getSourceExcerpt()`, `getFormattedTrace()`, `getFormattedDebugInfo()`, `arrayToTable()`, and `flattenArray()`. We'll defer a detailed discussion of these helper methods until after having looked at the `output()` method.

First, the method `output()` summarizes the error message, filename, and line number in plain English. It also uses utility method `DebugException::getSourceExcerpt()` to extract a partial source code listing of the file in which the error or exception occurred. If the `$ouputFormat` property is set to HTML, the `hightlight_string()` function will be used to apply syntax highlighting to the source code excerpt.

Another integral part of our output is the backtrace of functions or methods that were called from the top level of our script to get to the point where the exception or error occurred. Unless your object hierarchy is flat, it can happen pretty quickly that various objects are calling methods of other objects. Before you know it, your code has traversed seven or eight methods that all make their way into the backtrace. Viewing that much output can be overwhelming and confusing. The detail to help you fix your code might be lost in a flood of information.

The `output()` method enlists the help of the `DebugException::getFormattedTrace()` method to pull in information about each trace, which is formatted similar to the main exception/error information in that it contains a filename, line number, and a source code excerpt. Since each backtrace can provide quite a bit of information and there may be any number of these backtraces, we employ a little JavaScript to toggle the visibility of each backtrace. By default, the user only sees a hyperlink for each trace that will show the whole trace when clicked.

Next, the `DebugException::getFormattedDebugInfo()` method is in charge of aggregating the additional debug variables that were passed to the constructor of our class.

At the end, the only thing left is for the `output()` method to display the information that was collected in the `$output` array. If the requested output format is PLAIN, it will use the `flattenArray()` method to convert our multi-dimensional output array to a one-dimensional and simply implode the array of text. However, if the requested format is HTML, it will use `DebugException::arrayToTable()` to organize the output in an HTML table to make it more visually appealing and easier to read.

Having worked through the actions of the `output()` method, let's take a look at the cast of supporting methods that are doing much of the work. First, `getSourceExcerpt()` takes the absolute path to file on the server and a line number as input. It then reads that file and tries to extract the line number from the input parameter and any number lines preceding and following it. The default of how many additional surrounding lines to be returned is 10 and it is specified in the `DebugException::$sourceCodeSpan` property. The method is smart enough to know if fewer lines are available because the target line number is too close to the beginning or end of the file. The `getSourceExcerpt()` returns an array containing the source code extract; as well as the number of the first and last line actually extracted.

Next, `getFormattedTrace()` iterates over the array of backtraces. For each trace, it extracts the class, type, and function name. Finally, it also uses `getSourceExcerpt()` to include some lines of code surrounding the trace point.

`getFormattedDebugInfo()` starts off by checking the class of the exception being passed as a parameter. Since the `$addedDebug` property belongs to the `DebugException` class, we only need to proceed if the exception is of that class. However, once we have established that we are dealing with the correct class, we simply iterate over `$addedDebug` and use the `print_r()` function to return a human readable representation of the value of each item.

The second to last method we need to cover is `arrayToTable()`. This method will be invoked only when the `$outputFormat` property is set to HTML. Its purpose is to convert an array of output data to an HTML table for easier reading. The method expects an input array where each item corresponds to a row in the table to be constructed. There are two options for each item in the array. If the item is an array, it will be assumed that the first item in the sub-array is the label and the second item is the value. All other items in the sub-array will be ignored. The label and value will be converted to an HTML table row with two cells. Alternatively, if the item in the output array is not an array, it will simply be printed on an individual row of the table. `arrayToTable()` also takes some optional arguments: an ID to assign to the table for easier manipulation using JavaScript, a caption, and a Boolean flag determining whether the content of the table will first be rendered hidden or not.

Finally, the last method to look at is `flattenArray()`, which takes our multi-dimensional output array of debug info and converts it to a one-dimensional one that can be easily imploded to generate plain text output. This method is only used when `$outputFormat` is set to `PLAIN`, which is typically the case when you are working from the command line or saving the output to a log file.

Using DebugException

Wow—that was certainly a lot to digest! Luckily, for all the code we had to absorb, actually using the `DebugException` class couldn't be easier. All we have to do is include the class before we want to use it, registering the exception and error handler methods by calling `DebugException::init()`, and throwing a `DebugException` whenever we want to generate some output. Let's look at the simple example in the following listing:

```php
<?php
require_once('classes/DebugException.php');

class DebugExample
{
    private $imHiding = FALSE;

    public function trySomething()
    {
        $this->somethingWrong('dead');
    }

    public function somethingWrong($bang)
    {
        $ie = array('just'  => 'something',
                    'to'    => 'output',
                    'for'   => 'the',
                    'Debug' => 'Exception');

        throw new DebugException("exceptions are no good!",
                            null,
```

```
                                        array('A local associative array' =>
                                                                    $ie,
                                             'The current object is class '
                                                     . __CLASS__ => $this));
//          throw new Exception("exceptions are no good!");
//          trigger_error("errors are no good!");
     }
}

$debugExample = new DebugExample();

$debugExample->trySomething();
?>
```

The DebugExample class in the above listing doesn't really serve any purpose other
than to illustrate our DebugException class. After including the DebugException
class and instantiating DebugExample, the code calls method trySomething(),
which in turn calls method somethingWrong(). We're doing this merely to generate
a backtrace. Inside somethingWrong() we then proceed to throw a DebugException.
Note how the third argument to the constructor contains additional variables that we
would like to be displayed in the debug output.

If we were to throw a regular exception at this point, the output displayed in the
browser would look something like this:

> **Fatal error**: Uncaught exception 'Exception' with message 'exceptions are no
> good!' in /Users/dirk/Sites/phpdoc/c6/debug.php:20 Stack trace: #0 /Users
> /dirk/Sites/phpdoc/c6/debug.php(11): DebugExample->somethingWrong('dead')
> #1 /Users/dirk/Sites/phpdoc/c6/debug.php(34):
> DebugExample->trySomething() #2 {main} thrown in **/Users/dirk/Sites
> /phpdoc/c6/debug.php** on line **20**

The way a regular exception gets displayed is only somewhat informative. Much
of the available information is being omitted and what is being displayed is not
organized very well. Now let's take a look at the output our DebugException
class generates:

Debug Output

Summary: An exception occurred in file debug.php on line 23.

Error message: exceptions are no good!

Source code excerpt of lines 12 through 33 of file /Users/dirk/Sites/phpdoc/c6/debug.php:

```php
<?php
// ...

    public function somethingWrong($bang)
    {
        $ie = array('just'  => 'something',
                    'to'    => 'output',
                    'for'   => 'the',
                    'Debug' => 'Exception');
//      throw new Exception("exceptions are no good!",
//                          null);

        throw new DebugException("exceptions are no good!",
                                 null,
                                 array('A local associative array' => $ie,
                                       'The current object is class ' . __CLASS__ => $this));
//      throw new Exception("exceptions are no good!");
//      trigger_error("errors are no good!");
    }
}

$debugExample = new DebugExample();
```

Additional debug info:

A local associative array	`Array`
	`(`
	`    [just] => something`
	`    [to] => output`
	`    [for] => the`
	`    [Debug] => Exception`
	`)`

The current object is class DebugExample	`DebugExample Object`
	`(`
	`    [imHiding:private] =>`

Backtrace step 1 (click to toggle):

Backtrace step 2 (click to toggle):

Backtrace step 2:

Class:	DebugExample
Type:	->
Function:	trySomething
	with argument(s):

Source code excerpt of lines 23 through 36 of file /Users/dirk/Sites/phpdoc/c6/debug.php:

```php
<?php
// ...
                                 null,
                                 array('A local associative array' => $ie,
                                       'The current object is class ' . __CLASS__ => $this));
//      throw new Exception("exceptions are no good!");
//      trigger_error("errors are no good!");
    }
}
$debugExample = new DebugExample();
$debugExample->trySomething();
?>
```

As you can see, the new format is much more complete and informative. For starters, it includes source code excerpts that let you inspect the code right there in the browser without having to switch to your development environment. It also includes a complete hierarchy of backtraces. However, so as not to clutter the initial display, they are hidden until you decide to view them by clicking on the corresponding link. The above screenshot shows the second backtrace while the first one is still hidden.

There is also a section for "Additional debug info" that displays the extra parameters we passed to the DebugExceptions's constructor. And the best part of it is that all this happens without having to write any code in the file we are debugging.

What happens if PHP encounters an error or exception rather than us throwing an exception on purpose? You'll be happy to know that the output looks nearly identical. Although, we do lose the ability to pass in additional debug variables to be displayed.

As you know from our discussion of the DebugException class, it can also generate plain text output. Obviously you lose some of the niceties of the HTML version, but you still get the source code excerpts, backtraces, and thoughtful organization. All you have to do to enable plain text output is to set the $outputFormat property to PLAIN before any of the output gets generated.

```php
<?php
require_once('classes/DebugException.php');

DebugException::init();
DebugException::$outputFormat = DebugException::PLAIN

// debug output will be in plain text …
?>
```

Here is the same debug output formatted for plain text display. It is long enough that it made sense to only show the beginning and end while still gaining an understanding of the functionality of the underlying code.

```
Terminal — bash — bash — Dirk — ttys003 — 80×40 — ⌘2
DirkMacBook:chapter5 dirk$ php ./debug.php
Summary:
An exception occurred in file debug.php on line 21.
Error message:
exceptions are no good!
Source code excerpt of lines 10 through 31 of file /Volumes/Documents/Work/Wafer
Thin/Packt/Book/Code/chapter5/debug.php:
<?php
// ...
                $this->somethingWrong('dead');
        }

        public function somethingWrong($bang)
        {
                $ie = array('just'  => 'something',
                            'to'    => 'output',
                            'for'   => 'the',
                            'Debug' => 'Exception');

                throw new DebugException("exceptions are no good!");
        }
}

DebugException::init();
DebugException::$outputFormat = DebugException::PLAIN;


Source code excerpt of lines 18 through 31 of file /Volumes/Documents/Work/Wafer
Thin/Packt/Book/Code/chapter5/debug.php:
<?php
// ...
                            'Debug' => 'Exception');

                throw new DebugException("exceptions are no good!");
        }
}

DebugException::init();
DebugException::$outputFormat = DebugException::PLAIN;

$debugExample = new DebugExample();
$debugExample->trySomething();

?>
DirkMacBook:chapter5 dirk$ 
```

The way I use the DebugException class is that I include it in my bootstrap file or
a particular source file during development. Any exception or error will be displayed
nicely formatted. If I need more info at a particular line in the code, all I have to
do is throw a DebugException and pass it to all variables I wish to display in the
third parameter.

Remember to remove all references to the DebugException class
before deploying to production. Exposing your source code and
filesystem information to end-users in this way poses a serious
security vulnerability.

DebugException: Pros and cons

With everything the `DebugException` class does for us, we have also taken a couple of shortcuts that should not be ignored. First, how the information can be viewed is integrated into the class itself. We are essentially trading a tight coupling between the formatting of the output and the actual data against compactness. If we wanted to support additional ways of outputting, writing to a log file for example, we pretty much have to modify the class. `DebugExample` is not exactly a shining example of object-oriented design, but it is very compact and easy to use. That design decision was made intentionally. If you wanted to use `DebugException` as the basis for your own small debugging framework, you will probably want to create some classes to hold backtraces and other debug data and other classes to handle the view layer.

If you go back a couple of pages and review our original design goals, you will see that we have achieved all of them. `DebugException` is small and compact, easy to use, and generates both HTML and plain text output. The HTML version takes advantage of source code highlighting and dynamically showing/hiding content via JavaScript. Moreover, `DebugException` handles regular (uncaught) exceptions and converts errors to exceptions, which are then handled by the class itself. Finally, it displays backtraces, source code excerpts, and any number of additional debug variables.

Introducing Xdebug

So far we have been talking about debugging PHP scripts by outputting info at one or more places in your code. Now it is time to look at a professional tool that will facilitate that activity. It also allows us to take things a step further.

Xdebug is a Zend extension that is able to hook into the internals of the PHP interpreter. With that ability comes added power over simply outputting debug information with echo statements. Among its many features, in this chapter we want to focus on the ones specifically designed to find, diagnose, and fix bugs. In particular, we will be looking at improved output of stack traces, function traces, and variables; as well as support for interactively debugging scripts locally and remotely.

In addition to the Xdebug features to be discussed below, it offers the following tools that we will look at in other chapters of this book:

- **Code Profiling** allows you to optimize the performance of your application
- **Code Coverage Analysis** feature will be used to test applications

Xdebug is an Open Source project that was started and is being maintained by the main developer, Derick Rethans. This debugger has been around since about 2003 and is at version 2.0.5, which is PHP 5.3 compatible, as of this writing. It runs on Mac, Linux, and Windows and you can find out more about it at `http://www.xdebug.org/`.

Installing Xdebug

The preferred way of installing Xdebug is via PECL. PECL is a sister repository to PEAR and both share the same packaging and distribution system. While both PECL and PEAR command line clients support the same set of commands, they differ in which repository they access. Following is an excerpt of the output generated when using the PECL command to install Xdebug:

```
                Terminal — bash — bash — Dirk — ttys001 — 80×38 — ⌘2
DirkMacBook:bin dirk$ sudo pecl install xdebug
Password:
downloading xdebug-2.0.5.tgz ...
Starting to download xdebug-2.0.5.tgz (289,234 bytes)
....................................................done: 289,234 bytes
67 source files, building
WARNING: php_bin /usr/local/apache2/php/bin/php appears to have a suffix /bin/ph
p, but config variable php_suffix does not match
running: phpize
Configuring for:
PHP Api Version:        20090626
Zend Module Api No:     20090626
Zend Extension Api No:  220090626
configure.in:150: warning: AC_CACHE_VAL(lt_prog_compiler_static_works, ...): sus
picious cache-id, must contain _cv_ to be cached
../../lib/autoconf/general.m4:2018: AC_CACHE_VAL is expanded from...
... (many line of compiler output go here)
-root/install-xdebug-2.0.5/usr/local/apache2/php/lib/php/extensions
170268758    0 drwxr-xr-x  3 root  wheel    102 Dec 14 14:30 /var/tmp/pear-build
-root/install-xdebug-2.0.5/usr/local/apache2/php/lib/php/extensions/no-debug-non
-zts-20090626
170268759 560 -rwxr-xr-x  1 root  wheel 282936 Dec 14 14:30 /var/tmp/pear-build
-root/install-xdebug-2.0.5/usr/local/apache2/php/lib/php/extensions/no-debug-non
-zts-20090626/xdebug.so

Build process completed successfully
Installing /usr/local/apache2/php/lib/php/extensions/no-debug-non-zts-20090626/x
debug.so
install ok: channel://pecl.php.net/xdebug-2.0.5
configuration option "php_ini" is not set to php.ini location
You should add "extension=xdebug.so" to php.ini
DirkMacBook:bin dirk$ █
```

In addition to the PECL repository, there are other options for installing Xdebug. Windows users can download precompiled modules. The second option is to check the source code out of the project's CVS repository and compile it yourself. Detailed instructions for compiling the code can be found on the xdebug.org website.

Assuming the PECL installation ran without complaining, restart Apache, and check your phpinfo() output. To see your phpinfo() output, create the following simple PHP script and view it in your browser. It will display many details about how PHP was compiled, installed, and configured.

```
<?php
phpinfo();
?>
```

You should see Xdebug mentioned in the copyright/powered by box just below the summary information near the top of the page.

```
This program makes use of the Zend Scripting Language Engine:          Powered By
Zend Engine v2.3.0, Copyright (c) 1998-2009 Zend Technologies
   with Xdebug v2.0.5, Copyright (c) 2002-2008, by Derick Rethans
```

Further down the page, you will also see a section listing all the Xdebug configuration variables. Here is a shortened version of that section:

xdebug		
xdebug support		**enabled**
Version		2.0.4

Supported protocols		**Revision**
DBGp - Common DeBuGger Protocol		$Revision: 1.125.2.6 $
GDB - GNU Debugger protocol		$Revision: 1.87 $
PHP3 - PHP 3 Debugger protocol		$Revision: 1.22 $

Directive	Local Value	Master Value
xdebug.auto_trace	Off	Off
xdebug.collect_includes	On	On
xdebug.collect_params	0	0
xdebug.collect_return	Off	Off
xdebug.collect_vars	Off	Off
xdebug.default_enable	On	On
xdebug.dump.COOKIE	no value	no value
Many Options Omitted		
xdebug.var_display_max_children	128	128
xdebug.var_display_max_data	512	512
xdebug.var_display_max_depth	3	3

 You shouldn't use any other Zend extension at the same time as Xdebug—especially debuggers. They will most likely conflict with each other.

If there is no mention of Xdebug in your `phpinfo()` output, it means that Xdebug was not installed properly. Here are a few pointers on where to start troubleshooting the installation:

- Make sure that you properly restarted your web server after installing Xdebug.

- Check that your active `php.ini` file contains a line telling PHP to load the extension:

```
Terminal — more — bash — Dirk — ttys004 — 80×6 — ⌘2
DirkMacBook:lib dirk$ tail -37 php.ini | more
[xdebug]
; tell PHP where to find the Xdebug extension and load it
zend_extension=/usr/local/apache2/php/lib/php/extensions/no-debug-non-zts-200906
26/xdebug.so
```

(replace `zend_extension` with `zend_extension_ts` on system thread-safe installations of PHP prior to version 5.3). Also, make sure that the path in the above line points to an existing file.

- Scan you web server's and PHP's log files for any startup or initialization errors.

- Consult Xdebug's online installation documentation:
  `http://xdebug.org/docs/install`

Configuring Xdebug

I'm using Xdebug 2.0.5 to write this chapter. This version lists 44 configuration parameters in the `phpinfo()` output. Rather than looking at each and every configuration directive, we will limit ourselves to the ones that affect our task of debugging an application. Besides, the complete list of configuration directives can be viewed on the `xdebug.org` site.

Since Xdebug is a Zend extension, you can configure it by putting configuration settings in your `php.ini` file. Xdebug contains a default for each possible configuration option, which can then be overwritten in `php.ini`. Furthermore, you can then overwrite these settings in Apache's `httpd.conf/.htaccess` file or use the `ini_set()` function in any of your scripts to modify the behavior of Xdebug and the output it generates. Here is the Xdebug specific section I added to my `php.ini` config file:

```
[xdebug]
; tell PHP where to find the Xdebug extension and load it
zend_extension=/usr/local/apache2/php/lib/php/extensions/no-debug-non-
zts-20060613/xdebug.so
; protection
xdebug.max_nesting_level=100
; what to show when outputting variables & debug info
xdebug.show_local_vars=1
xdebug.collect_params=1
xdebug.var_display_max_children=128
xdebug.var_display_max_data=1024
```

```
xdebug.var_display_max_depth=5
xdebug.dump.COOKIE=*
xdebug.dump.FILES=*
xdebug.dump.GET=*
xdebug.dump.POST=*
xdebug.dump.REQUEST=*
xdebug.dump.REQUEST=*
xdebug.dump.SESSION=*
; enable & configure remote debugging
xdebug.remote_enable=1
xdebug.remote_host=127.0.0.1
xdebug.remote_port=9000
xdebug.remote_port=xdebug.remote_handler=dbgp
xdebug.remote_mode=req
xdebug.remote_log=/tmp/xdebug_remote.log
xdebug.remote_autostart=0
xdebug.idekey=dirk
; configure profiler - disabled by default, but can be triggered
xdebug.profiler_enable=0
xdebug.profiler_enable_trigger=1
xdebug.profiler_output_dir=/tmp
xdebug.profiler_output_name=xdebug.out.%s
```

 Remember that PHP can have multiple .ini configuration files. Often, this depends on which SAPI (Server Application Programming Interface) you are using. For example, if you are using PHP from the command line, you are likely using the CLI SAPI, which will by default look for the php-cli.ini config file. If Xdebug is not responding as expected, you might want to make sure that you added the configuration settings to the correct .ini file.

With the default settings in place, you can then fine-tune the configuration in your scripts on an as-needed basis.

```php
<?php
// configure Xdebug locally
ini_set('xdebug.var_display_max_children', 3);
ini_set('xdebug.var_display_max_data', 6);
ini_set('xdebug.var_display_max_depth', 2);
class DebugExample { ... }
?>
```

At this point, I hope that you are thinking back to the beginning of the chapter where we discussed the management of different sets of configuration settings. You might want to create a .ini file dedicated to your application's Xdebug setting. You can then have separate sections that correspond to environments, such as development, production, profiling, and so on.

Immediate benefits

Once Xdebug is configured properly, you can get some of the benefits it provides without having to do much.

var_dump() improved

First, Xdebug overwrites our old friend, the var_dump() function. The new and improved var_dump() function installed by Xdebug formats the output nicer and employs some other formatting and syntax highlighting to make the information easier to digest. Here is an example of what var_dump() output looks like without and with Xdebug enabled.

<table>
<tr><td colspan="2" align="center">var_dump(object) & var_dump(array) Comparison</td></tr>
<tr><td align="center">Without Xdebug</td><td align="center">With Xdebug</td></tr>
<tr><td>

```
object(DebugExample)#1 (2) {
  ["imHiding:private"]=>
  bool(false)
  ["slf"]=>
  object(DebugExample)#1 (2) {
    ["imHiding:private"]=>
    bool(false)
    ["slf"]=>
    *RECURSION*
  }
}
array(4) {
  ["just"]=>
  string(9) "something"
  ["to"]=>
  string(6) "output"
  ["for"]=>
  string(3) "the"
  ["Debug"]=>
  string(9) "Exception"
}
```

</td><td>

```
object(DebugExample)[1]
  private 'imHiding' => boolean false
  public 'slf' =>
    &object(DebugExample)[1]

array
  'just' => string 'someth'... (length=9)
  'to' => string 'output' (length=6)
  'for' => string 'the' (length=3)
  more elements...
```

</td></tr>
</table>

var_dump() settings

The following Xdebug configuration settings affect the behavior of the `var_dump()` function installed by Xdebug:

Setting	Description	Recommended value
`xdebug.var_display_max_children`	Number array elements and object properties to display.	128 (128)
`xdebug.var_display_max_data`	Maximum string length for values of object properties, array elements, and values of variables.	1024 (512)
`xdebug.var_display_max_depth`	How many levels to descend the object / array hierarchy.	5 (3)

Errors and exceptions beautified

The second out-of-the-box benefit Xdebug provides is that errors and uncaught exceptions will be formatted and displayed in HTML. This is similar to the `DebugExceptions` class we constructed previously. Here is an example of the resulting output when throwing an exception in our `DebugExample` class without registering `DebugException` and after enabling Xdebug. Notice how the output includes a listing of variables in local scope when the exception was thrown; as well as a dump of all local and global variables.

Stack trace settings

The following table lists some of the settings that affect how and what information is displayed in the stack trace when Xdebug encounters an error or exception. Rather than presenting a complete listing of all configuration settings, we will focus on the ones that are used most commonly and ones where it pays to change them from their installation default.

Setting	Description	Recommended value
x	Whether to output superglobals listed in `xdebug.dump.*`.	1 (1)
`xdebug.dump.*`	List of superglobals to dump if `xdebug.dump_globals` is enabled.	`xdebug.dump.COOKIE=*` `xdebug.dump.FILES=*` `xdebug.dump.GET=*` `xdebug.dump.POST=*` `xdebug.dump.REQUEST=*` `xdebug.dump.REQUEST=*` `xdebug.dump.SESSION=*`
`xdebug.dump_once`	Whether to dump superglobals on all errors or only on the first one.	1 (1)
`xdebug.dump_undefined`	Whether to include empty superglobals in dump.	1 (0)
`xdebug.show_local_vars`	Whether to dump all variables defined in the local scope (includes top-most scope).	1 (0)
`xdebug.collect_params`	Whether Xdebug should record variable names & values passed to functions.	2 (0)
`xdebug.collect_includes`	Whether to show names of include/require<_once> files in trace files.	1 (1)

Since stack traces make use of the `var_dump()` function when outputting information, the `var_dump()` settings affect the appearance of stack traces as well.

Protection from infinite recursion

If you have a piece of code where a method is being called recursively without the exit condition ever evaluating to TRUE, PHP can quickly exceed its allocated resources, which can result in unpredictable behavior, such as PHP segfaulting or in extreme cases the server locking up.

Luckily, Xdebug provides a configurable limit on the number of recursive calls that are allowed. Here is the corresponding configuration setting:

Setting	Description	Recommended value (default)
`Xdebug.max_nesting_level`	Maximum number of successive recursive function calls.	100 (100)

Remote debugging

One of the most powerful feature Xdebug provides is that of remote debugging. In this context, the term "remote" is somewhat misleading. It simply means that the code is executing in PHP and that the debugger code in the Xdebug extension on the server communicates with a separate debug client. It may be that the debug client and server are on separate machines, but it is not a requirement. If you have your development set up with a web server, such as Apache, executing locally, you can easily have debug client and server running on the same machine. This is the same as a web server and browser running on the same machine. Take a look at the following diagram:

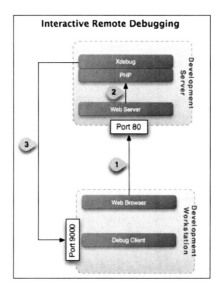

The above diagram illustrates the scenario of development workstation and development web server being two physically different machines. To start things off, the developer would open a web browser and request the page that is being debugged from the server (marker 1). This typically happens over standard port 80. The web server then determines that PHP is responsible for generating the requested page and hands processing off to the PHP executable (marker 2). This might happen based on the file extensions that are associated with PHP, for example. Within PHP, Xdebug figures out that it is supposed to start an interactive debug session. The developer is able to communicate this request to Xdebug by including an extra parameter in the URL. Now that Xdebug has claimed responsibility, it tries to open a connection to the host and port, usually port 9000, listed in the Xdebug configuration settings (marker 3). In this case, the machine running the debug client is the developer's workstation, but that is not a requirement.

The remote debugger provided by Xdebug is most likely what you have come to expect if you have used debuggers in other programming languages, such as C++ or Java. It allows you to issue commands to step through the code one line at a time. At any point, you can examine the variables and data structures that have been defined. It also allows you to set breakpoints where code execution will stop and give you an opportunity to evaluate and/or modify the state of the application before proceeding.

Remote server debug configuration

Before we can do any real remote debugging, we have to configure and enable that feature in Xdebug. Here are the configuration settings that determine the behavior of the debugger on the server:

Setting	Description	Recommended value (default)
`xdebug.remote_enable`	Toggle remote debugger.	`1 (0) - as needed`
`xdebug.remote_host`	The host name or IP address of the machine where the debug client is running.	`localhost (localhost)`
`xdebug.remote_port`	The port on which Xdebug tries to connect to the debug client.	`9000 (9000)`
`xdebug.remote_handler`	The debug protocol which Xdebug will use to communicate with the debug client. Valid settings are `php3`, `GDB`, and the `dbgp`.	`dbgp (dbgp)`

Setting	Description	Recommended value (default)
`xdebug.remote_mode`	Determines when Xdebug initiates the connection to the debug client. Valid settings are `jit` (on error condition) and `req` (as soon as the script starts execution).	`req (req)`
`xdebug.remote_log`	Absolute path to file where all debug communications will be appended.	`/tmp/xdebug_remote. log`
`xdebug.remote_autostart`	Whether Xdebug will always try to connect to the debug client.	`0 (0)`
`xdebug.idekey`	The idekey on the server and the client must match.	`phpdebug ()`

Remember to restart the web server after adding or changing the debug settings.

Debugging client configuration

Once the debugger is running on the server, it is time to fire up the client. Well, first we have to find a client that speaks the DBGp protocol we have configured previously. Luckily there are about twenty options available as of this writing. Xdebug even comes with a simple command line implementation of a DBGp client; however, using that version doesn't exactly make debugging a whole lot easier than using echo statements. The debug client executable that installs along with Xdebug can be used to interact with the server, but you have to know the commands to type on the command line and it is hard to grasp much information with purely text-based output. Furthermore, the responses are in XML, which adds an extra layer of complexity.

What we need is a debug client that takes some of the complexity out of the protocol and lets us focus on understanding and trouble-shooting our application. Tying back to one of the tools featured in another chapter, we'll use Eclipse with the PDT plug-in to give us a graphical UI for our debugging efforts. Although it is a bit challenging to locate all the settings required to get PHP debugging working in Eclipse, once you have it set up correctly, it works like a charm. What's more is that you will pretty much have to specify the same settings no matter which debug client you end up choosing. Following are the dialog boxes and their respective locations in Eclipse's menus that we need to configure remote debugging.

1. We have to let Eclipse know about our remote server. We do this via the **PHP Servers** screen located at **Preferences | PHP | PHP Servers**. This list of servers is used for a number of things, but we need to add our remote server here so we can later refer to it in our debug configuration.

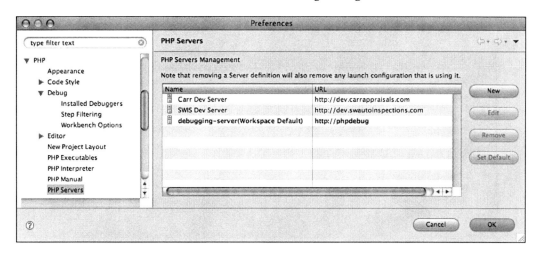

As part of defining a PHP Server, we also need to map a directory on our local workspace to a corresponding URL. You can do this under the **Path Mapping** tab from "**Preferences | PHP | PHP Servers**". For our purposes, I am mapping the code for this chapter to the URL `http://phpdebug` which actually resolves to localhost on my development machine.

2. We need to let Eclipse know about the debugger and its protocol we plan on using. PDT actually comes pre-configured with two debuggers, Xdebug and Zend Debugger. You can review and edit the complete list of debuggers by going to **Preferences | PHP | Debug | Installed Debuggers**. Similar to the servers, we have to make sure that our debugger appears in this list before we can use it in our debug setup.

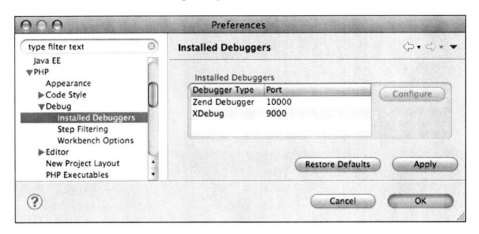

We should also review the detailed settings for Xdebug, the most important of which is the debug port. The **Max array depth** and **Max children** settings correspond to similarly named Xdebug configuration variables.

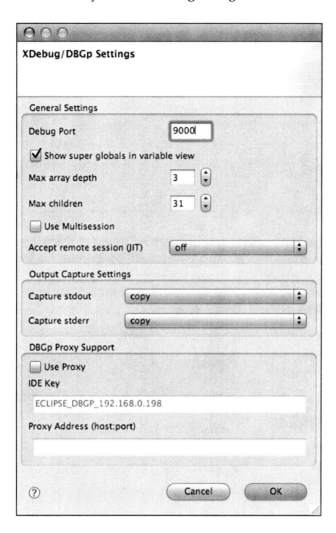

3. We need to tell Eclipse where it can find any local PHP executables. Eclipse will use the executable for parsing and syntax checking of the source code files. To edit or add to the list of PHP executables, open the **Preferences | PHP | PHP Executables** menu option.

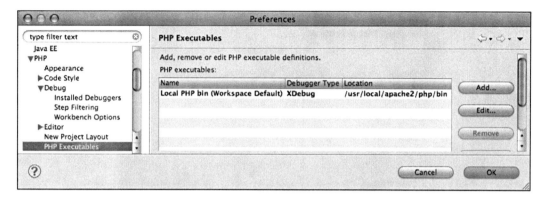

4. Now that we have all the preliminary setup out of the way, we can pull all the pieces together for the debug configuration for our project. Not surprisingly, the debugger, server, and PHP executable we defined in the prior steps make an appearance in this screen that you can find by going to **Project | Properties | PHP Debug**.

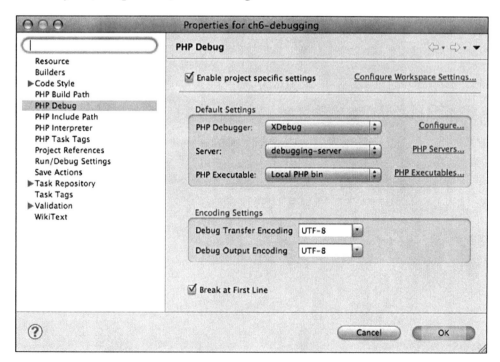

5. Let's select the **Run | Debug Configurations** option to define a debug launch configuration for our project. Select **PHP Web Page** and click on the document icon with a plus sign on it to create a new launch configuration.

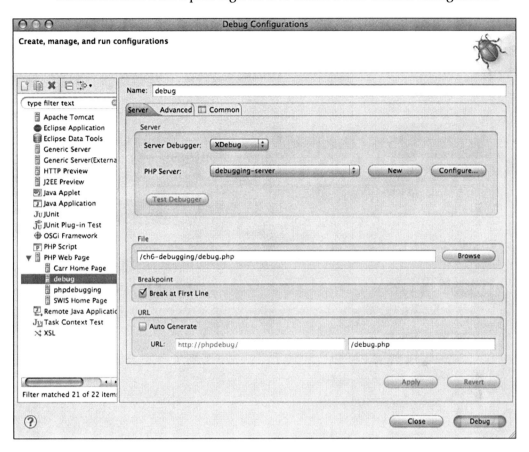

6. Now you can launch a debugging session from the previous dialog. Or, you can always start the same session by clicking on the little bug icon in the toolbar and select the name of the debug configuration you just defined. As soon as you do that, Eclipse will bring up the page to be debugged in the default browser (**Preferences** | **General** | **Web Browser**) and offer to switch to the PHP Debug Perspective.

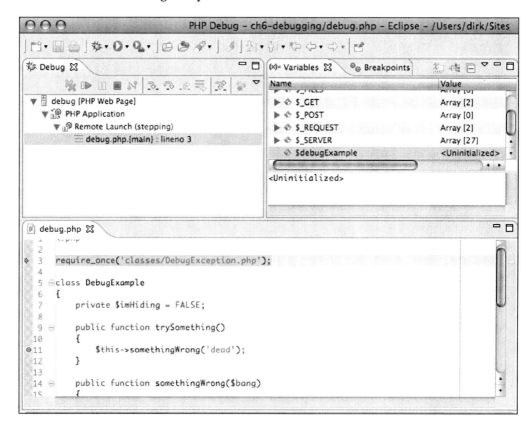

This is what we have been working for. We can now use the little icons in the debug view to step through the code one line at a time, step into functions, step over function, step out of functions, and inspect all local and global variables at the same time.

Setting a breakpoint is as easy as double-clicking in the margin. The little blue circle indicates a breakpoint and the **Breakpoints** view keeps track of all the breakpoints you have placed.

Summary

Just like programming itself, debugging is an art form. Also, the longer you do it, the better you get at it. After several years of developing software, experience and intuition will tell you which portion of the code to zoom in on when there is trouble. At the same time, experience isn't the only way to get better at debugging. Having the right tools at one's disposal and the knowledge to use them can cut down on debugging time significantly and can thus get you back to writing code more quickly. Hopefully, between learning to manage error logging configurations, developing a custom debug class that handles all exceptions and errors, and learning how to debug remotely, there are a few things we talked about in this chapter that you added to your arsenal.

I think that most developers who are not using a debugger are doing so because they think they don't need it. I'll be the first to admit that you can get a lot done with the combination of `echo()`, `var_dump()`, and `exit()`. However, there is something to be said for having all the debugging goodness wrapped into a nice GUI that is able to organize so much information in a digestible format. Another advantage of using a debugger is that you don't have to modify your code unlike when you insert `var_dump()` calls into your source files.

Hopefully, the concepts covered in this chapter will already make you better at debugging your code. Nevertheless, there are plenty of other tools and techniques out there that can make you even more efficient in hunting down those bugs. Ideally, you will use what you have just learned and use it as a starting point for building your own set of tools that are well suited to the way you like to work.

6
PHP Frameworks

Frameworks are a big topic because frameworks tend to be big (not all, though). We can't talk about all the available PHP frameworks because it would take too much space and time. That would be another book (or series). We can't even do any one of the frameworks justice in this chapter, but that is also not necessary for our purposes. There are three things I want to achieve in this chapter:

- Show you why you should consider using a framework
- Help you in determining which framework would be a good fit
- Create a sample project using a framework

Writing your own framework

Writing a framework is almost a rite of passage for most PHP developers. Granted, most frameworks don't end up being as comprehensive as the Zend Framework, but that doesn't mean they are not frameworks.

I have personally been through this cycle and I know several other developers that have done the same. You start by realizing that the same basic problems need to be solved in most of the applications you work on. Initially, you copy code to solve the problem from one project to another. Then you start to make enhancements and before you know it, you're working on your own framework.

Eventually, you come to realize that maintaining and optimizing a framework is a lot of ongoing work. Especially when you realize that some of your early design decisions are creating some problems in the long run. At this point, most developers start looking at and using other frameworks. Or better yet, you can start contributing to your framework of choice and have a say in the direction it takes and the features that get implemented.

Let's consider some basic advantages and disadvantages of using frameworks:

- **Advantages**
  - ° Jump-start development
  - ° Faster development due to code reuse
  - ° Cut down on errors by using proven code
  - ° Provide infrastructure and make it easy for other developers to get started
  - ° Provide design patterns for code quality and to speed up development

- **Disadvantages**
  - ° Makes design decisions for you (good and bad)
  - ° The time it takes to learn the framework or to set it up for each project

If you think about it a bit, you can probably easily add several more pros or cons to the above list. Let's take it a step further and frame our discussion in terms of the criteria you should consider when choosing a framework.

Evaluating and choosing frameworks

Depending on which source you trust (Google, Wikipedia, various PHP websites, and so on), there are around 50+ PHP frameworks available at the time of this writing. That is why I want to try and provide some criteria for finding one that will work best for you.

Most of the criteria for evaluating and choosing a framework discussed in this section apply not only to frameworks, but also to any software project in general. Availability of documentation and code quality are examples of such criteria. Other criteria are more closely related to the nature of a framework. The development philosophy and paradigms, for example, will have an impact on how you end up developing your own code at times, frameworks will nudge you to doing things a certain way. You have to be aware of those biases in order to make an informed decision.

Community and acceptance

One thing to look for is the breadth and depth of the communities that have grown around the framework. There are really two distinct communities that typically spring up around a framework—developers and users.

The more users who have invested time and resources into learning and using the framework, the easier it will be to get support if something goes wrong. However, while the sheer number of adopters is important, the caliber should be a factor as well. You want experienced, qualified, and motivated users to partake in the project. That way, if small bug fixes are required, experienced users can jump in and provide a solution rather than to simply report the problem.

The second community is made up of developers that participate in the core development of the framework itself. Here, too, you want to make sure that the community is large, active, and talented. For example, you want to be certain that the departure of a core team member does not bring the project to a halt. Also, framework developers should be experienced enough to address user concerns, incorporate emerging technologies, and turn out quality code.

Feature road map

What is the process for making design, architecture, and feature changes? Who gets to decide what feature gets implemented next or what bug fixes will be put on the fast track? The answers to these questions will greatly affect the future direction of the framework.

Some frameworks are driven by a small number of core developers. If they are the ones making the decisions, the quality of the resulting outcome directly corresponds to their competence. That can work out very well. If the core team is supremely competent, they will most likely design and code a framework that will do a beautiful job. On the flip side, having a small core team that makes the decisions and handles the coding also means that losing one or more team members can jeopardize the survival of the framework or at least jeopardize the development schedule. Furthermore, it also means that the team is lacking perspective. For a small group to anticipate all the needs of a large group using the framework is likely to result in some requirements being overlooked.

Other frameworks take a more democratic approach. Anybody that has something to contribute to the discussion can do so. In the end however, the decisions have to be made by qualified participants. Voting rights might be limited to official contributors to the project, but a public forum will allow different perspectives to be considered.

Personally, I lean towards the more democratic approach because it allows the people that actually use the framework to shape its direction. Ideally, new features get proposed and discussed in a public forum. Ideas are allowed to gestate before being turned into specifications. The more community members provide informed input, the better it is for everybody. A similar process should be in place for analyzing and criticizing technical specifications. Eventually, someone will have to decide what gets implemented and how, for the community at large to benefit.

Documentation

Before you commit to a framework, make sure you look at the developer and/or user documentation the project puts out. If the documentation is lacking, you will likely have to invest serious time in figuring out how things work by digging through source code and searching the Web. This pretty much negates one of the main reasons for having a framework—rapid development.

You want to be able to isolate the features of the framework you want to implement, look them up in the documentation, and pick up what you need to know without having to resort to any additional resources.

Hopefully, the documentation has been collected in a central location, which is the case with a user manual and API documentation. You are losing a lot of the convenience if you have to sift through hundreds of support forum messages to find an answer that you should be able to easily look up in a table of contents or index.

Lastly, documentation doesn't have to be coming from the project itself. It's nice to have free documentation, but if there are books available that do the job, that is probably acceptable as well. Either way, you want to make sure that the learning curve is not made any steeper than it already is by the lack of easily accessible and centralized documentation and examples.

Code quality

Being a developer, you should have no problem judging the quality of the code of the framework—especially after reading this book. It might not read exactly like your own code, but it is critical that the code be well thought out, easy to understand, and follow commonly accepted principles. After all, how can you be expected to build your own application on top of a framework that is made up of questionable code?

The easiest thing to do is to download the framework and start opening up some files. Here are some of the things I typically look for when doing a code survey:

- Plenty of helpful inline comments
- Use of object-oriented principles: inheritance, interfaces, and so on.
- Try-catch statements
- Short methods
- A minimum of required configuration and setup

You want to be able to peruse the source and come away thinking you would be proud turning out this kind of code. There is still no guarantee that it works correctly or suits your purpose, but it is a step in the right direction.

Coding standards and compliance

Although this criterion is closely related to overall code quality, I decided that it deserved its own treatment. As you already know from the corresponding chapter, coding standards have various benefits, but it becomes even more important in the case of a project that is being used and contributed to by many users. Coding standards become essential when contributions come from many different sources because they make integration of the code and reading it so much easier.

If you look at the prominent PHP frameworks, they all have their own coding standard. Some decide to spell their standards out in more detail. Others leave a lot of freedom to the individual developers. Either way, a coding standard will make it much easier for everybody's code to work together.

Also, if you ever have to consult the source code to see exactly how a feature works (or why not), you will have a much easier time navigating the source code tree if it follows a common layout and files adhere to a naming convention that has been spelled out.

Project fit

When comparing frameworks, you should start with a list of requirements for your application that you would expect the framework to handle for you. The more those requirements are met, the better the framework meets your needs.

There are frameworks that try to anticipate just about any need a developer might have while creating an application. Others are more narrowly focused in that they try to solve one specific problem. Zend Framework is an example of the former; whereas, Propel is an example of the latter. ZF offers many modules and continues to expand at a rapid pace. Propel, on the other hand, focuses on providing an ORM layer.

If you have a very specific need, you might not want to burden your project with a large framework. In that case, you might as well select the one framework that best addresses your need. However, if you are looking to leverage several of the framework's modules and anticipate adding more as your application grows, you probably want to look at frameworks that try to cover the gamut.

Easy to learn and adapt

Not having to solve the same problems over and over again for each project you undertake is a big motivation for using a framework. Just about everybody that develops software for a living has to justify the time spent on various tasks, whether it is to oneself or the person signing the paycheck. You can reasonably expect to have to spend some time to become familiar with the conventions, ideology, and specific tools of a framework, but you don't want it to slow you down too much.

Similarly, you will eventually encounter situations where the framework comes up short. If it is a solution that you expect to require again in the future, you will probably want to extend the framework rather than to code a one-off solution specific for your project. The question then becomes how easy is it to extend the framework and add the functionality you need? Did the designers of the framework plan for others to be easily able to extend the functionality? Is it easy to overwrite existing classes or implement interfaces to implement what you need?

Here are some signs that the framework may not be resulting in the time saving benefits for which you have been hoping:

- You find yourself consulting the same manual page over and over again. This might be a sign that the underlying concepts are too complex to be practical or that the documentation is insufficient.

- You discover that you have to implement several other features that you had not anticipated. Perhaps the modules of the framework are too tightly coupled?

- Does it seem like the easiest way of adding or changing functionality is to modify the framework's own code?

Open source

With PHP being an interpreted rather than a compiled programming language, it is kind of hard not to distribute the source code with an application. However, it's not impossible. There is a group of tools that allow developers to hide, obfuscate, or encrypt their code. Also, just because you have access to the source code doesn't mean that you are allowed to make changes. Depending on the license under which the framework is being distributed, you may or may not be allowed to modify and redistribute the source code.

Considering that we as PHP developers are benefiting from a whole stack of open source software (PHP, Apache, Linux, MySQL and so on) and the benefit we are getting from being able to change the source code if we want to, I prefer frameworks (and most other software I use) to be distributed under some flavor of liberal open source license.

Familiarity

There is something to be said for using a tool you already know can do the job. Consider the programming language(s) we use. All the time we invest in learning the features and idiosyncrasies of a programming language such as PHP pays off in the long run as we are able to produce better code faster. It is for that reason that the average developer doesn't switch his preferred language in which to code every year or so.

I would argue that the same applies to frameworks. If you already know how to use one framework, it may not be worth switching to another one if it is only expected to bring incremental improvements in functionality. If you know something well, stick with it until you can make a strong case for making a change.

Don't get me wrong, with the speed at which technology and the Internet change, we all have to stay vigilant and adopt new technologies. But, I would argue that we should go through a learning phase with each new technology before committing to it. Make an informed decision and leverage the strengths you already have.

Their rules

Developers of framework tend to make certain decisions for you. In an attempt to solve a problem or provide a tool to address a certain need, they are likely to implement it a certain way. More often than not, the solution they provide works well for the majority of the users. However, that doesn't mean that it will work well for you.

Popular PHP frameworks

Application development frameworks and comparing the feature they provide is a big topic—one that probably deserves its own book. Besides, considering the pace at which new frameworks have been springing up lately and at which features have been added to existing ones, such a comparison would quickly become outdated. For that very reason, this chapter is about giving you the tools to evaluate frameworks and choose the one best suited to your, your team's, or your application's needs. However, at the same time, it would be unforgivable not to at least mention the frameworks that have been working so hard at creating a following. Keep in mind that the following list is merely a subjective sampling of the more popular frameworks at the time I wrote this. Simply because a given framework does not appear on this list does not mean you should dismiss it from your consideration.

In no particular order, I want to quickly summarize the following frameworks: Zend, CakePHP, CodeIgniter, Symfony, and Yii.

Zend

Zend Framework is a collection of loosely coupled components that first saw the light of day in 2005. It is being distributed under a New BSD license. It was started and continues to be sponsored by Zend Technologies. However, ZF has added a number of big name sponsors to its roster, including IBM, Google, Microsoft, and Adobe Systems. According to the project's website, here are some of the design goals and benefits of using ZF:

- Simplicity and extensibility
- Well-tested code base
- Loosely coupled components and flexible architecture
- Zero configuration to start
- Support for latest Web 2.0 technologies:
    - AJAX
    - Search
    - Syndication
    - Web services
- Best practices through unit testing, code coverage analysis, and use of coding standards
- Continuously growing groups of components that address areas such as:
    - Model-View-Controller(MVC)
    - Rapid Application Development (RAD) and tooling
    - Database interaction
    - Internationalization and localization
    - Authentication, authorization, and session management
    - Consuming and exposing web services
    - Mail, formats, and search
    - Overall infrastructure

For more information on the project and to download a copy of its latest release version, you should visit their site here:

```
http://framework.zend.com/
```

CakePHP

CakePHP is an open source framework that has been available since 2005 under an MIT license. It was inspired by Ruby on Rails and shares much of the design philosophy with that framework. Some of the features of CakePHP as publicized on the project's website include:

- Model-View-Controller (MVC) architecture
- Application scaffolding (MVC-centric code generation)
- Command line utilities for generating code
- Support for easy handling of HTML, Forms, Pagination, AJAX, JavaScript, XML, RSS, and so on
- Support for **Access Control Lists (ACL)**, authentication, routing, URL mapping, model validation
- Components to help with security, session, and requests

For more information on the project and to download a copy of its latest release version, you should visit their site here:

```
http://cakephp.org/
```

CodeIgniter

CodeIgniter is a framework being developed by EllisLab, Inc. and has been available since 2006. The framework is being distributed under a home-brewed variety of an Apache/BSD-style open source license. According to the project's website, CI's claim to fame includes the following:

- Small footprint
- Fast performance
- Broad compatibility with various hosting environments and versions of PHP
- No requirements for:
    - Use of the command line
    - Coding rules
    - Complex configuration
    - A custom templating engine
- Simplicity over complexity
- Comprehensive documentation

For more information on the project and to download a copy of its latest release version, you should visit their site here:

```
http://codeigniter.com
```

Symfony

Symfony is an open source project that saw its first release in 2005 and it reached 1.0 release status in 2007. It is being developed by Sensio Labs under an MIT license. According to the project itself, Symfony's benefits include the following:

- Compatibility with many hosting environments due to few prerequisites
- Use of design patters; as well as clean and readable code
- Use of agile principles to develop:
    - **KISS (Keep It Simple Stupid)**
    - **DRY (Do Not Repeat Yourself)**
    - **XP (Extreme Programming)**
- Full control over configuration
- Incorporates many other open source projects:
    - PHP: Creole, Prado, Spyc, and Pake
    - JavaScript: Prototype, script.aculo.us, Dynarch.com, and TinyMCE

For more information on the project and to download a copy of its latest release version, you should visit their site here:

```
http://www.symfony-project.org/
```

Yii

Yii is a PHP framework with a strong emphasis on performance and scalability. Yii was started and first released in 2008, which makes it the youngest of the frameworks listed here. It is open source software being distributed under a new BSD license. According to the project's website, here is a list of benefits and features this framework offers:

- Emphasis on speed and scalability through extensibility

- Use of design patterns:
  - ○ Model-View-Controller architecture
  - ○ **Data Access Objects (DAO)**
  - ○ Active Record

- JavaScript support via jQuery
- Internationalization and localization
- Support for caching, logging, error handling, theming, authentication, authorization, form and input validation
- Console applications
- Web 2.0 widgets
- Web services

For more information on the project and to download a copy of its latest release version, you should visit their site here:

```
http://www.yiiframework.com/
```

Zend Framework application

All that theory is great as a foundation from which to start exploring and experimenting with the creation of actual framework-based applications. But what really serves to illustrate the usefulness of a framework is to build a small application that leverages a representative collection of the features provided by the framework.

We can't really do this for more than one framework for the simple reason that this chapter would become too long. I would like to preemptively offer my apologies to all proponents of other PHP frameworks. However, since ZF has certainly become one of the most widely adopted frameworks, we will be using it for our project.

The point of this exercise is to give you a whirlwind tour of some of the more commonly used components of ZF. We will see that we can achieve a lot of functionality without having to write a whole lot of code. If at some point, it seems like there is a lot of hand-waving going on, there are two reasons for that. First, we are leveraging a framework that is performing a lot of chores for us behind the scenes. We don't necessarily need or want to know all the details of what is going on, but without that knowledge it may seem a bit like magic. The second reason is that I am indeed skipping over many of the details of the various modules we will be using. There is not enough room to do an exhaustive treatment of the modules. Besides, that's not really the point of this chapter. However, for those who want to learn more about any of the ZF modules we will be using, I have enclosed links to the relevant sections in the excellent ZF *Programmer's Reference Guide*.

For a more complete treatment of how to develop applications using ZF, you might also want to consult Keith Pope's *Zend Framework 1.8 Web Application Development*:

```
http://www.packtpub.com/zend-framework-1-8-web-application-
development/book
```

Feature list

We will create a simple website, complete with the following features:

- MVC architecture
- A templating engine
- Database persistence
- Logging
- Authentication
- A form
- Email notification

If it sounds like a tall order to tackle in one chapter, fear not because that is exactly why we're using a framework to do all the heavy lifting. Specifically, the version of ZF I am using to create the application in this chapter is "Zend Framework Version: 1.9.3PL1".

Application skeleton

ZF comes with a module called `Zend_Application` to help you generate an application skeleton or augment existing applications with specific features. Since we are starting with a clean project, we will be using the `create project` option.

Under the hood `Zend_Application` actually uses two other ZF modules to do the work, namely `Zend_Tool_Framework` and `Zend_Tool_Project`. `Zend_Application` is a command line executable that can be found in the `bin` directory of the top-most directory of the ZF distribution. In other words, if you download and extract the most recent Zend Framework, you will find the `bin` directory just inside the main folder it created.

Take a look at the following transcript where `Zend_Application` creates an application skeleton for us with just one command. In the `bin` directory of the ZF distribution, you will find a couple of scripts that will handle the task of creating a blank project. The Unix/Linux/MacOS version is called `zf.sh`; whereas, the Windows equivalent is called `zf.bat`.

For lack of a better project name, I decided to use a sub-domain of my main domain name and call it zf.waferthin.com.

```
  ○ ○ ○              Terminal — bash — bash — Dirk — ttysOO5 — 80×40 — ⌘4
DirkMachine:Downloads dirk$ cd ZendFramework-1.9.3PL1/bin/
DirkMachine:bin dirk$ ls -l
total 32
-rwxrwxr-x  1 dirk  dirk  1258 Sep 22 12:43 zf.bat
-rwxrwxr-x  1 dirk  dirk  6362 Sep 22 12:43 zf.php
-rwxrwxr-x  1 dirk  dirk  1406 Sep 22 12:43 zf.sh
DirkMachine:bin dirk$ zf.sh create project ~/Sites/zf.waferthin.com/zf.waferthin
.com
Creating project at /Users/dirk/Sites/zf.waferthin.com/zf.waferthin.com

DirkMacBook:bin dirk$ tree ~/Sites/zf.waferthin.com/
/Users/dirk/Sites/zf.waferthin.com/
`-- zf.waferthin.com
    |-- application
    |   |-- Bootstrap.php
    |   |-- configs
    |   |   `-- application.ini
    |   |-- controllers
    |   |   |-- ErrorController.php
    |   |   `-- IndexController.php
    |   |-- models
    |   `-- views
    |       |-- helpers
    |       `-- scripts
    |           |-- error
    |           |   `-- error.phtml
    |           `-- index
    |               `-- index.phtml
    |-- library
    |-- public
    |   `-- index.php
    `-- tests
        |-- application
        |   `-- bootstrap.php
        |-- library
        |   `-- bootstrap.php
        `-- phpunit.xml

15 directories, 10 files
DirkMacBook:~ dirk$ █
```

This gives us a working skeleton of a website. There are only two things we want to do before firing up the web server and testing it out.

First, we need to create a directory for log files. Later we will be adding a log file where the application can log exceptions and such, but for now we only need the logs directory for the Apache web server to store access and error logs. Storing the web server's log files inside the application's directory structure is not a requirement, but rather a preference of mine. If you prefer to have Apache write to log files somewhere else on the filesystem, you can skip this next step.

```
Terminal — bash — bash — Dirk — ttys002 — 80×7 — ⌘3
DirkMachine:bin dirk$ cd ~/Sites/zf.waferthin.com/
DirkMachine:zf.waferthin.com dirk$ mkdir logs
DirkMachine:zf.waferthin.com dirk$ ls -l
total 0
drwxr-xr-x   2 dirk  dirk     68 Oct 11 09:13 logs
drwxr-xr-x   7 dirk  dirk    238 Oct 10 09:59 zf.waferthin.com
DirkMacBook:hooks dirk$ 
```

Second, we need to create a symbolic link to the ZF inside the newly created site's library folder. I prefer to store larger libraries that will not be checked into my version control system outside of the main code base.

```
Terminal — bash — bash — Dirk — ttys000 — 80×7 — ⌘2
DirkMachine:zf.waferthin.com dirk$ ln -s /usr/local/lib/php/ZendFramework-1.9.3P
L1-minimal zf.waferthin.com/library/Zend
DirkMachine:zf.waferthin.com dirk$ ls -al zf.waferthin.com/library/
total 8
lrwxr-xr-x 1 dirk  dirk   49 Oct 11 09:25 Zend -> /usr/local/lib/php/ZendFramew
ork-1.9.3PL1-minimal
DirkMacBook:~ dirk$ 
```

Now let's take a look at what the site looks like from a browser:

Important concepts

Before launching into an explanation of what all those directories and files that were generated automatically for us are, I think it will be helpful to cover some recurring concepts that help us tie things together.

Bootstrapping

Bootstrapping refers to the process of initializing the environment, components, and objects of the application. Bootstrapping is typically one of the first things to occur when a request is being processed. With our setup as generated by `Zend_Application` previously, we will encounter a `Bootstrap` class that uses a configuration file and helper classes to perform the bootstrapping.

MVC

MVC is the acronym for Model-View-Controller, a frequently used design pattern to separate business logic, request handling and routing, and displaying of information from each other. Discussing MVC in detail is beyond the scope of this chapter. Besides, judging by the fact that you are reading this book, I will assume that you have come across MVC in your career as a developer. Nevertheless, if you need a quick refresher on MVC, you might want to read up on it at Wikipedia:

`http://en.wikipedia.org/wiki/Model-view-controller`

What is noteworthy at this point is that MVC is an integral part of the application skeleton we generated above. You will see it reflected in the naming of the directories and classes.

Application structure detail

Let's take a look at the directory structure and files that were created automatically. If you look at the application directory, you will notice that aside from some additions, the components of the MVC pattern correspond directly to the contained directories. Here is a list of the directories, their purpose, and their default content.

Model: application/models/

This directory is meant to contain classes that encapsulate business logic and DB mappings. By default, it is empty.

View: application/views/

This directory contains views, which are responsible for displaying output and web pages to the user. Views are nothing more than HTML fragments interspersed by PHP. The sub-directories of `application/views/scripts/` are named after the modules of the application. For instance, later in our application, we will create a users module, accessible at `zf.waferthin.com/users/`, which will have a corresponding users directory in the `application/views/` directory.

Views produce HTML fragments that are assembled by a *layout* into a complete HTML page (more about that later).

By default, the `application/views/scripts/` directory contains views for the errors and the index page.

Controller: application/controllers/

This directory contains controller classes that correspond to the modules of the application. For example, the controller to handle requests from `zf.waferthin.com/users` would be called `UsersController.php`. Controllers handle user requests by instantiating models, asking them to perform certain actions, and displaying the result using views.

By default, `Zend_Application` creates an error and an index controller.

Configuration: application/configs/

This directory is meant to hold configuration files. By default, it contains the `application.ini` properties file with settings to initialize different environments: production, staging, testing, and development. This file is used by the bootstrapping process and classes. Based on the settings in this file the bootstrap process will set up the environment and initialize various components and objects.

application/configs/application.ini

```
[production]
phpSettings.display_startup_errors = 0
phpSettings.display_errors = 0
includePaths.library = APPLICATION_PATH "/../library"
bootstrap.path = APPLICATION_PATH "/Bootstrap.php"
bootstrap.class = "Bootstrap"
resources.frontController.controllerDirectory = APPLICATION_PATH "/
controllers"

[staging : production]

[testing : production]
```

```
phpSettings.display_startup_errors = 1
phpSettings.display_errors = 1

[development : production]
phpSettings.display_startup_errors = 1
phpSettings.display_errors = 1
```

Library

The `library` directory starts out empty, but is meant to contain external dependencies. You may be used to naming this directory `includes`, `classes`, or something similar. In our simple example, the only library we really require is the Zend Framework itself. We already took care of that dependency by creating a symbolic link to ZF in the `library` directory.

Public

This is the only directory that should be directly accessible to the user's browser. Files in the public directory are meant to be viewed. This is where you would put all your static content, including but not limited to:

- Images
- CSS
- JavaScript
- Static HTML pages
- Media: audio clips, video clips, and so on

When configuring a web server such as Apache, the public directory is the equivalent of your `DOCUMENT_ROOT`.

By default, `Zend_Application` creates two files in the public directory, `.htaccess` and `index.php`. The `.htaccess` file does two things. First, it sets the default environment. Second, it redirects all requests for files or directories that don't actually exist in the `public` directory to the `index.php` file. To do this, `.htaccess` requires the `mod_rewrite` Apache module to do some rules-based rewriting and redirecting. Here is the content of the `.htaccess` file:

zf_waferthin.com/public/.htaccess

```
SetEnv APPLICATION_ENV development

RewriteEngine On
RewriteCond %{REQUEST_FILENAME} -s [OR]
RewriteCond %{REQUEST_FILENAME} -l [OR]
RewriteCond %{REQUEST_FILENAME} -d
```

```
    RewriteRule ^.*$ - [NC,L]
    RewriteRule ^.*$ index.php [NC,L]
```

The `index.php` file is the application's entry point. Here is the corresponding listing:

zf_waferthin.com/public/index.php

```php
<?php
// Define path to application directory
defined('APPLICATION_PATH')
    || define('APPLICATION_PATH', realpath(dirname(__FILE__) . '/../
application'));

// Define application environment
defined('APPLICATION_ENV')
    || define('APPLICATION_ENV', (getenv('APPLICATION_ENV') ?
getenv('APPLICATION_ENV') : 'production'));

// Ensure library/ is on include_path
set_include_path(implode(PATH_SEPARATOR, array(
    realpath(APPLICATION_PATH . '/../library'),
    get_include_path(),
)));

/** Zend_Application */
require_once 'Zend/Application.php';

// Create application, bootstrap, and run
$application = new Zend_Application(
    APPLICATION_ENV,
    APPLICATION_PATH . '/configs/application.ini'
);
$application->bootstrap()
            ->run();
```

The `index.php` file defines the `APPLICATION_PATH` and `APPLICATION_ENV` constants that govern in which environment the application will run. It also sets the include path and uses `Zend_Application` to initialize the bootstrap process.

Tests

The `tests` directory is intended to contain unit tests. To start you off on the right foot, `Zend_Application` creates the sub-directories `application` and `library`, in which you are expected to create unit tests for the corresponding top-level directories of the application. By default, none of the unit tests are actually created.

Enhancements

Now that we have a basic feel for the structure of the application, let's continue by adding some pages that showcase the functionality provided by Zend Framework.

Adding a layout

There are many interface elements that appear on the individual web pages that repeat throughout the site. Examples of these recurring sections are headers, footers, advertising sections, and so on. It doesn't make sense to repeat the code to generate those sections on every page.

Earlier in this chapter, we encountered *views* that are responsible for formatting the information for display to the user. Although you can have a view generate a complete web page, it makes more sense to use views to generate the individual components and then assemble those components selectively to create the final web page. This is where `Zend_Layout` fits into the picture. A layout represents a particular arrangement and combination of individual components (views).

Although you can create any number of different layouts for a given site, we will concentrate on creating a single layout that will be used throughout the site. Our layout will have a header, footer, navigation, and a main content area. Visually, our layout breaks our pages into the following sections.

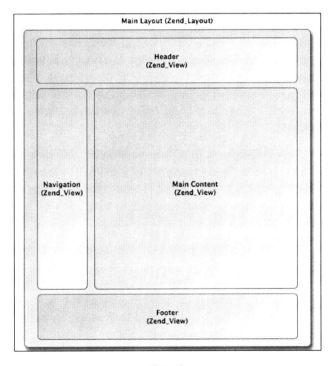

We start by creating a new directory for layout scripts, `application/layouts/scripts/`. There, we then create our layout script. Here is the listing.

Application/layout/scripts/layout.pthml

```
<!DOCTYPE HTML PUBLIC "-//W3C//DTD XHTML 1.0 Transitional//EN" "DTD/
xhtml1-transitional.dtd">
<html>
    <head>
        <link rel="stylesheet" type="text/css" href="/style.css"  />
        <?php echo $this->headTitle() ?>
        <?php echo $this->headScript() ?>
        <?php echo $this->headStyle() ?>
    </head>
    <body>
        <?php echo $this->render('header.phtml') ?>
        <?php echo $this->render('navigation.phtml') ?>

        <div id="maincontent">
            <?php echo $this->layout()->content ?>
        </div>

        <?php echo $this->render('footer.phtml') ?>
    </body>
</html>
```

The HTML in the above listing reflects the wireframe we diagrammed earlier. The body of the page consists of the header at the top, a navigation column on the left, the main content area to the right, and the footer at the bottom. You will also notice that we are referencing a stylesheet in the head section of the document, which takes care of some basic formatting, such as positioning the navigation and main content areas next to each other.

Another important thing to notice is the file extension of `.phtml` used for the previous listing, which is what Zend Framework's MVC implementation expects when looking for view templates. The above layout references various views, such as `header.phtml`, `navigation.phtml`, and `footer.phtml`. We will see where and how to create those in the next section where we take a look at views.

In the above listing, you will notice that we are using more than one object and method for populating the HTML template with content. Let's start with the `render()` method, which is provided to us by `Zend_View`. This method takes a view template, renders it, and returns the output, which makes it possible to nest views. In the above listing, we are asking `Zend_View` to render the `footer.phtml` view and include its output.

Another way of populating a view is to use view helper objects. Specifically, we are using some implementations of the `Placeholder` view helper. These objects are dedicated to a particular part of the page, such as the title or inline scripts, and provide convenience methods for aggregating content and outputting it. `headTitle()`, `headScript()`, and `headStyle()` are the placeholders we're using in our view. Also, note that `layout()` is another view helper and we are retrieving the main content to populate the template using the `content` key.

> For more detail about the `Zend_View_Helper` classes, consult the following ZF manual page:
> `http://framework.zend.com/manual/en/zend.view.helpers.html`

With all the layout directories and files in place, the last thing we need to do is to tell our MVC framework about the layout we created. Luckily, the bootstrap class that was created by default already contains a helper that knows all about layouts. The only thing we need to do is to add the following lines to our configuration file:

`application/configs/application.ini`

```
...
resources.layout.layoutPath = APPLICATION_PATH "/layouts/scripts"
resources.layout.layout = "layout"
...
```

> For more detail about the `Zend_Layout` module, consult the following ZF manual page:
> `http://framework.zend.com/manual/en/zend.layout.html`

Adding views

One feature of our application will be the ability for users to sign up for an account and use the same credentials to log in later. All that functionality will be grouped under the users module, which will correspond to a URL path by the same name. Specifically, we will add support for the following two URLs:

- `zf.waferthin.com/users/signup`: Users can create a new account
- `zf.waferthin.com/users/login`: Users can authenticate and log in to an existing account

To get the above two pages to appear, we need to create the corresponding views. Remember that views constitute only part of the page. The layout we defined in the previous section will provide the remaining HTML fragments to construct a complete page. Views live in the `application/views/scripts/<module/directory`.

Here is the listing for the sign-up page:

`application/views/scripts/users/signup.phtml`

```php
<?php
foreach ($this->message as $message) {
    echo "<strong>$message</strong><br />\n";
}

?>
<form action="/users/signup" method="POST">
    Email: <input type="text" name="email" value="<?php echo $this-
>params[email]; ?>" size="20" maxlength="30" /><br />
    Password: <input type="password" name="password" value="<?php echo
$this->params['password']; ?>" size="20" maxlength="30" /><br />
    Password (again): <input type="password" name="password_again"
value="<?php echo $this->params['password_again']; ?>" size="20"
maxlength="30" /><br />
    First Name: <input type="text" name="first_name" value="<?php echo
$this->params['first_name']; ?>" size="20" maxlength="30" /><br />
    Last Name: <input type="text" name="last_name" value="<?php echo
$this->params['last_name']; ?>" size="20" maxlength="30" /><br />
    <input type="submit" name="Submit" value="Submit" />
</form>
```

As you can see, `signup.phtml` is a simple sign-up form with text input fields for e-mail, password, first name, and last name. At the beginning of the script is a `foreach` loop that will allow us to output messages to the users. The values of the input fields can have a default depending on the stage of the sign-up process. For example, if the user incorrectly retyped his password, we would want to show him the sign-up form again without him having to retype all entries.

We will see shortly how the default values and messages to the user become available as variables in the view.

Now, here is the listing for the login page:

`application/views/scripts/users/login.phtml`

```php
<?php
foreach ($this->message as $message) {
    echo "<strong>$message</strong><br />\n";
}
```

```
?>
<form action="/users/login" method="POST">
    Login: <input type="text" name="email" value="<?php echo $this-
>params['email']; ?>" size="20" maxlength="30" /><br />
    Password: <input type="password" name="password" value=""
size="20" maxlength="30" /><br />
    <input type="submit" name="Submit" value="Submit" />
</form>

<p>If you don't have an account yet, you can <a href="/users/
signup">sign up here</a>.</p>
```

With the above two .phtml scripts we created the "V" part of MVC. We now have a way of displaying information. In the next section, we will work towards getting the "M" portion working as well; we will be creating a model for the user account data.

Before we wrap up our brief look at views, we have to remember to create the views referenced in the layout we created earlier. Since these views aren't really associated with a particular module of the application, they will reside in the application/views/scripts/ directory. Here are the corresponding listings:

application/views/scripts/header.phtml

```
<div id="header">
    <p>ZF Sample Site</p>
</div>
```

application/views/scripts/navigation.phtml

```
<div id="navigation">
    <p><strong>Navigation</strong></p>
    <p><a href="/">home</a></p>
    <p><a href="/users/login">login</a></p>
    <p><a href="/users/signup">signup</a></p>
</div>
```

application/views/scripts/footer.phtml

```
<div id="footer">
    <p>copyright 2009</p>
</div>
```

For more detail about the Zend_View module, consult the following ZF manual page:
http://framework.zend.com/manual/en/zend.view.html

Adding logging

Whether for debugging during development or in production, being able to log data and messages during the different stages of your application's execution can be extremely valuable. For that reason, we want to create a logger-type object that is accessible throughout the application's various components and lifecycle. Doing the instantiation in the Bootstrap class comes to mind for the following reasons:

- Bootstrapping takes place early and thus our logger will be available almost immediately.

- By creating and accessing our logger object through the bootstrap class, we can make sure that it gets treated as a Singleton.

- Although not in the global namespace, it is possible to access the bootstrap resources from just about anywhere in the application.

- The bootstrap process takes care of the overhead. All we have to worry about is the code to actually create the logger and use it throughout our code.

Here is the complete listing of the Bootstrap class. The __iniAutoload() method was generated automatically by Zend_Application. We only added the highlighted __initLog() method.

application/Bootstrap.php

```php
<?php
class Bootstrap extends Zend_Application_Bootstrap_Bootstrap
{
    protected function _initAutoload()
    {
        $autoloader = new Zend_Application_Module_Autoloader(array(
                    'namespace' => '',
                    'basePath'  => dirname(__FILE__),
                    ));

        return $autoloader;
    }

    // bootstrap log resource
    protected function _initLog()
    {
        // construct path to log file; name includes environment
        $logFile = realpath(APPLICATION_PATH . '/../../logs/') .
                DIRECTORY_SEPARATOR . APPLICATION_ENV . '.log';
```

```
        // create writer object needed by Zend_Log
        $writer = new Zend_Log_Writer_Stream($logFile);

        // instantiate Zend_Log and tell it to write to log file
        $log = new Zend_Log($writer);

        return $log;
    }
}
```

Any method in the bootstrap class name __init<Resource>() will be called automatically during the bootstrap process. Any return value from such a method will be stored in a registry. In our case, __initLog() will be called when bootstrapping takes place at the beginning of the request lifecycle. The object of type Zend_Log that the method returns will now be an available throughout the remainder of the request lifecycle.

Without going into too much detail, the way that Zend_Log works is that it supports any number of logging methods simultaneously, such as text files, databases, or debuggers. Each type of logging method requires an object of type Zend_Log_Writer to handle the actual logging. It is also possible to specify different priorities with each logged message.

In our case, we create a simple text file in the zf_waferthin.com/logs/ directory and we name it after the environment in which the application operates. So, if we are running in the development environment, the APPLICATION_ENV would be set to "development" and our log file will be called zf_waferthin/logs/development. log. Once we have instantiated a Zend_Log_Writer, we can also instantiate the Zend_log instance and tell it to use the text file writer.

We will encounter this again later, but here is a quick example of how to use the bootstrap object available from within a controller object to obtain a reference to the log object and write a message to the log file.

```
// get bootstrap object -> get log resource -> log message
$this->getInvokeArg('bootstrap')->getResource('log')->log('Logging
application startup.'));
```

 For more detail about the Zend_Log module, consult the following ZF manual page:
http://framework.zend.com/manual/en/zend.log.html

Adding a database

After creating a view, we have a way for users to enter their information into a form. However, we know that we will need to persist this account data in some kind of long-term storage. Let's use a MySQL database to save the data and authenticate against it later.

I started by creating a "db" directory under the root directory of the project. This directory contains two additional directories, separating the schema from the data. The "tables" directory contains a text file with SQL command to create a table matching the name of the file. Analogously, the "data" directory contains files with insert statements to populate individual tables within the database. Here too, files are named after the table they populate.

Starting with a single table called "users," here is the resulting directory structure:

```
DirkMacBook:zf.waferthin.com dirk$ tree db
db
|-- data
|   `-- users.sql
`-- tables
    `-- users.sql
DirkMacBook:~ dirk$
```

The structure for table users is defined in file `db/tables/users.sql`. Here is the create table statement in that file:

```
--
-- Table structure for table `users`
--
DROP TABLE IF EXISTS `users`;
CREATE TABLE `users` (
  `id` int(10) unsigned NOT NULL AUTO_INCREMENT COMMENT 'Primary key',
  `email` varchar(30) NOT NULL DEFAULT '' COMMENT 'Email address for authentication & notification purposes',
  `password` varchar(50) NOT NULL DEFAULT '' COMMENT 'Password for authentication purposes',
  `first_name` varchar(30) NOT NULL DEFAULT '' COMMENT 'User first name',
  `last_name` varchar(30) NOT NULL DEFAULT '' COMMENT 'User last name',
  `active` tinyint(4) unsigned NOT NULL DEFAULT '1' COMMENT 'Boolean active flag',
```

```
  `deleted` tinyint(3) unsigned NOT NULL DEFAULT '0' COMMENT
'Boolean deleted flag (logical delete)',
  `created_date` datetime NOT NULL COMMENT 'Creation / sign up
date',
  `update_date` timestamp NOT NULL DEFAULT CURRENT_TIMESTAMP
COMMENT 'Date and time on which the record was last updated',
  PRIMARY KEY (`id`),
  UNIQUE KEY `unique_login` (`login`)
) ENGINE=MyISAM AUTO_INCREMENT=2 DEFAULT CHARSET=latin1;
```

Without going into too much detail, we have an `id` column that we use as a primary key. There are self-explanatory text fields for `email`, `password` (hashed), `first_name`, and `last_name`. Furthermore, there are two Boolean flags used for logically deleting users and activating/deactivating them. Next, there are date-time and timestamp fields to capture the creation and modification date of the account, respectively. The last thing worth noting is the unique index placed on the login field. After all, we don't want to allow more than one user to have the same username.

You will have to create a database and run the above statement to create the `users` table. Once we have a table we can populate it with some default test data. In our case, the file `db/data/users.sql` has the following content to create a single test account for myself:

```
--
-- Dumping data for table `users`
--
LOCK TABLES `users` WRITE;
INSERT INTO `users` VALUES (1, 'dirk@wafertin.com',
SHA1('mylilsecret'), 'Dirk', 'Merkel', 1, 0, NOW(), NOW());
UNLOCK TABLES;
```

The only thing noteworthy about the above insert statement is the fact that we are not storing the password itself, but rather a cryptographic hash of it using the `SHA1()` function.

That's it for creating the database and table itself. Now let's work on letting our application know about it. Lucky for us, this is another chore the bootstrapping sequence can handle for us. All we need to do is to put the corresponding configuration settings into our main settings file and our base bootstrap class will use a helper class responsible for initializing a database resource. Add the following lines to your `application.ini` file, but substitute the credentials applicable to the database you created:

`application/configs/application.ini`

```
. . .
resources.db.adapter = "pdo_mysql"
resources.db.params.host = "localhost"
resources.db.params.username = "<db_user_name>"
resources.db.params.password = "<db_user_password>"
resources.db.params.dbname = "<db_name>"
resources.db.isDefaultTableAdapter = true
. . .
```

Our application now has a reference to a database connection stored in the bootstrap class. We can use that connection directly, but as we will see in the next section, there are other components of ZF that can use that connection as well.

 For more detail about the Zend_Db module, consult the following ZF manual page:

http://framework.zend.com/manual/en/zend.db.html

Adding a model

At this point, we have a database and a users table to store account information for our users. We also have a connection to the database provided by our bootstrap process. What we don't yet have is a class to actually create, retrieve, update, and delete records from our users table.

In addition to providing basic **CRUD (Create, Read, Update, and Delete)** functionality, such a class should also encapsulate our business logic. For example, the class we are about to create will contain logic to determine whether logins and password match the required format. In the context of MVC, such a class constitutes the "M" letter of the acronym. In other words, we need to create a model to represent users as an object in PHP.

Since we are dealing with user accounts, some of the actions our model will be expected to perform have to do with account creation, checking of login credentials, and validating input data.

Models live in the application/models/ directory. Here now is the listing for the Model_Users class:

application/models/Model_Users.php

```php
<?php
/**
 * Model_Users
```

```
 *
 * CRUD functionality and business logic for
 * user accounts.
 *
 * @package zf_waferthin
 * @author Dirk Merkel
 **/
class Model_Users extends Zend_Db_Table_Abstract
{
    // DB table name
    protected $_name = 'users';

    // primary ID of table
    protected $_primary = 'id';

    // store feedback messages
    public $message = array();

    // constructor provided for completeness
    public function __construct()
    {
        parent::__construct();
    }


    /**
     * This is where all the validation happens.
     * This method is consulted before inserting
     * or adding entries or directory by the user.
     */
    public function validate(Array $data = array())
    {
        $this->message = array();

        // validate email
        if (!isset($data['email'])
            || empty($data['email'])
            || !preg_match('/^[a-zA-Z0-9_\.@]{6,}$/', $data['email']))
{

            $this->message[] = 'Email is required and must consist of
                                at least 6 alphanumeric characters.';
        }
```

```
        // validate password format
        if (!isset($data['password'])
            || empty($data['password'])
            || !preg_match('/^[a-zA-Z0-9_]{6,}$/', $data['password']))
    {

            $this->message[] = 'Password is required and must consist
                               of at least 6 alphanumeric characters.';

        // validate password was retyped correctly
        } elseif ($data['password'] != $data['password_again']) {

            $this->message[] = 'You did not retype the password
                                                    correctly.';
        }
        return !count($this->message);
    }

    // create a new user account
    public function insert(Array $data = array())
    {
        // call insert method provided by Zend_Db_Table_Abstract
        return parent::insert($data);
    }

    // validate credentials
    public function login($email, $password)
    {
        // minimal input validation
        if (empty($email) || empty($password)) {
            return false;
        }

        // get Zend_Db_Table_Select object for query
        $select = $this->select();

        // construct query
        $select->where('email = ?', $email)
               ->where('password = SHA1(?)', $password)
               ->where('active = ?', 1)
               ->where('deleted = ?', 0);

        // did we find a result
        $row = $this->fetchRow($select);
```

```
        if (!empty($row)) {
            return $row;
        } else {
            return false;
        }
    }
}
```

By extending `Zend_Db_Table_Abstract`, our model class will be able to provide basic CRUD functionality out-of-the-box. For example, the `insert()` method we provide does nothing more than to call the parent class's method by the same name. Of course, I didn't need to include this method here at all because inheritance would have ensured that the parent method would be called automatically. I merely included it to make it obvious what is going on. Really all we have to do is add our business logic.

The protected properties `$_name` and `$_id` specify the name and primary key of the database table we are encapsulating respectively. Any queries we directly or indirectly generate in any of the methods will automatically include that information.

In terms of business logic, we add the three methods, namely `validate()`, `insert()`, and `login()`. `validate()` performs some regular expression matching on the e-mail address and password submitted by the user. This is just some basic input validation that would have to be expanded if this code were to ever reach a production system. Any error messages are stored in the `$messages` property where the controller can retrieve it and display it to the users.

We already mentioned that `insert()` does nothing more than to let the parent class, `Zend_Db_Table_Abstract`, do all the work necessary to insert a new row into the users table and thus create a new user account.

Lastly, the `login()` method takes an e-mail and password pair and, after some very simple input validation, queries the users table for such an account that is also active and has not been deleted. If it is able to retrieve the record, it returns the calling code in the controller, which can then presumably start a session for the user. If an active account cannot be found, `login()` merely returns a Boolean false.

 For more detail about using the `Zend_Db_Table` module to create model, consult the following ZF manual page:

http://framework.zend.com/manual/en/zend.db.table.html

Adding a controller

The controller's job is to orchestrate everything. It tells layouts and views to display pages to the user. On the backend, it instantiates and operates on models that represent the business objects of your application. In our case, we want to create a controller that can handle user signups and logins.

In ZF's MVC implementation, controllers live in the `application/controllers/` directory, which is where we are creating our `UsersController.php`. Take a look at the following listing:

application/controllers/UsersController.php

```php
<?php
// ZF MVC controller class for users module
class UsersController extends Zend_Controller_Action
{
    public $log = null;

    // controller initialization
    public function init()
    {
        // get local reference to logger object
        $this->log = $this->getInvokeArg('bootstrap')-
                                            >getResource('log');
    }

    // this method will be called is no action was
    // specified in the URL
    public function indexAction()
    {
        // forward to login
        $this->_redirect('/users/login');
    }

    public function signupAction()
    {
        // get request object
        $request = $this->getRequest();

        // handle new signups
        if ($request->isPost()) {

            // instantiate users model
            $users = new Model_Users();
```

```php
        // get submitted data
        $record = $request->getParams();

        // validate data before inserting
        if ($users->validate($record)) {

            // remove data we don't need
            unset($record['password_again'],
                $record['Submit'],
                $record['controller'],
                $record['action'],
                $record['module']);

            // create the new record
            try {
                $users->insert($record);

            // account created confirmation message
            $this->view->message = array('The account for ' .
        $record['email'] . ' has been created successfully.');

                // send confirmation email
                $this->sendConfirmationEmail($record['email'],
                        $record['first_name'] . ' ' .
                                    $record['last_name'],
                                    'admin@zf.waferthin.com',
                                    'Admin',
                                    'Account Created',
                                    'confirm_email.phtml');

            // something went wrong
            } catch (Exception $e) {

                // log the problem ...
                $this->log->info('Unable to create new user
        account: ' . $record['email'] . "\nError message: " . $e-
                                    >getMessage());

                // .. and notify the user
                $this->view->message = array('An error
occurred. The account for ' . $record['email'] . ' could not be
                                    created.');
            }
```

```
                    // validation failed
                    } else {

                        // assign parameters back to view
                        $this->view->params = $record;

                        // assign success / failure message to view
                        $this->view->message = $users->message;

                    }

                }

            }


    public function loginAction()
    {
        // get request object
        $request = $this->getRequest();

        // handle login request
        if ($request->isPost()) {

            // instantiate users model
            $users = new Model_Users();

            // validate credentials
            if ($user = $users->login($request->getParam('email'),
$request->getParam('password'))) {

                    // log successful login ...
                    $this->log->info('Login success: ' . $request-
                                            >getParam('email'));

                    // show welcome message
                    $this->view->message = array('Welcome back, ' .
            $user['first_name'] . ' ' . $user['last_name'] . '. You
                                    have successfully logged in.');

                // credentials not accepted
                } else {

                    // log unsuccessful login attempt ...
                    $this->log->info('Unsuccessful login attempt: ' .
                                    $request->getParam('email'));
```

```
                    // ... and display error message
                    $this->view->message = array('Your email or
    password do not correspond to an active user account. Please
              try again or <a href="/users/signup">signup</a>');

              // assign parameters back to view
              $this->view->params = $request->getParams();
          }
      }
}

// send email with body of message rendered with Zend_View
protected function sendConfirmationEmail($recipientEmail,
                    recipientName,
                    $senderEmail,
                    $senderName,
                    $subject,
                    $emailViewName)
{
    // create a view
    $view = new Zend_View();

    // tell view where to look for templates
    $view->setScriptPath(APPLICATION_PATH .
                                '/views/scripts/users/');

  // assign an array of key-value pairs to be rendered in view
    $info = array(
                    'recipientName' => $recipientName,
                    'recipientEmail' => $recipientEmail
                    );
    $view->assign($info);

    // render view
    $message = $view->render($emailViewName);

    // instantiate Zend_Mail obmect
    $mail = new Zend_Mail();

    // use fluid interface to send confirmation message
    $mail->setBodyText($message)
        ->setFrom($senderEmail, $senderName)
```

```
                          ->addTo($recipientEmail, $recipientName)
                          ->setSubject($subject)
                          ->send();

                // log email sent
            $this->log->info('Sent email template ' . $emailViewName . '
                                        to ' . $recipientEmail);
        }
    }
```

In ZF's MVC implementation, controllers subclass `Zend_Action_Controller`. Before any other methods get called, the `init()` method gets a reference to the log object we created during the bootstrap process and makes it available as a local property.

Methods in the controller class are named after the action of the module they are handling. In our case, that means that the URL `/users/signup` will be handled by the `signupAction()` method of the `UsersController` class. Analogously, the `loginAction()` handles requests for the `/users/login` path.

Our controller has two main action handler methods, `signupAction()` and `loginAction()`. The `signupAction()` method starts by obtaining a reference to the Request object. It then uses the Request object to determine whether the request method is POST and to retrieve the posted variables. It then instantiates a `Model_Users` object and uses it to validate the user-submitted values. If the data passes validation, the controller uses the model to create a new user record. The validation error message(s) or successful account creation message are then displayed to the user.

The `loginAction()` method follows a similar logic with the main difference being that it calls the model's `login()` method to verify the user's credentials.

In addition to `<name>Action()` methods that are automatically mapped to certain URLs, you can add any kind of method to a controller. We have, for example, added the `sendConfirmationEmail()` method. This is called from the `signupAction()` method and is responsible for sending a confirmation e-mail to the e-mail address of a successfully added new account. `sendConfirmationEmail()` is worth a second look because it introduces a new ZF module, `Zend_Mail`, and illustrates further use of the already familiar `Zend_View` module.

The `sendConfirmationEmail()` takes the parameters of recipient and sender e-mail address and name; as well as the message's subject and name of the view to be used for the body of the message. After instantiating a `Zend_View` object, we assign the recipient's name and e-mail address to the view, and ask the object to render the view whose name was passed in as a parameter. `Zend_View` is essentially taking a template, processing it by making some substitutions, and returning the complete text. This text will be used when sending the e-mail later on in this method. Here is a listing of the template, or view script in ZF MVC lingo being used:

application/views/users/confirm_email.phtml

```
    Thank you for signing up with zf.waferthin.com, <?php echo $this-
                                        >params['first_name']; ?>!
    The email address used for this account is <?php echo $this-
                                        >params['email']; ?>.
```

As you can see, the use of Zend_View in this case is more explicit as compared to how it is used in the <name>Action() methods of the controller. There we never actually have to call the render() method.

Now that we have the body of the message, we can use the Zend_Mail module to send the e-mail. This example hardly illustrates the advantages Zend_Mail provides over PHP's built-in mail() function, but it does the job of actually sending the message just fine. Here are some of the advanced features provided by Zend_Mail:

- MIME-compliant
- Multipart messages
- Various transport methods
- Secure SMTP
- Retrieving messages via local store (mbox etc.), POP3, and SMTP
- Highly customizable and extensible

For more detail about the Zend_Mail module, consult the following ZF manual page:
http://framework.zend.com/manual/en/zend.mail.html

Lastly, there is also the indexAction() method that does nothing more than redirect the user's browser from one location to another. Specifically, it redirects requests for URL /users/ to /users/login.

For more detail about the Zend_Controller module, consult the following ZF manual page:
http://framework.zend.com/manual/en/zend.controller.html

Putting it all together

To summarize, we created a controller that uses a layout and various views to display pages to the user. We created two views and two corresponding methods in the controller class to handle the URLs /users/signup and /users/login. Upon submitting either the signup or login form, the controller instantiates the Model_Users class and uses it to validate the input and either create a new account or validate against an existing one.

It's time to try out our application. Here is a screenshot of the signup page with the information filled in.

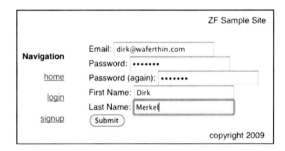

And here is the resulting page after clicking the **Submit** button. I can also confirm that I received the confirmation e-mail sent out after successfully creating an account.

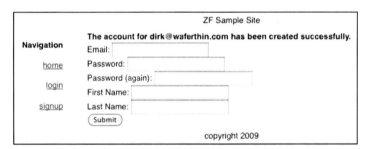

Now let's take a look at the login page. After creating a new account, we can now use the same e-mail and password to log in. Here is the result screen:

As you can see, a user is now able to create an account and use the corresponding credentials to log-in to our site. Granted, there isn't much functionality that would entice a visitor to sign up, but with the help of our framework of choice, Zend Framework, developing such a site can progress at a rapid pace.

Summary

Although there are many things to consider when picking a development framework, you can't really go wrong with most of the established and actively maintained ones. Frameworks like Cake, Symfony, and Zend Framework overlap to a large degree in terms of the problems they solve. However, you can make your life easier by doing your homework and selecting a framework that suits your development philosophy and style. After reading this chapter, you should be able to look at the offering of frameworks out there and ask the right questions to narrow down the field.

Although I used Zend Framework as an example to show what a framework can add to your development effort, I certainly urge you to consider other options. I like that most of the ZF components are pretty loosely coupled. Although, the `Zend_Application` module in conjunction with ZF's full MVC implementation doesn't feel quite as loosely coupled as ZF used to. Either way, it is still possible to add individual ZF modules to your existing applications in situations where it doesn't make sense to convert the whole application just so it can run on ZF.

I'm hoping that you will invest the time to find the framework that suits you best. Then learn how to get the most out of it. Finally, when you are starting to push things to the limit, you should think about contributing to the project if possible to make it a better tool for everybody.

7
Testing

The software we write is constantly being tested—at least we hope it is. That is because every time someone uses a piece of code, a class, or a website you created, he or she is implicitly testing it as well. We will take a look at the different types of testing that are performed during a typical software development cycle.

One thing that types of testing have in common is that their goal is to ferret out problems with the software. The earlier we are able to catch a bug, the cheaper it is to fix it. If the developer can find, diagnose, and fix a bug during the development stage, it will happen much faster than if it happens during user acceptance testing when the client gets his hands on the final product. As we will see later in the chapter, once unit tests have been set up, it is relatively cheap to run them; whereas, it is fairly expensive if a problem gets uncovered during regression or integration testing. One reason for that is because the former test is automated and the latter one requires a professional tester to spend valuable time on testing activity.

This chapter is really about unit testing because it is closest to our activity, that is, writing code. However, we also need to be keenly aware of the other testing activities that are going on because they directly affect our end product.

Testing methods

The following sections briefly look at how to approach testing in general. The basic question is whether it is best to focus on how the code is supposed to behave or whether the tester should be aware of what the code is actually doing. That is to say, should you test the code from the outside with the actual implementation hidden or should you be aware of how the programmer implemented the required functionality? As we will see, both approaches have their pros and cons and in the end it is possible for you to choose your own combination, as the two sides are not mutually exclusive.

It might not be obvious at first, but considering the general approach first will help us in understanding how others might be testing our code. It also helps us when we get into the heart of this chapter and start writing unit tests.

Black box

Black box testing treats the code that is being tested as a complete unknown. The tester only needs to know how the code is supposed to behave, not how it achieves that behavior. For example, sufficiently detailed functional specifications should be enough for a tester to construct test cases and observe the behavior of the code.

On one hand, the advantage of black box testing is that the tester is not biased by any knowledge of the implementation and the results can be considered somewhat more impartial. On the other hand, it is not uncommon for a black box tester to construct multiple test cases that essentially test the same piece of code, which results in a duplication of effort and a waste of resources.

White box

Unlike the black box approach, **white box** testing requires access to the source, understanding of the code, and the use of that knowledge to construct the test cases. Moreover, it usually involves testing of parts of the code that is not usually accessible from "outside the box." For example, a tester might write a test case for a protected method in a class that is not really visible to the user of the system or any code interfacing with the class being tested.

I prefer the term *transparent box testing* because it more accurately describes the fact that the tester can see through the conceptual box that contains the code and can understand the inner workings.

With an increased understanding of the code comes the ability to write better and more targeted test cases. A downside to this approach is that it requires a tester with significant development skills to properly understand the code. Another drawback that is often overlooked is that fact that the tester runs the risk of making the same assumptions as the developer. If any of those assumptions proves to be incorrect, it could result in an untested scenario, or worse, an uncaught bug.

Gray box

As the name suggests, this approach is a combination of the black box and white box approaches. A tester using this method would be knowledgeable about the inner working of the application, just like in the white box method. However, similar to the black box method, testing would be done completely from outside the application without being able to manipulate the codes inner data structures.

Gray box testing is essentially a compromise between black box and white box testing. I wouldn't go so far as to say that it combines the best of both worlds. If that were the case, there would no longer be the need for either of the other methods. Instead, gray box testing is a compromise that tries to reap the benefits of having access to and understanding of the code while still being limited to interfacing with the application from the point of view of a user.

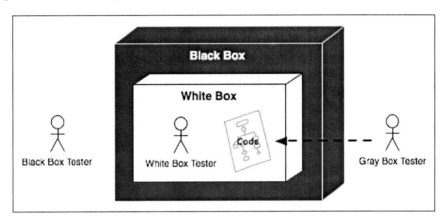

This brings us to my last note on the subject, namely that the three approaches described previously aren't at all as mutually exclusive as they may appear at first glance. They all have their advantages. Assuming you have the resources available, it often make sense to do both black box and white box testing at the same time—they complement each other. Another option is to have a tester develop black box test cases first and white box ones second. That way, his thinking won't be tainted by knowledge of the code's inner workings until he starts working on the back box test cases. Of course, this will really only work for a limited amount of time. Once the tester is familiar with the code, he has essentially been tainted and his ability to write black box tests will have been compromised. This approach is of limited value to larger and agile projects where the base of test scripts continues to grow throughout the project's lifetime.

Types of testing

There are many different types and methods for testing software. Following are some brief definitions of the most common terminology you might find in developer circles or enterprise settings.

You should keep in mind that different types of testing don't necessarily compete with each other. They often simply address different aspects of the software and can therefore complement each other.

Unit testing

As the name suggests, this type of testing occurs at the most granular level of software development, typically right before and/or after coding time. It targets the basic building blocks of software or units. In PHP, these building blocks are classes and methods.

Usually, multiple test cases are written to test the functionality of a class or method. Individual test cases are then grouped together into test suites. Writing a test case commonly involves some form of coding — typically in the same programming language in which the main application is being written anyway. Later in this chapter, we will be testing PHP classes by constructing the **Unit Test** in PHPUnit, which leverages all the syntax and idioms an experienced PHP developer already knows.

Since unit testing targets relatively small parts of a complete application, it is not uncommon to have dozens or hundreds of tests, thus making manual execution of these tests impractical. Instead, it is common to try and automate the execution of these tests so the whole battery of tests can be executed quickly and often.

The attentive reader will have noticed that I mentioned that it is possible to create unit tests before writing code. In essence, you use a unit test to describe exactly how a piece of software should behave. Having created a test, you then proceed to implement the code necessary to satisfy it. This approach is called test-driven development and is often found as part of agile software development methodologies, such as Extreme Programming (just one of many buzz words in this area).

To me, test-driven development always appears as kind of a backward black box testing. You start by describing the behavior of the component with knowing the implementation details because it doesn't exist yet. Then you go about turning your black box into a white box by writing the code that your unit test requires to run without reporting an error.

Unit testing is extremely useful and necessary for any but the smallest software development projects. However, for all the benefits it provides, it also has some drawbacks. For starters, it takes discipline to consistently write unit tests, no matter whether it is before or after you write the code. However, once you are in the habit of creating tests, you will quickly find that it actually enhances your productivity. Also, you need to be aware of what unit testing is intended to do, namely it aims to test implementation details in an automated fashion. Knowing that, it is understandable that it misses the big picture. Even though individual methods or classes pass their unit test with flying colors does not mean that application actually does what it is supposed to. It only means that the methods and classes do what the developer thought they were supposed to do. However, keep in mind that this is not what unit testing is designed to do. There are other methods of testing software that look at the whole application and derive their approach from the user's perspective.

Used in the right way while being aware of its strengths and weaknesses, unit testing becomes an incredibly powerful tool to make us more productive as developers, and our code more robust.

Integration testing

Unit testing is geared towards the building blocks of the application, whereas **integration testing** aims to test how well those pieces fit together. Larger systems are typically broken up into modules. Modules are often groupings of related functionality in a system. For example, in a shopping cart application, you might have catalog browsing, payment processing, and checkout modules. To speed up development, each of these modules can be handled in parallel by a separate group of developers. However, once all the modules have been completed, it is necessary that they indeed work together as intended. There are several things that can be done to make sure that this testing phase goes as smoothly as possible. For example, clearly defined APIs that describe how the modules are supposed to communicate with each other will be beneficial in reducing disconnects in the logic.

Another approach to this problem is **continuous integration**, which aims to put the modules together as early as possible. When practicing continuous integration, an automated process is responsible for checking out the latest changes to the project, building it, staging it, running any automated tests, and making the results available to all interested parties. This automatic process happens as frequently as possible— often multiple times a day. Since continuous integration can be such a productivity booster and nicely combines many of the topics we are covering in this book, I have devoted the final chapter to this topic.

Regression testing

Unfortunately, it happens quite frequently that we as developers break a perfectly good piece of software in the process of implementing a new feature or fixing a bug. A previously working feature or function that gets broken this way is called a software regression and it is the responsibility of **regression testing** to uncover these regressions before they reach the user and make us look bad. After all, we have all heard the complaint that "it used to work before you upgraded the system."

Most developers think of testing when they fix a bug or add a new feature. However, testing is often being neglected when refactoring existing code. One's familiarity and understanding of the existing code or functionality can often lead to a false sense of security. It happens all too often that a developer changes a couple of lines around to "streamline performance" or "make the code more elegant." Those are all desirable and necessary actions, but you should not forego more rigorous testing merely because your changes pass a quick test.

The typical approach to regression is the straight forward re-testing of existing functionality with each change to the software. It is also common to re-verify previously fixed bugs to make sure they have not resurfaced.

As systems mature the number of features and fixed bugs increases. As a corollary, manual retesting of both each time some work is done on the code becomes prohibitively expensive in terms of money and time. Consequently, automated testing is often employed as part of regression testing. Each time a new feature has been added or a bug has been fixed, a corresponding automated test should be added to the test suite. That way, the test can easily be executed every time something in the code changes—even if it is seemingly unrelated.

System testing

Having tested the individual pieces of the code during the unit testing phase; as well as having tested how well those pieces come together during the integration testing phase, it is finally time to test how the system performs as a whole. Since this phase considers the final product that will be delivered to the customer, it is driven by the functional specifications. In other words, does the system behave the way the customer expects and how that expectation was captured in the functional specifications?

At this point of testing, focus is put on how the system behaves, not how it operates behind the scenes.

User acceptance testing

Finally— the coding is done and the QA team is happy with the test results. It's time to hand the product of your sweat and tears over to the client. Well, not so fast. There is still one more type of testing that needs to be performed before we can call the project a success. In particular, the client (or the client's subject matter expert) needs to assure themselves that the delivered product does indeed meet the expectations originally set in the functional spec created for this purpose. This kind of testing is called **user acceptance testing**. It is usually a kind of black box testing performed by the client with a test script that was developed based on the functional specifications. Often normal users of the system are recruited to test the system before they actually get to use it.

Although the client will always be expected to sign off on the final product, the impact of user acceptance testing is being lessened with the advent of agile development methodologies and continuous integration. The earlier and more consistently we can get the client exposed to the product in the making, the fewer nasty surprises we will encounter during the later stages of the project. Despite having said that, this is not meant to be a chapter on development methodologies or the software development lifecycle. At the same time, nobody can argue the fact that testing is an integral part of both topics.

Following is a simple diagram that illustrates the testing types discussed previously in a hierarchical manner in which they relate to each other.

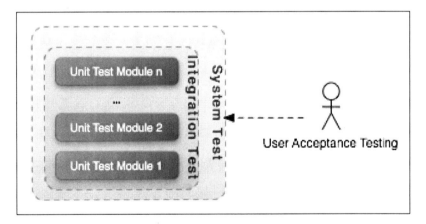

Introducing PHPUnit

PHPUnit is a testing framework that aims to make it as easy as possible to create, maintain, and execute individual, or more commonly, whole batteries of tests for components of code.

Installing PHPUnit

Although you can download the source code for PHPUnit directly and install it that way, we will follow the only officially supported method for installing PHPUnit, which is via the `pear` installer utility. The developers of PHPUnit maintain their own PEAR channel, which we will have to let PEAR know about before we can install packages from it. To learn more about the **PHP Extension and Application Repository (PEAR)** and the `pear` command-line utility used to manage channels and application packages, you can visit their site at:

```
http://pear.php.net/
```

Following is a transcript of using the `pear` installer to discover the PHPUnit channel and install the package.

Let's start by taking a look at what channels are currently available on my system.

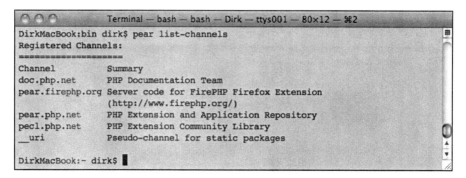

Since `pear.phpunit.de`, the Pear channel for PHPUnit is not included in the list, let's ask Pear to add it.

```
DirkMacBook:bin dirk$ sudo pear channel-discover pear.phpunit.de
Adding Channel "pear.phpunit.de" succeeded
Discovery of channel "pear.phpunit.de" succeeded

DirkMacBook:~ dirk$ 
```

Now that PEAR knows where to find the PHPUnit ackage, let's go ahead and install it.

```
DirkMacBook:bin dirk$ sudo pear install phpunit/PHPUnit
Did not download optional dependencies: pear/Image_GraphViz, pear/Log, use --all
deps to download automatically
phpunit/PHPUnit can optionally use package "pear/Image_GraphViz" (version >= 1.2
.1)
phpunit/PHPUnit can optionally use package "pear/Log"
phpunit/PHPUnit can optionally use PHP extension "xdebug" (version >= 2.0.0)
downloading PHPUnit-3.3.17.tgz ...
Starting to download PHPUnit-3.3.17.tgz (272,418 bytes)
...................................................done: 272,418 bytes
install ok: channel://pear.phpunit.de/PHPUnit-3.3.17

DirkMacBook:~ dirk$
```

That's all there is to it. A quick directory listing of the `bin` directory in my PHP installation directory reveals the `phpunit` command line utility.

```
DirkMacBook:bin dirk$ ls -l
total 68072
-rwxr-xr-x  1 root  wheel       859 Aug 18 04:43 pear
-rwxr-xr-x  1 root  wheel       880 Aug 18 04:43 peardev
-rwxr-xr-x  1 root  wheel       796 Aug 18 04:43 pecl
lrwxr-xr-x  1 root  wheel        36 Jul  6 15:38 phar -> /usr/local/apache2/php/
bin/phar.phar
-rwxr-xr-x  1 root  wheel     14839 Jul  6 15:38 phar.phar
-rwxr-xr-x  1 root  wheel   9069408 Jul  6 15:38 php
-rwxr-xr-x  1 root  wheel      2908 Jul  6 15:38 php-config
-r-xr-xr-x  1 root  wheel  18340260 Sep 25  2007 php.bck
-rwxr-xr-x  1 root  wheel   7376944 Aug 11  2008 php.dSYM
-rwxr-xr-x  1 root  wheel       966 Aug 18 04:43 phpcs
-rwxr-xr-x  1 root  wheel      1476 Apr  3 13:36 phpdoc
-rwxr-xr-x  1 root  wheel      4530 Jul  6 15:38 phpize
-rwxr-xr-x  1 root  wheel      2133 Aug 23 05:28 phpunit
drwxr-xr-x  3 root  wheel       102 Aug 18 04:43 scripts

DirkMacBook:~ dirk$
```

If you ran into problems retracing the above steps, you might want to consult the PEAR online manual. Assuming that everything went without a hitch and we now have all PHPUnit tools installed, we need to start writing unit tests and test suites.

String search project

As we have done in prior chapters, we will work with a running example that will be modified as we dive deeper into the features of PHPUnit. As this whole chapter is about testing code, there really is no way around working with actual code. Explaining how to test code in a vacuum without actually doing it is fairly useless in my opinion.

I was thinking that it might be interesting to have a compact piece of code that nevertheless hides some pitfalls because it is non-trivial to understand the intricacies of what is actually going on. This description seems to fit algorithms in general. Although it might be easy to understand a given algorithm conceptually, a lot more attention to detail is required when actually implementing it.

Our sample project will involve string search algorithms. Specifically, the algorithm we will be looking at is known as the Boyer–Moore–Horspool algorithm. Simply put, we will be searching a string (also known as "the buffer") for one or more occurrences of a smaller string (also known as "the substring"). Take, for example, the last two stanzas of John Frederick Nims's "Love Poem:"

> *Forgetting your coffee spreading on our flannel,*
> *Your lipstick grinning on our coat,*
> *So gaily in love's unbreakable heaven*
> *Our souls on glory of spilt bourbon float.*
>
> *Be with me, darling, early and late. Smash glasses —*
> *I will study wry music for your sake.*
> *For should your hands drop white and empty*
> *All the toys of the world would break.*

If we take the above text to be our buffer, we might ask how many times the substring "our" occurs within the buffer.

This particular algorithm is a standard in computer science and has been around for a while. There are some slightly refined variations of the basic algorithm available, but for the sake of simplicity we will be sticking to the version that only requires a single lookup table. Don't worry—you'll better understand what I'm referring to once we get into the guts of the code and the algorithm.

BMH algorithm basics

The human approach to this problem would be quite sequential. Most of us would probably scan the text from beginning to end while looking for occurrences of "our" or at least the letter "o." We can easily write some code that mimics the way we would search for a string within a larger one. However, as it turns out, this would be an inefficient way of doing it.

The BMH algorithm recognizes the fact that it is not necessary to look at each character of the buffer. With the help of a pre-calculated lookup table, it is possible to jump several characters and speed up the search process. For more details, you might want to read the explanation of this algorithm on Wikipedia:

```
http://en.wikipedia.org/wiki/Boyer-Moore_algorithm
```

The Boyer-Moore-Horspool algorithm we will be using in our example is actually a slightly simplified version of the full Boyer-Moore algorithm.

Implementing BMH

For the time being, let's ignore the fact that string search functionality has been implemented in the core PHP functions much more efficiently than we can by writing it in PHP. First we define an interface, let's call it `StringSearchable`, which dictates how string search functionality is supposed to be implemented in any class providing that functionality.

```
interfaces/StringSearchable.php
```

```php
<?php
interface StringSearchable
{
    // define method signature with args like needle, haystack
    public function search($substring, $buffer);
}
?>
```

Next, we create class `BoyerMooreStringSearch` that implements the `StringSearchable` interface in the form of the BMH algorithm described previously.

```
classes/BoyerMooreStringSearch.php
```

```php
<?php
class Search_String_BoyerMoore implements StringSearchable
{
  // the substring for which to search
  public $substring = 'null';

  // the buffer that will be searched for any occurrences of the
   substring
  public $buffer = '';

  // jump table derived from substring
  public $jumpTable = array();

  // array of results
  protected $results = array();

  public function __construct()
  {
      // intentionally left blank
```

```
    }

    public function __destruct()
    {
      // intentionally left blank
    }

    // implement interface method
    // with args like needle, haystack
    public function search($substring, $buffer)
    {
      // reset results array
      $this->results = array();

      $this->substring = $substring;
      $this->buffer = $buffer;

      // get jump table
      $this->deriveJumpTable();

      $currentCharacter = strlen($this->substring) - 1;
      $substringLength = strlen($this->substring);
      $bufferLength = strlen($this->buffer);

      while ($currentCharacter < $bufferLength) {

        for ($i = $substringLength - 1; $i >= 0; $i--) {

          // character matches, continue ...
          if ($this->buffer{($currentCharacter - $substringLength + $i
                          + 1)} == $this->substring{$i}) {

      // did all letters match?
        if ($i == 0) {
          $this->results[] = $currentCharacter -$substringLength;
          $currentCharacter +=$this->getJumpLength
                              ($this-buffer{$currentCharacter});

            } else {
              continue;
            }

          // mismatch, jump ahead ...
          } else {
```

```
        $currentCharacter += $this->getJumpLength
                            ($this->buffer{$currentCharacter});
        break;
      }
    }
  }

  // return true if any matches occurred, false otherwise
  return (sizeof($this->results) > 0);
}

// create lookup table that determines how far we can
// jump ahead if a character doesn't match
 protected function deriveJumpTable()
{
  $maxJump = strlen($this->substring);

  // loop over letters of
  for ($i = strlen($this->substring) - 2; $i >= 0; $i--) {
    if (!array_key_exists($this->substring{$i}, $this->jumpTable)) {
      $this->jumpTable[$this->substring{$i}] = $maxJump - $i - 1;
    }
  }
}

// return the jump table
public function getJumpTable()
{
  return $this->jumpTable;
}

// return the results array
public function getResults()
{
  return $this->results;
}

// how many matches did we find?
public function getResultsCount()
{
  return sizeof($this->results);
}

// use the jump table to determine how far
```

```
    // to move ahead in the buffer
    public function getJumpLength($character)
    {
      if (array_key_exists($character, $this->jumpTable)) {
        return $this->jumpTable[$character];
      } else {
        return strlen($this->substring);
      }
    }
  }
?>
```

The `BoyerMooreStringSearch` class starts out by setting a couple of instance variables to hold the string to search (`$buffer`), the string to search for (`$substring`), the jump table array that will allow us to traverse the target string faster (`$jumpTable`), and an array to store found matches (`$results`). The constructor and destructor methods are empty and only included for completeness. However, the `search()` method contains most of the functionality and is the one that actually implements the algorithm, except for calculating the jump table which is being handled by a separate method.

After assigning the buffer and substring to instance variables, the `search()` method then asks method `deriveJumpTable()` to calculate the jump table array. It then initializes some local variables (`$bufferLength`, `$substringLength`, and `$currentCharacter`) that will be used to track our progress as we're traversing the buffer while searching for the substring. As we search the buffer from beginning to end, we use the jump table to determine by how many characters we should jump ahead.

There are also several accessor methods that allow us to retrieve the jump table and the results.

Unit testing BoyerMooreStringSearch

We could write a short script to exercise our new string searching class. However, we want to be able to do more than simply convince ourselves that it works. Let's start by outlining the whole unit testing procedure when using PHPUnit. With some basic knowledge under our belt, we will then create the actual tests and flesh out some of the details of all the available options and tools.

The test class

Classes and tests for those classes come in pairs. For a given class `MyClass`, you should have a corresponding class `MyClassTest` that consists of a collection of tests to be performed on `MyClass`. Whereas the original class has methods and properties to perform its regular function, `MyClassTest` has methods that represent individual tests. The test class typically extends `PHPUnit_Framework_TestCase` and each method name in the test class ends with the string "Test." When invoked, PHPUnit will instantiate `MyClassTest` and execute every test method in that class.

Assertions

Tests use assertions to perform the actual comparison or conditional that determines whether a test succeeded. You can think of assertions as an abbreviated syntax for if-then-else statements that integrate with the PHPUnit testing framework. I am using version 3.3.17 of PHPUnit to write this chapter and there are a total of 59 different assertions available.

The last argument to an assertion call is always a message to be displayed in case the assertion fails and PHPUnit needs to inform the user that the corresponding unit test was unsuccessful.

Some examples of assertions are:

- `assertArrayHasKey($key, array $array, $message = '')`: Tests whether key `$key` is defined in array `$array` and outputs message `$message` if not. This test is equivalent to using the native PHP functions `array_key_exists($key, $array)` or `isset($array[$key]) || is_null($array[$key])`.

- `assertFileExists($filename, $message = '')`: Tests whether a file `$filename` exists and displays message `$message` if the file cannot be found.

- `assertObjectHasAttribute($attributeName, $object, $message = '')`: Tests whether object `$object` has a property named `$attributeName` and displays message `$message` if it doesn't.

As the sample selection above illustrates, there are assertions to handle all kinds of tests, including comparisons (equal, less/greater than, is null, is true, and so on), reflection of objects and classes (existence of properties, methods, and so on), and XML (attributes and strings versus files).

For the complete list of assertions and their functionality, please consult the PHPUnit manual that can be viewed or downloaded from the project's site. Here is the link to a list of all assertions listed in the appendix of the documentation for version 3.3.

```
http://www.phpunit.de/manual/3.3/en/appendixes.assertions.html
```

Organization

Although it is more of a convention than a requirement, you should structure your unit tests so that they mirror the structure of your classes. If you are conscientious about creating unit tests, there should be a one-to-one correspondence between your classes and the respective unit tests. However, this is more of a guideline. Sometimes a unit test is not required for a class. At other times, it makes sense to write more than one unit test class for a given regular class. In the latter case, you should create a directory named after the original class to contain the unit tests.

Here is an example of a slightly fictitious class hierarchy and the corresponding test classes. I call it "slightly fictitious" because we will not actually be implementing all of these test classes in this chapter—only some of them. Let's start by listing the class hierarchy.

```
Terminal — bash — bash — Dirk — ttys001 — 80×11 — ⌘2
DirkMacBook:code dirk$ tree classes
classes
`-- Search
    |-- Array
    |   `-- Quick.php
    `-- String
        |-- BoyerMoore.php
        `-- Sequential.php

3 directories, 4 files
DirkMacBook:code dirk$ ▮
```

Following is the corresponding hierarchy of unit tests.

```
Terminal — bash — bash — Dirk — ttys001 — 80×13 — ⌘2
DirkMacBook:code dirk$ tree tests/
tests/
`-- Search
    |-- Array
    |   `-- QuickTest.php
    `-- String
        |-- BoyerMoore
        |   |-- MultipleTest.php
        |   `-- ResultCountTest.php
        `-- SequentialTest.php

4 directories, 6 files
DirkMacBook:code dirk$ ▮
```

As you can see, the `Search_Array_Quick` class has a corresponding `Search_Array_QuickTest` class. However, for the `Search_String_BoyerMoore` class, we have a corresponding directory that contains more than one corresponding test class. In this case, our two test classes are called `Search_String_BoyerMoore_MultipleTest` and `Search_String_BoyerMoore_ResultCountTest`.

Thanks to the way the `phpunit` executable works, it is straightforward to execute subsets of all the tests you have created. If you give the path to an individual test class, only that class will be executed. The following command line call to `phpunit`, for example, will only execute the tests in the `MultipleTest` class.

DirkMachine$ phpunit tests/Search/String/BoyerMoore/MultipleTest

In contrast, if you direct `phpunit` to a directory, it will traverse all sub-directories and execute any test file it finds. Thus, the following command line results in all tests in classes `MultipleTest`, `ResultCountTest`, and `Sequential` to be executed.

DirkMachine$ phpunit tests/Search/String

There are also two alternative ways of organizing and grouping tests. First you can define groupings in an XML file that you then pass to the `phpunit` executable as an option. Second, you can extend the `PHPUnit_Framework_TestSuite` class provided by PHPUnit. You can add any group of individual tests to a test suite. This approach has the additional advantage that `PHPUnit_Framework_TestSuite` provides methods to allow sharing of fixtures across test classes (more about fixtures shortly).

For more details on how to use the XML or class-defined test suite, please consult the excellent PHPUnit manual.

Our first unit test

Now that we know about the basic class structure of a unit test and how to use assertions, let's put that knowledge to work and create our first basic unit test.

classes/BoyerMooreStringSearchTest.php

```php
<?php
require_once 'PHPUnit/Framework.php';

require_once('../interfaces/StringSearchable.php');
require_once('../classes/BoyerMooreStringSearch.php');

// test class are named after the class they test
// and extend PHPUnit_Framework_TestCase
class BoyerMooreStringSearchTest extends PHPUnit_Framework_TestCase
{
  // methods are individual test and start with the string "test"
  public function testNumberOfMatches()
    {
    $poem = <<<POEM
Forgetting your coffee spreading on our flannel,
Your lipstick grinning on our coat,
So gaily in love's unbreakable heaven
```

```
Our souls on glory of spilt bourbon float.

Be with me, darling, early and late. Smash glasses—
I will study wry music for your sake.
For should your hands drop white and empty
All the toys of the world would break.
POEM;

    // create an instance of the search class
    $bm = new BoyerMooreStringSearch();

    // execute the search using our algorithm
    $bm->search('our', $poem);

    // assert that the algorithm found the correct
    // number of substrings in the buffer
      $this->assertEquals(8, $bm->getResultsCount(),
            'The algorithm did find the correct number of matches.');
    }
  }
?>
```

We start by requiring the definitions of the class and interface we will be testing, StringSearchable and BoyerMooreStringSearch; as well as the PHPUnit class we are extending, PHPUnit_Framework_TestCase. The unit test class we are creating, BoyerMooreStringSearchTest, is named after the class that we are testing. The only difference is that it has "Test" appended to the class name. Our test class extends PHPUnit_Framework_TestCase because that is how we are leveraging all the goodies of the PHPUnit framework.

The actual test is performed in method testNumberOfMatches(), which will be invoked automatically when we ask PHPUnit to execute our test class. The only requirement is that the method name starts with "test."

The test itself is pretty straightforward. We define a variable $poem which we will be searching for the occurrence of a substring. We are using the assertion assertEquals() to compare the number of matches reported by the class we are testing to the number of matches we know to be correct, namely eight.

That's it! Now, let's run this test from the command line. Assuming that the `phpunit` executable is in your path, you type the following command and observe the output.

```
Terminal — bash — bash — Dirk — ttys001 — 80×10 — ⌘2
DirkMacBook:tests dirk$ phpunit BoyerMooreStringSearch/ResultCountTest
PHPUnit 3.3.17 by Sebastian Bergmann.

.


Time: 0 seconds

OK (1 test, 1 assertion)

DirkMacBook:Search dirk$
```

PHPUnit starts out by identifying itself, its author, and the version that is running. The single dot on the next line represents a successfully executed unit test. In particular, the assert statement in our `testNumberOfMatches()` method turned out to be true. If the assert had failed, the dot would have been replaced by a letter "F" for failure. PHPUnit would also provide us with some details about which test failed and display the corresponding error message.

Temporarily modifying our test to expect a different number of results, we can force the unit test to fail. The corrsponding output is as follows:

```
Terminal — bash — bash — Dirk — ttys001 — 80×18 — ⌘2
DirkMacBook:tests dirk$ phpunit tests/Search/String/BoyerMoore/ResultCountTest.p
hp
PHPUnit 3.3.17 by Sebastian Bergmann.

F

Time: 0 seconds

There was 1 failure:

1) testNumberOfMatches(ResultCountTest)
The algorithm did find the correct number of matches.
Failed asserting that <integer:8> matches expected value <integer:7>.
/DirkMachine/UnitTesting/tests/Search/String/BoyerMoore/ResultCountTest.php:35

FAILURES!
Tests: 1, Assertions: 1, Failures: 1.
DirkMacBook:Search dirk$
```

Extended test class features

Having a test class with a single test is not quite in the spirit of unit testing. Our goal is to create enough tests to cover most or all of the scenarios our code is likely to encounter in production use. In this section, we will work towards that goal by adding additional test methods and by using different sets of data for the tests we have created.

Fixtures

One of the basic tenets of unit testing is that the environment should be exactly the same each time the test is being performed. PHPUnit gives us a pair of special methods that complement each other for exactly that purpose. The methods setUp() and tearDown() are provided to us by the PHPUnit_Framework_TestCase class we are extending and these methods are responsible for setting up the environment before and after each test is performed.

The important thing to note is that setUp() is called before each test method to give you a chance to reset the environment if necessary and desired. In that sense, setUp() is different from a constructor method, which only gets called once during the lifetime of an object. To illustrate this point, take a look at the following mock unit test class.

SetUpTearDownTest.php

```php
<?php
require_once 'PHPUnit/Framework.php';

class SetUpTearDownTest extends PHPUnit_Framework_TestCase
{
  // illustrating call to setUp method
  protected function setUp()
  {
    echo "executing " . __FUNCTION__ . "\n";
  }

  // first generic test method
  public function test1()
    {
    echo "executing " . __FUNCTION__ . " \n";
    }

  // second generic test method
  public function test2()
    {
    echo "executing " . __FUNCTION__ . " \n";
    }

  // illustrating call to tearDown method
  protected function tearDown()
  {
    echo "executing " . __FUNCTION__ . " \n";
  }
}
?>
```

Executing the above code doesn't perform any unit tests, but it does show us exactly the order of execution of the unit test methods and the methods that prepare and clean up the environment, setup() and teardown(). Here is what we see when executing our mock unit test class from the command line:

```
DirkMacBook:tests dirk$ phpunit ./SetUpTearDownTest
PHPUnit 3.3.17 by Sebastian Bergmann.

executing setUp
executing test1
executing tearDown
.executing setUp
executing test2
executing tearDown

.

Time: 0 seconds

OK (2 tests, 0 assertions)

DirkMacBook:Search dirk$
```

As you can conclude from the above output, setUp() gets called twice, once before each unit test method (test1 and test2). Analogously, tearDown() also gets called twice right after each of the unit test methods have completed.

Practical applications for these two methods are to set up the **fixture** of the unit tests. In other words, you get a chance to reset the environment to exactly the state required to run the tests. Only in a controlled environment is it possible to obtain reliable results.

In reality, setUp() is used much more frequently than tearDown(). You will see this as we add setUp() to our sample unit test class. We use setUp() to instantiate the class we are testing before each test. However, due to automatic garbage collection upon dereferencing objects, there is no corresponding action required of the tearDown() method.

Although generally not advisable, it is possible to share fixtures across different sub-classes of PHPUnit_Framework_TestCase. If you are looking to implement these kinds of global fixtures, take a look at adding setUp() and tearDown() to the PHPUnit_Framework_Testsuite instead of the PHPUnit_Framework_TestCase class we have been working with up to this point.

Before we add fixtures to our project, let's look at another useful feature that we will be implementing at the same time.

Annotations

In the context of coding, annotation are directives to the compiler, interpreter, or any other kind of parser. However, annotations take the form of phpDocumentor tags and are thus embedded in the comments of the source and don't really affect the execution of the code. PHPUnit 3.3.x, which is what I used to write this chapter, supports annotations for managing code coverage analysis (`@cover`, `@codeCoverageIgnoreStart`, and `@codeCoverageIgnoreEnd`), automated creation of assert-based tests (`@assert`), grouping of test classes (`@group`), marking methods as tests (`@test`), and marking tests as part of a scenario for behavior-driven development (`@scenario`).

In the following section, I would like to highlight the two annotations you are most likely to use, namely data providers (`@dataProvider`) and exception testing (`@expectedException`).

Data providers

Data providers are a shortcut for performing what is essentially the same test, but with different test data. The idea is that the PHPUnit framework knows to execute a given test method multiple times, each time passing it different parameters to be used during the test.

To let PHPUnit know where to get the data, you have to add a special phpDocumentor tag that identifies the name of a public method that returns either an array or an object which implements the `Iterator` interface. Either way, PHPUnit is then able to iterate over the array or object and call the corresponding test method for each item returned.

This may sound complicated, but a quick example illustrates the concept pretty convincingly:

tests/Search/String/BoyerMoore/MultipleTest.php

```
<?php
require_once 'PHPUnit/Framework.php';

require_once('interfaces/StringSearchable.php');
require_once('classes/Search/String/BoyerMoore.php');

class MultipleTest extends PHPUnit_Framework_TestCase
{
  protected $bm;

  protected function setUp()
    {
```

```
        // create the new search class
    $this->bm = new BoyerMoore();
    }


/**
 * @dataProvider provider
 */
    public function testNumberOfMatches($buffer, $substring, $matches)
    {
    // execute the search
    $this->bm->search($substring, $buffer);

        // assert that the algorithm found the correct
    // number of substrings in the buffer
        $this->assertEquals($matches, $this->bm->getResultsCount());
    }


    // This method provides data to be used when calling
    // method testNumberOfMatches()
 public function provider()
    {
    return array(
            array('abcdeabcdabcaba', 'abc', 3),
            array(<<<POEM
Forgetting your coffee spreading on our flannel,
Your lipstick grinning on our coat,
So gaily in love's unbreakable heaven
Our souls on glory of spilt bourbon float.

Be with me, darling, early and late. Smash glasses—
I will study wry music for your sake.
For should your hands drop white and empty
All the toys of the world would break.
POEM
            , 'our', 7)
        );
    }
}
?>
```

Class `MultipleTest` performs essentially the same as did class `ResultCountTest` we encountered earlier in this chapter. It uses our algorithm to locate all matches for a given substring and compares the result to a value known to be correct. However, we also see some of the new features we just learned about, being implemented in this class.

First, rather than having to instantiate `BoyerMooreStringSearch` in the test class, we let the `setUp()` method take care of that for us. This way, when we add additional test methods to the class, we won't have to worry about having to obtain a reference to the object we are testing.

Second, we created a `provider()` method that returns an array. Each array member is in turn an array itself consisting of three values: the buffer, the substring, and the number of occurrences of the substring within the buffer. The number of items in the array corresponds to the number of arguments required by method `testNumberOfMatches($buffer, $substring, $matches)`. What this means is that `testNumberOfMatches()` will get called twice, once with the string "abcdeabcdabcaba" as the buffer and once with the excerpt from the poem with which we have been working.

At this point, adding another buffer-substring-result count test has become trivial. All we have to do is add another three-member array to the array in the `provider()` method and PHPUnit will take care of the rest.

Following is the output from running this unit test class. As expected, we see two dots representing two successfully executed tests (really the same test with two different sets of data).

```
Terminal — bash — bash — Dirk — ttys001 — 80×10 — ⌘2
DirkMacBook:tests dirk$ phpunit tests/Search/String/BoyerMoore/MultipleTest
PHPUnit 3.3.17 by Sebastian Bergmann.

..

Time: 0 seconds

OK (2 tests, 2 assertions)
ons: 1, Failures: 1.
DirkMacBook:Search dirk$
```

Exceptions

Testing exceptions can be kind of tricky. If you code some method call or data that will cause the code being tested to throw an exception, you can then wrap that code into a try-catch-statement and let the test case fail if it never reaches the catch statement. However, PHPUnit offers a much more elegant, concise, and explicit way of testing exceptions, the `@expectedException` annotation.

By preceding the test case with an `@expectedException` annotation, you can let PHPUnit know that the test case should be considered a failure unless an exception is being thrown. Since there is nothing like an example to clear up confusion, here we go.

Let's say we add the following code at the beginning of the `BoyerMoore::search()` method to make sure the parameters we are getting are acceptable:

```php
<?php
  // ... the rest of the class's code goes here ...


    // implement interface method
    // with args like needle, haystack
  public function search($substring, $buffer,
                          $caseSensitive = self::CASE_SENSITIVE)
  {
    // validate input
    if (!is_string($substring) || strlen($substring) < 1) {
      throw new Exception("Substring to search for must be a string
                                  with one or more characters.");
    } elseif (!is_string($buffer) || strlen($buffer) < 1) {
      throw new Exception("Buffer through which to search must be a
                                  string with one or more characters.");
    } elseif (!is_bool($caseSensitive)) {
      throw new Exception("The third argument to function " .
                                  __FUNCTION__ . " must be a boolean.");
    }

  // ... the rest of the class's code goes here ...
?>
```

Following is the test class that allows us to test the various scenarios where an exception might get thrown due to invalid parameters being passed to the search function.

```php
<?php
require_once 'PHPUnit/Framework.php';

require_once('interfaces/StringSearchable.php');
require_once('classes/Search/String/BoyerMoore.php');

// test class are named after the class they test
// and extend PHPUnit_Framework_TestCase
class ExceptionsTest extends PHPUnit_Framework_TestCase
{
    protected $bm;

    protected function setUp()
    {
        // create the new search class
```

```php
        $this->bm = new BoyerMoore();
    }


    /**
     * Testing that an exception being thrown if the buffer,
     * substring, or 3rd argument don't pass validation.
     *
     * @dataProvider provider
     * @expectedException Exception
     */
    public function testExceptions($buffer, $substring,
$caseSensitive)
    {
        // execute the search using our algorithm
        $this->bm->search($substring, $buffer, $caseSensitive);
    }


    // This method provides data to be used when calling
    // method testNumberOfMatches()
    public function provider()
    {
        return array(
                    array('', 'find me', BoyerMoore::CASE_SENSITIVE),
// empty buffer
                    array(null, 'find me',
BoyerMoore::CASE_SENSITIVE), // null buffer
                    array(array(), 'find me',
BoyerMoore::CASE_SENSITIVE), // array buffer
                    array('search me', '',
BoyerMoore::CASE_SENSITIVE), // empty substring
                    array('search me', null,
BoyerMoore::CASE_SENSITIVE), // null substring
                    array('search me', array(),
BoyerMoore::CASE_SENSITIVE), // array substring
                    array('search me', 'find me', 'whatever'), //
wrong 3rd arg
                    );
    }
}
?>
```

Once again we are using a data provider to call the `testExceptions()` method multiple times. Since `testExceptions()` accepts buffer, substring, and a Boolean case-sensitive flag as arguments, we can test exceptions being thrown due to any of the three arguments not passing validation.

Here is the output from running the new test:

```
○ ○ ○              Terminal — bash — bash — Dirk — ttys001 — 80×11 — ⌘2
DirkMacBook:tests dirk$ phpunit tests/Search/String/BoyerMoore/ExceptionsTest.ph
p
PHPUnit 3.3.17 by Sebastian Bergmann.

.......

Time: 0 seconds

OK (7 tests, 7 assertions)

DirkMacBook:Search dirk$ █
```

As you can see from the dots, the test code expected and caught seven exceptions, which means that all seven tests passed.

Automation: generating tests from classes

Among other useful features, PHPUnit's command-line client has one that stands out as a big time saver in my opinion. Given a class, phpunit can use reflection on that class and generate the skeleton of a corresponding test class. If you are thoroughly committed to test-driven development, you might be shuddering in horror right now. If you think about it, this is pretty much the opposite of what many modern and agile methods preach these days. You are supposed to write your test cases first and then code accordingly. However, that is not the reality we developers face most days. There are many reasons why you might end up with complete code before even a single test case has been written.

There is the situation where you inherit an existing project that does not come with unit tests. Perhaps the developer was not nearly as enlightened as we are. Or, the project simply predates the practice of creating unit tests. Whatever the case, you are now asked to make significant changes to the project and you want to make sure that your new contributions don't break existing functionality. You can start writing unit tests from scratch or you can use phpunit to give you a hand.

Another possibility is that management has committed to a deliverable that puts you in serious time constraint. Maybe you have been asked to prototype a solution over a couple of days that simply does not allot the time to create proper unit tests as well. We all know it happens, but we also know that we should really make an effort to return to the project as soon as the workload lightens to create those missing unit tests. The coding is the fun part, of course, which is why we want to make creating unit tests at the tail end of the project as quick as possible. Again, PHPUnit comes to our rescue.

Using the `--skeleton-test` command line option to `phpunit`, we can easily generate a bare bones test class. Fleshing out an automatically generated test class is a significant time saver compared to generating one from scratch.

Here is the command line output from generating a test class based on our BoyerMoore class:

```
           Terminal — bash — bash — Dirk — ttys001 — 80×5 — ⌘2
DirkMacBook:tests dirk$ phpunit --skeleton-test BoyerMoore
PHPUnit 3.3.17 by Sebastian Bergmann.

Wrote skeleton for "BoyerMooreTest" to "./BoyerMooreTest.php".
DirkMacBook:Search dirk$ █
```

The test code that was generated by the above command is as follows:

```php
<?php
require_once 'PHPUnit/Framework.php';

require_once 'BoyerMoore.php';

/**
 * Test class for BoyerMoore.
 * Generated by PHPUnit on 2009-09-01 at 12:45:03.
 */
class BoyerMooreTest extends PHPUnit_Framework_TestCase
{
    /**
     * @var     BoyerMoore
     * @access protected
     */
    protected $object;

    /**
     * Sets up the fixture, for example, opens a network connection.
     * This method is called before a test is executed.
     *
     * @access protected
     */
    protected function setUp()
    {
        $this->object = new BoyerMoore;
    }

    /**
```

```
     * Tears down the fixture, for example, closes a network
connection.
     * This method is called after a test is executed.
     *
     * @access protected
     */
    protected function tearDown() { }

    /**
     * @todo Implement test__destruct().
     */
    public function test__destruct()
    {
        // Remove the following lines when you implement this test.
        $this->markTestIncomplete(
          'This test has not been implemented yet.'
        );
    }

    /**
     * @todo Implement testSearch().
     */
    public function testSearch()
    {
        // Remove the following lines when you implement this test.
        $this->markTestIncomplete(
          'This test has not been implemented yet.'
        );
    }

    /**
     * @todo Implement testGetJumpTable().
     */
    public function testGetJumpTable()
    {
        // Remove the following lines when you implement this test.
        $this->markTestIncomplete(
          'This test has not been implemented yet.'
        );
    }

    /**
     * @todo Implement testGetResults().
     */
```

```
public function testGetResults()
{
    // Remove the following lines when you implement this test.
    $this->markTestIncomplete(
      'This test has not been implemented yet.'
    );
}


/**
 * @todo Implement testGetResultsCount().
 */
public function testGetResultsCount()
{
    // Remove the following lines when you implement this test.
    $this->markTestIncomplete(
      'This test has not been implemented yet.'
    );
}


/**
 * @todo Implement testGetJumpLength().
 */
public function testGetJumpLength()
{
    // Remove the following lines when you implement this test.
    $this->markTestIncomplete(
      'This test has not been implemented yet.'
    );
}
}
?>
```

As you can see, PHPUnit generated nicely formatted object-oriented PHP code that contains placeholders for the body of the test methods. It even includes some helpful phpDocumentor tags, such as @access, @var, and @todo.

Unimplemented and skipped tests

The test class skeleton generated by PHPUnit above illustrates how to mark a test as being unimplemented. By calling markTestIncomplete([$message]), you can let the PHPUnit framework know that the corresponding test should neither be considered a success nor a failure—it simply hasn't been implemented yet.

Asking PHPUnit to run the test class above results in the folowing output:

```
000           Terminal — bash — bash — Dirk — ttys001 — 80×11 — ⌘2
DirkMacBook:code dirk$ phpunit tests/Search/String/BoyerMooreTest
PHPUnit 3.3.17 by Sebastian Bergmann.

IIIIII

Time: 0 seconds

OK, but incomplete or skipped tests!
Tests: 6, Assertions: 0, Incomplete: 6.
" to "./BoyerMooreTest.php".
DirkMacBook:Search dirk$ █
```

As you can see, incomplete tests have been marked with a capital letter "I".

Similarly, you can use a call to `markTestSkipped([$message])` to let PHPUnit know that a given test should be considered skipped. In the output of `phpunit`, skipped tests are indicated by a capital letter "S."

As a guideline, you should call `markTestSkipped()` if an otherwise complete unit test is not being executed due to some condition. In other words, you should have a conditional statement, such as an if-statement, wrapping calls to `markTestSkipped()`. Otherwise, if the body of the test is empty or the test logic has only been implemented partially, you should use `markTestIncomplete()`.

Automation: generating classes from tests

Now that we know how to generate test case skeleton classes from code classes, let's consider the opposite direction and use that as an entry point into a discussion of test-driven development.

Using the `--skeleton-class` command line option, you can get PHPUnit to generate a bare class file based on the test class you have written. PHPUnit parses your test class and knows which class is being tested based on the name of the file.

The idea of writing the test before the code is not at all as crazy as it may seem. It is actually the foundation of a methodology that has grown in popularity over the last couple of years.

Test-driven development

Test-driven development is not completely new, but it has seen resurgence in conjunction with agile and extreme programming methodology over the last couple of years. The basic premise is simple: write the unit test(s) first and then write the code to satisfy the test.

Proponents of this approach claim that it results in simpler and easier to maintain code. Furthermore, it breaks the development process into relatively small and manageable iterations. Here is a flowchart of what one such iteration might look like:

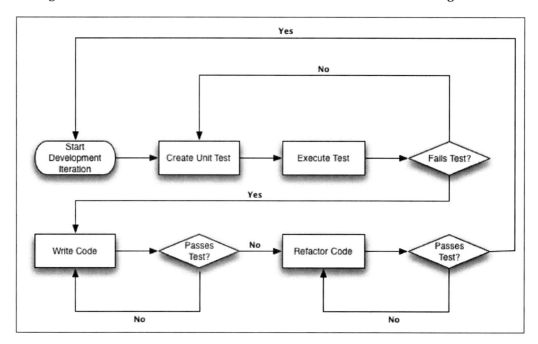

 The typical sequence of activities when using test-driven development is the following:

1. Write a unit test.
2. Execute the test and make sure it fails (because the corresponding code has not yet been written).
3. Write the code to satisfy the test.
4. Execute the test again to make sure the code passes. If not, return to step 3.
5. Refactor the code while continuing to run the unit test to make sure none of the changes break the newly added functionality.

Enhancing our example with TDD

I hope that by now you have picked up on the fact that I don't believe in operating in a vacuum of theory. Therefore, let's apply our newfound knowledge to our string search class by giving it an option to make the search either case-sensitive or case-insensitive. At the moment, the algorithm considers all characters to be different, which means it is currently case-sensitive.

Here is the test method we would add to perform a case-insensitive search. For brevity, I have omitted the rest of the test class that we have already seen.

```php
<?php
    // … the rest of the test class goes here

    // testing case-insensitive search
    public function testCaseInsensitive()
      {
      // get data array from provider method
      $dataArr = $this->provider();

      // execute the search
      $this->bm->search('our', $dataArr[1][0],
                                    BoyerMoore::CASE_INSENSITIVE);

          // assert that the algorithm found the correct
      // number of substrings in the buffer
          $this->assertEquals(8, $this->bm->getResultsCount());
      }

    // … the rest of the test class goes here

?>
```

By calling the `provider()` method directly, we are able to retrieve a reference to the poem excerpt we have been using in our tests thus far. In methods `testNumberOfMatches()` we expected 7 occurrences of "our" because the search was case-sensitive. For a case-insensitive search, however, we would expect eight occurrences of "our" to be found because the buffer contains the word "Our" at the beginning of a sentence and consequently the first letter has been capitalized.

Actually, if you look at how we are calling the search, you will notice that we have added a third argument—a class constant to signify whether the search is to be case-sensitive or not. Since the test will be prevented from even running as the result of a parse error, let's add class constants `CASE_SENSITIVE` and `CASE_INSENSITIVE` to the `BoyerMoore` class before asking `phpunit` to run the test class.

Executing the test class with the new test method meets our design goal: the previous tests pass; whereas the newly added test method results in a failure. Here is the output phpunit gives us:

```
DirkMacBook:code dirk$ phpunit tests/Search/String/BoyerMoore/MultipleTest
PHPUnit 3.3.17 by Sebastian Bergmann.

..F

Time: 0 seconds

There was 1 failure:

1) testCaseInsensitive(MultipleTest)
Failed asserting that <integer:7> matches expected value <integer:8>.
/Volumes/Documents/Work/WaferThin/Packt/Book/Code/chapter8/tests/Search/String/B
oyerMoore/MultipleTest.php:63

FAILURES!
Tests: 3, Assertions: 3, Failures: 1.
DirkMacBook:Search dirk$
```

We can now move on to the third step of our test-driven development iteration, which is to write the code to satisfy the new test. We might modify the search() method as follows. Again, for brevity I have omitted the rest of the class code listing because it hasn't changed.

```php
<?php
// class constants
const CASE_SENSITIVE = true;
const CASE_INSENSITIVE = false;

    // the substring for which to search
    public $substring = 'null';
public $originalSubstring = 'null';

    // the buffer to be searched for any occurrences of the substring
    public $buffer = '';
public $originalBuffer = '';

    // ... the rest of the test class goes here

    // implement interface method
    // with args like needle, haystack
  public function search($substring, $buffer, $caseSensitive =
self::CASE_SENSITIVE)
```

```
{
    // reset results array
    $this->results = array();

    $this->substring = $substring;
$this->originalSubstring = $substring;
    $this->buffer = $buffer;
$this->originalBuffer = $buffer;


// change the working buffer & substring to lower case
// if the search is to be case-insensitive
if ($caseSensitive != self::CASE_SENSITIVE) {
  $this->substring = strtolower($this->substring);
  $this->buffer = strtolower($this->buffer);
}

    // get jump table
    $this->deriveJumpTable();

    $currentCharacter = strlen($this->substring) - 1;
    $substringLength = strlen($this->substring);
    $bufferLength = strlen($this->buffer);

    while ($currentCharacter < $bufferLength) {

      for ($i = $substringLength - 1; $i >= 0; $i--) {

        // character matches, continue ...
        if ($this->buffer{($currentCharacter - $substringLength +
        $i + 1)} == $this->substring{$i}) {

          // did all letters match?
          if ($i == 0) {
            $this->results[] = $currentCharacter - $substringLength;
            $currentCharacter += $this->getJumpLength
                                 ($this->buffer{$currentCharacter});

          } else {
            continue;
          }

        // mismatch, jump ahead ...
        } else {
```

```
            $currentCharacter += $this->getJumpLength
                              ($this->buffer{$currentCharacter});
        break;
      }
    }
  }

  // return true if any matches occurred, false otherwise
  return (sizeof($this->results) > 0);
}

// ... the rest of the test class goes here
?>
```

Additions to the code have been highlighted in the above listing. Our solution is to simply keep unmodified copies of the buffer and substring (`$bufferOriginal` and `$substringOriginal`) and convert our working buffer and substring to lower case before performing the search.

Running the exact same unit test that failed before now displays the following successful output.

```
000                 Terminal — bash — bash — Dirk — ttys001 — 80×9 — ⌘2
DirkMacBook:code dirk$ phpunit tests/Search/String/BoyerMoore/MultipleTest
PHPUnit 3.3.17 by Sebastian Bergmann.

...

Time: 0 seconds

OK (3 tests, 3 assertions)
DirkMacBook:Search dirk$ █
```

In our example, we can skip the last step typical of test-driven development. Our test and new feature are simple enough that not much refactoring is required to move from merely satisfying the test to a state where you can proudly show it off to other developers without being ridiculed.

Code coverage

If you happen to also have Xdebug installed, PHPUnit can easily be made to generate code coverage data. Adding the option `--coverage-html <output_dir>` to the command-line execution of `phpunit` will result in a coverage report being generated in HTML. For example, I ran the following command line:

```
phpunit --coverage-html ./report tests/Search/String/BoyerMoore/
```

This executed all unit tests found in the BoyerMoore directory and generated the HTML page as follows:

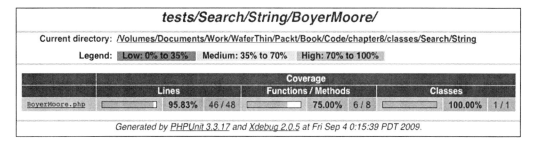

For the BoyerMoore class, we can get more detailed information from the report by clicking on BoyerMoore.php.

tests/Search/String/BoyerMoore/

Current file: /Volumes/Documents/Work/WaferThin/Packt/Book/Code/chapter8/classes/Search/String /BoyerMoore.php

Legend: executed   not executed   dead code

	Coverage		
	Classes	Functions / Methods	Lines
Total	100.00% 1 / 1	75.00% 6 / 8	95.83% 46 / 48
BoyerMoore	100.00% 1 / 1	75.00% 6 / 8	95.83% 46 / 48
public function __construct()		100.00% 1 / 1	100.00% 1 / 1
public function __destruct()		100.00% 1 / 1	100.00% 1 / 1
public function search($substring, $buffer, $caseSensitive = true)		100.00% 1 / 1	100.00% 33 / 33
protected function deriveJumpTable()		100.00% 1 / 1	100.00% 7 / 7
public function getJumpTable()		0.00% 0 / 1	0.00% 0 / 1
public function getResults()		0.00% 0 / 1	0.00% 0 / 1
public function getResultsCount()		100.00% 1 / 1	100.00% 1 / 1
public function getJumpLength($character)		100.00% 1 / 1	100.00% 3 / 3

There is even a listing of the source code with highlighting that shows which lines have been tested and which have not. Here is an excerpt.

```
35            :      public function search($substring, $buffer,
36            :      {
37            :          // validate input
38        11  :          if (!is_string($substring) || strlen($s
39         3  :              throw new Exception("Substring to se
40         8  :          } elseif (!is_string($buffer) || strlen
41         3  :              throw new Exception("Buffer through
42         5  :          } elseif (!is_bool($caseSensitive)) {
43         1  :              throw new Exception("The third argu
44            :          }
45
```

For obvious reasons, the higher the percentage of lines that have been tested, the more confidence you can have in the quality of your code.

TestCase subclasses

PHPUnit provides several subclasses of `PHPUnit_Framework_TestCase` that provide specialized functionality. Although we do not have time and space enough to cover these in detail, I want you to be aware that these advanced features exist and know that you can read up on them when the time comes when you need them in your unit tests. Following is a list of `PHPUnit_Framework_TestCase` subclasses and corresponding descriptions:

- `PHPUnit_Extensions_PerformanceTestCase` allows you to limit the execution time of a process. This class is helpful if you are testing performance and execution times.

- `PHPUnit_Extensions_OutputTestCase` lets you construct tests for the output generated by the code being tested.

- `PHPUnit_Extensions_Database_TestCase` allows you to test database connections and sets of data.

- `PHPUnit_Extensions_SeleniumTestCase` enables you to test your code through the web interface it provides. This is done with the help of Selenium, a popular web application testing system.

Summary

We started this chapter with an overview of different types of testing. Hopefully, this background knowledge will help you to better relate to the various people that have a stake in the software development process. Different motivations result in different types of testing. A functional expert cares whether the system produces the correct result, but may care little about the details of the implementation on a code level. It's not his job.

Our job as developers, however, is closely tied to the lowest level of testing, namely unit testing. With the help of the PHPUnit framework, we learned how to quickly construct simple tests, organize them, and execute them. We even covered advanced topics such as test-driven development and code coverage analysis.

Paired with a little discipline, PHPUnit is sure to make it easier to catch bugs early in the development process when it is still comparatively cheap to fix them. I challenge you to write the first line of code on your next project for a unit test instead of regular code.

8

Deploying Applications

Once you have finished developing your applications and have gotten everybody invested in the project to sign off, it is time to deploy. Actually, by then, you should have already deployed the application many times and the whole process should be more or less automated.

Most of the projects in which I have been involved lately have benefited from frequently deploying the application to various environments, such as development, test, and production. Automating this process allows you to quickly get new instances of the application up and running.

Not only is this a good way of shaking out any potential problems with the eventual production deployment, it is also a great step toward having new developers be productive. If you have the deployment process optimized and well documented, new members of the development team will not have to spend countless hours setting up their development environment. Instead, they can follow some simple steps to get the application working and ready for development.

Goals and requirements

Let's consider what our goals should be in deploying or upgrading an application. Put another way, how do we measure success? One might be tempted to say that how well the application performs is equivalent to how well the deployment went. However, that would be misleading. At this stage, we don't concern ourselves anymore with functional design, programming, or testing. We are operating on the assumption that we have a fully functional application that needs to be deployed. Whether it works as expected may or may not still be our problem, but it has nothing to do with the deployment itself.

How then, you may ask, will we determine whether the deployment went well? What shall we strive for in coming up with a deployment plan? As you may have guessed, I have a couple of ideas on the topic.

First, a deployment should happen quickly. If you have been deploying applications manually, you will be surprised as to how much of that activity can be automated if only it is planned carefully. The first time you deploy an application, you can typically take your time and make sure you get it right before notifying the client or users of the availability of the application. Not surprisingly, a quick deployment becomes significantly more important when upgrading an application that is actively being used. In that situation, our goal should be to minimize or completely avoid any interruption of service to the existing user base. That is when speed becomes a factor.

The second goal is for the deployment to be completely reversible. You might want to start thinking of an application upgrade as atomic transaction that you may have encountered when working with databases. If something goes wrong during the deployment, you should be able to reverse all steps taken so far and restore the application to the exact state it was in before the deployment started. As much sense as that seems to make, sometimes it is easier said than done.

Take for example the case where you have to modify an existing database table. You might have to run some queries to modify the table structure or manipulate the data. If you mess up or some other unforeseen problem occurs, how do you back out? Assuming you planned ahead, you can restore the database from a backup you took before you started the upgrade. However, depending on the size of your database, loading the definitions and data for all tables might take several minutes. Alternatively, you can restore only the compromised table, but only if you have the right tools to do that. If you have backed up your database to a single monolithic dump file, it might not be that easy to extract a single table and restore it. Another option yet is to run prepared queries to reverse the changes that led to the problem. If that is your approach, you will want to prepare those queries ahead of time so you don't have to come up with them in crisis mode when the pressure is on.

As you can see by the above example, there are often many approaches you can take to make your deployment or upgrade reversible. Careful planning is required to be able to do this for each of the steps involved.

To summarize, our requirements for a deployment or upgrade are:

1. Speed and automation to minimize user impact and eliminate human error
2. Complete reversibility of all actions

I'm repeating myself here because our subsequent discussion of deployment plans, individual actions, and actual code we develop to make it happen, will be framed against the backdrop of these requirements. They will be a yardstick in deciding how successfully we have accomplished our goal.

Deploying your application

In the previous section, we've talked about being able to reverse individual steps during a deployment, but which steps exactly are we talking about. Let's take a look at some activities that are typical of deploying or upgrading an application. Later in the chapter, we will work on actually implementing these tasks and automating them as much as possible.

The following sequence diagram illustrates the steps of deploying an application or website. Certainly, depending on your application, there are steps that you can add or ignore, but these steps should present a good starting point for most deployments and can be tweaked as necessary.

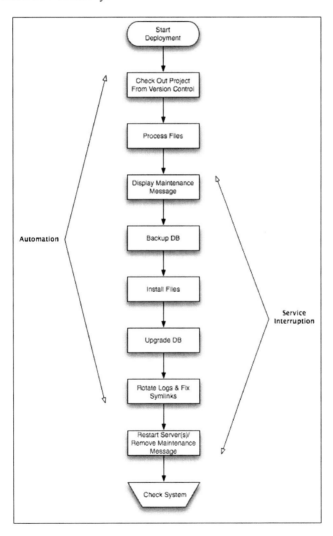

Before looking at each of these steps in detail, let's consider the big picture represented by the previous diagram. We start by checking the whole project out of our version control system. To accommodate the environment in which the application will be deployed, some of the files, primarily configuration files, will have to be modified. We then put up a message on our existing website that informs users of the ongoing maintenance. After installing the files, making the corresponding changes to the underlying database, and rotating the log files, we take down the under maintenance message, restart the server, and once again open the site to our users. Lastly, we inspect the site to verify that the application is functioning properly.

Checking out and uploading files

Assuming that your project resides in some kind of source code control system, you will have to first pull it out to a version of the project that can be deployed to a production server. If you are using Subversion to house your projects as discussed in another chapter in this book, you need to perform an *export* of your project to get a copy that is stripped of all the Subversion meta data typically hidden in invisible files within each of the project's directories. Other version control systems may use different terminology, but the idea remains the same. You need a copy of your projects that is clean of any meta data or other files that are not meant to be deployed.

In contrast, you might want the deployment process to be able to deploy source code that is still connected to the repository. In Subversion terminology, you might be checking the code out into a local or remote working copy. The benefits of that approach are twofold. First, you can use the information in the repository to make future upgrades easier. For example, you might be able to simply run a command to update the checked out version to the most recent version of the code. Second, if your deployment process supports repository checkouts, it can be used to quickly set up development environments, thus getting new development team members productive more quickly. Therefore, the process that we will be developing in this chapter will allow you to perform either type of deployment, production or development.

It is also more than likely that you will have to change one or several of the configuration files with settings that reflect the production environment. For example, you may need to set the home directory of your project, database connection credentials, base URL, and so on.

You might want to take a look at the chapter on application frameworks because the sample application we developed in that chapter was intentionally designed to support multiple environments with the help of corresponding sections in the configuration file. This was done in anticipation of having an automated deployment process targeting different environments.

Once you have a deployable version of your project, you will need to transfer it to the server. This is typically done using the FTP, SFTP, or SCP (SSH) protocols. Hopefully, you will be using one of the secure options that don't expose credentials in the clear.

If you are working the installation from the productions server, you might be able to combine the two steps of exporting and uploading the project by leveraging the fact that all modern version control systems support remote operations. Simply check out your project from the repository directly to the target machine and you're done with this step.

Displaying an under-maintenance message

Before actually pulling the figurative switch, you should notify your users that you will be performing some work on the server. I usually redirect users temporarily to a generic HTML page that informs them that the server is undergoing maintenance and that they should retry their request in a couple of minutes.

If you plan and automate your upgrades well, the service interruption your users experience should be minimal or non-existent. So what's the point of putting up a maintenance page you may ask? Well, the maintenance page suddenly becomes important if something should derail your carefully planned deployment. At that point, you are probably scrambling to figure out what went wrong so you can fix it. When this situation occurs, you will be thankful for not having to worry about warning the users and can instead spend your time on the task that really requires your attention, namely the troubleshooting.

Once the upgrade has been completed, the maintenance page needs to be taken down. Again, this should be automated because it is a step you don't want to forget.

Upgrading and installing files

Once the files are on the server, you will need to make them available to your users. Replacing the existing files with the new ones violates our requirement of reversibility. You could rename them or move the folder with the old files and then replace them with the new ones. However, there is an even quicker way of doing this.

On systems that support symbolic links (or *aliases* or *shortcuts*), it is good practice to have a symlink that points to the directory containing the application files. When it is time to upgrade, you merely have to point the symlink at a different directory and the new files become visible instantly.

Upgrading database schema and data

Most applications these days rely on some kind of permanent database storage, with MySQL being the frontrunner in that category, simply because of its popularity. When you first deploy an application, you are usually also responsible for making sure that the database gets created correctly and is accessible. In the case where you are upgrading an existing installation, you will have to come up with a way of modifying the schema and/or data. A typical way of doing that is to have a text file to which developers add queries to make the database changes required by their code. During deployment, a database administrator or developer is then responsible for executing those queries during the upgrade window in which the rest of the deployment tasks are taking place as well.

Although this approach might work well enough for upgrading or creating a database, it does not satisfy our deployment requirements. It is not easily reversible—unless you plan for it. Also, as you deploy subsequent releases, additional changes to the database will be required and it will become increasingly difficult to roll it back to a previous state.

One possible answer to these problems can be found in a tool that allows us to define, manage, and execute incremental changes to the database. These incremental changes are called migrations and the tool we will be using to manage our migrations is called *DbDeploy*. Since each incremental upgrade to a database has a corresponding incremental downgrade, it is possible to step through the changes to the database in either direction at any time you wish. Moreover, changes can be applied in an automated fashion, thus satisfying both our requirements of a successful deployment.

We will dive into the details of DbDeploy when we get to define actual DB migrations later in this chapter.

Rotating log files and updating symbolic links

Depending on where and how your application saves log information, it may be necessary or at least advisable to rotate the log files. For one, you need to make sure that they are still writable by the server, which may not be the case if the log files reside within your application's directory and you have pointed the production symlink to another directory.

Miscellaneous other libraries or supporting applications might need to be copied or symlinked to the newly deployed application. For example, I have a Web interface for reading e-mail that is accessible from the document root directory of my website. However, it is not part of the site's project in the Subversion repository and this needs to be copied or symlinked whenever a new version of the site is being deployed.

Verifying the deployed application

This last step may be obvious, but at the same time it is not one you want to overlook. There should be checks that everything that was deployed is actually working as expected. This is the one step where we have to allow for a slight deviation from our requirements. Although we can and want to automate some checks, such as testing HTTP response headers, some things just have to be checked manually. Sometimes the easiest way of making sure that everything is working is to pull up the site in a web browser or execute the application in whichever way it was meant to be accessed. Often, any major problems can be spotted right away.

Automating deployment

Now that we are clear on what we are trying to achieve, let's start exploring the tools we will be using to implement and automate our deployment plan. Although we will enlist a handful of supporting utilities to get the job done, the tool we will be looking towards to automate the whole process and perform most of the tasks is called Phing.

Phing

Phing is a project build system. The name is actually a recursive acronym and stands for "**PH**ing **I**s **N**ot **G**nu Make." Phing allows you to perform all kinds of tasks associated with building software. It's especially great for automating tasks, which is exactly what we have been discussing in the first part of this chapter.

Although Phing goes so far as to disavow any association with the utility *make*, it is pretty safe to say that *make* is part of Phing's heritage. However, Phing has been modeled much more closely after *Ant*, Java's predominant build tool, than anything else.

Using Phing instead of Ant has the advantage that it supports various tasks specific to PHP development. Also, Phing is written in PHP, which makes it easy for a PHP developer to extend its functionality.

Phing is driven by targets that are defined in an XML file. Targets are essentially actions that Phing can perform. The XML file that defines these targets and their interdependence is usually called `build.xml`. Targets in turn are composed of one or more tasks, but we will learn more about either a little later in this chapter.

From the command line it is then easy to ask Phing to execute any of the defined targets and handle the dependencies automatically. Examples of user-defined targets might include:

- `create-skeleton`: Create some directories needed by the site
- `checkout-site`: Perform a Subversion checkout
- `update-db`: Run some pre-defined queries to update the database structure and/or data

These targets are actually some of the ones we will be creating and using on our test project as follows.

Installing Phing

There are a couple of different ways of installing Phing. The easiest and least painful one would be to do it via the Pear installer. We have encountered the Pear repository and the accompanying command line tool numerous times throughout this book. The reasons for that are simple—it works and it has found wide acceptance to the effect that most of the third party tools I discuss can be downloaded and installed that way.

Rather than just run Pear at this point, I want to point out what a perfect fit this tool is for the current chapter. If you stop to think about it, by typing `pear install phing/phing`, we're doing exactly what this whole chapter is about—we deploy (install) an application, namely Phing. In other words, depending on your type of application, distributing it via a Pear channel might be another approach to deploying it.

For now, let's proceed with the practical aspects (because it just works!) and use Pear to install Phing. The following is a transcript of me installing Phing from the command line:

```
DirkMachine:bin dirk$ sudo pear channel-discover pear.phing.info
Adding Channel "pear.phing.info" succeeded
Discovery of channel "pear.phing.info" succeeded
DirkMachine:bin dirk$ sudo pear install phing/phing
Package "pear.phing.info/phing" dependency "pear.php.net/Xdebug" has no releases
Did not download optional dependencies: pear/VersionControl_SVN, pear/Xdebug, pe
ar/PEAR_PackageFileManager, use --alldeps to download automatically
phing/phing can optionally use package "pear/VersionControl_SVN" (version >= 0.3
.0alpha1)
phing/phing can optionally use package "pear/Xdebug" (version >= 2.0.0beta2)
phing/phing can optionally use package "pear/PEAR_PackageFileManager" (version >
= 1.5.2)
downloading phing-2.3.3.tgz ...
Starting to download phing-2.3.3.tgz (422,298 bytes)
..................................................................
.....done: 422,298 bytes
install ok: channel://pear.phing.info/phing-2.3.3

DirkMacBook:hooks dirk$
```

There are really only two commands here. First, pear channel-discover `pear.phing.`
`info` tells the pear installer that there is a Pear repository at `pear.phing.info.`
Second, `pear install phing/phing` tells the executable to install the package
called phing (second occurrence of "phing") from the channel called phing
(first occurrence of "phing").

Another option of getting Phing is to check it out of the project's CVS repository
directly. The advantage there is that you get the latest and greatest code base,
including unreleased enhancements and bugs. This is what you will have to do if
you plan on contributing to the project because it will allow you to commit your
changes back to the repository—assuming you have been given commit privileges.

Basic syntax and file structure

The build file contains XML that defines all the actions and targets available to
the user. By convention, this file is named `build.xml`. However, if you use the
`-buildfile [builfile]` command-line option, you can name it anything you
like. For our examples, we will stick with the default naming convention.

Let's take a look at the basic structure of a Phing build file. The following skeleton of
a Phing build file doesn't actually do anything. It is only meant to illustrate the basic
structure of those files. However, we will flesh out the various sections of the build
file as we make our way through this chapter towards the goal of a fully automated
deployment process.

```xml
<?xml version="1.0"?>

<project name="projectName" description="Optional description of the
build file." default="defaultTargetName">
    <property name="someGlobalProperty" value="value" override="true"
/>
    <type>
        <!-- global type definition -->
    </type>

    <target name="defaultTargetName" depends="supportingTarget"
description="Describe the default task here.">
        <property name="aLocalProperty" value="someValue"
override="true" />
                <!-- local type definition -->
        </type>

        <task>
            <!-- task definition -->
        </task>
```

```
                <!-- more tasks (optional) -->
        </target>

        <target name="supportingTarget" description="Describe the
supporting target here.">
            <task>
                <!-- task definition -->
            </task>
            <!-- more tasks (optional) -->
        </target>
</project>
```

As developers, we are all well versed in XML, which is why I think we can step through this skeleton of a Phing build file rather quickly. Moreover, I think it makes most sense to discuss the tag hierarchy from the inside out.

Tasks

At the heart of a build file are tasks. These are the tags that directly correspond to actions. This is where work actually gets done. You can think of tags as the most specific work unit. The Phing manual defines core tasks as those that are needed to build projects. In contrast, optional tasks are ones that are not strictly required to build projects. I find this distinction rather artificial, especially considering that PHP is an interpreted language, which means that any build process doesn't even include a compilation phase.

Examples of core tasks include the following:

- **CopyTask**: Copies individual or groups of files or directories from one location in the filesystem to another, while optionally renaming them

- **ForeachTask**: Iterates over a list and allows you to wrap one or more tasks to execute for each of the items in the list

- **InputTask**: Prompts the user for input that can be used in the execution of subsequent tasks

Examples of optional tasks include the following:

- **SvnExportTask**: Exports a project from a subversion repository to a local directory

- **ZipTask / UnzipTask**: This set of complementary tasks either creates a zip archive from a group of files or extracts files from an existing archive

- **PHPUnit2Task**: Runs test cases or test suites using the PHPUnit2 unit test framework

Tasks are similar to functions in that they can take arguments. We will see some examples of actual tasks as soon as we start putting together our own build script to deploy an application.

Rather than trying to list all available tasks along with each of their options, I urge you to consult the well-written online manual for the latest and greatest listing and description of tasks:

```
http://phing.info/docs/guide/
```

Lastly, if the set of tasks available in Phing don't satisfy your requirements, you can easily add your own. As an Open Source tool, Phing was intended to be extensible. I would imagine that the fact that it was written in PHP makes it all the more easy for readers of this book to be able to code their own tasks. It is actually surprisingly easy to add your own task in the form of a single class that accepts the parameters and performs the desired action.

Targets

Targets are logical groupings of tasks. Tasks are grouped together under a target to achieve a common goal. For example, you might have a target called `backup-db`, which has tasks that create a backup of the database, compress the resulting dump file, and transfer it by FTP to a location where such backups are typically stored.

Tasks listed within the opening and closing target tags will be executed in the order in which they appear. Targets have three attributes, namely "name", "description", and "depends." The name attribute allows you to execute the corresponding target from the phing command-line client. Here is an example of calling target `upgrade-db` in the default build file `build.xml`:

```
$ phing upgrade-db
```

The target name is optional and if omitted the default target defined in the project tag (discussed as follows) will be executed.

The "description" attribute of the target tag is simply a brief textual summary of what the tasks do.

Finally, the "depends" attribute lets the author specify other targets that need to be executed before the current target. Phing keeps track of which targets have been called already and automatically calls the targets that still need to be performed to meet the requirement. In our `build.xml` skeleton as seen previously, target `defaultTargetName` depends on target `supportingTarget`. When you call `defaultTargetName`, Phing would make sure to first execute `supportingTarget`. Multiple target dependencies can be listed as long as they are separated by commas. Just as with tasks, target dependencies will be executed in the order in which they are listed.

Properties and property files

Properties are Phing's equivalent of variables. They can be defined in the global namespace or in the local one for each of the targets. Global property definitions must occur outside of any of the target tags; whereas, local property or type definitions belong between an opening and closing target tag.

This is followed by some global definitions of properties and types. Properties are essentially variables, most of which don't change throughout the execution of the script. Other properties, however, will be created dynamically and used by the build script to keep state within or between the execution of individual targets.

Properties are defined and used within the `build.xml` file with the following syntax:

```
<property name="svn.url" value=
"https://${svn.server}/home/svn/${svn.project}" override="true" />
```

In this example, we are defining a property called `svn.url`. The value assigned to `svn.url` is a URL that is in turn composed of some strings and two previously defined properties, `svn.server` and `svn.project`. As you can see, the syntax for using the value assigned to a property is the dollar sign followed by the property name inside of curly brackets: `${prop.name}`.

It is possible and very convenient to keep properties in separate files that contain nothing but name value pairs. These files follow the naming convention of ending in `.properties`. Here is an example of a simple properties file:

```
# Subversion
svn.server=waferthin.com
svn.proto=https://

# ... many other properties defined here ...

# database connection settings & credentials
db.server=localhost
```

```
db.user=root
db.password=psstdonttell
db.name=state_secrets
```

As you can see, the syntax is straightforward. Values are assigned to property names with an equal sign and there is only one name-value pair to each line. Importing such a properties file is supported by the file attribute of the property task like this:

```
<property file="propfile.properties"/>
```

That's all it takes to set all the properties listed in file `propfile.properties` in the same namespace as the property task.

There are at least two advantages of using property files. First, it helps to keep the `build.xml` more compact. XML tends to be a bit verbose anyway and keeping most properties in a separate file makes it easier to read and understand the build file. Second, property files add a level of abstraction in the same way that a central configuration file or object might do for a PHP application. To deploy the application to a different location, you edit the properties without having to touch the `build.xml` file.

To further extend that idea and provide support for different environments. As we will see in our example a little later, we can simply tell Phing to which environment we want to deploy and the rest of the setup can be handled by including a properties file to match the environment. It is not uncommon to have property files named `dev.properties`, `staging.properties`, or `production.properties` to reflect the environment for which they configure the build or deployment process.

Types

Types are capable of representing data elements that are more complex than properties. For example, a type can be a reference to files in a given directory whose name matches a supplied regular expression. Here is an example of the `fileset` type that will contain a reference to all `.property` files in the project's `build` directory, except for the one named `deprecated.properties`.

```
<fileset dir="${project.home}/build" >
    <include name="*.properties" />
    <exclude name="deprecated.properties" />
</fileset>
```

The built-in types in Phing include the following:

- `FileList`: An ordered list of files on the filesystem. Files are not required to exist in the filesystem.
- `FileSet`: An unordered list of files that exist in the filesystem.
- `Path` / `Classpath`: Used to represent collections of directory paths.

For detailed descriptions of their functionality and attributes of these types, please consult the Phing manual.

Filters

As the name suggests, filters allow you to filter and transform file content in some way. As of this writing, there are 14 core filters included in Phing that let you take such diverse actions as to:

- Expand properties within a file
- String line breaks, line comments, or PHP comments
- Remove/add lines from/to a file based on location within the file or content of the line

Filters have to be wrapped inside an opening and closing `filterchain` tag. The build file excerpt under the mappers sub-section also contains an example of a filter in action. Later in the chapter, we will see another example of applying filters to change the content of one or more files.

Mappers

Whereas filters operate on file content, mappers do the same for filenames. There are currently five core mappers in Phing that allow us to operate on paths and filename by doing one or all of the following:

- `FlattenMapper`: Remove directories from a path, leaving only the filenames
- `GlobalMapper`: Move files while renaming them
- `IdentityMapper`: Change nothing
- `MergeMapper`: Change multiple files to have the same name
- `RegexpMapper`: Change filename using regular expressions

Here is an example of renaming template files to actual PHP files while using the expandproperties filter and renaming the files using the GlobalMapper:

```
<copy todir="/includes">
    <filterchain>
        <expandproperties />
    </filterchain>
    <mapper type="glob" from="*.php.tpl" to="*.php"/>
    <fileset dir="templates">
        <include name="*.php.tpl" />
    </fileset>
</copy>
```

For complete listings of all filters and mappers; as well as detailed descriptions of their use and attributes, I once again ask you to refer to the excellent online Phing manual. For now, our time will be better spent working through some examples and get a feel for actually doing some work with Phing.

The project tag

The outer most tag is the project tag, which supports attributes to define the project name and description; as well as the name of the target that will be executed by default. As we will see shortly, it is always possible to instruct Phing to execute a specific target instead of the default one defined here. Also, Phing uses the project name when providing feedback to the user.

Deploying a site

Now let's put all our newfound knowledge about tasks, targets, properties, types, filters, mappers, and projects to good use by creating a build file that will seamlessly deploy an upgrade to a website. We will also create some templates and data that will allow us to upgrade and downgrade the database at will. Rather than to experiment with someone else's site, I decided to automate the deployment of my own site, `waferthin.com`. Here is the directory structure of the currently deployed site:

```
Terminal — bash — bash — Dirk — ttys005 — 80×42 — ⌘2
waferthin.com
|-- clients
|   |-- images
|   `-- invoices
|-- db
|   `-- templates_c
|-- htdocs
|   |-- admin
|   |-- cgi-bin
|   |-- clients
|   |-- images
|   |-- js
|   |-- mail -> roundcubemail-0.3-RC1
|   |-- mantis -> mantis-1.1.1
|   |-- mantis-1.1.1
|   |   |-- api
|   |   |-- core
|   |   |-- css
|   |   |-- doc
|   |   |-- graphs
|   |   |-- images
|   |   |-- javascript
|   |   `-- lang
|   |-- overlib
|   |-- roundcubemail-0.3-RC1
|   |-- stats
|   `-- suspended.page
|-- includes
|   |-- classes
|   `-- libraries
|       |-- Smarty
|       `-- Zend
|-- logs
`-- smarty
    |-- cache
    |-- configs
    |-- plugins
    `-- templates
        |-- admin
        `-- clients

DirkMacBook:~ dirk$
```

Separating external dependencies

It makes sense to separate external dependencies that don't reside in your version control system with the rest of your project. Those are likely files and directories that don't necessarily need to be updated each time you deploy. By separating out these dependencies, you don't have to worry about accidentally overriding or breaking them. In the case of my site, there are some directories and files that have simply been copied into the site during the original manual install, such as Zend Library, Mantis (an issue tracker), and RoundCube (a web-based e-mail reader). These will either have to be moved from one release to the next or simply be replaced by a symbolic link. For the same reason, the `logs` directory will have to be moved outside of the project itself. Once our build script is finished and we have successfully deployed the site, we will take a look to see how the structure has changed from what we started with.

Creating a build script

Let's start by creating a basic build script. Luckily, targets break the whole script into manageable pieces. We will be creating one target at a time until we have all the pieces of the puzzle in place and are ready to deploy the whole site with a single command.

Environment and properties

I typically work on a local copy of my projects, but end up deploying test and production instances remotely. Perhaps your workflow isn't exactly the same as mine, but chances are that you find yourself having to deploy the same application to a variety of different servers or environments. It would be nice if our Phing script could be flexible enough to accommodate these different requirements transparently to the user. Since most, if not all, of the actions that need to be performed are essentially the same, we write our script so that we can deploy to the different environments by simply changing some properties, such as the domain name, the path to the project on the server, database settings, and so on.

A common solution to this problem is to create property files that correspond to the different environment that we wish to support. We can then create targets to load the corresponding properties file, or prompt the user for which environment's properties file he wants to use.

Here is the `dev.properties` file, which contains the settings for deploying a development version of the site to my local machine:

```
# deployment
site.fqdn=dev.waferthin.com
site.fqdn.secure=dev.secure.waferthin.com
site.home=/Users/dirk/Sites/${site.fqdn}
site.root=/Users/dirk/Sites/${site.fqdn}/${site.fqdn}
```

```
# Subversion
svn.bin=/usr/bin/svn
svn.fqdn=svn
svn.user=dirk
svn.repo=/svn/
svn.proto=https://
svn.project=waferthin.com/trunk
svn.password=mylilsecret

# database connection settings & credentials
db.user=root
db.password=shdonttell
db.name=waferthin
db.fqdn=localhost
db.port=3306
db.bin=/usr/local/mysql/bin/mysql
db.backup.dir=${site.home}/backups

# location of application log file
log=${site.home}/logs/waferthin.log

# smarty template engine
smarty.templates_dir=${site.root}/smarty/templates
smarty.compile_dir=${site.root}/smarty/templates_c
smarty.configs_dir=${site.root}/smarty/configs
smarty.cache_dir=${site.root}/smarty/cache
smarty.plugins_dir=${site.root}/smarty/plugins
smarty.plugins2_dir=${site.root}/includes/libraries/Smarty/plugins
smarty.force_compile=true

# extenal utilities
extern.apachectl=/usr/sbin/apachectl
extern.sudo=/usr/bin/sudo
extern.ln=/bin/ln
extern.mysqldump=/usr/local/mysql/bin/mysqldump

# libraries
zend_dir=/usr/local/lib/php/Zend
```

As you can see, there are six sections with the following logical breakdown:

1. Properties starting with `site.` deal with where on the server to deploy the site.

2. Properties starting with `svn.` deal with how to access the Subversion repository where the code resides.

3. Properties starting with `db.` deal with connection parameters and authentication credentials for accessing the database.

4. Properties starting with `smarty.` deal with configuring the Smarty template engine.

5. Properties starting with `extern.` deal with the location of external executables on which the build script depends.

6. The `log` and `zend_dir` properties are used to satisfy additional external dependencies by creating symbolic links (more about that later).

I also have corresponding files for the production environment called `prod.properties` and for the test environment called `test.properties`. All three files reside in the same directory as `build.xml`. Once support for properties files and environments has been implemented, you can add as many deployment environments as you wish by simply creating a corresponding properties file.

Now let's start by creating a `build.xml` file that does nothing more than initializing the environment:

```xml
<?xml version="1.0"?>
<project name="waferthin.com" description="Targets for maintaining and
deploying the waferthin.com web site." default="deploy">

    <!-- initialize timestamp that will be used in naming of various
files & directories -->
    <tstamp/>

    <target name="deploy" depends="get-env" description="Deploy
the site to the web server and perform necessary build and upgrade
tasks.">
    </target>

    <target name="get-env" description="get the environment for an
action">
        <!-- has the environment been set already? -->
        <if>
            <not>
                <isset property="environment" />
```

```
            </not>
            <then>
                <!-- prompt the user to select from a list of
supported environments -->
                    <input propertyname="environment"
validargs="dev,test,prod" promptChar=":">Enter environment </input>
            </then>
        </if>

        <!-- make sure the properties file for the environment exists
-->
        <available file="${environment}.properties"
property="env_prop_exists" type="file" />
        <if>
            <equals arg1="${env_prop_exists}" arg2="true" />
            <then>
                <!-- parse the properties files -->
                <property file="${environment}.properties"/>
            </then>
            <else>
                <!-- die with an error message -->
                <fail message="No properties file for selected
environment exists (${environment}.properties)" />
            </else>
        </if>
    </target>

    <target name="deploy-dev" description="Deploy the site to the
development environment.">
        <property name="environment" value="dev" override="true" />
        <phingcall target="deploy" />
    </target>

    <target name="deploy-prod" description="Deploy the site to the
production environment.">
        <property name="environment" value="prod" override="true" />
        <phingcall target="deploy" />
    </target>

    <target name="deploy-test" description="Deploy the site to the
test environment.">
        <property name="environment" value="test" override="true" />
        <phingcall target="deploy" />
    </target>
</project>
```

The project tag contains a description of the targets in the build.xml file and identifies the deploy target as the default. The only interesting thing about the deploy target is the depends attribute, which in this case lets Phing know that the get-env target must be executed first. Now let's examine the get-env target, which is the only one doing any actual work so far.

Here is what happens if we run our initial build.xml from the command line:

```
Terminal — bash — bash — Dirk — ttys002 — 80×17 — ⌘3
DirkMacBook:~ dirk$ phing -f build_1.xml
Buildfile: /Volumes/Documents/Work/WaferThin/Packt/Book/Code/chapter8/build_1.xm
l

waferthin.com > get-env:

Enter environment (dev,test,prod): dev
  [property] Loading /Volumes/Documents/Work/WaferThin/Packt/Book/Code/chapter8/d
ev.properties

waferthin.com > deploy:


BUILD FINISHED

Total time: 2.9911 seconds
DirkMacBook:hooks dirk$
```

Lastly, we also have three convenience targets, deploy-dev, deploy-test, and deploy-prod. These targets set the environment property to dev and prod, respectively, and then continue by calling the deploy target. This way, it is possible to deploy to either the development or production environment without having Phing prompt you to manually enter the name of the environment.

Directory skeleton

The way we are deploying our application assumes a certain directory structure. If we are deploying for the first time, we will have to create the directories we will need in subsequent steps. If we are upgrading, we will still want to create any directories that are missing at that point.

Here is the target that will handle the creation of the directories for us:

```
<!-- create directories; no existing ones will be overridden -->
<target name="create-skeleton" description="Create the basic directory
structure for the site.">
    <mkdir dir="${site.home}" />
    <mkdir dir="${site.home}/build" />
    <mkdir dir="${site.home}/backups" />
```

```
        <mkdir dir="${site.home}/logs" />
        <mkdir dir="${site.home}/tmp" />
    </target>
    ...
```

The `mkdir` task creates the directory that is specified in the `dir` attribute.

Subversion export and checkout

Now it is time to get the code out of our version control system. Since we have focused on Subversion for version control in a previous chapter of this book, we will be relying on it here as well. However, if your project resides in CVS, Git, Perforce, or any other such tool, the steps would be very similar. Although, as it happens, Phing has some built-in optional task for interacting with Subversion; whereas, if you are dealing with a slightly less common repository type, you might to create your own Phing task or use the `ExecTask`, which lets you run other command-line executables.

Here is an excerpt from our `build.xml` that defines the `svn-export` target.

```
    ...
    <target name="svn-export" description="Export the site's files from
    subversion to the local target directory.">

        <!-- construct proper Subversion URL -->
        <property name="svn.url"
    value="${svn.proto}${svn.fqdn}${svn.repo}${svn.project}"
    override="true" />

        <!-- was the subversion password given in the properties file? -->
        <if>
            <not>
                <isset property="svn.password" />
            </not>
            <then>
                <!-- prompt the user for the subversion password -->
                <input propertyname="svn.password promptChar=":">Enter
    password for user ${svn.user} to get project ${svn.project} from
                Subversion repository ${svn.fqdn}${svn.repo}</input>
            </then>
        </if>

        <!-- checkout project for development -->
        <if>
```

```
            <equals arg1="${environment}" arg2="dev" />
            <then>
                <echo>Beginning svn checkout ...</echo>
                <svncheckout svnpath="${svn.bin}"
                    repositoryurl="${svn.url}"
                    todir="${site.root}.${DSTAMP}${TSTAMP}"
                    username="${svn.user}"
                    password="${svn.password}" />
            </then>
            <!-- export project for deployment -->
            <else>
                <echo>Beginning svn export ...</echo>
                <svnexport svnpath="${svn.bin}"
                    repositoryurl="${svn.url}"
                    todir="${site.root}.${DSTAMP}${TSTAMP}"
                    username="${svn.user}"
                    password="${svn.password}" />
            </else>
        </if>
    </target>
```

We start by using the `property` task to construct the proper Subversion URL pointing to our project and store it in the property `svn.url`.

Next, we check whether the `svn.password` property has been set. It is good security practice not to hard-code passwords into property files, but it impedes automation. This way supports both options. If the `svn.password` has not been given, Phing will prompt the user to enter it using the `inputTask` tag.

If you don't want to be required to enter your SSH username and password all the time, you have the option of installing your public SSH key on the server where the Subversion repository resides and modifying the `build.xml` file to not prompt you for credentials.

How we actually get the code out of the repository depends on what we are going to be doing with it. We have an if-then-else conditional because the actions we want to take are slightly different for a development environment as compared to the others. On one hand, if we are working with a development environment, we perform a Subversion checkout using the `svnexport` task that will allow us to commit subsequent changes back to the repository. On the other hand, if we are deploying that application, we want to use the `svnexport` task that excludes any Subversion artifacts throughout the directory structure of the project.

Building files from templates

Every site or application has some kind of configuration information and there are various ways of storing that information and making it available to the application. You will see authors using property files, XML files, and global PHP variables for configuration. In my site, I happen to have a Config class defined in file Config.php where the configuration settings are stored either as class constants or private static properties. Normally, this means that one would have edited this file by hand to set the correct values for the deployment environment. However, since we are looking to automate all deployment steps, we need to come up with a different approach.

Our solution is to create a template for the Config.php file, which could then be used to create a Config.php customized for the deployment environment. Here are the first couple of lines of the Config.php template:

```
class Config
{
    // DB connection settings & credentials
    const DB_VENDOR = 'mysql';
    const DB_HOSTNAME = '${db.fqdn}';
    const DB_PORT = ${db.port};
    const DB_USERNAME = '${db.user}';
    const DB_PASSWORD = '${db.password}';
    const DB_DATABASE_NAME = '${db.name}';

    // application log file location
    const LOG_FILE = '${log}';
    ...
```

Hopefully you have already recognized the placeholders for the values being assigned to the class constants as nothing more than Phing properties. The following listing then takes the Config.php template and replaces the placeholder properties with their assigned values, which are coming straight from the corresponding properties file.

```
<target name="stamp-config" description="Populates the Config.php
class with config properties.">
    <copy todir="${site.root}.${DSTAMP}${TSTAMP}/includes/classes">
        <filterchain>
            <expandproperties />
        </filterchain>

        <fileset dir="${site.root}.${DSTAMP}${TSTAMP}/config/
templates">
            <include name="Config.php" />
        </fileset>
    </copy>
</target>
```

The copy task takes care of moving the `Config.php` template to the `includes/classes/` directory where the application expects it to be. However, there are a couple of extra steps involved in this task that warrant a second look.

There are two sub-tags that are being used inside the copy task. First, the `filterchain` task allows you to process the files that are being copied. In our case, we are using the `expandproperties` task to replace all placeholders with properties. Second, the `fileset` task allows us to construct a list of files by including or excluding individual files based on various criteria, such as regular expressions that match the path or name of the files. For our purposes, the list consists of only a single file, `Config.php`, which we include by name.

Maintenance page

At this point, we have completed all preliminary steps for upgrading the site. For the actions, we want to ensure that normal traffic to the site cannot interfere. Simultaneously, it is now necessary to let the users know that the site will be temporarily unavailable by redirecting all traffic to a maintenance page that informs the user that the site is temporarily unavailable due to maintenance. I have such a page called `maintenance.html` in the root of the publicly accessible directory, `htdocs`.

I use Apache as my web server, which supports per-directory configuration files, typically called `.htaccess` files. For this to work, you have to make sure that `.htaccess` files are enabled. The following code also requires the `mod_rewrite` module to be enabled in Apache, which we use to change request URLs and redirect the user's browser. Basically, we are creating a local Apache configuration file that uses `mod_rewrite` to temporarily redirect all requests to the `maintenance.html` page.

```
<target name="disp-maint" description="Export the site's files from
subversion to the local target directory.">
    <!-- check whether there already is an .htaccess file -->
    <available file="${site.root}/htdocs/.htaccess"
property="htaccess_exists" type="file" />
    <if>
        <equals arg1="${htaccess_exists}" arg2="true" />
        <then>
            <!-- .htaccess file exists; move/rename it -->
            <move file="${site.root}/htdocs/.htaccess"
                tofile="${site.home}/htdocs/.htaccess.bck"
                overwrite="false" />
        </then>
    </if>
    <!-- new .htaccess file for maintenance screen -->
    <echo file="${site.root}/htdocs/.htaccess" append="false">
```

```
Options +FollowSymlinks
RewriteEngine on
RewriteCond %{REQUEST_URI} !/maintenance.html$
RewriteCond %{REMOTE_HOST} !^127\.0\.0\.1
RewriteRule $ /maintenance.html [R=302,L]
    </echo>
</target>
```

Rather than just create the .htaccess file, however, the code first checks whether such a file already exists. If so, it renames the existing file using the move task. Then we use the echo task with the file attribute to write the necessary Apache configuration directives to the newly created .htaccess file.

Database backup

As we have disabled regular traffic to the site, we can be assured that the underlying database is not being accessed anymore. If the site you are deploying has any automated jobs that access the database, you will most likely want to tweak the previous target to temporarily disable those jobs as well.

It is now time to back up the database. Even though the tool we are using for database migrations supports incremental upgrades and downgrades, it is common practice to always create a complete backup of the database whenever anything changes. Hopefully you have a routine that backs up the database along with the rest of the site anyway.

The following listing takes care of the database backup:

```
<target name="backup-db" description="Backup the database before
upgrade.">
    <!-- was the database password given in the properties file? -->
    <if>
        <not>
            <isset property="db.password" />
        </not>
        <then>
            <!-- prompt the user for the database password -->
            <input propertyname="db.password" promptChar=":">Enter
        password for user ${db.user} for database ${db.name}</input>
        </then>
    </if>

    <!-- execute external command mysqldump to backup database -->
    <exec command="${extern.mysqldump} --quick --
            password=${db.password} --user=${db.user} ${db.name} >
```

```
                                        ${db.name}.${DSTAMP}${TSTAMP}.sql"
            dir="${db.backup.dir}"
            escape="false" />

        <!-- compress the DB dump file -->
        <zip
    destfile="${db.backup.dir}/${db.name}.${DSTAMP}${TSTAMP}.sql.zip">
            <fileset dir="${db.backup.dir}">
                <include name="${db.name}.${DSTAMP}${TSTAMP}.sql" />
            </fileset>
        </zip>
        <!-- delete the original DB dump file to save space -->
        <delete file="${db.backup.dir}/${db.name}.${DSTAMP}${TSTAMP}.sql"
    />
    </target>
```

We start by checking whether the database password was provided in the properties file. If not, we interactively prompt the user to enter it from the command line. This logic should appear familiar to you because it is the same thing we did for getting the Subversion password.

We then use the `exec` task to run an external command, namely the `mysqldump` utility to export the schema and data to a text file. This text file is a complete snapshot of the database and can be used to reset the database to exactly the state it was in when the snapshot was created. Once again we are incorporating the timestamp into the name of the file so we know exactly when it was created.

The `command` attribute of the `exec` task is the command line that will be executed after changing the working directory to the path specified in the `dir` attribute. The `escape` attribute is a Boolean that determines whether shell meta characters will be escaped before executing the command. Please consult the manual for additional attributes supported by the `exec` task.

Database dump files are just text files and as such ideal targets for saving disk space by compressing their content. Luckily, Phing provides a task for compressing files using the zip algorithm. Similar to the `copy` task we saw earlier, the `zip` task contains a `fileset` tag to specify which files are to be included in the archive. In our case, we are compressing a single file.

Lastly, after the database dump file has been compressed, we can delete the original (uncompressed) file using the `delete` task. Although the `delete` task supports several other attributes, the only one we are using here is the `file` attribute to indicate the file that is to be the target of the deletion.

One last note regarding database backups is that the directory we use to store the backups is one of those which we created in the `create-skeleton` target earlier.

Database migrations

After backing up the database, we can apply any changes to the schema and/or data. For such purposes, Phing provides the very handy `dbdeploy` task. The way `dbdeploy` works is that you create an individual file for any change to the database. In that file, you put the SQL needed to upgrade the database; as well as the SQL needed to downgrade the database again. The two sets of SQL are separated by this character sequence: `-- //@UNDO`.

The name of the file should be descriptive of what it does. It also must start with an integer that indicates the order in which the individual migration files are to be processed. The lower numbered ones are executed before the higher ones.

To keep track of which migrations have been applied, `dbdeploy` requires its own tracking:

```
CREATE TABLE `changelog` (
  `change_number` bigint(20) NOT NULL,
  `delta_set` varchar(10) NOT NULL,
  `start_dt` timestamp NOT NULL DEFAULT CURRENT_TIMESTAMP ON UPDATE
CURRENT_TIMESTAMP,
  `complete_dt` timestamp NULL DEFAULT NULL,
  `applied_by` varchar(100) NOT NULL,
  `description` varchar(500) NOT NULL,
  PRIMARY KEY (`change_number`,`delta_set`)
) ENGINE=MyISAM DEFAULT CHARSET=latin1;
```

For example, to create a table called users, I created the following file:

`db/deltas/1-create-users.sql`

```
CREATE TABLE `users` (
  `id` int(11) unsigned NOT NULL AUTO_INCREMENT,
  `login` varchar(50) NOT NULL,
  `password` varchar(100) NOT NULL,
  `email` varchar(100) DEFAULT '',
  `active` tinyint(1) NOT NULL DEFAULT '1',
  `date_modified` timestamp NOT NULL DEFAULT CURRENT_TIMESTAMP ON
UPDATE CURRENT_TIMESTAMP,
  `date_added` timestamp NOT NULL DEFAULT '0000-00-00 00:00:00',
  PRIMARY KEY (`id`),
  UNIQUE KEY `unique_login` (`login`)
) ENGINE=MyISAM AUTO_INCREMENT=4 DEFAULT CHARSET=latin1;
```

```
--  //@UNDO

DROP TABLE IF EXISTS `users`;
```

The CREATE TABLE statement is the upgrade path and the DROP TABLE is the opposite action and thus provides us with the downgrade path.

The dbdeploy task doesn't actually execute the SQL. It only creates it. That is why an exec task is required to execute the generated upgrade SQL via the MySQL command line client. Here is the target to upgrade the database:

```
<target name="deploy-db" description="Runs the SQL migrations to
update the DB schema and data.">
    <!-- load the dbdeploy task -->
    <taskdef name="dbdeploy"
classname="phing.tasks.ext.dbdeploy.DbDeployTask"/>

    <!-- generate SQL to upgrade the DB to the most recent migration
-->
    <dbdeploy url="mysql:host=${db.fqdn};dbname=${db.name}"
        userid="${db.user}"
        password="${db.password}"
        dir="${site.root}.${DSTAMP}${TSTAMP}/db/deltas"
        outputfile="${site.home}/build/db-upgrade-
                                    ${DSTAMP}${TSTAMP}.sql"
        undooutputfile="${site.home}/build/db-downgrade-
                                    ${DSTAMP}${TSTAMP}.sql" />

    <!-- execute SQL using mysql command line client -->
    <exec
        command="${extern.mysql} -h${db.fqdn} -u${db.user} -
        p${db.password} ${db.name} &lt; ${site.home}/build/db-upgrade-
                                    ${DSTAMP}${TSTAMP}.sql"
        dir="${site.home}/build"
        checkreturn="true" />
</target>
...
```

Going live

We are almost there. We have checked out and modified the site, backed up and upgraded the database. All that is left is to make the actual switch from the previous version of the site to the one we just created. That is the job of the `publish-site` target in the following listing:

```
<target name="publish-site" description="Activates new version of site
and restarts Apache for all changes to take effect.">
    <!-- symlink in external library dependencies -->
    <exec command="${extern.ln} -s ${zend_dir}"
        dir="${site.root}.${DSTAMP}${TSTAMP}/includes/libraries"
        escape="false
    <!-- delete symlink to currently active copy of the site -->
    <delete file="${site.root}" />
    <!-- symlink to newest version of site -->
    <exec command="${extern.ln} -s ${site.fqdn}.${DSTAMP}${TSTAMP}
                                                      ${site.fqdn}"
        dir="${site.home}"
        escape="false" />
    <!-- restart the Apache web server gracefully for all changes to
                              take effect: we are live now!!! -->
    <exec command="${extern.sudo} ${extern.apachectl} graceful"
                                              escape="false" />
</target>
```

First, using the `exec` task again, we create a symbolic link to a copy of Zend Framework that is required for this site to function. Second, using the `delete` task, we remove the symbolic link that points to the previous version of the site. Third, again using the `exec` task, we create a new symbolic link to the version of the site we just checked out of Subversion and prepared for deployment.

As a final step, we tell the Apache web server to reload its configuration to make sure that all changes will take effect right away. Since Apache doesn't run under my login, I need to use the `sudo` command, which will prompt me for the root / administrator password to perform this action.

Putting it all together

Now that we have constructed all the individual targets, we assemble all to create the final `build.xml` file. For the complete listing, please refer to the `build.xml` file in the code bundle for this chapter.

When I run this file for the development environment from the command line, I get the following output, which I broke up into two separate screenshots to accommodate the length of the listing.

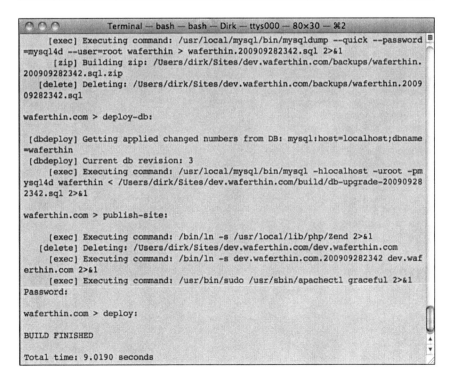

Not bad. Within slightly more than nine seconds, I was able to check out a project from Subversion, create some files from templates, put up a maintenance page, back up and upgrade the database, create various symbolic links and directories, and finally restart the web server. And that includes me having to type the administrator's password to be allowed to restart the server.

Now let's take look at the site's changed directory structure. If you flip back a couple of pages, you can compare it to what it looked like before we restructured it to make upgrades easier.

As a testament to the ease with which we can now deploy the site, I included in the listing the database upgrade/downgrade scripts (db-upgrade.xxxx.sql and db-upgrade.xxxx.sql); as well as, the top-level directories of the previously deployed applications that are now backed up (dev.waferthin.com.xxxx). Unfortunately, this means that the listing is so long that I had to split it into two separate screenshots.

```
dev.waferthin.com/
|-- backups
|   |-- waferthin.200909262254.sql.zip
|   |-- waferthin.200909271853.sql.zip
|   |-- waferthin.200909282241.sql.zip
|   `-- waferthin.200909282342.sql.zip
|-- build
|   |-- db-downgrade-200909282259.sql
|   |-- db-downgrade-200909282305.sql
|   |-- db-downgrade-200909282306.sql
|   |-- db-downgrade-200909282342.sql
|   |-- db-upgrade-200909282259.sql
|   |-- db-upgrade-200909282305.sql
|   |-- db-upgrade-200909282306.sql
|   `-- db-upgrade-200909282342.sql
|-- dev.waferthin.com -> dev.waferthin.com.200909282342
|-- dev.waferthin.com.200909262254
|-- dev.waferthin.com.200909271853
|-- dev.waferthin.com.200909282241
|   |-- clients
|   |   |-- images
|   |   `-- invoices
|   |-- config
|   |   `-- templates
|   |-- db
|   |   `-- deltas
...
DirkMacBook:~ dirk$
```

```
 ○ ○ ○                Terminal — bash — bash — Dirk — ttys005 — 80×33 — ⌘2
...
|   |-- htdocs
|   |   |-- admin
|   |   |-- billing_policy.html
|   |   |-- case_studies.html
|   |   |-- clients
|   |   |-- clients.html
|   |   |-- contact_us.html
|   |   |-- file.php
|   |   |-- how_does_it_work.html
|   |   |-- images
|   |   |-- index.html
|   |   |-- js
|   |   |-- overlib
|   |   |-- privacy_policy.html
|   |   |-- services.html
|   |   `-- style.css
|   |-- includes
|   |   |-- classes
|   |   |-- global_init.php
|   |   `-- libraries
|   |-- smarty
|   |   |-- cache
|   |   |-- configs
|   |   |-- plugins
|   |   |-- templates
|   |   `-- templates_c
|   `-- webdav-passwdfile
|-- logs
|   |-- dev.waferthin.com-access_log
|   `-- dev.waferthin.com-error_log
`-- tmp
DirkMacBook:~ dirk$ █
```

The directory at the top of our hierarchy, `dev.waferthin.com`, now holds the following subdirectories:

- `backups`: contains pre-upgrade database backups
- `build`: contains incremental database upgrade and downgrade SQL scripts
- `dev.waferthin.com.YYYYMMDDHHMM`: site source code with date stamp
- `dev.waferthin.com`: symbolic link pointing to the current release
- `logs`: logs files
- `tmp`: temp directory for file manipulations

Deploying the application to a test or production web server is equally simple. As long as you have Phing installed, all you have to do is copy the `build.xml` and environment properties files to the destination machine and run the corresponding target.

Backing out

After the new site is live, we need to inspect it to make sure everything is running as intended. What if there are problems? If the issue isn't something we can fix immediately, the plan is to back out of the upgrade and revert to the previous version. With the way our site is structured, this is merely a matter of changing the symbolic link to point to the old version of the application and to restart the web server. Optionally, depending on what upgrades were applied, you might also want to run the script to downgrade the database. That's it. Within a few seconds you can switch between two or more different versions of the site.

Summary

I hope that in reading this chapter you have gained a new perspective on how to deploy an application. Although deployment is often the last step in the development process, you need to start planning for it right from the start. Organizing your site's files in such a way that it lends itself to an automated deployment process is half the battle.

We started out by discussing application deployment and trying to come up with some guidelines for measuring success. The process we developed managed to fulfill both goals we had set ourselves. It is completely automated so as to minimize human errors and the time during which users of the application are negatively affected.

Along the way of automating the deployment process, we learned about Phing and how it can be used to automate all kinds of tasks. Although we used it to deploy a site, Phing can really do a whole lot more. You can create targets to perform all kinds of maintenance on your code or site. For example, you have Phing synchronize files and directories or generate phpDocumentor documentation. There is no end to how much you can do with it.

9
PHP Application Design with UML

UML is one of those buzz words that has been in the software development industry for several years. The hoopla surrounding the UML has died down over the years, but it would be a mistake to assume the same is true for its usefulness. Although you are somewhat more likely to encounter the UML in development environments that experience longer software development life cycles, there is no reason that PHP developers shouldn't benefit from it as well. Granted that as a web-centric scripting language, much in PHP's eco-system is geared towards getting the job done. As a matter-of-fact, I think that's how PHP got started—as a tool to get the job done. However, my goal is that after reading this chapter you will come to realize that if you pick the most appropriate parts of the UML and take the time to master them, they will be a great addition to your tool chest. In particular, you will be able to plan your own development efforts better; as well as be able to share vital information with other developers and architects easily and in a visual manner.

My goal in this chapter will be to define the UML, give an overview of the technology, and take a survey of the available tools. Rather than to take a purist's approach, we will try to approach UML so that we, as PHP developers can get the most out of it. We will then take a closer look at class diagrams, sequence diagrams, and use cases. To bridge theory and practice, we will work through an example to illustrate the use of these diagrams.

 As of this writing, the official UML standard is at version 2.2 and work continues toward 2.3. Also, there is no indication that this will be the last revision as this general-purpose, software-modeling tool continues to evolve.

Meta-model versus notation versus our approach

When talking about the UML, it is important to distinguish between the meta-model and the notation. The meta-model consists of definitions and descriptions of the various components and their possible relationships. For example, the meta-model describes exactly what is meant by an "association." As PHP developers who are well versed in object-oriented technology, we know intuitively what we mean when we talk about an association between two classes. However, since the UML is a general-purpose modeling language, the specifications have to contain a definition for "associations" that applies to all areas where the UML can be used. Moreover, the definition has to be rigorous enough for the whole interdependent system to make sense. In other words, it needs to be rigorous in a mathematically logical sense.

Although the UML would not be possible without the meta-model, it is the notation in which we as practitioners are really interested. The UML notation is made up of the signs and symbols used to represent elements in a UML diagram. It is what most people think of when they hear talk of the UML. For us programmers, the notation is the practical side of the UML that allows us to visualize abstract relationships between objects on a high level.

To put it another way, the meta-model is the general and theoretic component that allows one to extend the UML and apply it to different areas. For a PHP developer trying to make practical use of the UML, it is much more important and useful to understand the notation.

For the rest of this chapter, we will cover as much of the meta-model as is necessary to have usable definitions of the object-oriented technology as it applies to PHP. For instance, we will briefly cover the definition of an "association" as it applies to PHP, but then we will spend more time learning how to use the UML notation to represent an association. Our ultimate goal is to be able to construct UML diagrams (notation) that help us better understand the complex relationships and behavior of the objects and other concepts in our code. Naturally it is important that how we use the notation conforms to the meta-model for it to be usable and consistent, but we will not spend much time on general theory and instead focus our attention on the practical side of the UML.

As long as we are talking about practical notions, we might as well consider to what degree it makes sense to limit ourselves to the graphical elements that are meant for a particular diagram type. In my opinion, one should take a pragmatic approach. In other words, use whatever works. Most developers and architects are not formally trained in the UML and whatever working knowledge they have was accumulated while working on projects. Of course, that is perfectly fine. Theory should be used as a tool when it suits the purpose, but it should not be limiting users in terms of how they can express themselves. So, if a particular design process calls for elements from a sequence diagram, an object diagram, and a use case diagram, so be it. The goal should be to get the message across, not to make the designers of the UML happy by limiting oneself to the elements that were intended for a particular diagram type.

The notation for each diagram type described in the UML specifications should serve as a common foundation for all users. However, everybody should feel free to borrow additional elements from other diagram types if it serves the end of communicating an idea or concept more clearly. Consequently, that is the approach we will be taking throughout the rest of this chapter. Actually, you may not be aware of it, but we have been doing that already. For example, if you look at the chapter on source code and version control, you will see that the `Basic Version Control Workflow` diagram was inspired by a UML activity diagram. However, it also deviates significantly from what the UML standard defines as an activity diagram by incorporating elements of flow charts and entity relationship diagrams. Note that this is not a problem, but rather one of the benefits of the UML. Depending on the relationships, processes, or activities you are trying to describe, it is perfectly acceptable to mix different types of diagrams.

Levels of detail and purpose

How much detail you put into a UML diagram is typically directly proportional to the amount of time it takes to author the diagram. Sometimes it makes sense to spend more time on it, at other times it doesn't. The level of effort you put into it should be determined by the purpose of the diagram. On the lower end of the effort scale is the situation where you are sketching a process or relationship of your software to quickly communicate functionality or design details to other members of your team. This might happen during design meetings with one team member sketching something out on a white board or a piece of paper for others to see.

A technical lead or architect might spend a little more time refining a diagram and give it to a coder to implement the design. In such a case, it makes sense to spend a bit more time considering some of the details of the diagram. Whatever the diagram conveys to the coders doesn't need to be etched in stone, but the more consistent it is, the more sense it will make to the developer. Also, it will result in fewer follow-up discussions with the architect. This type of use of UML diagrams is called a blueprint.

Lastly at the high end of the effort scale, UML can be used to write software directly. Obviously, standards have to be observed much more rigorously and the amount of time spent on working through various scenarios and testing the program, rival that of writing software in any other programming language.

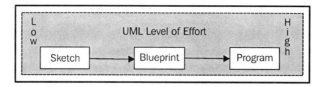

For our purposes, we can safely ignore the high end of the effort scale. We will be using PHP to write our code. Just because you can use UML to write functional code doesn't mean that it is the best tool for the job. However, using UML to sketch out behavior, capability, and elements of the software we are designing makes a lot of sense. With a little more effort we can easily turn our sketches into blueprints that we can hand over to another developer to have him or her turn out some PHP that conforms to the design we had in mind.

Round-trip and one-way tools

At a basic level, you can use pen and paper to sketch out your UML diagrams. However, there is a good selection of software-based tools that will let you take things a step further by turning the diagram into basic code or vice versa. For example, a class diagram (which we will cover in detail later) describes the structure of various classes and their relationships. A properly constructed class diagram can be used to generate the classes represented by the diagram. Since the UML is a programming language agnostic tool, it is up to the UML authoring tool you are using whether a converter for your language of choice exists. If you look at UML diagramming tools, you will find that nearly all of them support Java. Your selection narrows if you are looking for a tool that is capable of generating PHP 5+ compliant PHP code. However, such tools are definitely available and we will be working with one later on in the chapter.

If supported by the tool, it is also possible to reverse the process and generate UML diagrams from existing source code. In the case of PHP, this process typically involves reflection and programmatic parsing of class and phpDoc tags. Assuming that you have a tool that can automate this process, you will end up with a UML diagram that allows you to easily see high-level information about the classes and how they relate to each other. This can come in extremely handy if you are new to a complex project or application and are trying to understand the existing functionality. It also helps you to bring new development team members up to speed.

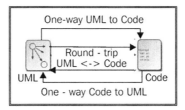

UML authoring tools that only generate code from diagrams are called one-way tools. Similarly, tools that only generate UML diagrams from existing code are also called one-way tools. In contrast, tools that work in both directions are often referred to as round-trip tools.

At this point, you don't need to be worried that your job of writing code will be outsourced to a UML authoring tool. The code that gets generated by these UML tools is not nearly as complete or detailed as anything a developer can write. Code generated from class diagrams, for example, merely reflects that basic properties and method names specified in the diagram. It will take an experienced developer to add all the business logic that really turns lines of code into an application that people can use.

Basic types of UML diagrams

There are 14 basic types of UML diagrams defined by UML 2.2, the current standard as of this writing. These 14 diagrams are divided into two groups of seven each, namely structure diagrams and behavior diagrams.

Structure diagrams are static in nature and describe the major components of the system and their relationships. In contrast, behavior diagrams are dynamic and depict how components interact with each over time.

The following diagram shows the hierarchy of the UML diagrams followed by a brief description of each diagram type.

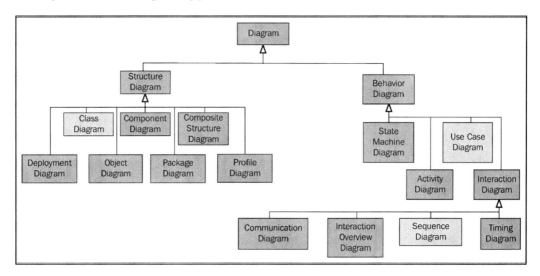

In the previous diagram, the diagram types that we will be examining in more detail in the rest of this chapter have a lighter background than the rest. Here is a brief description of all diagram types included in version 2.2 of the UML.

Structure diagrams:

- **Class diagrams** deal with classes, interfaces, and their properties and methods. They depict how the different classes and interfaces relate to each other, in a hierarchical fashion.

- **Component diagrams** show the main components that comprise a system and their interdependencies.

- **Composite structure diagrams** depict the inner state of components or classes and their interaction during execution of the system.

- **Deployment diagrams** are used to show the hardware on which the system is being deployed, the software executing on each piece of hardware, and the connectivity between them.

- **Object diagrams** show the state of object instances at a particular point in time during the execution.

- **Package diagrams** show logical groupings (packages) of software components and how they relate to each other.

- **Profile diagrams** show stereotypes, which are used to extend UML and their relationships.

Behavior diagrams:

- **State machine diagrams** are used to model the behavior limited to a finite set of states.

- **Use case diagrams** are used to describe the desired behavior of a system and how various participants interact with it.

- **Activity diagrams** are used to illustrate the control and flow of information through the system.

- **Communication diagrams** show the interaction of system components in terms of the messages they exchange and the sequence in which they exchange them.

- **Interaction overview diagrams** express control flow as a collection of interconnected nodes, where each node represents an interaction diagram.

- **Sequence diagrams** show how processes or components interact with each other by focusing on the sequences of actions and messages between them.

- **Timing diagrams** depict the interaction of components with a focus on timing of the individual interactions.

It is pretty hard to understand the true nature of each of the diagrams listed above without looking at an example. Although we cannot afford (and don't need to) look at all of them, we will examine three types of diagrams in enough detail so you can start using them in your work.

Diagrams

In the following section, we will look at three of the most common and useful diagrams for PHP development: class diagrams, sequence diagrams, and use cases. For each of these, we will learn about the individual components and we will illustrate their use in a running example.

Class diagrams

By far, the most common UML diagram type you are likely to encounter is the class diagram. It is also the one that I use most often. It allows you to describe classes and objects in your projects. For example, a class diagram might show you the properties and methods for a given class, including visibility, default values, and additional details. Furthermore, class diagrams can specify the relationship between the various classes. For example, it might indicate a parent-child relationship between two classes and/or an interface (inheritance). Or, it might indicate how some objects are used as attributes of other classes (composition).

Elements of a class

A class in a UML diagram is divided into three sections: the class name, properties, and methods. From top to bottom, the first section contains the name of the class. The second one lists the properties. And, the third section lists the methods of the class.

Properties (Attributes)

In general, properties take the following format. Note that the UML refers to these as "attributes," but since we have been using the term "property" in our context of object-oriented PHP, we will stick with that terminology.

```
visibility name: type multiplicity = default {property-string}
```

- `visibility` can be one of public, protected, or private.

- `name` is the name you give the variable.

- `type` is the data type of the variable.
  Note: Since PHP is not a strongly typed language, this keyword is not binding. However, it is of value to the programmer to know how to treat the variable.

- `multiplicity` indicates how many elements are expected to constitute the property. Multiplicity can be a single number or a range. For example, `String [3]` denotes an array of 3 strings, `int [0..5]` indicates an array of 0 to 5 integers, and `bool [*]` would be an array of Booleans that can be any size.

- `default` is the default value that will be assigned to the property. It should match the type indicated earlier in the property notation.

- `property-string` can be used to indicate additional language or implementation dependent attributes or notes to the developer, such as "read-only." In reality, I rarely see the property string used.

The name is the only part of the property that is not optional. Here is an example of the UML notation for a typical property found in a class:

```
public countArr: int[*] = null
```

In this example, the visibility is `public`, the name is `countArr`, the type is `int`, the multiplicity is an array of any size, and the default value is `null`. In other words, `countArr` is an array of integers that is allowed to grow to any size and will initially be set to null. Note that this example has no `property-string`.

Methods (Operations)

Here are the general elements that constitute a method. In general UML, these are considered "operations", but since we are focusing on object-oriented PHP, we will call them what they really are to us, namely methods.

```
visibility name (paramter-list) : return-type {property-string}
```

- `visibility` can be one of public, protected, or private.

- `name` is the name you give the method.

- `parameter-list` enumerates the arguments the method accepts, both required and optional. Arguments are specified in a format similar to properties but shorter: `name type = default value`.

- `return-type` is the data type of the variable being returned by the method. **Note**: Since PHP is not a strongly typed language, this keyword is not binding. However, it is of value to the programmer to know how to treat the variable.

- `property-string` can be used to indicate additional language or implementation dependent attributes or notes to the developer, such as "read-only". In reality, I rarely see the property string used.

Once again, here is a quick example of what a method definition might look like in UML notation.

```
private getCounterByIndex(index int): int
```

Here we are describing a method with visibility `private`, name `getCounterByIndex`, and return type `int`. In addition, the method takes one parameter named `index`, which is also of type `int`. That is to say, the private method `getCounterByIndex` takes an integer as parameter and returns an integer.

Static methods and properties

Methods and properties that are static are indicated in UML diagrams by underlining the name of the respective property or method. As an example, the only instance of the object in the implementation of a singleton design pattern in PHP might be stored in a property described like the UML:

```
private instance: DbConnection[1] = null
```

A class diagram example

Let's start our example with a single class to see how properties and methods are specified before expanding our scope by adding additional classes and relationships. Our particular example will be a class that is capable of probing a remote machine's port. If the port is active, the class can be used to look up the service that is most commonly associated with the port. In other words, given a host name or IP address and port, our class will attempt a connection. For example, given port domain name "google.com" and port number "80", we would expect the class to open a connection to the Google search engine and tell us that HTTP services are active on port 80.

Here is what a class diagram for such a class might look like:

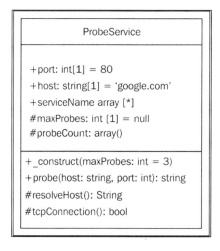

The previous diagram is a representation of a single PHP class called `ProbeService`. As you will recall from our above discussion, the other two sections are dedicated to the properties and methods of the class. This diagram also uses some notation that we haven't discussed before, namely single characters to abbreviate notation for visibility.+ indicates public, # protected, and - private (not shown above) visibility. This particular class has five properties:

- `port` is a single integer with default 80 and public visibility. It holds the port number that will be probed at the remote system.

- `host` is a single string with default 'google.com' and public visibility. It holds the host name or IP address of the remote system to be probed.

- `serviceName` is an associative array with public visibility. It represents a mapping of port numbers to common service names.

- `maxProbes` is a single integer with default null and protected visibility. It represents the maximum number of times any given host may be probed so as to avoid overloading the server and possibly incurring the wrath of the system administrator.

- `probeCount` is an array with protected visibility. It will be used to keep track of how many times a particular host or IP address has been probed.

In addition, our class also has the following methods:

- `construct()` is the public constructor for `ProbeService`, which takes the maximum number of probe attempts as an optional parameter.

- `probe()` is a public method that takes the host name (a string) and port number (an integer) as parameters and returns a string. This method is the one that will be called as an entry point for actually probing a remote system.

- `resolveHost()` is a protected method that requires no parameters and returns a string. Its function is to do a lookup on domain names and return an IP address.

- `tcpConnection()` is a protected method that undertakes the actual connection attempt and returns Boolean to indicate success or failure. It will use the host name and port number passed to the `probe()` method.

Like most concepts, discussing UML on a purely theoretical level will only lead to misunderstandings. Besides, I would like to keep this discussion as practical as possible. Consequently, here is an actual implementation of the above class:

```
/ProbeService.php
    <?php
    class ProbeService
    {
        // port to probe
        public $port = 80;

        // host to probe
        public $host = 'google.com';
```

```
// map of port numbers to common service names
public $serviceName = array(23     => 'telnet',
            25      => 'smtp',
            80      => 'http',
            110 =>  'pop3',
            443     => 'https'
            );

// maximum number of probes allowed per host per port
protected $maxProbes = null;

// multi-dimensional array storing the number
// of probes per host per port
protected $probeCount = array();

// constructor initializes maxProbes to 3
public function __construct($maxProbes = 3)
{
  $this->maxProbes = $maxProbes;
}

// probe host and port
public function probe($host, $port)
{
  // save port and host for other methods to access
  $this->host = $host;
  $this->port = $port;

  try {

    // get a list of IP addresses associated with the host
    $ipAddresses = $this->resolveHost();

    // iterate over all found IP addresses
    foreach ($ipAddresses as $ip) {

      // check max probing limit
      if ($this->probeCount[$this->host]
        [$this->port] < $this->maxProbes) {

        // increment the number of times this host & port were
                                              probed
        $this->increasePortCount();

        // got a responsive port
        if ($this->tcpConnection()) {

          echo "$this->host is responding on port $this->port.";
```

```
                     // try to look up the service name base on the port
                                                            number
                 if (array_key_exists($this->port, $this->serviceName)) {
                   echo " This port is typically associated with the
                         {$this->serviceName[$this->port]} service.\n";
                 } else {
                   echo " Unfortunately, we don't have a name for the
                                    service responding on that port.\n";
                 }
                 break;

               // unable to establish a connection
               } else {
                 echo "The host $this->host is not responding on port
                                               $this->port.\n";
               }

             // throw max number of probes exceeded exception
             } else {
               throw new Exception("Maximum probe limit of
                   $this->maxProbes exceeded for host $this->host on port
                                                   $this->port.");
             }
           }

         // catch exceptions and notify user
         } catch (Exception $e) {
           exit("Unable to probe $this->host:$this->port:
                                         {$e->getMessage()}");
         }
     }

     // lookup IP addresses corresponding to a given host name
     protected function resolveHost()
     {
       if ($ipAddresses = gethostbynamel($this->host)) {
         return $ipAddresses;
       } else {
         throw new Exception('Unable to resolve host ' .
             $this->host . '. Check network connection and validity of
                                              host name.');
       }
     }
 }
```

```php
    // method to keep track of connections by host & port
    protected function increasePortCount()
    {
      // check whether an entry already exists
      if (array_key_exists($this->host, $this->probeCount)
        && array_key_exists($this->port,
                                  $this->probeCount[$this->host])) {

          $this->probeCount[$this->host][$this->port]++;

        // create new entry
        } else {
          $this->probeCount[$this->host][$this->port] = 1;
        }
    }


    // attempt to open socket connection
    protected function tcpConnection()
    {
      // try to open a socket
      $socket = fsockopen($this->host, $this->port, $errorNumber,
                                          $errorString, 30);

      // unable to open socket
      if (!$socket) {
        return FALSE;

      // success!
      } else {

        // gracefully close the connection & return true
          fclose($socket);

        return TRUE;
      }
    }
  }
?>
```

Here is a quick example of how to use this class. We instantiate it and probe Yahoo! on port 80.

```php
<?php
require_once('ProbeService.php');

$probe = new ProbeService(3);
$probe->probe('yahoo.com', 80);
?>
```

The previous code snippet yields the following output:

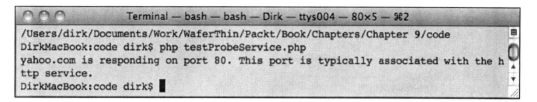

Encouraged by our ability to discern a service running on a remote machine, let's expand our project a little bit and build a network scanner that is able to do the following:

- Scan a range of ports for a given host
- Determine which ports respond and which services are likely to correspond to those ports
- Collect service-specific information for each port-service combination

After adding a couple of classes, our UML might look like this now:

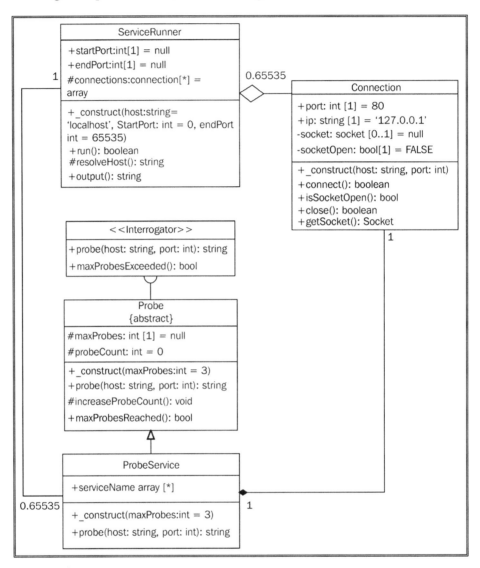

With the basic knowledge of how to represent an individual class in a UML diagram, our expanded diagram is starting to look a bit more interesting and complex. We have some additional types of classes (abstract and interface) and we are introducing the concept of relationships, such as compositions, implementation, inheritance, and dependence. Let's look at each of these concepts in combination with how we have applied them in our diagram.

For starters, we have refactored the `ProbeService` class. Since our network scanner might be implementing all kinds of different probing and scanning classes, we defined an `Interrogator` interface, which guarantees that any implementing class will provide a probe method that accepts a host name and port as arguments. Moreover, it will also require a method to be implemented to verify that the maximum number of probes has not been exceeded. We want to be nice netizens and not step on any system administrator's toes. This method is called `maxProbesExceeded()`.

In a UML diagram, you denote an interface by surrounding the name of the interface with "<<" and ">>" as we have done with the `Interrogator` interface. Not surprisingly, the section for properties is missing from `Interrogator` because interfaces cannot have properties.

In our sample project, abstract class `Probe` implements the `Interrogator` interface. `Probe` implements the `probe()` method required by the `Interrogator` interface. However, it also adds properties `$maxProbes` and `$probeCount` and some constructor logic to initialize the properties. The idea is to provide the basics of tracking the probe count and compare it to a maximum value that is set at object instantiation.

Abstract classes are marked as such by italicizing the class name. Since it is often hard to discern whether a word is in italics, it is also allowed to put the keyword {abstract} below the class, which is what we have done in our diagram of the `Probe` class.

Further down the inheritance hierarchy, we get to our old friend the `ProbeService` class. Having moved some functionality to the abstract parent class, it is now somewhat lighter. Furthermore, socket connection handling has been moved to a new class, `Connection`. The relationship between the two classes is such that `ProbeService` is composed of a `Connection` object (among others). In a UML diagram, this kind of relationship is indicated by a line ending in a filled diamond touching the class that represents the whole part of the relationship.

`Connection` will be used to hold the host name and port information for individual connections. It also has methods for opening, closing, returning, and getting status on socket connections.

The class that ties everything together is `Service Runner`. The idea is that the user provides `ServiceRunner` with a host name and target port range. `ServiceRunner` then creates `ProbeService` objects to probe each remote port sequentially. Active ports, that is remote ports that have been identified to have a service running, will have their corresponding `Connection` object collected in the `$connections` array.

The relationship just described is that `ServiceRunner` aggregates `Connection` objects. This type of relationship is indicated in a UML diagram with a line that ends in an unfilled diamond.

Relationships

Let me start by saying that 'relationships' is not the proper UML terminology. However, I like to use it as an umbrella term to collect ways in which parts of a class diagram can interact with each other. Terms that I decided belong into this category include association, aggregation, generalization (inheritance), dependency, and composition.

All of these relationships manifest themselves in a class diagram in the form of a line connecting one or more components, such as classes or interfaces. Symbols at the endpoint of the line indicate with which kind of relationship we are dealing. Multiplicity notations can accompany any of the lines.

I want to briefly cover these concepts with an eye on how they relate to PHP.

Association

The loosest kind of relationship is an **association**, which is indicated by a single solid line connecting two classes. If you add an arrow to one of the endpoints of the line, it indicates that the end with the arrowhead represents the part and the other end the whole of the relationship. It is also possible to name associations.

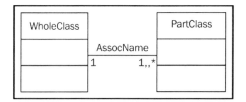

In our sample application, the `ServiceRunner` and `ProbeService` classes are connected by association. `ServiceRunner` iterates over a range of port numbers and instantiates a `ProbeService` object for each of them.

Aggregation

Aggregation is somewhat stronger than an association and generally indicates a "has a" relationship. Aggregation is indicated in a UML diagram by adding an unfilled diamond to the end of the connecting line that belongs to the whole part of the relationship.

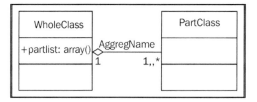

In our example, a `ServiceRunner` object has an array that may or may not contain any number of `Connection` objects. Thus the two classes are related by aggregation and the unfilled diamond is touching the `ServiceRunner` class.

Composition

Composition is the strongest of these relationships. In composition, the lifecycle of the part is typically determined by the lifecycle of the whole of the relationship. Composition is indicated with the connecting line terminating in a filled diamond shape touching the whole of the relationship.

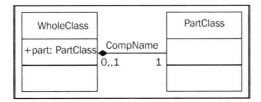

In the case of our network scanner project, each `ProbService` object has a `Connection` object. In other words, the two classes are connected by composition. In the corresponding UML diagram above, the line connecting the two classes has a filled diamond at the end touching the `ProbeService` class.

For the most part, the difference between the relationships described above is one of degree. All of them indicate some kind of dependency on another component. Consequently, it isn't always a clear-cut decision as to whether a relationship should be characterized as an association, an aggregation, or a composition.

Dependency

Actually, **dependency** is another relationship you can indicate in a UML diagram. It is somewhat less specific than the above relationships, which typically imply dependency. If you want to signify that one class depends on another, you draw a dotted line from one class to the one on which it depends. An open arrowhead should point to the one on which another depends.

Another way to think about dependency is that it indicates coupling. The more dependency arrows your diagram has, the more tightly coupled the components are.

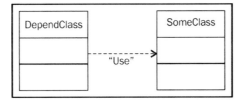

Generalization

There is one other kind of relationship I want to cover, namely that of **generalization**. In the context of object-oriented PHP, generalization takes the form of inheritance and the implementation of interfaces.

Inheritance takes the form of a line going from the child class to the parent class with an unfilled arrowhead pointing at the parent.

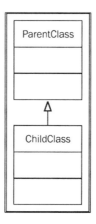

In our running example, the ProbeService extends the abstract Probe class. Consequently, the arrow points from the child class to the parent class with the unfilled arrowhead touching the Probe class.

Interfaces

In our example, we have already seen an interface. In particular, the Probe class implements the Interrogator interface. However, there are other ways of indicating how individual classes provide (implement) or require certain interface. The notation that is used to denote that a class provides an interface is a little stub sticking out of the class. It is a line with an unfilled circle. For obvious reasons, it is often called a lollipop.

The complement to a class providing (implementing) an interface is one that requires an interface. The graphical notation for such a class is the same as for an implementing class, but with half of the circle missing.

Following is a simplified UML diagram with a matching pair of classes. One implements the interface that the other requires.

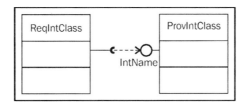

Example refactored

After covering some more theoretical ground and constructing a UML diagram for the much-improved version of our network scanner, I was able to rewrite the code for our project. For complete listings, please look at the following files in the source code package accompanying this chapter:

- `ServiceRunner.php`
- `interfaces/Interrogator.php`
- `classes/Probe.php`
- `classes/ProbeService.php`
- `classes/Connection.php`

Code generators

I chose to write the above code from scratch. However, as mentioned in the introduction to this chapter, there are tools that will take class diagrams and generate classes that contain all the components and relationships depicted in the diagram. You will still have to add business logic to really make the classes functional, but these tools can save you a lot of time—if you are creating UML diagrams anyway.

The quality of the code varies from one UML authoring tool to another. While working on this chapter, I created some class diagrams in ArgoUML, one of the oldest and best-known UML diagramming tools. I was pleasantly surprised that the PHP code it output was fully PHP5 object-oriented and quite usable. You can learn more about ArgoUML and download this open source tool at:

`http://argouml.tigris.org/`

For this chapter, however, I chose a tool that was better at handling graphics. It had plenty of stencils that made it easy to draw a good-looking diagram. Unfortunately, my layout software had no code generating features at all.

Sequence diagrams

Whereas class diagrams describe how various components of a system relate to each other on a design or architectural level, **sequence diagrams** show the interaction of these components as the code is being executed. As execution flows from one component to another, methods get called, properties get set, and objects get created, modified, and destroyed. You can find all these actions on a properly constructed sequence diagram.

Scope

As every developer knows, there is a lot of handing off control from one component class to another going on during the typical invocation of a PHP script. You attempt to capture all that interaction in a single sequence diagram, it would probably be useless because it will end up nearly as complex as the code itself. Instead, the challenge consists of isolating the parts of the system that would actually benefit from a sequence diagram. You might want to focus on the most commonly requested code, based on your analysis and expectation. Alternatively, you might zero in on the most complex piece of code. Often, seeing a diagram of a complex interaction can really enhance one's understanding of the concept. Yet another possibility is to do a sequence diagram of the application as a whole. Although you would be foregoing much of the detail, it would allow you to quickly communicate the overall functionality of the application.

A sequence diagram of the network scanner

Rather than starting by diving into a bunch theory, let's take a look at a sequence diagram of our running example, the network scanner. Although sequence diagrams can be quite complex in themselves, there are relatively few elements that are used to construct them. Lucky for us, this means that it is pretty easy to understand a sequence diagram, even if you have not been formally trained in that area.

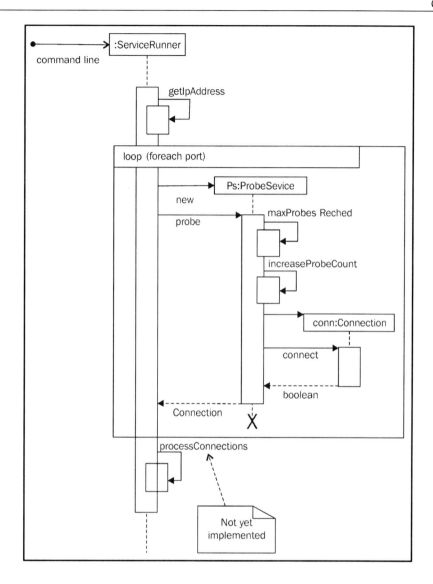

The above diagram merely reflects the flow of execution of the most recent implementation of our network scanner project. Let's step through the diagram while learning about the elements at your disposal when constructing a sequence diagram.

Objects and lifelines

Each vertical column belongs to the lifeline of a different object. In additional to an object, you think of these as roles or participants. The rectangle at the top contains the role and type (class) of the object. Lifelines, and thus time, runs from top to bottom. A serrated line means that the object exists, but that it is not currently active. Times of activity are indicated by unfilled rectangles overlaying the lifelines. An "X" at the end of the lifeline means that the object is being destroyed, which can happen when some process calls the object's destructor. More often than not however, destruction happens simply because the last existing reference to the object has been dereference and garbage collection destroys the object during its regular housekeeping activity.

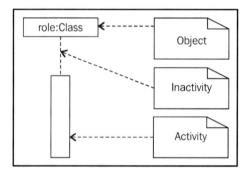

Our sample project has three objects: ServiceRunner, ProbeService, and Connection. Since ServiceRunner is the object that drives the whole application, it has the longest lifeline and area of activity. The Connection class, in contrast, has a short lifeline because it gets created later.

Methods

Indicating a method call in a sequence diagram is done simply by drawing an arrow from the calling object to the object that contains the method being called. The method name should be added as a label to the arrow. If an object is calling one of its own methods, the arrow simply loops back to the object from which it originated.

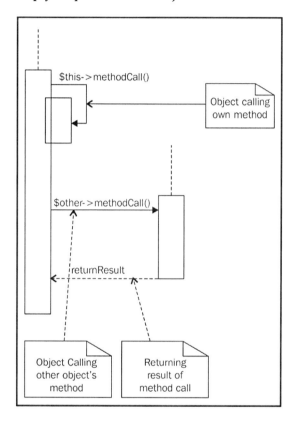

In the UML diagram of our example application, `ProbeService` is calling its own method `increaseProbeCount()`. An example of an object calling a method belonging to a different object is when `ProbeService` calls `Connection`'s `connect()` method.

Creating and destroying object

Creating a new object uses the same type of arrow as a regular function call; however, there are two differences. First, the arrow points to the rectangle containing the object role and name instead of the activity rectangle. Second, instead of a method name, the label accompanying the arrow reads "new."

An "X" at the end of the lifeline indicates destruction of an object.

In the UML diagram of our sample application, you can see the new-arrow when `ServiceRunner` instantiates `ProbeService`. Further down the diagram, at the end of `ProbeService`'s lifeline, you see the "X" indicating the `ProbeService` has been dereferenced and is being destroyed.

Loops and conditionals

I often think of time flowing from top to bottom in a sequence diagram. However, the analogy breaks down when you introduce looping to the diagram. It is therefore better to think of the flow of execution instead of time as you interpret the diagram from top to bottom. Even then, loops and conditional aren't a natural fit for sequence diagrams, but sometimes they are necessary to fully reflect what the functioning code is supposed to be doing.

Nevertheless, to indicate a looping construct (`foreach`, `for`, `while`, and so on) or a conditional (`if-then-else`, `switch`, and so on), you use **interaction frames**. The frame encloses the section of the diagram affected by the conditional or looping. The label located at the top of the interaction frame contains a keyword indicating the nature of the frame and often some pseudo code to indicate the execute condition (for conditions) or the exit condition (for looping constructs).

The following diagram is a sequence diagram that shows how to recursively calculate the factorial of an integer (for example, "4 factorial" = 4! = 4 x 3 x 2 x 1 = 24).

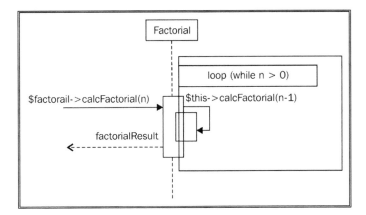

The interaction frame describes a while loop that will execute as long as the argument **n** is greater than zero.

There are several keywords you can use to describe the nature of an interaction frame, but the most frequently used ones and the ones relevant to PHP are:

- **alt** (**alternatives**): Multiple conditionals, such as if-then-else statement
- **opt** (**optional**): Single conditional, such as an if-statement
- **loop**: Looping construct, such as foreach or while statements

The sample network scanner project UML diagram uses an interaction frame to illustrate how the code loops over every port number between the start and end port numbers.

Synchronous versus asynchronous calls

Although PHP alone doesn't provide a multi-threaded environment for your scripts, your whole application may very well be considered multi-threaded if you have an HTML UI that issues asynchronous AJAX calls to your PHP backend. That is why I want to briefly talk about the last element of sequence diagrams we will be covering. The difference between a synchronous and an asynchronous call is indicated by the tip of the method call arrow. On one hand, if the tip is filled out, it is a synchronous call. On the other hand, if the tip consists of only two lines, we are dealing with an asynchronous call.

The following diagram illustrates both types of calls. A JavaScript script might issue an asynchronous call from a web page. Within PHP however, the objects communicate using synchronous calls.

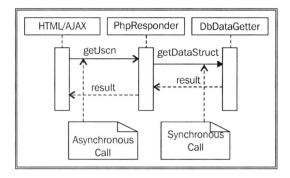

The UML diagram for our sample application contains only synchronous calls.

Use cases

Class diagrams gave us an insight into the hierarchy and organization of the project's classes in terms of inheritance and dependence on each other. In contrast, sequence diagrams showed us the actual activity between instantiated objects, not just classes. The third member of the UML family I want to look at is used to describe how the application behaves (or should, anyway) from the outside. **Use Cases** detail interactions with the application from a user's perspective.

Use cases—diagrams optional

Although part of the UML, use cases aren't typically that beneficial in diagram form. Instead, use cases are often formulated as a sequence of steps. We are essentially talking about a list of short sentences that describe actions by the user and the application's resulting behavior. Language is actually more appropriate to communicate this information than images. However, that is not to say there are no diagrams involved in use cases at all—there are. Use case diagrams are good at showing the participants (or "actors" in the UML parlance), the activities in which they engage, and their relationships. Nevertheless, you will have to read (or write if you are authoring a use case) the text of the use case to really appreciate the details of the interactions being described.

When to create use cases

It makes sense to create a use case when you are collecting the functional requirements for an application. Since you are essentially describing the users' actions, it makes sense to create the diagram and textual description as you are discussing the application with them.

Later in the development process, use diagrams can be referred to by developers that are working on particular parts of the code that touch upon the scenarios described in the use case. They are also very useful for testing. Use cases can be used as the basis for putting together functional and regression test scripts, as well as to develop unit tests.

It is often advisable to review and update the use cases before and during development and testing. A lot of requirements can change between the initial functional requirements gathering and when the application gets to the coding and testing stages.

Example use case

True to our approach to the other two types of UML diagrams, we will create a use case for our sample project. By now, you should have a pretty good idea of what this tool is designed to do. However, the code we have written so far doesn't really make for a very complex interaction with the user. Clearly, the above code was meant merely as a starting point for a network scanner type application. Consequently, we will describe some more advanced features that are not present in the above code, but that can easily be added by expanding on the existing code base.

Background

The user's employer is about to deploy two newly installed servers. Working together, they will be used to deploy the company's flagship website. One machine will host the PHP code and all static files, such as images, CSS, and so on. The other machine will be a dedicated database server. Both servers have two IP addresses, one public facing IP and another connected to a network that handles order processing and fulfillment.

Before publicly launching the site, management has decided to authorize a security audit of the servers to make sure that customer information and the machines on the order processing and fulfillment network cannot be compromised. As part of this audit, our user has been asked to figure out which ports are exposed on these two new servers and what services are running on them.

Typical scenario

- User launches network scanner application, giving it 4 IP addresses and a maximum port range from 0 to 65535.

- Application scans IP addresses and ports and generates a list of open ports.

- Inspecting the list of ports, the user asks the application for typical services deployed on the respective ports. For example, asking for a description of port 123, the application responds with a description of **NTP**, the **Network Time Protocol**.

- User compares the port and service list generated by the application to a known list of ports required by the website to handle its tasks.

- Ports and services not on the preapproved list will be added to a potential exception list.

- For each of the IP address and port numbers on the exception list, the user asks the application to verify that the expected service is actually running on that port.

- The application generates a list of IP addresses and port numbers, highlighting ports that have non-standard or unidentifiable services running.

- Using the exception report generated by the application, the user asks the website servers' system administrator to look if any unexplained services are being exposed.

Example use case diagram

The following is a use case diagram that provides a visual interpretation of the actors and activities involved in the process described previously.

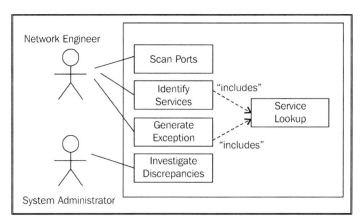

There are really only a couple of elements used to construct a use case diagram. Let's look at them in the context of our example.

Actors

Participants, or "actors" as they are called in the UML, are represented as little stick figures. These are the users of the system that interact with it in various ways as they go about their business.

In our case, the network engineer asked to scan the two servers and the system administrator with which he consults are the actors in this use case.

System boundary

The optional system boundary is simply a box around the elements of the system to separate it visually from the actors.

In our diagram, I have chosen to put a boundary box around the activities conducted by the network scanning application.

Use cases

It shouldn't really come as a surprise that a use case could contain one or more use cases. By going down the hierarchy, you are simply breaking the activities into more detail. Use cases or activities are depicted by ovals that contain the name of the use case/activity. A simple line is used to connect actors with activities/use cases.

In our example, we have an activity named "Scan Ports". In the textual description of our use case, this was one of the activities. However, scanning a port can be a use case in itself if you break it into its components, such as collecting information, opening a socket, waiting for a response, and so on.

Relationships

Similar to components of a class diagram, use cases can have relationships with each other. The UML specifications describe relationships between use cases, such as generalization, association, extension, and inclusion. In reality, these can add a lot of unnecessary complexity to an otherwise simple diagram. Consequently, the only use case relationship I have ever used is "includes." Relationships are identified by a serrated arrow with two short lines for the head. The arrow head should touch the use case that is being included.

Our sample project's use case diagram shows that the **Identify Services** and **Generate Exceptions** activities/use cases include the **Service Lookup** activity/use case.

Summary

In this chapter, you have seen some of the most commonly used types of UML diagrams, namely class diagrams, sequence diagrams, and use case diagrams. If you hadn't been exposed to the UML before, I hope that you have come to realize the value this tool adds in terms of easily communicating functionality, design, and behavior.

Also, we have barely touched the surface of the UML. There are plenty of other UML diagram types to explore, some more useful to a PHP developer, others less so. Like most topics in this book, our look at UML was not meant to be exhaustive, but rather driven by pragmatism. With what you have learned in this chapter, you should be able start using the UML in your every day development activities. At the same time, you have a solid foundation for learning more details if you want or need to. Good starting points for learning more about the UML in general are the web pages of the OMG, which oversees the advancement of the UML:

http://www.omg.org

The UML's home page is another online resource you will most likely want to consult:

http://www.uml.org

My advice at the end of this chapter echoes what I had said in the beginning. Start using the UML where it seems to make sense. Don't be bogged down by details of the specifications and adopt it to show your work as a PHP developer. However, it makes sense to spend a little time to master the common vocabulary and diagram elements so you don't run into misunderstanding when working with other developers.

10
Continuous Integration

For any large scale development project, making the pieces fit together is a challenge. If you are the only developer working on a project, you don't have to worry about your changes creating a conflict with those of other developers (you can think of it the other way around if you prefer). However, when there are several or even dozens of developers modifying the same code base, you are likely to run into all kinds of problems. A maxim that we have seen in Unit Testing, and that applies here just as well, is that the longer you wait to address the problem, the harder and more expensive it becomes.

Developers and software architects started thinking about how to integrate the changes from different sources early, quickly, and on an ongoing basis. The practice of 'Continuous Integration' is one that was developed in an attempt to address the above problem. In a nutshell, you set up a process to automate the build process and provide feedback on the results. There are various ways of notifying interested parties, some of them include online reports, e-mails, and RSS feeds. The idea is that if anything goes wrong, whoever is responsible or affected by the problem gets notified right away. For example, in the case of a piece of code failing a unit test, the developer who last modified the corresponding source code would be notified to take a look at his output and fix the problem before it affects other developers working on related tasks.

This process often runs on its own server, but it doesn't have to. There is no reason smaller development teams can't get away with combining a CI server with a staging or testing server. You can even run the CI instance on a developer's machine as long as you take care not to cross-pollute the two environments.

Another way to think of CI is that it is the calculus of software integration and testing. The more frequently the automated process runs, the less likely it is that any bugs or incompatibilities can take hold in the system and sneak their way into a release. Just like Calculus looks at increasingly smaller incremental changes to get a result that is increasingly more accurate, CI also tries to shrink the time between successive builds. The earlier a problem is caught and brought to attention, the easier and more likely it is to fix it.

Another benefit of continuous integration is that it significantly reduces the need for dedicated integration testing. Since this kind of testing will happen continuously during the development process, it is very unlikely that actual integration testing will uncover any major problems later on.

Here is a diagram that attempts to illustrate some of the perceived benefits of implementing continuous integration compared to an approach that separates development from integration and testing:

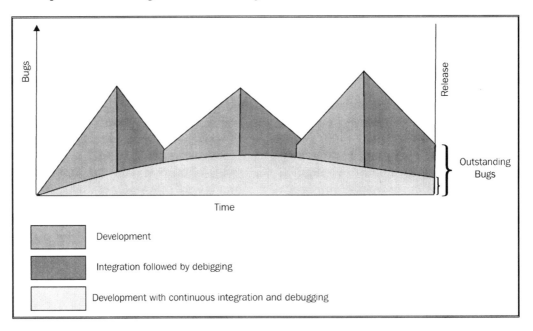

Let's first look at the more traditional approach. During periods of development (medium grey), the number of bugs increases. Then, after integrating the parts that make up the application, a debugging phase (dark grey) brings down the overall number of bugs again. This cycle repeats until the product is released with some of the defects having gone unnoticed.

In contrast, a software development cycle that includes continuous integration exhibits a curve that is much smoother (light grey). There is no clear separation between coding, integrating, and fixing bugs. As bugs are detected and fixed earlier, the overall number of them is never allowed to grow as big as with the other approach. In the above diagram, we are also left with fewer bugs once the application is released. That is the promise of continuous integration, but whether this will indeed be the case will depend on how effectively we implement it.

In essence, the goal is to produce fewer bugs and more stable code by integrating changes early and fixing problems as soon as they arise. This process becomes continuous by automating the process of building, testing, and providing feedback.

In this chapter, we will set up a continuous integration server and configure it to automatically build a project and report on the results.

The satellite systems

In one way or another, continuous integration touches upon all the other topics we covered in this book. You will see and use all the tools that we learned about and you will be able to put them to good use. Let's briefly review the tools themselves and take a look at how we will use them for CI.

Version control: Subversion

I'm hoping that the chapter on source code and version control already showed you the benefits of using such systems. In connection with CI, a source code repository becomes important because it contains a central and authoritative copy of the source code that we will need to actually build the project. This task would be impossible to automate if all the changes to the project were to reside on the machines of different developers or if they were not centrally accessible.

Our choice of a source and version control system has been Subversion. Any tools with comparable features (CVS, Perforce, and so on) will work as well, however, if you are planning on using a CI server as we will do in this chapter, you might want to check the server's documentation to see which source control systems are supported natively. Subversion is a natural choice because I don't know of a CI server that does not support it. Of course, I say that being fully aware that I have only worked with a couple of CI server out of a couple dozen that are listed on the Wikipedia page on continuous integration.

As we are implementing a sample automated CI process in this chapter, we will first use Subversion to check whether there have been any changes to the source code since the last time the process executed. You can use that information to decide whether to execute the process anyway. After all, it is possible that external factors have changed and that would affect the success of another build. For example, data in an external database or web service might have changed that might affect the outcome of certain unit tests. Of course, having external dependencies of this nature should be avoided in unit tests, but sometimes you can't get around it.

Commit frequency

One of the questions that I encounter a lot in connection with version control systems is: "How often should I commit?" As usual, the answer to that question starts with "it depends." There are different schools of thought, but my answer is usually the following:

- Commit at least once a day
- Commit at the end of a task, such as a new feature implementation or bug fix
- If you know your commit will break the build, you should hold off on committing

Once we introduce continuous integration into our development process, I would add the following guidelines:

- Time your commits to see whether it breaks the automated build (in case you need to fix it)
- Increase your commit frequency as much as possible to take CI to its natural conclusion

These guidelines are motivated by one of the guiding principles of open source software, which is to release early and often. You can think of a continuous integration environment as a micro open source project. The earlier other developers and users get their hands on your code, the sooner you can get productive feedback and make necessary changes early and easily.

Testing: PHPUnit

"Building" a project is a big part of the CI process. For languages like Java or C++, building implies compiling the source code to an executable state. Although the fact that a project compiles doesn't mean it is working as intended (or working at all!), it is nevertheless an important stepping-stone towards success. After all, if it doesn't compile we know for certain that it will not run.

Since PHP is an interpreted rather than a compiled language, we don't have the luxury of looking towards compilation to judge whether a project "built" successfully. That is why unit tests become so much more important during continuous integration. After all, checking a project out of Subversion into a local directory on the CI server tells us nothing about whether the application is actually working or not. Executing a suite of unit tests; however, will tell us a whole lot about how successfully the application is behaving.

If you were slacking off on writing unit tests either before or after working on changes to your source code, you now have an added incentive. Not only is it good practice to write unit tests for the sake of your code, it is absolutely essential for setting up a CI environment.

Think about it this way—if you are looking to benefit from a CI process, chances are that there is more than one cook in the kitchen. In other words, the team working on your application probably consists of at least several developers, analysts, testers, and so on. Even if your code in itself is flawless, think about all those times when others manage to break your code. No matter how loosely coupled your code is, there are dependencies that can cause your unit tests to fail even if another developer is making changes to his code. Having unit tests in place and executing them automatically during the periodic CI process will let all interested parties know if a test fails—especially the owner of the unit test and the developer whose code broke the test.

So, if you are cherry picking chapters in this book and you haven't taken in the chapter on unit testing or don't know about it already, I urge you to do so now. Of course, if you are primarily interested in setting up a continuous integration process, while other team members have to worry about coding and writing unit tests, feel free to continue reading.

Automation: Phing

Integration has always been a necessary part of software development and testing. You can and often have to do this manually. But to effectively make the process continuous, we will look towards automation. It only makes sense to remove manual tasks as much as possible if our goal is to execute the integration process as frequently as possible.

You can think of the other tools mentioned previously, such as version control, unit testing, code coverage, as the building blocks of CI. Automation then provides the plumbing to make sure everything fits together and the information flows from one component to the next. I think this point is well illustrated in the following flow diagram:

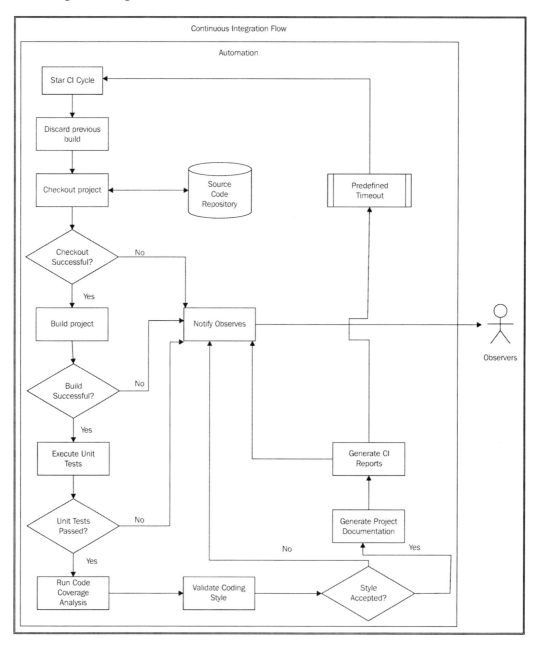

You can pretty much use any automation tool you want. But, you should first make sure that it is a good fit with the rest of your suite of CI tools. You can even put together some PHP command line script to control this process, but there are other tools that we have encountered before that are a bit more suitable for the task at hand.

If this were a book about Java, we would probably be working with Ant, but since we call ourselves PHP developers, we will be doing this with Phing. Besides, you have already mastered automating release and build related tasks in Phing after reading the chapter on deploying applications (haven't you?). So, it's time to put your new Phing scripting skills to use.

Coding style: PHP_CodeSniffer

Although the primary goal of the CI process is to make sure that the code base builds, executes, and passes the automated tests, it is also a great place to run project-wide tasks that also aim to improve the quality of the code and make it more maintainable in the long run. Validating the coding style you have defined for your project is one of those tasks.

As we have seen in the corresponding chapter on coding style, PHP_CodeSniffer can be made to check all source files against a pre-defined coding standard. Any discrepancies will be reported and the developer who owns the file(s) or the one who last worked on it can be made responsible to bring the code into compliance as a matter of policy.

The CI environment for our sample project will provide a PHP_CodeSniffer Report in the web-based UI; as well as, a graph to illustrate coding style violations versus compliance.

Documentation: PhpDocumentor

Generating and staging the project's code-level documentation is another non-essential task for a successful build. However, if developers are expected to create inline documentation, we should be consistent enough to generate and stage the documentation. Besides, this way the CI server becomes the perfect central place for locating the most up-to-date documentation.

Code coverage: Xdebug

Even though we have devoted a whole chapter to debugging and the use of Xdebug, we didn't really touch upon the functionality Xdebug provides in terms of code coverage analysis. In relation to automated software testing, code coverage provides one or more metrics to measure how much of the code was actually exercised when running the test suite.

You can state code coverage by focusing on different parts of software, including but not limited to the following:

- **Statement coverage** measures how many executable lines (that is, excluding whitespace or comment lines) were executed: "6,936 of 11,291 lines were executed."
- **Function coverage** measures how many of your source code's functions were executed: "398 of 465 functions were called."
- **Decision coverage** measures how many conditionals (if-then-else statements, switch statements, and so on.) have been evaluated to all possibilities: ."243 of 312 if statements have been evaluated to both TRUE and FALSE."
- **Path coverage** measures how many of the possible paths of execution of the software actually occurred: " 4,939 of a possible 18,837 paths were executed."

You get the idea. We basically want to know how much of the code in the project is actually being tested by our test cases.

Complete code coverage (that is, 100%) is quite hard to achieve and requires extensive time spent on writing unit tests and verifying coverage. As a rule of thumb, code coverage of 80% to 90% is quite respectable.

In our sample project, we will report code coverage by having a CI tool that is able to interpret the data output by Xdebug during unit test suite execution and generate the corresponding reports.

Environment setup considerations

In all chapters thus far, we have focused on a single tool to get the job done. Although I tried to select the most established and mature PHP-centric tools, at times it simply came down to preference or perspective. The case in this chapter is even more complicated than that.

Do I need a dedicated CI server?

Continuous integration can be done on any machine, including a developer's workstation. If you can spare the resources in terms of memory, disk space, and CPU cycles, you can make the CI process the responsibility of an existing machine, perhaps a file server or even your version control system. Another factor in making this decision is the size of the team. If you are the primary observer of the CI output, it might be convenient to have the automated builds performed on your machine. However, if your team size were slightly larger, it would be important to have the CI server centrally accessible. Carrying it around on your laptop might benefit yourself, but wouldonly serve to frustrate the rest of your team as they are trying to check the latest build output or consult the generated documentation.

Do I need a CI tool?

Continuous Integration is primarily a process and you don't necessarily need an application to follow it. For example, if your existing project has sufficient automation in the shape of Phing build scripts, you might be able to expand on the existing functionality and create a CI process without much fuss. After all, the tasks that need to be performed during the CI process are all ones that developers perform manually at one stage of the development process or another.

In contrast, there are several reasons for adding yet another tool to the mix. A tool that provides the framework for automating CI builds. As you are deciding whether to add such a tool, you might want to consult the following list of questions:

- Do I have multiple projects that need to be built and reported on?
- Do I need textual and graphical reports on the CI process?
- Do I already have a process that generates documentation from inline comments and makes it available to developers?

If you decide that a specialized continuous integration tool is called for, you will learn how to install, configure, and run just such a tool later on in this chapter.

CI tools

Continuous Integration is still a fairly new phenomenon in PHP. Nevertheless, as PHP continues to make inroads into the development departments of large corporations worldwide and larger PHP teams are being assembled, I'm sure that CI will play an increasingly bigger role. Correspondingly, I expect more CI tools supporting or written in PHP to crop up. Simultaneously, the current offerings will most likely continue to mature.

CI tools typically provide us with a framework for implementing the whole process. These tools provide a unified interface to the variety of lower level tools that are operating behind the scenes. In addition, they typically provide additional functionality in the area of accumulating metrics, reporting, and notification.

When the time came to decide which tool to use for setting up a CI environment and sample project, I had to choose between two serious contenders.

XINC (Xinc Is Not CruiseControl)

Yet another entry in the list of recursive acronyms used in software development, Xinc is a continuous integration server written in PHP 5 for PHP. As such, the focus has been on supporting PHP-centric tools, such as Phing. Xinc has built-in support for Subversion and PHPUnit.

phpUnderControl

The good news about phpUnderControl is that it was built on top of an established and proven CI platform. The bad news is that we will have to stray from our favorite programming language and use a Java tool instead. I am of course talking about Cruise Control, which is the tool underlying phpUnderControl.

Continuous integration with phpUnderControl

To properly illustrate continuous integration, we really need a project that meets the following requirements:

- Unit tests have been created for all or most of the project
- The source code resides in version control repository
- Inline documentation has been written to conform to phpDocumentor syntax
- There exists a well-defined coding style that can be validated using PHP_CodeSniffer

Creating such a project from scratch is completely out of scope for this chapter, however, there are plenty of open source projects available that will serve perfectly as guinea pigs for our purposes. Since it has repeatedly come up in our discussion of coding style and frameworks, we are going to implement a continuous integration process for the Zend Framework because it satisfies all our requirements above. Besides, it will be nice to get some hard numbers on code coverage and unit test for a development framework that is aiming at wide adoption.

Installation

phpUnderControl is built to modify an existing installation of CruiseControl and getting it installed is a three-step process. In particular, we have to:

1. Install CruiseControl.

2. Install phpUnderControl and its supporting files.

3. Run the command that tells phpUnderControl to modify the CruiseControl installation to allow us to properly display output for PHP-based projects.

Installing CruiseControl

CruiseControl is a continuous integration server written in Java. Since it was one of the earliest CI tools, it has reached a certain level of maturity. It is also being used by a lot of development teams, which is why it is a valuable tool with which to be familiar—even if you are not working in PHP or Java.

Being a Java based application, you will have to have a working **Java Runtime Environment (JRE)** installed on the machine on which you are configuring the CI environment. Detailed instructions on how to install Java are beyond the scope of this chapter, but a good starting point will be Sun's Java download page:

```
http://www.java.com/en/download/manual.jsp
```

Assuming that Java has been installed, we can proceed by downloading a binary distribution of CruiseControl. If you are feeling adventurous, have experience with CruiseControl already, or know your way around Java source code, you can download one of their source code distributions or go directly to their Subversion repository. However, the binary distribution represents a quick and painless way of getting CruiseControl up and running. Here is the download page for CruiseControl. At the time of this writing, the most recent version is 2.8.2, but I urge you to download the most recent version:

```
http://cruisecontrol.sourceforge.net/download.html
```

Once the download finishes, simply extract the archive. Depending on your platform, simply execute the `cruisecontrol.bat` or `cruisecontrol.sh` script file in the application's home directory and barring any complications, CruiseControl should be up and running. Actually, hold that thought—before we are ready to start the server, we need to overlay CruiseControl with phpUnderControl and configure it to build our project.

Installing phpUnderControl

The easiest way to install phpUnderControl is via the PEAR installer.
phpUnderControl is being hosted at the PHPUnit repository. So, don't let the
occurrence of PHPUnit in the following transcript confuse you — we are still
only installing phpUnderControl.

```
DirkMacBook:~ dirk$ pear config-get preferred_state
stable
DirkMacBook:~ dirk$ sudo pear config-set preferred_state beta
config-set succeeded
DirkMacBook:~ dirk$ sudo pear channel-discover components.ez.no
Adding Channel "components.ez.no" succeeded
Discovery of channel "components.ez.no" succeeded
DirkMacBook:~ dirk$ sudo pear channel-discover pear.phpunit.de
Channel "pear.phpunit.de" is already initialized
DirkMacBook:~ dirk$ sudo pear install --alldeps phpunit/phpUnderControl
downloading phpUnderControl-0.4.7.tgz ...
Starting to download phpUnderControl-0.4.7.tgz (558,873 bytes)
.............................................................
............................done: 558,873 bytes
downloading Graph-1.4.3.tgz ...
Starting to download Graph-1.4.3.tgz (3,389,133 bytes)
...done: 3,389,133 bytes
downloading Base-1.7.tgz ...
Starting to download Base-1.7.tgz (226,881 bytes)
...done: 226,881 bytes
install ok: channel://components.ez.no/Base-1.7
install ok: channel://components.ez.no/Graph-1.4.3
install ok: channel://pear.phpunit.de/phpUnderControl-0.4.7

DirkMacBook:~ dirk$
```

The important lines are highlighted in the above terminal session transcript. Basically,
we have to do the following:

- Let PEAR know that we are looking for beta packages, rather than the default
  stable ones: `pear config-set preferred_state beta`. We have to do this
  because we are installing version 0.4.7 of phpUnderControl, the latest as of
  this writing, which is nevertheless considered a beta release.

- Inform PEAR of the existence of the `components.ez.no` and `pear.phpunit.
  de` channels:
  - `pear channel-discover components.ez.no`
  - `pear channel-discover pear.phpunit.de`

- Tell the pear command line utility to install phpUnderControl from
  the PHPUnit repository along with all its dependencies: `pear install
  --alldeps phpunit/phpUnderControl`. phpUnderControl relies
  extensively on the following tools, which will be installed with the
  `--alldeps` switch if they are not present already. You should recognize
  these because I have devoted a chapter in this book to each of them:

- ∘ phpDocumentor
- ∘ PHPUnit
- ∘ PHP_CodeSniffer

If everything goes ok, you should see output similar to the above and phpUnderControl will be installed.

Although we installed phpUnderControl using PEAR, you should visit the project's home page because it contains a lot of useful detail, only some of which we will be able to cover in this chapter. If the configuration of the project you are trying to build doesn't exactly match the one we are working through in this chapter, you should certainly start by looking at the documentation page:

```
http://phpundercontrol.org
```

Overlaying CruiseControl with phpUnderControl

At this point, we have installed CruiseControl and phpUnderControl, but so far there is no connection between the two. We need to let phpUnderControl register itself with CruiseControl and allow it to make some modifications, such as changing some of the output template and style sheet; as well as adding some images.

The `phpuc` command line executable for phpUnderControl supports these commands:

- `install`: Installs or upgrades CruiseControl with phpUnderControl
- `clean`: Removes old builds and artifacts
- `example`: Installs a small sample PHP project in CruiseControl
- `delete`: Deletes a project and related files from CruiseControl
- `graph`: Generates the metric graphs
- `merge-phpunit`: Merges multiple PHPUnit output files into a single one
- `project`: Creates a new PHP project within CruiseControl

Unfortunately, not all these commands have been documented in the online manual. Fortunately, the `phpuc` command line utility includes help information for each of the commands. Simply type the following at the command line to get a description of the command and a listing of all the options. You will have to replace `<command>` with the actual name of the command for which you are trying to get help.

```
DirkMacBook$ phpuc <command> --help
```

The most important command of those seven is easily the `install` command, which we will be using to register phpUnderControl with CruiseControl. Please take a look at the following listing:

```
○○○         Terminal — bash — bash — Dirk — ttys001 — 80×19 — ⌘2
DirkMacBook:~ dirk$ which phpuc
/usr/local/apache2/php/bin/phpuc
DirkMacBook:~ dirk$ phpuc install ~/Sites/cruisecontrol
Performing CruiseControl task.
    1. Creating directory "webapps/cruisecontrol/images/php-under-control
    2. Creating directory "webapps/cruisecontrol/js

Performing modify file task.
    1. Creating backup "/webapps/cruisecontrol/buildresults.jsp".
    2. Modifying file "/webapps/cruisecontrol/buildresults.jsp"
    ...
   16. Modifying file "/webapps/cruisecontrol/xsl/modifications.xsl"

Performing create file task.
    1. Creating file "/webapps/cruisecontrol/dashboard.jsp"
    2. Creating file "/webapps/cruisecontrol/error.jsp"
    ...
   48. Creating file "/webapps/cruisecontrol/WEB-INF/lib/php-under-control.jar"
DirkMacBook:~ dirk$ ▮
```

We start out by making sure that the `phpuc` command line utility is indeed available and our shell confirms that it is located inside my machine's PHP `bin` directory at `/usr/local/apache2/php/bin/phpuc`.

The install command requires only one argument, namely the path to the CruiseControl installation on which to operate. It then performs a series of file manipulations, some of which I replaced with "..." to keep the above listing short.

That's it for the installation. If we wanted, we could start up CruiseControl, but there wouldn't be anything to report yet. We still need to go through the configuration to get it to build our project and display the metrics it collects during that process.

Also, from this point on, I will be using CruiseControl and phpUnderControl interchangeably because the two have become fused. Although the underlying platform is still CruiseControl, the user interface identifies itself as phpUnderControl. In a sense, both are working together to provide us with a rich continuous integration environment tailored for PHP.

CruiseControl configuration

In this section, we will focus on getting both our project(s) and CruiseControl configured to do their work automatically. Before we dive into the guts of the corresponding configuration files, let's start by considering the high-level picture.

Overview of the CI process and components

To understand how CruiseControl works, you need to understand three components: the project build file, the CruiseControl configuration files, and the log directory.

First, the project build file is an Ant file that defines the project-specific tasks that need to be performed each time the project is being build in the CI environment. This XML file is responsible for initiating such tasks as retrieving the code from your version control system, running the test suite, and compiling the API level documentation.

Second, the CruiseControl configuration file is another XML file that dictates how and when the build process is executed for each project. Once the project build is complete, the output will be processed, digested, formatted, and reported on. There are also various channels through which the analysis results will be made available, such as e-mail, online reports, and RSS feeds. The details of which are all configured in CruiseControl's `config.xml` file.

Third, although it is only one of the many directories involved in the whole CI process, the logs directory deserves special mention because it is through it that CruiseControl and the project communicate with each other. During the build process, output is generated in a format that CruiseControl understands and written to the logs directory. CruiseControl patiently waits for the build process to complete, after which it processes the output in the logs directory.

To understand how things work, we will be looking at the overall project layout so we know where to find components that are part of CruiseControl and phpUnderControl; as well as, output that is generated by the build process. Then we construct the project specific build file. Finally, we configure Cruise Control to execute the process and keep an eye on things.

CruiseControl and project layout

Before we start automating the build process and defining the project within CruiseControl, I want to spend a little time getting a sense of the filesystem layout of CruiseCrontrol and the projects themselves. This will help in understanding how to set up additional projects; as well as the flow of data between the project's build process and phpUnderControl's reporting facilities.

Here is a hierarchical listing of the CruiseControl folder. Files and sub-folders not relevant to our discussion have been removed:

```
                  Terminal — bash — bash — Dirk — ttys001 — 80×36 — ⌘2
cruisecontrol
|-- apache-ant-1.7.0
|-- artifacts
|   |-- connectfour
|   `-- zend_framework
|       `-- 20091107051820
|           |-- api
|           |-- coverage
|           `-- graph
|-- config.xml
|-- etc
|-- lib
|-- logs
|   |-- connectfour
|   |   `-- _cache
|   `-- zend_framework
|       `-- _cache
|-- projects
|   |-- connectfour
|   `-- zend_framework
|       |-- build.xml
|       |-- build
|       |   |-- api
|       |   |-- coverage
|       |   `-- logs
|       `-- source
|           |-- bin
|           |-- demos
|           |-- documentation
|           |-- externals
|           |-- incubator
|           |-- library
|           |-- resources
|           |-- src
|           `-- tests
`-- webapps
```

The first thing to notice is that CruiseControl comes with its own distribution of Ant, which is located in the `apache-ant-1.7.0` directory. Ant is the default Java-based build tool used by CruiseControl. Ant is a good tool for the job, but it's certainly not the only one. Luckily, due to CruiseControl's modular nature it is pretty easy to install and take advantage of additional build tools. In our case, we will create a build script, using Ant then port it to the more PHP-centric replacement Phing. This may seem like a roundabout way of doing things, but there are several reasons. First, the phpUnderControl documentation uses build script examples written for Ant and not Phing. Second, CruiseControl itself uses Ant scripts to automate the process and it is necessary to be familiar with its syntax. Lastly, there is a feature relating to running unit tests that was not working properly in Phing, but we will look at a workaround for that later.

At this point, you may wonder why we would want to bother with Phing at all. The answer is simply that Phing has much better and intuitive support for PHP centric tasks than Ant does. Phing was built with PHP5 for PHP5 and you will see how that pays off when we convert the build script from Ant to Phing.

Next, the artifacts directory contains data and reports generated by the build process. The data is organized in sub-folders named after the project and build date. In the example listing above, we can find build data for the zend_framework project for a build that took place on 11/07/2009 at 5:18:20 a.m. The data itself is broken into three categories. The `api` folder contains the documentation generated by phpDocumentor, the `coverage` directory contains code coverage reports generated by PHPUnit during the execution of the unit test suite. Finally, the `graph` directory contains various images of graphs generated by phpUnderControl summarizing results from the unit tests, build attempts, and coding standard validations.

The `logs` directory contains plain text and XML log files on the status of each of the projects.

As you might have guessed, each of the projects configured in phpUnderControl are stored in the `projects` directory. The complete code that gets checked out from your source code control system gets stored in the source directory. In contrast, the `build` directory contains files that get generated during the build process. Here we see that same three sub-directories as under the artifacts directory. After a build finishes, CruiseControl moves the contents of the `build` directory to the corresponding sub-directory of the `artifacts` directory.

In addition to the directories we have mentioned so far, I included the two most important files in the above hierarchical representation of the CruiseControl directory. First, the build file for each project is located in the project's top-level directory. In our case, this means that the `build.xml` file is in the `projects/zend_framework` directory. Second, the main CruiseControl file, `config.xml`, is located in the topmost directory.

The directory structure and the location of the project directory itself are completely configurable CruiseControl's `config.xml` configuration file. For example, you might choose to locate the project directory outside of the CruiseControl directory to make upgrades easier.

Getting the project source

As you saw from the directory structure discussed in the previous section, we need to create a few directories to set up our project.

Starting from the `projects` directory, let's create a folder to store all files related to a continuous integration build of Zend Framework. We will then checkout the ZF source code from the project's Subversion repository and put it into the "source" subfolder. All output generated by the build process will go into the `build` directory. Here is a short transcript of me creating those directories and performing a Subversion checkout of ZF:

```
                  Terminal — bash — bash — Dirk — ttys001 — 80×20 — ⌘2
DirkMacBook:~ dirk$ cd ~/Sites/cruisecontrol/projects
DirkMacBook:projects dirk$ mkdir zend_framework
DirkMacBook:projects dirk$ mkdir zend_framework/build
DirkMacBook:projects dirk$ mkdir zend_framework/build/api
DirkMacBook:projects dirk$ mkdir zend_framework/build/coverage
DirkMacBook:projects dirk$ mkdir zend_framework/build/logs
DirkMacBook:projects dirk$ mkdir zend_framework/source
DirkMacBook:projects dirk$ svn checkout http://framework.zend.com/svn/framework/
standard/trunk ./zend_framework/source
A       zend_framework/source/LICENSE.txt
A       zend_framework/source/tests
A       zend_framework/source/tests/TestConfiguration.php.dist
...
A       zend_framework/source/externals/dojo/util/shrinksafe/shrinksafe.jar
A       zend_framework/source/externals/dojo/util/shrinksafe/README
U       zend_framework/source/externals/dojo
Checked out external at revision 20724.

Checked out revision 18868.
DirkMacBook:~ dirk$ █
```

I omitted several thousand lines that were scrolling down my screen while Subversion was performing the checkout and informing me about each individual file it was downloading. Depending on your connection speed, it might take several minutes for `svn` to checkout the trunk of ZF into the `projects/zend_framework/source` folder. Luckily with the way we will be setting up the build process, this is a one-time process. From here on, we will simply update this local working copy of ZF before continuing with the rest of the build process.

Configuring the project: build.xml

Each project has one build file. Ant, the Java-based automation tool used by CruiseControl, uses this file to perform the build process. You can learn more about Ant in general by visiting the project's website. Especially useful will be the manual pages, as well as the alphabetical listing and description of core and optional tasks:

```
http://ant.apache.org/
```

We will put our build.xml file in the project's directory:

```
projects/zend_framework/build.xml
```

A build file typically defines multiple targets. In our case, we will be defining targets to handle and Subversion update of the project, generating phpDocumentor documentation, validating our coding standard using PHP_CodeSniffer, and executing the unit test suite using PHPUnit.

Here is the listing of the first target named svn-update:

```
cruisecontrol/projects/zend_framework/build.xml
    . . .
    <!-- update the local working copy of the project -->
    <target name="svn-update">
      <exec executable="svn" dir="${basedir}/source">
        <arg line="up"/>
      </exec>
    </target>
    . . .
```

We are executing the Subversion command line client, svn, by telling it to update the local working copy of the project located in ${basedir}/source. Of course, this target only succeeds because we checked the project out of Subversion manually in the previous step.

As you are tinkering with your `build.xml` file, you can easily test individual targets by executing ant and specifying the target name on the command line. For example, here is a console transcript of me testing the `svn-update` target:

```
○ ○ ○          Terminal — bash — bash — Dirk — ttys001 — 80×15 — ⌘2
DirkMacBook: dirk$ tree -d -L 4 cruisecontrol

DirkMacBook:projects dirk$ ../apache-ant-1.7.0/bin/ant svn-update
Buildfile: build.xml

svn-update:
     [exec]
     [exec] Fetching external item into externals/dojo
     [exec] External at revision 20724.
     [exec]
     [exec] At revision 18868.

BUILD SUCCESSFUL
Total time: 12 seconds
DirkMacBook:~ dirk$ ▮
```

This next listing is for target `php-documentor`:

`cruisecontrol/projects/zend_framework/build.xml`

```
...
<!-- have phpDocumentor generate API documentation -->
<target name="php-documentor">
  <exec executable="phpdoc">
    <arg line="-ct
          -ue
          -t ${basedir}/build/api
          -tb /Users/dirk/Sites/phpdoc/phpUnderControl/data/phpdoc
          -o HTML:Phpuc:phpuc
          -d ${basedir}/source/library/Zend"/>
  </exec>
</target>
...
```

Here we are executing the `phpdoc` command line utility to parse the source files in `source/library/Zend` and put the generated documentation into directory `projects/zend_framework/build/api`. We also tell it to use phpDocumentor output templates provided by phpUnderControl because they better match the CruiseCrontrol design. Those templates were put in `/Users/dirk/Sites/phpdoc/phpUnderControl/data/phpdoc` by the phpUnderControl installation process. The `-o` switch is also required for phpDocumentor to use the custom output templates.

Next, we define the target for PHP_CodeSniffer to validate the source code against the Zend coding standard.

cruisecontrol/projects/zend_framework/build.xml

```
    . . .
    <!-- validate against Zend coding style using PHP_CodeSniffer  -->
    <target name="php-codesniffer">
      <exec executable="phpcs" dir="${basedir}/source/library"
                           output="${basedir}/build/logs/checkstyle.xml">
        <arg line="--report=checkstyle
                   --standard=Zend Zend"/>
      </exec>
    </target>
    . . .
```

This target executes the phpcs command line utility to process all files found in the Zend directory, which can be found in the source/library/ directory. The source files that are found will be evaluated against the Zend coding standard. Results are saved to the build/logs/checkstyle.xml file in the checkstyle format, which is the format phpUnderControl requires to generate reports on coding standard validations.

Now for our last target, here is the listing for running the unit tests:

cruisecontrol/projects/zend_framework/build.xml

```
    . . .
    <!-- run unit test suite using PHPUnit -->
    <target name="phpunit">
      <exec executable="phpunit" dir="${basedir}/source"
                                                    failonerror="on">
        <arg line="--log-xml ${basedir}/build/logs/phpunit.xml
              --log-pmd ${basedir}/build/logs/phpunit.pmd.xml
              --log-metrics ${basedir}/build/logs/phpunit.metrics.xml
              --coverage-xml ${basedir}/build/logs/phpunit.coverage.xml
              --coverage-html ${basedir}/build/coverage
                 phpucAllTests tests/Zend/AllTests.php"/>
      </exec>
    </target>
    . . .
```

In this target, we are executing the phpunit command line utility on the project's source directory. The various arguments generate corresponding reports on code coverage, metrics, and unit test results in XML format that will be converted to a web-based report by phpUnderControl.

In testing this phpunit target individually from the command line, I discovered that PHPUnit is somewhat memory intensive. I had to increase the memory_limit config setting in my php.ini file to 2GB for PHPUnit to be able to finish all the tests and write the output to file! In my tests, whenever the process of executing the unit tests ran out of memory, it would appear to finish the tests, but no output was generated. This memory requirement is extremely steep. At the same time, most projects don't have thousands of unit tests the way Zend Framework does.

Finally, here is the complete listing of the build file for our Zend Framework project:

cruisecontrol/projects/zend_framework/build.xml

```xml
<?xml version="1.0" encoding="UTF-8"?>
<project name="zend_framework" default="build" basedir=".">

  <!-- main build target that executes a sub-targets -->
  <target name="build" depends=
              "svn-update,php-documentor,php-codesniffer,phpunit"/>
  <!-- update the local working copy of the project -->
  <target name="svn-update">
    <exec executable="svn" dir="${basedir}/source">
      <arg line="up"/>
    </exec>
  </target>

  <!-- have phpDocumentor generate API documentation -->
  <target name="php-documentor">
    <exec executable="phpdoc">
      <arg line="-ct
            -ue
            -t ${basedir}/build/api
            -tb /Users/dirk/Sites/phpdoc/phpUnderControl/data/phpdoc
            -o HTML:Phpuc:phpuc
            -d ${basedir}/source/library/Zend"/>
    </exec>
  </target>

  <!-- validate against Zend coding style using PHP_CodeSniffer  -->
  <target name="php-codesniffer">
    <exec executable="phpcs" dir="${basedir}/source/library"
output="${basedir}/build/logs/checkstyle.xml">
      <arg line="--report=checkstyle
```

```
                --standard=Zend Zend"/>
    </exec>
  </target>


  <!-- run unit test suite using PHPUnit -->
  <target name="phpunit">
    <exec executable="phpunit" dir="${basedir}/source"
                                          failonerror="on">
      <arg line="--log-xml ${basedir}/build/logs/phpunit.xml
            --log-pmd ${basedir}/build/logs/phpunit.pmd.xml
            --log-metrics ${basedir}/build/logs/phpunit.metrics.xml
            --coverage-xml ${basedir}/build/logs/phpunit.coverage.xml
            --coverage-html ${basedir}/build/coverage
            phpucAllTests tests/Zend/AllTest.php"/>
    </exec>
  </target>
</project>
```

In addition to the targets already discussed previously, you can see default `build` target, which simply serves to combine the other targets. That means that we only have to call the default target to have all the other tasks executed in sequence.

All targets are wrapped into a `project` tag, which also has attributes to define the name of the project (`zend_framework`), the default target to execute (`build`), and the base directory that is used to specify other paths throughout the various targets (`"."`).

Configuring CruiseControl

Now that we have the build file for our project just so that does everything we expect during a continuous integration build, we still need to let CruiseControl know about our project. Specifically, we need to configure CC so it knows about the various directories and files of our project, when to run the continuous integration build, and who to notify of the results and how.

Following is the complete XML-based CruiseControl configuration file. The `cruisecontrol` tag brackets all further configuration directives. Similarly, the `project` tag does the same for all configuration directives for an individual project. Our configuration contains only a single project, but it could contain any number of projects—all of them framed by a starting and ending `project` tag:

cruisecontrol/config.xml

```
  <cruisecontrol>
    <!-- start of Zend Framework project -->
    <project name="zend_framework" buildafterfailed="false">
```

```
    <!-- check for svn changes, but wait 3 min. until last
         commit before starting the build -->
    <modificationset quietperiod="180">
      <svn localWorkingCopy="projects/${project.name}/source/"/>
    </modificationset>

    <!-- execute an Ant script to build; check every hour for
                   changes builds only happen if changes occurred -->
    <schedule interval="3600">
      <ant anthome="apache-ant-1.7.0"
                   buildfile="projects/${project.name}/build.xml"/>
    </schedule>

    <!-- write status data to text file -->
    <listeners>
      <currentbuildstatuslistener
                              file="logs/${project.name}/status.txt"/>
    </listeners>

    <!-- merge status data from build log -->
    <log dir="logs/${project.name}">
      <merge dir="projects/${project.name}/build/logs/"/>
    </log>

    <!-- preserve data published / generated during build -->
    <publishers>
      <artifactspublisher dir="projects/${project.name}/build/api"
              dest="artifacts/${project.name}" subdirectory="api"/>
      <artifactspublisher
           dir="projects/${project.name}/build/coverage"
          dest="artifacts/${project.name}" subdirectory="coverage"/>
      <execute command="phpuc graph logs/${project.name}
                                   artifacts/${project.name}"/>
    </publishers>
  </project>
</cruisecontrol>
```

The project tag itself contains attributes for the name of the project (zend_framework) and whether to continue trying to build after a failed build (yes).

The modificationset tag lets us define the kind of circumstances that would trigger a new build. In our case, since the Zend Framework source code is being maintained in Subversion, we use the svn tag to trigger a new build three minutes after the latest new commit. This way, we give the committer some time to finish committing all his files and hopefully we don't start a build mid-commit. The localWorkingCopy attribute obviously tells CruiseControl where the local version of the source is located.

You get to tell CruiseControl how to build the project using the `schedule` tag. In our case, we are telling CC to execute the `build.xml` file, which is an Ant build file. The installation of Ant to use is located in `apache-ant-1.7.0`. Lastly, the `interval` attribute will cause the system to check whether a new build is required. Remember that we are using the `svn modificationset`. In other words, CruiseControl checks hourly whether changes have been submitted to the Subversion repository, in which case it initiates a new build sequence.

The `listeners` get notified of build events and are typically designed to handle a particular one. Our `currentbuildstatuslistener` simply writes some status data about the current build to a text file in the `logs` directory.

The `log` tag tells CruiseControl where the main log file for the project is located. The nested `merge` tag tells CC that the log file generated by each build should be merged into the main log file upon completion.

After a build completes, the tasks listed within the `publisher` task will be run. They are typically used to propagate the results to someone or somewhere. All we are doing is copying some information generated during the build to a directory where it is accessible to CruiseControl's reporting function. The two `artifactspublisher` tasks we see copy the API-level documentation generated by phpDocumentor and the code coverage reports generated by PHPUnit to the corresponding sub-directories of the `cruisecontrol/artifacts/<project_name>` directory. You should recognize these directories from our discussion in the section entitled "CruiseControl and Project Layout." Finally, the `exec` task calls `phpuc`, the phpUnderControl command line client to generate metric graphs that we will see shortly as part of the online reports.

I am using version 2.8.2 of CruiseControl to write this chapter and this particular version supports 25 different publishers. Obviously, we are using only the bare minimum in our publishers tag. Other publishers allow you to transfer build results or send notifications via e-mail, HTTP, FTP, instant messenger, and various others.

The CruiseControl configuration file supports dozens of different tags and even more attributes. All these options provide a lot more flexibility and power than we are taking advantage of here in our basic `config.xml` file. For a complete listing and description of all the options, you should consult the online reference for the `config.xml` on the CruiseCrontrol project's website:

`http://cruisecontrol.sourceforge.net/main/configxml.html`

Advanced options

I want to briefly highlight some of the more useful of the many CruiseControl configuration options. Even though we will not be adding them to our simple `config.xml` file, it will be valuable to know about thse because you are likely to require one or multiple ones when the time comes to configure your own project.

Bootstrappers

Bootstrappers execute before the build. `execboostrapper` is one of the 20+ bootstrappers supported by CruiseControl, which means that you can do just about anything you want. However one of my favorite boostrappers is the `svnbootstrapper` (there are equivalent ones for other version control systems), because it lets you retrieve resource from Subversion before the build. The more common use for `svnbootstrapper` is to retrieve the `build.xml` file from Subversion. That way, you can keep all of your project's files in one location.

Unfortunately, this task is useless in our sample setup because I don't have commit privileges for the Zend Framework, which means that I cannot commit my `build.xml` to the ZF repository.

Publishers

CruiseControl supports a plethora of publishers. You can push out your CI build results via RSS, FTP uploads, or HTTP pages. In addition to getting the phpUnderControl reports built, the publisher I use the most is the `email` one. It lets you send an e-mail with a link to the build results. Hopefully, this way the recipients of the e-mail will check the build results occasionally.

Running CruiseControl

With the configuration files for our project and CruiseControl in place, it is finally time to fire up CruiseControl and let it start the continuous integration process by building the project for the first time. The CruiseControl root directory contains platform-specific scripts that will launch the server, after which you will be able to connect to it with your browser. If your CC environment is on a Windows machine, you want to execute the `cruisecontrol.bat` batch file. Analogously, if your environment is on any flavor of Unix, Linux, or OS X, you will want to give the `cruisecontrol.sh` shell script a try.

Unless you started the server in the background, you will see all kinds of status information output to the terminal. This output is handy in case you have to troubleshoot any part of the CI process. Give the server a couple of seconds to launch and then point your browser to the following URL:

```
http://localhost:8080/cruisecontrol/
```

CruiseControl uses port 8080 by default. If that port conflicts with another service you have running on your machine, you can supply the following optional command line switch to change it:

```
cruisecontrol.<sh|bat> -webport [new web port]
```

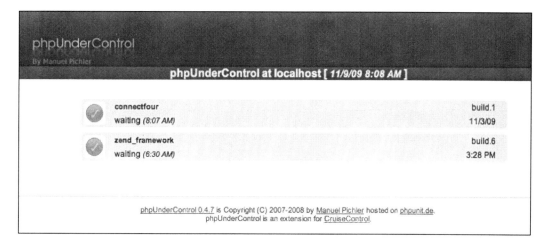

When you first bring up CruiseControl in your browser, you will notice how the interface has been customized by phpUnderControl. The default page contains a listing of all projects being managed by CruiseControl and their current build status. In the screenshot above, you can see two projects listed: `connectfour` and `zend_framework`. The former is a sample project that comes with CruiseControl and the latter is of course our own project. We can see that the last build, number 6, took place on 3:28 pm and the CC is waiting until 6:30 am until potentially starting another build. Clicking on the round green checkmark icon will start a new build right away. Clicking on the name will display more detailed reports about the project.

The overview page

This page provides a summary of all activity for a given project. Let's take a look at the overview page for the zend_framework project and how it summarizes some of the more detailed reports:

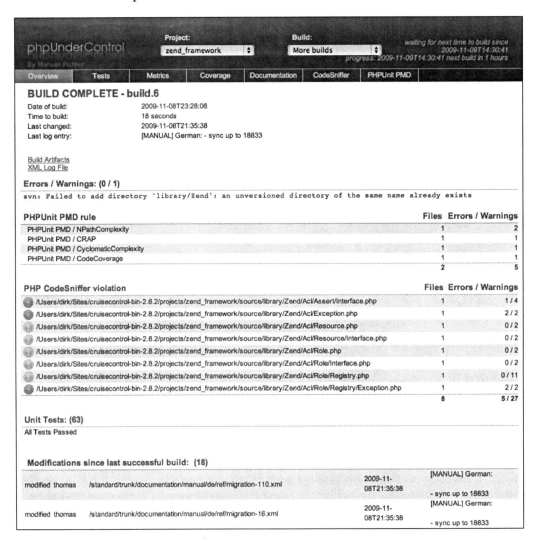

At the top, you can see data about the last build: when it started, how long it took, and so on. Below that we see an error message that alerts us to a problem Subversion encountered during the build process. Then there are three sections listing unit test results, coding standard violations identified by PHP_CodeSniffer, and changes to the source code that have been made since the previous build.

The tests page

Clicking on the **Tests** tab brings up a page listing the results of the unit tests. The following screenshot shows the unit tests for the zend_framework project that CruiseControl ran automatically as part of its build process:

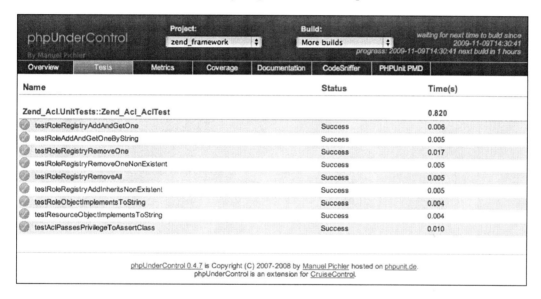

Unlucky for us, Zend Framework seems to be doing a good job because there is not a single failed unit test in the previous screenshot. There were actually a lot more unit tests, but I edited them out of the previous image for brevity's sake.

Metrics

The Metrics tab reveals a set of beautiful looking graphs that chart the results
of the various build tasks over time:

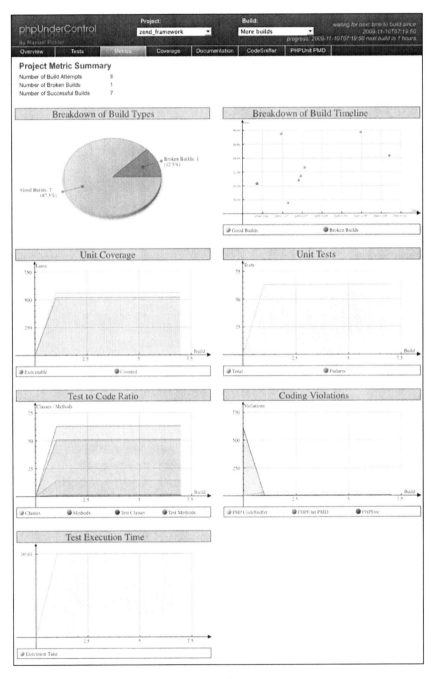

We can see how code coverage, unit test pass / fail ratio, build success versus failure, test to code ratio, number of coding standard violations, and test execution time change with each additional build.

Coverage

The **Coverage** page displays statistics on what kind of code coverage was achieved by the unit test suite:

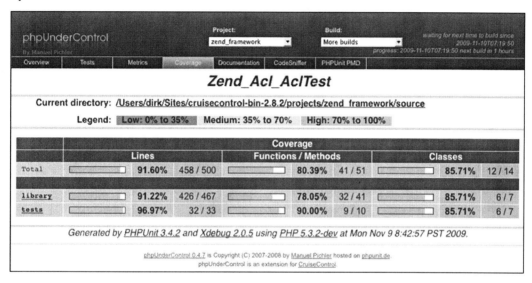

As you can see, the numbers for Zend Framework are very respectable. You can tell that writing unit tests is an integral part of the development process for this project.

Documentation

The **Documentation** tab leads to the API-level documentation generated by phpDocumentor. The theme installed by phpUnderControl matches the rest of the site quite nicely. This is the same documentation that phpDocumentor would have generated if you had run it from the command line:

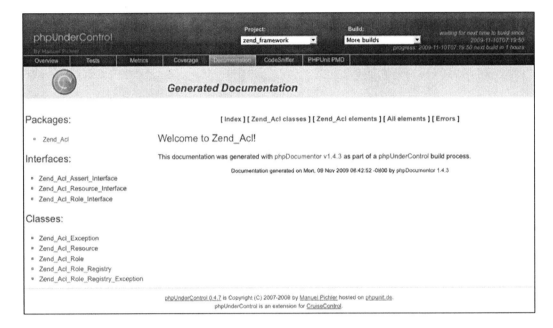

CodeSniffer

The **CodeSniffer** page lists all violations of the Zend coding standard
PHP_CodeSniffer could find. Again, I truncated this page to save space.
There are quite a few listings, but note that most of them are warnings
and significantly fewer of them are actual errors:

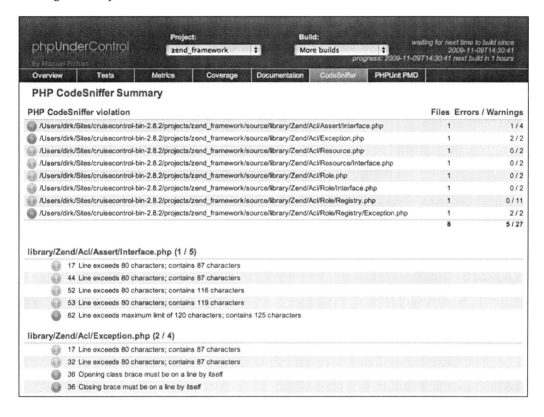

PHPUnit PMD

The **PHPUnit PMD** tab shows the result of the heuristic tests and rules that were applied to determine the complexity and quality of the code:

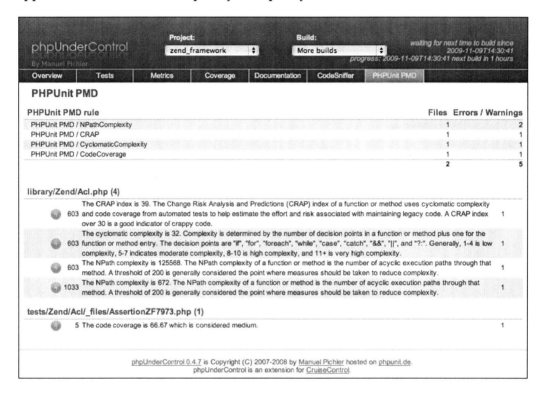

Replacing Ant with Phing

Did you notice how all targets in the Ant `build.xml` file we constructed contained tasks of type `exec`? That is because most of the targets are pretty PHP-centric. Ant is a general build tool, but its roots lie in Java development, which explains why it knows nothing about PHPUnit, PHP_CodeSniffer, and phpDocumentor. Although Subversion is used in many projects, including Java, support for it in Ant can often only be achieved by adding an optional extension.

What is a PHP developer to do? Well, we already saw in a previous chapter that Phing is an Ant replacement that supports all the goodness a PHP developer's heart could desire (at least as far as the project build process goes). Therefore, in this section, I would like to outline the steps necessary to replace Ant with Phing as a build tool for CruiseControl/phpUnderControl.

Unfortunately, the news isn't all good. On one hand, due to its extensible nature, CruiseControl can support Phing as a build tool. On the other hand, Phing doesn't support all the tasks and options required to work with phpUnderControl.

If you recall, the way we told CruiseControl to use Ant as a build tool was with the `ant` tag inside the `schedule` tag in the `config.xml` file. CruiseCrontrol's configuration parameters provide for a corresponding tag for Phing support. Following is a partial listing of CC's config.xml where the `ant` tag has been replaced with a `phing` tag:

cruisecontrol/config.xml

```
...
<schedule interval="300">
<phing phingscript="/usr/local/apache2/php/bin/phing"
    phingworkingdir="projects/${project.name}"
     buildfile="projects/${project.name}/build-phing.xml"
     uselogger="true"
     usedebug="false"/>
</schedule>
...
```

For a complete listing of the attributes supported by the `phing` tag, you can consult CruiseControl's exhaustive list of `config.xml` parameters that is part of the project's documentation pages.

That's all it takes to execute a Phing file to handle the build process, however, we still need to port our current Ant file build file to Phing.

We have four critical tasks that need to be executed during the build process: `svn-update`, `php-documentor`, `php-codesniffer`, and `phpunit`. And if you have been using Phing ever since you read the chapter about it in this book, you will remember that each of these targets has a corresponding task in Phing. In theory, we should be able to replace each of the ant targets with single Phing tasks. That does indeed work well using the `svnupdate` task to handle updating the local working copy from the Subversion repository, as well as, generating API-level documentation using the `phpdoc` task. Here is the listing with the corresponding Phing targets:

cruisecontrol/projects/zend_framework/build-phing.xml

```
...
<!-- update the local working copy of the pr<target name="svn-update">
  <svnupdate
      svnpath="/usr/local/bin/svn"
      nocache="true"
      todir="${basedir}/source"/>
</target>
```

```
<!-- have phpDocumentor generate API documentation -->
<target name="php-documentor">
  <phpdoc title="API Documentation"
    destdir="${basedir}/build/api"
    sourcecode="no"
    customtags="true"
    undocumentedelements="true"
    templatebase="/Users/dirk/Sites/phpdoc/phpUnderControl/data/
phpdoc"
    output="HTML:Phpuc:phpuc">
     <fileset dir="${basedir}/source/library/Zend/">
        <include name="*" />
     </fileset>
     <projdocfileset dir=".">
        <include name="README" />
        <include name="INSTALL" />
        <include name="CHANGELOG" />
     </projdocfileset>
  </phpdoc>
</target>
...
```

The challenge I faced in creating the Phing build file was with the other two targets: `php-codesniffer` and `phpunit`.

The `php codesniffer` task does everything we need it to—except that it does not support the `--reportfile` attribute, which is needed for us to save the output to exactly the file that phpUnderControl expects. It looks like this oversight has been corrected in some beta versions, but a peek at the source of the version that I was using to write this chapter revealed that it had not yet been included in the release. Fortunately, while we are waiting for support of the `--reportfile` attribute to make it into the release of Phing, there is a workaround. We can simply do the same thing we did in the Ant file, which is to use the `exec` task to call `phpcs`, the phpDocumentor command line client. Here is a listing of the Phing version of that target:

`cruisecontrol/projects/zend_framework/build-phing.xml`

```
...
<!-- validate against the Zend coding style using PHP_CodeSniffer -->
<target name="php-codesniffer">
  <exec dir="${basedir}/source/library"
    command="/usr/local/apache2/php/bin/phpcs
       --report-file=${basedir}/build/logs/checkstyle.xml
       --report=checkstyle
       --standard=Zend Zend"/>
</target>
...
```

My problems with Phing's `phpunit` task were similar to the issue I encountered with the `phpcodesniffer` task. With the attributes support by the `phpunit` task, I was not able to get PHPUnit to generate all the metrics and coverage reports in the format required by phpUnderControl. Until the phpunit Phing task receives some additional functionality, we will have to resort to the same workaround as for the `phpcodesniffer` task, which is to use the exec task instead to call the `phpunit` command line client directly. Here is a listing of the corresponding target in Phing vernacular:

cruisecontrol/projects/zend_framework/build-phing.xml

```
...
<!-- run unit test suite using PHPUnit -->
<target name="phpunit">
  <exec dir="${basedir}/source" checkreturn="on"
      command="/usr/local/bin/phpunit
         --log-xml ${basedir}/build/logs/phpunit.xml
         --log-pmd ${basedir}/build/logs/phpunit.pmd.xml
         --log-metrics ${basedir}/build/logs/phpunit.metrics.xml
         --coverage-xml ${basedir}/build/logs/phpunit.coverage.xml
         --coverage-html ${basedir}/build/coverage
         phpucAllTests tests/Zend/Acl/AclTest.php"/>
</target>
...
```

Finally, here is the complete Phing build file, complete with headers, project tags, and default target:

cruisecontrol/projects/zend_framework/build-phing.xml

```
<?xml version="1.0" encoding="UTF-8"?>
<project name="zend_framework" description="Continuous Integration
build script for Zend Framework" default="build">

  <property name="basedir" value="." override="true"/>

  <!-- main build target that executes a sub-targets -->
  <target name="build" depends="svn-update,php-documentor,php-
                                            codesniffer,phpunit"/>

  <!-- update the local working copy of the project -->
  <target name="svn-update">
    <svnupdate
        svnpath="/usr/local/bin/svn"
        nocache="true"
        todir="${basedir}/source"/>
  </target>
```

```xml
  <!-- have phpDocumentor generate API documentation -->
  <target name="php-documentor">
    <phpdoc title="API Documentation"
      destdir="${basedir}/build/api"
      sourcecode="no"
      customtags="true"
      undocumentedelements="true"
      templatebase="/Users/dirk/Sites/phpdoc/phpUnderControl/data/
phpdoc"
      output="HTML:Phpuc:phpuc">
       <fileset dir="${basedir}/source/library/Zend/">
          <include name="*" />
       </fileset>
       <projdocfileset dir=".">
          <include name="README" />
          <include name="INSTALL" />
          <include name="CHANGELOG" />
       </projdocfileset>
    </phpdoc>
  </target>

  <!-- validate Zend coding style using PHP_CodeSniffer  -->
  <target name="php-codesniffer">
    <exec dir="${basedir}/source/library"
      command="/usr/local/apache2/php/bin/phpcs
        --report-file=${basedir}/build/logs/checkstyle.xml
        --report=checkstyle
        --standard=Zend Zend"/>
  </target>

  <!-- run unit test suite using PHPUnit -->
  <target name="phpunit">
    <exec dir="${basedir}/source" checkreturn="on"
      command="/usr/local/bin/phpunit
        --log-xml ${basedir}/build/logs/phpunit.xml
        --log-pmd ${basedir}/build/logs/phpunit.pmd.xml
        --log-metrics ${basedir}/build/logs/phpunit.metrics.xml
        --coverage-xml ${basedir}/build/logs/phpunit.coverage.xml
        --coverage-html ${basedir}/build/coverage
        phpucAllTests tests/Zend/AllTests.php"/>
  </target>
</project>
```

With the above two workarounds in place, the combination of CruiseControl overlaid with phpUnderControl, and using Phing as a build tool works just fine. I switched my builds from Ant to Phing after a couple of days and none of the report or graphs showed any sign of interruption.

Also, as Continuous Integration becomes common practice in enterprise PHP development and these tools mature a bit more, I am confident that these slight incompatibilities will be worked out.

Summary

Continuous Integration is simply a combination of tasks that you are likely to perform anyway during the development and release of a project. The difference, however, is that with continuous integration, you do it earlier and more frequently. Decreasing the time between automated builds allows you to view the development of the project over time rather than to look at a single snapshot of the code. It allows you to keep a finger on the pulse of your project and catch any problems early on.

We learned about some of the advantages of adding CI to your development process. First, configuring the CI process once will bring benefits throughout the project's lifetime. Second, CI encourages and practically requires best practices, such as unit testing, inline documentation, and coding standards.

We also learned about CruiseControl and phpUnderControl—two tools that when combined extend a mature CI server to support PHP and its cast of supporting players: phpDocumentor, PHPUnit, Phing, and PHP_CodeSniffer.

While we were able to put together a PHP-centric CI system, we also noticed that this kind of tool is still maturing in the PHP world. This was the only chapter in this book where we had to resort to a tool that was developed in a programming language other than PHP. I am referring to CruiseControl, of course, which was developed in Java. However, over time, I hope that one of the crop of PHP-based continuous integration servers will challenge CruiseControl for the title. The Xinc project is leading the way, but it seems that it will take a bit more time and effort for it to reach a level of maturity and flexibility to rival that of CruiseControl.

Now that you have been given a tour of the benefits of continuous integration and have been shown how to set it up, I hope that you will take the time to explore this valuable tool some more and give it a chance to become part of your day-to-day development process.

Index

var_dump(mixed $expression [, mixed $expression [, $...]]) and print_r(mixed $expression [, bool $return= false]) 210, 211, 212

G

generalization, relationship 382
get_class_methods(mixed class_name), PHP function 212
get_class([object object]), PHP function 212
get_class_vars(string class_name), PHP function 212
getConfigDirs() method 206
getExcludedSniffs() method 32
getFormatted DebugInfo() method 225
getFormatted Trace() method 225
getIncludedSniffs() method 32
getIniFiles() method 206
getInstance() method 164
get_object_vars(object object), PHP function 212
getOpt() function 164
getSourceExcerpt() method 225
GlobalMapper 342
gray box testing 293

H

headScript() placeholder 271
headStyle() placeholder 271
headTitle() placeholder 271
help, svn subcommands 151
highlight_string(string str [, bool return]) and highlight_file(string filename [, bool return]), PHP function 212
history/log, Subversion 147
hooks
  about 159, 190
  coding standards enforcing, pre-commit hook used 191-193
  commits developers notifying, post-commit hook used 194
host property 373
html_errors option 201

I

IdentityMapper 342
if-elseif-else statements 13
ignore_repeated_errors option 201
ignore_repeated_source option 201
import, svn subcommands 152
indenting 8
indexAction() method 287
info, svn subcommands 152
ini_get_all() function 200
ini_set() function 235
init() method 286
inline documentation 23, 24
inline tags, tag reference
  about 83
  {@Example} 84
  {@id} 85
  {@id}, inline tags 85
  {@inheritdoc} 87
  {@internal}} 86
  {@link} 88
  {@source} 88, 89
  {@toc} 90
  {@tutorial} 91
InputTask 338
inputTask tag 351
insert() method 281
inspection, PDT
  files 114
  PHP explorer 114
  projects 114
  type hierarchy 115
installation, PHPUnit 298, 299
integration testing 295
interaction overview diagrams 369
interfaces 382

J

Java Runtime Environment (JRE) 96

L

line endings 8
line length 8
list, svn subcommands 152

Thank you for buying
Expert PHP 5 Tools

Packt Open Source Project Royalties

When we sell a book written on an Open Source project, we pay a royalty directly to that project. Therefore by purchasing Expert PHP 5 Tools, Packt will have given some of the money received to the PHP Group project.

In the long term, we see ourselves and you—customers and readers of our books—as part of the Open Source ecosystem, providing sustainable revenue for the projects we publish on. Our aim at Packt is to establish publishing royalties as an essential part of the service and support a business model that sustains Open Source.

If you're working with an Open Source project that you would like us to publish on, and subsequently pay royalties to, please get in touch with us.

Writing for Packt

We welcome all inquiries from people who are interested in authoring. Book proposals should be sent to author@packtpub.com. If your book idea is still at an early stage and you would like to discuss it first before writing a formal book proposal, contact us; one of our commissioning editors will get in touch with you.

We're not just looking for published authors; if you have strong technical skills but no writing experience, our experienced editors can help you develop a writing career, or simply get some additional reward for your expertise.

About Packt Publishing

Packt, pronounced 'packed', published its first book "Mastering phpMyAdmin for Effective MySQL Management" in April 2004 and subsequently continued to specialize in publishing highly focused books on specific technologies and solutions.

Our books and publications share the experiences of your fellow IT professionals in adapting and customizing today's systems, applications, and frameworks. Our solution-based books give you the knowledge and power to customize the software and technologies you're using to get the job done. Packt books are more specific and less general than the IT books you have seen in the past. Our unique business model allows us to bring you more focused information, giving you more of what you need to know, and less of what you don't.

Packt is a modern, yet unique publishing company, which focuses on producing quality, cutting-edge books for communities of developers, administrators, and newbies alike. For more information, please visit our website: www.PacktPub.com.

PHP Team Development

ISBN: 978-1-847195-06-7   Paperback: 184 pages

Easy and effective team work using MVC, agile development, source control, testing, bug tracking, and more

1. Work more effectively as a team by breaking up complex PHP projects into manageable sub-parts

2. Develop code that is much easier to maintain with source control, agile principles, and project tracking

3. Apply techniques related to process models, collaboration among team members, and continuous long-term improvement

PHP 5 E-commerce Development

ISBN: 978-1-847199-64-5   Paperback: 356 pages

Create a flexible framework in PHP for a powerful ecommerce solution

1. Build a flexible e-commerce framework using PHP, which can be extended and modified for the purposes of any e-commerce site

2. Enable customer retention and more business by creating rich user experiences

3. Develop a suitable structure for your framework and create a registry to store core objects

4. Easily add exciting and powerful features

Please check **www.PacktPub.com** for information on our titles

LaVergne, TN USA
14 April 2010
179153LV00003B/42/P